*"The Path that leadeth on, is lighted by one fire—
the light of daring, burning in the heart."*

◆ * ●

Reincarnation in World Thought

A Living Study of Reincarnation in All Ages;
Including Selections from the World's Religions,
Philosophies and Sciences, and Great Thinkers
of the Past and Present

Compiled and Edited by

JOSEPH HEAD
S. L. CRANSTON

◆ * ●

JULIAN PRESS
NEW YORK

Preface

Among the probing questions that persistently knock at the door of maturing minds are enigmas such as these: Who and what is Man? Is there a meaning for his existence? Does he have a future beyond the grave? All such questions obviously revolve around one pivotal problem: Is man mortal or immortal?

The hesitancy with which modern man approaches these subjects is readily understandable considering the naïve level of popular opinions regarding the soul and the hereafter. Nevertheless, as Lewis Loeser points out, "Death and our attitudes toward it are man's number one preoccupation. We devote more time to thinking about, talking about, and avoiding this subject than any other. It is time we faced up to it realistically in our Western culture." [1]

While it is true that a surprising number of distinguished thinkers of every era have considered the problem in terms of repeated existence upon earth—as this work serves to demonstrate—such testimony hardly establishes reincarnation as a fact. But it does suggest that the doctrine merits investigation. It should also prove challenging to look into the objections to reincarnation theory raised by Aristotle, Freud, Julian Huxley, and other well-known writers. All these aspects, pro and con, are to be found in the present volume, which save for the more significant passages retained from its predecessor work, *Reincarnation, an East-West Anthology*, is composed of new material from both ancient and modern sources.

[1] *Mental Hygiene*, July, 1965, p. 470.

Discussing reincarnation and pre-existence in *The Imprisoned Splendour*, the British physicist, Raynor Johnson, remarks:

Some people seem curiously and almost instinctively interested in these topics, others, frequently religious-minded people, feel antagonistic, as though some strange pagan faith were subtly menacing their cherished beliefs. The average thoughtful Western man has in general given little consideration to these matters, although his reticence does not always match his knowledge. In any attempt to formulate a philosophy of life and endeavour to see meaning in our pilgrimage, these ancient beliefs cannot be lightly set aside. It is our duty to weigh them carefully, and without prejudice, in order to see if they will illuminate for us tracts of experience which would otherwise remain dark and mysterious. . . . The idea of reincarnation presents no logical difficulties, whatever be the emotional reaction to it. What the soul has done once by the process of incarnation in a physical body, it can presumably do again.[2]

"By the term 'soul,' " Dr. Johnson explains, "we mean that individualised aspect of the Self, including . . . the Intuitive Self and Higher Mind, all of which are regarded as immortal. We should of course bear in mind that what is meant by the phrase 'have lived before' is not that the physical form [and personality] Raynor Johnson has lived on earth previously, but rather that Raynor Johnson is only a particular and temporary expression of an underlying immortal soul which has adopted previous and quite possibly different appearances." Reincarnationists tend to believe that between these appearances a lengthy period of assimilative rest and inner revitalization usually intervenes.

Among the synonyms used for reincarnation by the authors quoted are palingenesis, transmigration, pre-existence, and metempsychosis. In Sanskrit the terms are *punar-janman*—again birth—and *samsâra*—the round of births and deaths. The Greek equivalent for *punar-janman* is palingenesis, from *palin*, back or again, and *genesis*, origin or production. The word "transmigration" has been so frequently misused to suggest the birth of humans into animal forms—a complete reversal of the natural evolutionary processes—that it is hardly satisfactory for general use. Some churchmen make a limited use of "pre-existence" and do not relate it to reincarnation. This is discussed in Part Two under "Christianity." According to Dean Inge, metempsychosis—from *metem*, change and *psyche*, soul—is an incorrect expression "since it is the bodies, not the souls, that are changed at rebirth."[3] However, if we equate "change" with "growth," the term "metempsychosis" can meaningfully be used to indicate the evolution of soul through a process of rebirth.

[2] New York: Harper and Row, 1953, Chap. 18.
[3] W. R. Inge, The Philosophy of Plotinus (London: Longmans Green, 1948), I, 86 fn.

As the reader moves through the centuries he finds unfolding the little known but completely engrossing story of how reincarnation became divorced from the Christian teachings, and through what channels, hidden and open, it survived the Dark Ages. Also, the Platonic line of influence is traced from Greece and Alexandria to Arabia and Persia—when the Platonists were expelled from Europe for nearly a thousand years—and then to Renaissance Italy, France, Germany, England, and eventually America. A fascinating picture of reincarnation teaching in Western and Middle East philosophy thus emerges, for wherever Plato and the Neoplatonists have exerted an influence there the idea of rebirth inevitably gains fresh currency.

To preserve the continuity of the Western story, authors are presented in birth-year sequence and not according to nationality as was done in *Reincarnation, an East West Anthology*. However, all Western writers quoted are now classified according to national origin in the Index. One need but check under such headings as: American, British, French, German, Irish, Italian, Russian, the various Scandinavian countries, and so on.

Also, in order that material on important topics be readily accessible, subject headings have been extensively used in the Index. (See list at the beginning of Index.) Thus, to ascertain what authors have said on Karma as related to rebirth, look under "Karma." Similarly with subjects like Brotherhood, Education, Evolution, Memory of Past Lives, Music and Composers, Purpose of Rebirths, etc.

Turning now for a moment to Part Two of the book itself and the opening sections on oriental religions, it seems essential to distinguish between the views of the great religious teachers included therein, and the later conventional emphasis on the attainment of the bliss and quietude of Nirvana as the supreme aim of man's incarnations on earth. There seems little psychological difference between the latter belief—perhaps a distortion of the real meaning of Nirvana—and the escape promised by Western religions, since in both instances the goal is usually a static state of happiness where striving and learning cease. If any religion encourages a race to Heaven or Nirvana, the philosophy of reincarnation of course fails to communicate its central message of eternal growth.

This non-escapist approach seems implicit in the selections from Plato and his successors; the German and American Transcendentalists; the nineteenth-century Theosophists; and such modern philosophers as Nietzsche, John McTaggart, Macneile Dixon, Jung, Radhakrishnan, C. J. Ducasse, and Herbert Fingarette. In his psychoanalytic work, *The Self in Transformation*, Dr. Fingarette devotes some seventy pages to reincarnation and karma as applied to the here and now of man's psychological life. (See Part Six.)

Perhaps a few words should be said about "proof." Several scientists—pre-eminently the psychiatrist, Ian Stevenson, Chairman of the Department of Neurology and Psychiatry at the University of Virginia School of Medicine—have been investigating hundreds of case histories of persons supposedly remembering former lives, to determine if decisive evidence concerning survival may be forthcoming. This patient research will receive treatment in Part Six. However, in view of the obvious limitations of "physical" proof for nonphysical reality, many persons believe that the real case for or against reincarnation rests chiefly on its capacity to provide a rational explanation of life and its mysteries. Truth always explains and unifies, as Schopenhauer so pertinently indicates when offering this criterion for the demonstration of truth:

> The theory which can decipher the relations between the world and all things that it contains, should find the warrant of its truth in the unity so established between the many different natural phenomena—a unity which is not apparent apart from that theory. When we have to deal with an inscription whose alphabetical characters are unknown, we make successive trials until we reach a combination that gives intelligible words and coherent sentences. No doubt then remains that the decipherment is correct. . . . In the same way the reading of the world-cipher should carry its own proof.[4]

Jung calls rebirth "an affirmation that must be counted among the primordial affirmations of mankind," [5] while the seventeenth century divine, Thomas Burnet, startled by the universal prevalence of the belief, declared it "fatherless, motherless, and without genealogy." [6] In Part Four, "Reincarnation Among Peoples of the World," anthropologists add their testimony to this effect.

But how shall one regard the widespread *current* interest in the doctrine of many lives? Is it an apprehensive return to the thinking of a bygone age, a hopeless pursuit of lost securities? Or is it possibly an intuitive reaching out to repossess a heritage belonging to every man, now to be recovered at the level of both critical intelligence and affirmative daring? On these and other questions our writers speak for themselves—not as "authorities" to be respectfully believed, but to set the stage for a living dialogue about man and his universe, in which the reader is invited to be the chief participant.

THE EDITORS

---

[4] Gustave Geley, *From the Unconscious to the Conscious.* New York: Harper and Row, 1920, p. 324.
[5] See pp. 415–416.
[6] Isaac de Beausobré, *Histoire Critique de Manichée et du Manicheisme.* Amsterdam: 1734–1739, II, 491.

Contents

◆ * ●

◆ * ●

Introduction

We have never been as openmouthed and inquisitive, never as astonished and embarrassed at our ignorance about man. We know what he makes, but we do not know what he is or what to expect of him. Is it not conceivable that our entire civilization is built upon a misinterpretation of man? Or that the tragedy of man is due to the fact that he is a being who has forgotten the question: Who is Man? The failure to identify himself, to know what is authentic human existence, leads him to assume a false identity, to pretend to be what he is unable to be or to not accept what is at the very root of his being. Ignorance about man is not lack of knowledge but false knowledge.

ABRAHAM J. HESCHEL[1]

1 The author's words as they appear on the jacket of his book *Who is Man?* (Stanford University Press, 1965).

The Pivot of the Human Situation

[The selections here presented are from the book *The Human Situation*,[1] comprising the Gifford Lectures (1935–1937) of the British philosopher and educator W. Macneile Dixon. Dixon has been called a Confucius for the West, uniting its several currents of metaphysical thinking in one unified philosophy. The extracts are taken mostly from the last chapter, "The Verdict," and lead gradually to a consideration of reincarnation. Marks to indicate omissions in the text have not been used. Further selections will be given in Part Six. One of Dixon's predecessors in this famous Gifford Lectures series at the University of Glasgow was William James whose talks were published in his well-known work *The Varieties of Religious Experience*.]

There is a saying that nature does nothing in vain. Yet if she created automatic machines, and some thinkers like the behaviourists insist we are no more, why did she proceed to blunder, for assuredly a blunder it was, of conferring upon them an unnecessary sensitivity to pain and pleasure? Without sensitivity machines work very well. But we are not stones or trees, and in making sensitive beings nature went clean out of her way. Consciousness is an unpardonable blot upon her scheme.

The modern and shortest way with the soul or self is to deny it out-

[1] London: Edward Arnold, 1937 and 1957; New York: St. Martin's Press. Galaxy paperback, New York: Oxford University Press, 1958.

right. Can we suppose "that a ship might be constructed of such a kind that entirely by itself, without captain or crew, it could sail from place to place for years on end, accommodating itself to varying winds, avoiding shoals, casting and weighing anchor, seeking a haven when necessary, and doing all that a normal ship can?" Yes, we are told, in the human or animal body we have precisely such a ship, which handles itself admirably without captain or navigator.

You have heard of this curious doctrine, of this psychology which rejects the psyche and retains only the "ology," the science of the self without the self. Thus, in summary fashion, the great authorities deny and dispose of us, and incidentally of themselves. Where we imagined the "I" or self to be, there is only, they tell us, a series of fleeting impressions, sensations, fancies, pains and pleasures, which succeed each other with amazing rapidity, but without any support, any connection or tie between them, no entity over and above them that as centre or subject thinks, feels or desires. It is then a mirage or hallucination, this notion of the self. And an interesting and peculiar illusion, which till yesterday successfully played the impostor's part upon the whole human race, philosophers included. And not only so, but after this prodigious feat of deception, it laid a snare for itself and caught itself out. This illusion, the most extraordinary that ever was, discovered itself to be an illusion.

On every side today you meet with an exaltation of the intellect at the expense of the spirit. You may trust, it is said, your thoughts, but not your aspirations. Nature is rent asunder. You enthrone the measuring, weighing, calculating faculty of the human creature. His remaining attributes are irrelevant. But who told you that nature had drawn this line? Where did you learn of this preference? Nature has no preferences. If she has given us deceiving souls, how can you argue that she has given us trustworthy intellects? We should at least, then, aim at a conclusion which the intellect can accept and the heart approve.

And how wide, how grotesquely wide of the mark are they who indulge in childish and insensitive chatter, babbling of the hope for a future existence as a petty, personal desire, born of selfishness. For what, to put no gloss on things, are the implications of its rejection? The story of humanity becomes the story of a long procession of sufferers, for whose suffering no justification is offered, of poor souls intellectually and morally confounded, who entered existence blind to any reason for their coming and will leave it blind, who cannot so much as conjecture their origin, or the meaning of their lives, whose elevation above the lower creatures has been their direst misfortune, their ideals an accentuation of their griefs. And the revolt of reason against this happy consummation is labeled selfishness. What kind of selfishness is that which asks no more for oneself than for all men and creatures ever born? Let us have no more of this.

To live is by universal consent to travel a rough road. And how can a rough road which leads nowhere be worth the travelling? Mere living, what a profitless performance; mere painful living, what an absurd! There is then, nothing to be hoped for, nothing to be expected and nothing to be done save to await our turn to mount the scaffold and bid farewell to that colossal blunder, the much-ado-about-nothing world. Beyond all peradventure it is the thought that death appears to proclaim, the thought of frustration and final unreason at the heart of things, that is itself the root of the pessimist's despair. Give assurance that it is not so, and the scene is changed. The sky brightens, the door is left open for unimagined possibilities, things begin to fall into an intelligible pattern.

If you have not here among men who reflect, however unwilling they are to acknowledge it, the pivot of the human situation, the question upon the answer to which all turns, I know not where to look for it. Immortality is a word which stands for the stability or permanence of that unique and precious quality we discern in the soul, which, if lost, leaves nothing worth preservation in the world. "If immortality be untrue," as Buckle wrote, "it matters little whether anything else be true or not."

What kind of immortality is at all conceivable? Of all doctrines of a future life, palingenesis or rebirth, which carries with it the idea of pre-existence, is by far the most ancient and most widely held, "the only system to which," as said Hume, "philosophy can hearken." Many things are hard to believe, and a future life, some say, is quite incredible, and the mere thought of it a sort of madness. But what hinders if we have already found a present? Well, I should myself put the matter rather differently. The present life is incredible, a future credible. "Not to be twice-born, but once-born is wonderful." To be alive, actually existing, to have emerged from darkness and silence, to be here today is certainly incredible. A philosopher friend of mine could never, he told me, bring himself to believe in his own existence. A future life would be a miracle, and you find it difficult to believe in miracles? I, on the contrary, find it easy. They are to be expected. The starry worlds in time and space, the pageant of life, the processes of growth and reproduction, the instincts of animals, the inventiveness of nature, they are all utterly unbelievable, miracles piled upon miracles. If there be a sceptical star I was born under it, yet I have lived all my days in complete astonishment.

Our interest in the future, how strange it is if we can never hope to see the future. That interest rarely seems to desert us, and in itself appears inexplicable were we not possessed of an intuition which tells us that we shall have a part in it, that in some sense it already belongs to us, that we should bear it continually in mind, since it will be ours. So closely are all human ideals associated with futurity that, in the absence of the faith that man is an immortal being, it seems doubtful whether they could ever have come to birth. "In the further depth of our being we are secretly conscious of our share in the inexhaustible spring of eternity, so that we can always hope to find life in it again."

If things as they are have not a feature in common with things as they will be, we have no basis for thought at all regarding that future. As Leibniz said, "a leap from one state to another infinitely different state could not be natural." The experiences of time and of our present condition could, one feels, only be valuable in an existence not wholly unlike it; and any doctrine which insists upon a totally dissimilar existence, an indescribable spiritual life as a sequel to the present, makes of the present an insoluble enigma. [Although the doctrine of periodic returns to earth life] has for European thought a strangeness, it is in fact the most natural and easily imagined, since what has been can be again. This belief seems, indeed, to be in accordance with nature's own favourite way of thought, of which she so insistently reminds us, in her rhythms and recurrences, her cycles and revolving seasons. "It presents itself," wrote Schopenhauer, "as the natural conviction of man whenever he reflects at all in an unprejudiced manner."

W. MACNEILE DIXON

Is There a Future Life?

[These excerpts are from an article in The Yale Review[1] by J. Paul Williams, Chairman of the Department of Religion at Mt. Holyoke College. Among the ideas considered, Dr. Williams touches on a point raised by Dixon but from a new approach, and concludes with two unusual thoughts on rebirth.]

One cause for the current skepticism concerning the future life is that many people have given up a belief in the soul. Probably there is no ques-

[1] Spring, 1945.

tion in philosophy which has more in it of meaning for practical living than the question, "What is the nature of human nature?" or, in the terms of theology, "What is the nature of man?" Is a man just a body, as some of our contemporaries believe? Or is he just a soul, as some others hold? Or is he a body that has a soul? Or (and this is a different proposition) is he a soul that has a body? . . .

The argument for the future life which logically precedes all others is the simple one that if man is a soul it is not unreasonable to suppose that he survives death. If man is simply a body, a physio-chemical reaction, and nothing more, it is obvious that he does not live again as such a body. If, however, man is—or perhaps has—a soul, the door is left open to the possibility that the soul persists after death. Thus the case for the future life is no stronger than is the case for the existence of the soul. Are human beings souls?

There are two ways to prove a thing. One is to show how it follows logically from other things that [are true]. The other is just to point and say, "There it is." . . . I am among those who feel that they must believe in souls simply because they experience them. It may be that my family, the students I meet on the campus, the friends I play cards with are just bodies, machines, not essentially different from the images I see on a movie screen, images that move and talk. But I find that a very hard position to accept. It is much easier to account for one's experience of people and for one's knowledge of himself on the assumption that the essential human being is more than just a physio-chemical reaction. Is man a living soul? For answer observe people: watch a group of boys playing football; read Shakespeare; look into the eyes of one beloved.

The idea that human beings are just bodies is one phase of the notion that nothing exists but matter, that spirit is nonexistent, that mind is but matter in motion. This position is one that some scientists have expounded dogmatically. Because of the prestige of these men, many people have jumped to the conclusion that anyone who is thoroughly abreast of modern thought will discard faith in a soul. Yet there are other scientists, men of equal prestige, who do not accept the faith that the universe is composed exclusively of matter and assert their belief that faith in a future life is rational. But as a matter of fact scientists are in no better position than are the rest of us to decide whether matter and mind are both real. That is a question for philosophy. And we must all, consciously or unconsciously, be philosophers. . . .

Accept if you can the belief that we are souls; that still does not mean that a future life is proved. Do these souls survive death? Our only experience of life is in connection with the body. Some people would contend that we must deduce from this simple fact the conclusion that where there is no body there is no life. But this is not a necessary conclusion. William James pointed out that we can take two positions concerning the relation between the body and life: one is that the body *produces* life; the other that the body *reflects* life. Light is produced by a candle; if the candle is put out its light disappears. Light is reflected by a mirror; if the mirror is taken away the light still continues. Now is it not at least as easy to suppose that the body reflects the soul as it is to suppose that it produces the soul? It may be that this human carcass, full of aches and diseases, heir to boils and rheumatism, produces things like "Hamlet," the theory of evolution, psychoanalysis, and the fortieth chapter of Isaiah, but it is a great deal easier for me to believe that these things are the work of living souls who used bodies as instruments. . . .

If we assume that the soul is reflected rather than is produced by the body, then it is rational to believe that the soul can exist apart from the body. The fact that we have no direct experience of souls which do exist apart from matter is a serious weakness in the argument, but it need not force us to the conclusion that they cannot so exist. The typical reaction of the materialists to this kind of reasoning in an appeal to stick to the known facts. But the materialistic scientist certainly does not limit himself to immediately experienced data. The limits of our experience are so narrow that if we did not permit our thinking to go beyond them, human thought would be puny indeed. Who ever experienced an atom or an electron? . . . The whole conception of the atomic structure is an inference; it is believed because it is consistent with the way in which the elements combine, because it explains why under certain conditions peculiar markings appear on photographic plates. . . . Yet we do not accuse the physicist of irrationality when he says that the solid matter of a rock is really composed of tiny solar systems in which electrons revolve at incredible speed around protons. . . . Let no one think that he has reached perfection in his habits of thought if he accepts inferential logic in physics but rejects it in theology. . . .

One's emotional orientation to the problem of the future life is materially advanced when one realizes that the two great religions of the East—Hinduism and Buddhism—assume that the future life is a fact. They teach that man is reborn into the world over and over again, and they view the prospect with much anxiety. Thus one major function of these religions is to teach men how to avoid being reborn. It is not "wishful thinking" from the Hindu or Buddhist point of view to expect to live again; rather it is stark realism. But it would be "wishful thinking" from their point of view really to believe that religion has found a way to get man off of the "Wheel of life." . . .

Another argument in favor of a future life is the simple fact that we are alive now. Here we are, set in the midst of an infinity of time. It is impossible for us to imagine a limit to time. . . . If that is true, then the chances are infinitely against us that we should be alive at any specific time. But here we are. The only way to get rid of the infinity of chances which are against us is to assume that we are like time; that is, that we too are infinite. . . .

Usually thinking about personal immortality takes this form—a human being is created somewhere near the time of his birth, finally he dies, and then he becomes immortal. The conception I am suggesting, however, is that in addition to living after this life is ended we have lived before it began. This is a logically necessary assumption, if one accepts the force of the argument in any measure. For since infinity is infinitely greater than any part of infinity, the chances of living during any part of eternity, say forever after birth, are infinitely against one. Thus the possibility that we have lived before this life is as good as the possibility that we will live after this life. But, it may be said, we have no memory of any former existence. True, and therefore, if one accepts the argument, one is forced into the conclusion that some means has operated to prevent memory of previous existences.

J. PAUL WILLIAMS

Objections to Reincarnation

[The main objections to reincarnation are here discussed by C. J. Ducasse, former Chairman of the Department of Philosophy at Brown University, and a past President of the American Philosophical Association. The selections are taken from the last chapter of *Nature, Mind, and Death*,[1] portions of the chapter having been part of Dr. Ducasse's University of California, 1947 Foerster Lecture on the Immortality of the Soul. The author also discusses reincarnation at length in his book *A Critical Examination of*

[1] La Salle, Illinois: Open Court, 1951. The Paul Carus Lectures, Eighth Series.

the Belief in a Life After Death,[2] and in his Garvin Lecture, "Life After Death Conceived As Reincarnation." [3]

In discussing rebirth in Nature, Mind, and Death, Ducasse states that "no claim is made that this conception of survival is known to be true, or even known to be more probably true than not." His purpose in introducing the subject is to explore the merits of the charge that there is no survival hypothesis which "would be both theoretically possible and significant enough to be worth our caring now whether it is a fact or not." The latter part of the charge is considered first.]

The hypothesis of survival as rebirth (whether immediate or delayed) in a material world (whether the earth or some other planet) is of course not novel. . . . As W. R. Alger declares, "No other doctrine has exerted so extensive, controlling, and permanent an influence upon mankind as that of the metempsychosis—the notion that when the soul leaves the body it is born anew in another body, its rank, character, circumstances, and experience in each successive existence depending on its qualities, deeds, and attainments in its preceding lives." [4]

Although the hypothesis of such [Karmic] dependence is in large part logically distinct from and additional to that of rebirth in another material body, it has in fact been virtually always conjoined with the latter—probably because the transmigration hypothesis then is, as Alger further says, "marvelously adapted to explain the seeming chaos of moral inequality, injustice, and manifold evil presented in the world of human life. . . . Once admit the theory to be true, and all difficulties in regard to moral justice vanish . . . the principal physical and moral phenomena of life are strikingly explained; and, as we gaze around the world, its material conditions and spiritual elements combine in one vast scheme of unrivalled order, and the total experience of humanity forms a magnificent picture of perfect poetic justice."

This conception of survival, moreover, is the most concrete. Because what it supposes is so like the life we know, it can be imagined most clearly. . . . But since, in respect of practical significance for us now, the transmigration hypothesis apparently would have in addition to concreteness the merits Alger describes, it will be worth while now to inquire in some detail whether it really is theoretically tenable, or on the contrary faces insuperable difficulties. . . .

[2] Springfield, Illinois: Chas. C. Thomas, 1961, Chapters 20–26.
[3] Garvin Lectures of Abraham N. Neuman and others, In Search of God and Immortality (Boston: Beacon Press 1961), pp. 142–65.
[4] W. R. Alger, A Critical History of the Doctrine of a Future Life, p. 475.

The hypothesis of survival as rebirth—let us say, on this earth—at once raises the question whether one's present life is not itself a rebirth; for logically, even if not in point of practical interest, the hypothesis of earlier lives is exactly on a par with that of later lives. Hence, assuming transmigration, to suppose that one's present life is the first of one's series of lives would be as arbitrary as to suppose that it is going to be the last. . . .

Now the supposition that one's present life not only will have successors but also has had predecessors, immediately brings up the objection that we have no recollection of having lived before. But if absence of memory of having existed at a certain time proved that we did not exist at that time, it would then prove far too much; for it would prove that we did not exist during the first few years of the life of our present body, nor on most of the days since then, for we have no memories whatever of the great majority of them, nor of those first few years. Lack of memory of lives earlier than our present one is therefore no evidence at all that we did not live before.

Moreover, there is occasional testimony of recollection of a previous life, where the recollection is quite circumstantial and even alleged to have been verified. One such case may be cited here without any claim that it establishes pre-existence, but only to substantiate the assertion that specific testimony of this kind exists. . . . If pre-existence should happen to be a fact, it is obvious that the only possible empirical evidence of it would consist of verifiable recollections such as testified to in the case about to be described.

It is that of "The Rebirth of Katsugoro," recorded in detail and with many affidavits respecting the facts, in an old Japanese document translated by Lafcadio Hearn.[5] The story is, in brief, that a young boy called Katsugoro, son of a man called Genzo in the village of Nakanomura, declared that in his preceding life a few years before he had been called Tozo; that he was then the son of a farmer called Kyubei and his wife Shidzu in a village called Hodokubo; that his father had died and had been replaced in the household by a man called Hanshiro; and that he himself, Tozo, had died of smallpox at the age of six, a year after his father. He described his burial, the appearance of his former parents, and their house. He eventually was taken to their village, where such persons were found. He himself led the way to their house and recognized them; and they confirmed the facts he had related. Further, he pointed to a shop and a tree, saying that they had not been there before; and this was true.

Testimony of this kind is directly relevant to the question of rebirth. The recollections related in this case are much too circumstantial to be

[5] Lafcadio Hearn, *Gleanings in Buddha Fields*, Chap. X.

dismissed as instances of the familiar and psychologically well-understood illusion of *déjà vu*, and although the testimony that they were verified is not proof that they were, it cannot be rejected *a priori*. Its reliability has to be evaluated in terms of the same standards by which the validity of testimonial evidence concerning anything else is appraised.

A second objection to the transmigration hypothesis is that the native peculiarities of a person's mind as well as the characteristics of his body appear to be derived from his forebears in accordance with the laws of heredity. McTaggart . . . makes clear that "there is no impossibility in supposing that the characteristics in which we resemble the ancestors of our bodies may be to some degree characteristics due to our previous lives." [Likening the inherited body and mental tendencies to a hat, and the wearer thereof to the reincarnating soul] he points out that "hats in general fit their wearers with far greater accuracy than they would if each man's hat were assigned to him by lot. . . . A man's head is never made to fit his hat, and, in the great majority of cases, his hat is not made to fit his head. The adaptation comes about by each man selecting, from hats made without any special reference to his particular head, the hat which will suit his particular head best." And, McTaggart goes on to say: "This may help us to see that it would be possible to hold that a man whose nature had certain characteristics when he was about to be reborn, would be reborn in a body descended from ancestors of a similar character. . . . It would be the character of the ancestors of the new body, and its similarity to his character, which determined the fact that he was reborn in that body rather than another." [6]

McTaggart's use of the analogy of the head and the hats if taken literally would mean, as a correspondent of mine suggests, that, like a man looking for a hat to wear, a temporarily bodiless soul would shop around, trying on one human foetus after another until it finds one which in some unexplained manner it discovers will develop into an appropriate body. McTaggart, however, has in mind nothing so far-fetched, but rather an entirely automatic process. He refers to the analogy of chemical affinities in answer to the question how each person might be brought into connection with the new body most appropriate to him.

But although McTaggart's supposition is adequate to dispose of the difficulty which the facts of heredity otherwise constitute, the rebirth his supposition allows is nevertheless not personal rebirth if, by a man's personality, one means . . . the habits, the skills, the knowledge, character, and memories, which he gradually acquires during life on earth. . . . If our

[6] McTaggart, *Some Dogmas of Religion*, p. 125.

present birth is indeed a rebirth, they certainly are not brought to a new earth life; for we know very well that we are not born with the knowledge, habits, and memories we now have, but gained them little by little as a result of the experiences and efforts of our present lifetime.

But this brings up another difficulty, namely, what then is there left which could be supposed to be reborn? A possible solution of it . . . is definable in terms of the difference familiar in psychology between, on the one hand, *acquired* skills, habits, and memories, and on the other *native* aptitudes, instincts, and proclivities; that is, in what a human being is at a given time we may distinguish two parts, one deeper and more permanent, and another more superficial and transient.

The latter consists of everything he has acquired since birth: habits, skills, memories, and so on. This is his personality.[7] The other part, which, somewhat arbitrarily for lack of a better name we may here agree to call his individuality, comprises the aptitudes and dispositions which are native in him. These include not only the simple ones, such as aptitude for tweezer dexterity, which have been studied in laboratories because they so readily lend themselves to it, but also others more elusive: intellectual, social, and esthetic aptitudes, dispositions, and types of interest or of taste. Here the task of discriminating what is innate from what is acquired is much more difficult, for it is complicated by the fact that some existent aptitudes may only become manifest after years have passed, or perhaps never, simply because not until then, or never, did the external occasion present itself for them to be exercised—just as aptitude for tweezer dexterity, for instance, in those who have it, must remain latent so long as they are not called upon to employ tweezers.

There can be no doubt that each of us, on the basis of his same individuality—that is, of his same stock of innate latent capacities and incapacities—would have developed a more or less different empirical mind and personality if, for instance, he had been put at birth in a different family, or had later been thrust by some external accident into a radically different sort of environment, or had had a different kind of education, or had met and married a very different type of person, and so on.

Reflection on this fact should cause one to take his present personality with a large grain of salt, viewing it no longer humorlessly as his absolute self, but rather, in imaginative perspective, as but one of the various personalities which his individuality was equally capable of generating had it happened to enter phenomenal history through birth in a different envi-

---

[7] Lat. *persona* = a mask for actors (*per* = through, and *sonus* = sound); thus, the mask or appearance through which the voice speaks.

ronment. Thus, to the question: What is it that could be supposed to be reborn? an intelligible answer may be returned by saying that it might be the core of positive and negative aptitudes and tendencies which we have called a man's individuality, as distinguished from his personality. And the fact might further be that, perhaps as a result of persistent striving to acquire a skill or trait he desires, but for which he now has but little gift, aptitude for it in future births would be generated and incorporated into his individuality. . . .

Another objection which has been advanced against the transmigration hypothesis is that without the awareness of identity which memory provides, rebirth would not be discernibly different from the death of one person followed by the birth of another. In this connection, Lamont quotes Leibniz's question: "Of what use would it be to you, sir, to become king of China, on condition that you forgot what you have been? Would it not be the same as if God, at the same time he destroyed you, created a king in China?" [8]

But continuousness of memory, rather than preservation of a comprehensive span of memories, is what is significant for consciousness of one's identity. Thus, for example, none of us finds his sense of identity impaired by the fact that he has no memories of the earliest years of his present life. . . . That the sense of identity depends on *gradualness of change in ourselves*, rather than on preservation unchanged of any specific part of ourselves, strikes one forcibly when he chances to find letters which he wrote thirty or forty years before. Many of them may awaken no recollections whatever, even of the existence of the persons to whom they were addressed or whom they mentioned, and it sometimes seems incredible also that the person who wrote the things they contain should be the same as his present self. In truth, it is not the same in any strict sense, but only continuous with the former person. . . .

One more difficulty in the conception of survival as transmigration remains to be examined. It concerns not so much the theoretical possibility of transmigration as its capacity to satisfy certain demands which death appears to thwart—such capacity being what alone gives to a conception of survival practical importance and interest for us in this life.

One of these demands, as we have seen, is that the injustices of this life should somehow be eventually redressed; hence, conceptions of survival have generally included the idea of such redress as effected in the life after death. And, when survival has been thought of as later lives on earth, the redress has been conceived to consist in this—that the good and evil deeds,

[8] Corliss Lamont, *The Illusion of Immortality*, p. 22; Leibniz, *Philosophische Schriften*, ed. Gerhardt, IV, 300.

the strivings, the experiences, and the merits and faults of one life, all would have their just fruits in subsequent lives. . . .

Now, however, it may be objected that, without memory of what one is being rewarded or punished for, one learns nothing from the retribution, which is then ethically useless. . . . But the eye-for-eye and tooth-for-tooth mode of moral education is not the only one there is, nor necessarily always the most effective. If, for example, impatience caused Tom to do Dick an injury, the morally important thing as regards Tom is that he should acquire the patience he lacks; but the undergoing by him of a similar injury at the hand of Dick is not the only possible way in which he could come to do so. Indeed, it would contribute to this only in proportion as Dick's retaliation were prompt and were known to be retaliation for the injury resulting from Tom's impatience. Other ways in which Tom might learn patience are conceivable. He might, for example, eventually find himself in a situation psychologically conducive to the development of patience —one, for example, where his love for someone would cause him to endure year after year without resentment the vagaries or follies of the loved person —or, more generally, some situation which for one reason or another he would be powerless to alter or to escape and in which only patient resignation would avail to bring him any peace. . . .

It is further conceivable that Tom's eventual landing into a situation forcing him to practice patience should be a perfectly natural consequence of his vice of impatience. Each of us that is old and mature enough to view the course of his life in perspective can see that again and again his aptitudes, his habits, his tastes or interests, his virtues or his vices—in short, what he was at a given time—brought about, not by plan but automatically, changes in his material or social circumstances, in his associates, in his opportunities and so on; and that these changes in turn, quite as much as those due to purely external causes, contributed to shape for the better or the worse what he then became. This, which is observable within one life, could occur equally naturally as between the present and the subsequent bodied lives of a continuous though gradually changing self. . . .

We have now considered the chief of the difficulties in the way of the transmigration form of the survival hypothesis. In attempting to meet them . . . we have gradually defined a form of survival which appears possible and which, if it should be a fact, would have significance for the living.

C. J. DUCASSE

What reincarnates is a mystery to many minds because they find a difficulty in understanding such a permanency as must stand behind repeated incarna-

tions. Their minds are so identified with the body in its relations and surroundings that they are unable to dissociate themselves from it. We must first understand that there is in us That which never changes at all, whatever changes are brought about by it. We never are the things we see, or feel, or hear, or know, or experience. No matter how many the experiences may be, we are still unchanged with the possibility of infinite other experiences. That the Self in us is changeless may seem difficult for the Western mind to grasp, thinking that without change there is no progress; but it may be perceived by the fact of our identity (or I-am-I consciousness) remaining ever the same in a child's body and through all the changes of body that have occurred since childhood. If the identity ever changed, it could never observe change. Only that which is permanent and stable can see change, can know it, can make it.

Robert Crosbie
The Friendly Philosopher

Karma as Related to Rebirth

[From *The Religions of Man*[1] by Huston Smith, Professor of Philosophy at Massachusetts Institute of Technology, and a widely traveled lecturer on comparative religion.]

In the Hindu view, spirit no more depends on the body it inhabits than body depends on the clothes it wears or the house it lives in. When we outgrow a suit or find our house too cramped we exchange these for roomier ones that offer our bodies freer play. Souls do the same. . . . The mechanism that ties these new acquisitions together is the law of karma. . . .

Karma means, roughly, the moral law of cause and effect. Science has alerted the Western world to the importance of causal relationships in the physical world. Every physical event, we are inclined to believe, has its cause, and every cause will have its determinate effects. India extends this concept of universal causation to include man's moral and spiritual life as well. To some extent the West has also. "As a man sows, so shall he reap"; or again, "Sow a thought and reap an act, sow an act and reap a habit, sow a habit and reap a character, sow a character and reap a destiny"—these are

[1] New York: Harper & Row, 1958, Chap. II.

ways the West has put the point. The difference is that India tightens up and extends its concept of moral law to see it as absolutely binding and brooking no exceptions. The present condition of each individual's interior life—how happy he is, how confused or serene, how much he can see—is an exact product of what he has wanted and got in the past; and equally, his present thoughts and decisions are determining his future states. Each act he directs upon the world has its equal and opposite reaction on himself. Each thought and deed delivers an unseen chisel blow toward the sculpturing of his destiny.

This idea of *karma* and the completely moral universe it implies . . . commits the Hindu who understands it to complete personal responsibility. . . . Most persons are unwilling to admit this. They prefer, as the psychologists would say, to project—to locate the source of their difficulties outside themselves. . . . This, say the Hindus, is simply immature. . . .

Because *karma* implies a lawful world, it has often been interpreted as fatalism. However often Hindus may have succumbed to this interpretation, it is untrue to the doctrine itself. *Karma* decrees that every decision must have its determinate consequences, but the decisions themselves are, in the last analysis, freely arrived at. Or, to approach the matter from the other direction, the consequences of a man's past decisions condition his present lot, as a card player finds himself dealt a particular hand, but is left free to play that hand in a number of ways. This means that the career of a soul as it threads its course through innumerable human bodies is guided by its choices. . . . We live in a world in which there is no chance or accident; the words are simply covers for ignorance.

HUSTON SMITH

Nowhere within the frame of the archaic civilizations are suffering and pain regarded as "blind" and without meaning. . . . In the light of the law of karma, sufferings not only find a meaning but also acquire a positive value. . . . A man not totally devoid of intelligence can serenely tolerate the sufferings, griefs, and blows that come to him . . . because each of them solves a karmic equation that had remained unsolved in some previous existence.

Mircea Eliade
The Myth of the Eternal Return

◆ ∗ ●

PART I

Reincarnation
in Myth and Symbol

Throughout the inhabited world, in all times and under every circumstance, the myths of man have flourished; and they have been the living inspiration of whatever else may have appeared out of the activities of the human body and mind. . . . Myth is the secret opening through which the inexhaustible energies of the cosmos pour into human cultural manifestations. Religions, philosophies, arts, the social forms of primitive and historic man, prime discoveries in science and technology, the very dreams that blister sleep, boil up from the basic, magic ring of myth. . . . The symbols of mythology are not manufactured; they cannot be ordered, invented, or permanently suppressed. They are spontaneous productions of the psyche, and each bears within it, undamaged, the germ power of its source.

JOSEPH CAMPBELL
The Hero with a Thousand Faces

The dreams of ancient and modern man are written in the same language as the myths whose authors lived in the dawn of history. . . . Yet this language has been forgotten by modern man. Not when he is asleep, but when he is awake. Is it important to understand this language also in our waking state? . . . I believe that symbolic language is the one foreign language that each of us must learn. Its understanding brings us in touch with one of the most significant sources of wisdom, that of the myth, and it brings us in touch with the deeper layers of our own personalities. . . . Indeed, both dreams and myths are important communications from ourselves to ourselves. If we do not understand the language in which they are written, we miss a great deal of what we know and tell ourselves in those hours when we are not busy manipulating the outside world.

ERICH FROMM
The Forgotten Language

◆ ✳ ●

Reincarnation
in Myth and Symbol

"The cycle of birth, death, and rebirth is about the most basic theme of myth and religion," writes Alan Watts in his introduction to Henderson and Oakes' *The Wisdom of the Serpent—The Myths of Death, Rebirth, and Resurrection.*[1] "Nothing is more provocative than the idea of death," he adds. "It is because men know that they will die that they have created the arts and sciences, the philosophies and religions. For nothing is more thought-provoking than the thought which seems to put an end to thought: 'What will it be like to go to sleep and never wake up?' Irresistibly this seems to suggest a corollary: 'Where and who was I before my father and mother conceived me?' For the unthinkable-after-death appears to be the same as the unthinkable-before-birth, so that if once I came out of nothing, the odds are that I can come again and again." (P. xi.)

Although some of the myths and symbols considered in this section were used by later forms of Christianity in teaching a once-for-all resurrection, orginally they were conceived by people who believed in a process of continual rebirth of both man and the universe, and their symbols, we shall see, most obviously reflected that outlook. (In Part Five, under "The Greek Mysteries," other reincarnation myths will be considered.)

The Eternal Return

"The myth of eternal return," remarks Joseph Campbell, "displays an order of fixed forms that appear and reappear through all time. The daily round

[1] Joseph L. Henderson and Maud Oakes. New York: Braziller, 1963.

of the sun, the waning and waxing moon, the cycle of the year, and the rhythm of organic birth, death, and new birth, represent a miracle of continuous arising that is fundamental to the nature of the universe. . . . [The world] will disintegrate presently in chaos, only to burst forth again, fresh as a flower, to recommence spontaneously the inevitable course. . . . The dreamlike spell of this contemplative, metaphysically oriented tradition, where light and darkness dance together in a world-creating cosmic shadow play, carries into modern times an image that is of incalculable age." [1]

The prevalence of these ideas in the West is summarized by Mircea Eliade in his much-translated work, *The Myth of the Eternal Return*:[2]

In the third century B.C., Berosus popularized the Chaldean doctrine of the "Great Year" in a form that spread through the entire Hellenic world (whence it later passed to the Romans and the Byzantines). According to this doctrine, the universe is eternal but it is periodically destroyed and reconstituted every Great Year. . . . This doctrine of periodic universal conflagration . . . dominates the thought of Zeno and the entire Stoic cosmology.

The myth of universal combustion was decidedly in fashion throughout the Romano-Oriental world from the first century B.C. to the third century of our era; it successively found a place in a considerable number of gnostic systems derived from Greco-Irano-Judaic syncretism. Similar ideas . . . are found in India and Iran, as they are among the Mayas of Yucatan and the Aztecs of Mexico. We shall have to return to these questions; but, even now, we are in a position to emphasize . . . the optimistic character of these ideas. In fact, this optimism can be reduced to a consciousness of the normality of the cyclical catastrophe, to the certainty that it has a meaning and, above all, that it is never final.

Of course the rigid views of the Stoics of an unaltered repetition of cycles—even to the minutest particular—are logically untenable and scientifically impossible. Cycles—human and cosmic—are never circles but spirals. The earth in yearly orbit around the sun returns not to the path previously traversed, for the sun in its tremendous journey around its own moving center in the Milky Way galaxy has meanwhile drawn the planets to "new" portions of space.

Campbell speaks of perpetual recurrence in this way: "Those who have identified themselves with the mortal body and its affections will necessarily find that all is painful, since everything—for them—must end [even if subsequently to be reassembled]. But for those who have found the still point of eternity, around which all—including themselves—re-

<hr>

[1] *The Masks of God: Oriental Mythology.* New York: Viking, 1962, pp. 3–4.
[2] New York: Pantheon, 1954, pp. 87–88.

volves, everything is acceptable as it is; indeed, can even be experienced as glorious and wonderful." [3] Elsewhere in the same volume he states that the West's "concept of the hero . . . is of the actual, particular individual, who indeed is mortal and so doomed. Whereas in the Orient the true hero of all mythology is not the vainly striving, empirical personality, but that reincarnating one and only transmigrant, which, to quote a celebrated passage [from The Bhagavad-Gita] 'is never born; nor does it ever die; nor, having once been, does it ever cease to be. Unborn, eternal, changeless and of great age, it is not slain when the body is slain.' " (P. 137.)

The Dance of Shiva

In Hinduism the theme of the Eternal Return finds illustration in the stories centering around the God Shiva, the destroyer and regenerator. The myth that follows, sensitively reviewed by Nobel prize author, Hermann Hesse, in his novel *Magister Ludi*,[1] is equally applicable in Indian philosophy to immense cycles embracing worlds and galaxies, and to smaller yugas involving the death and rebirth of races and civilizations:

> The world as [the Hindu] myths portray it was in the beginning divine, radiant and happy, beautiful as spring—a golden age. But suddenly it grows sick and begins to degenerate, becomes more and more coarsened and wretched, until finally, at the end of four ever declining aeons, it is ripe to be stamped underfoot and destroyed by the dancing feet of Shiva. That is not the end of the world, however. It begins anew with the smile of the dreaming Vishnu. . . . It is truly marvelous: these people discerning and capable of suffering as hardly any other, looked upon the gruesome game of world history with horror and shame —the ever turning wheel of lust and suffering. They saw and understood the decay of creation, the lust and devilry of man and simultaneously his deep longing for purity and harmony, and discovered this glorious allegory for the whole beauty and tragedy of creation—the aeons and the decline of creation, the powerful Shiva who tramples the putrefying world to pulp and the laughing Vishnu who lies in slumber and allows a new world to be born of his divine golden dreams.

Some illuminating remarks are to be found on this myth in the just quoted work, *The Wisdom of the Serpent*. One of the authors, Joseph Henderson—whom we find occasion to quote several times in this section —is an American psychiatrist, and a former colleague of Jung. The authors state:

[3] *The Masks of God: Oriental Mythology*, p. 3.

[1] New York: Frederick Ungar, 1957, pp. 285–287.

Amongst the greatest of the names of Shiva is Nataraja, Lord of Dancers, or King of Actors. The cosmos is His theatre, there are many different steps in His repertory. He Himself is actor and audience. . . . In the night of Brahma, Nature is inert, and cannot dance till Shiva wills it: He rises from His rapture, and dancing sends through inert matter pulsing waves of awakening sounds, and lo! matter also dances appearing as a glory round about Him. Dancing, He sustains its manifold phenomena. In the fulness of time, still dancing, he destroys all forms and names by fire and gives new rest. This is poetry; but none the less, science. . . .

It is not man who has to placate an all-powerful god in this story, but the god who has to put himself in order, after the chaos engendered by the strife of opposites. And there is no end to this cycle which will be repeated throughout eternity in the dance of death and rebirth. The Western world has also had its myths of destruction with an equivalent myth of recreation, expressed either as rebirth or resurrection, or as the return of the dead to life, providing an echo of the Eastern belief in transmigration or reincarnation. But nothing we have in our cultural tradition seems quite to equal the overwhelming power of the destructive and its inevitable and unending power of rebirth as do the Eastern mythical systems. (Pp. 10, 78, 82.)

The words "this is poetry; but none the less, science," make it appropriate to mention that astronomers now consider it likely that the universe is reborn numerous times. As *The New Yorker*[2] reports: "Scientists are coming around to the view that the universe has a heart-beat. . . . The cosmos expands and contracts much as a heart does, pumping once every eighty-two billion years, and destroying and bringing to life a succession of universes with each lub-dup, or 'big bang.'" The magazine comments: "We congratulate science on finally beginning to discover its true identity, as an agency for corroborating ancient wisdom. Long before our century, before the Christian era, and even before Homer, the people of India had arrived at a 'big-bang' cosmogony."

The Resurrecting Sun

In the daily rise of the sun, and its yearly "return" at solstice time and at the vernal equinox, we have a symbol that has had universal appeal among all races. In *Man and His Symbols*, edited by C. G. Jung and others[1], Joseph Henderson writes:

We read the myths of the ancient Greeks or the folk stories of American Indians, but we fail to see any connection between them and our attitudes to the "heroes" or dramatic events of today. Yet the connections are there. And

[2] July 17, 1965.

[1] New York: Doubleday, 1964, pp. 106–108.

the symbols that represent them have not lost their relevance for mankind. . . . [A] striking example should be familiar to anyone who has grown up in a Christian society. At Christmas we may express our inner feeling for the mythological birth of a semidivine child, even though we may not believe in the doctrine of the virgin birth of Christ or have any kind of conscious religious faith. Unknowingly, we have fallen in with the symbolism of rebirth. This is a relic of an immensely older solstice festival, which carries the hope that the fading winter landscape of the northern hemisphere will be renewed. For all our sophistication we find satisfaction in this symbolic festival, just as we join with our children at Easter in the pleasant ritual of Easter eggs and Easter rabbits.

But do we understand what we do, or see the connection between the story of Christ's birth, death, and resurrection and the folk symbolism of Easter? Usually we do not even care to consider such things intellectually. Yet they complement each other. Christ's crucifixion on Good Friday seems at first sight to belong to the same pattern of fertility symbolism that one finds in the rituals of such other "saviors" as Osiris, Tammuz, Orpheus, and Balder. They, too, were of divine or semidivine birth, they flourished, were killed, and were reborn. They belonged, in fact, to cyclic religions in which the death and rebirth of the god-king was an eternally recurring myth.

Dr. Henderson then makes an interesting point: "But the resurrection of Christ on Easter Sunday is much less satisfying from a ritual point of view than is the symbolism of the cyclic religions. For Christ ascends to sit at the right hand of God the Father: His resurrection occurs once and for all. It is this finality of the Christian concept of the resurrection (the Christian idea of the Last Judgment has a similar 'closed' theme) that distinguishes Christianity from other god-king myths. It happened once, and the ritual merely commemorates it." "But this sense of finality," Henderson continues, "is probably one reason why early Christians, still influenced by pre-Christian traditions, felt that Christianity needed to be supplemented by some elements of an older fertility ritual. They needed the recurring promise of rebirth; and that is what is symbolized by the egg and the rabbit of Easter." [2] The pagan Easter, of course, was a sun festival, as it coincided with the vernal equinox, when nature gloriously resurrects. The word Easter comes from Ostara, the Scandinavian goddess of spring, and Easter eggs were called eggs of Ostara.

During the winter-solstice celebrations in honor of the reborn Sun, the fir tree, we know, played an important part. The evergreen trees, ever renewing themselves, are a highly suggestive symbol for immortality and rebirth, and likewise the lighting of the candles that adorn them. The Jewish Hanukkah, the festival of lights, is also celebrated around this period.

At Christmas, or solstice time, most of the ancient sun gods were re-

[2] P. 108.

born: the Persian Mithra, Egyptian Osiris, Greek Bacchus, the Roman and Greek Apollo, the Phoenician Adonis, the Phrygian Atys. Both physically, as the sun, and spiritually, as Great Teachers, or luminaries of wisdom, "they came in the midst of the cold and dark, and were the hidden, secret promise of spring." It may be significant that Jesus—called by some the Christ Sun—was eventually said to be born at this widely celebrated solstice cycle. Before the fifth century various dates were assigned for his birth: January 6, March 25, April 19, May 20, December 25. St. Clement of Alexandria set it at November 17.[3]

The Lunar Myth

[From The Myth of the Eternal Return, by Mircea Eliade:] [1]

The phases of moon—appearance, increase, wane, disappearance, followed by reappearance after three nights of darkness—have played an immense part in the elaboration of cyclical concepts. We find analogous concepts especially in the archaic apocalypses and anthropogonies; deluge or flood puts an end to an exhausted and sinful humanity, and a new regenerated humanity is born, usually from a mythical "ancestor" who escaped the catastrophe. . . .

In the "lunar perspective," the death of the individual and the *periodic* death of humanity are necessary, even as the three days of darkness preceding the "rebirth" of the moon are necessary. The death of the individual and the death of humanity are alike necessary for their regeneration. Any form whatever, by the mere fact that it exists as such and endures, necessarily loses vigor and becomes worn; to recover vigor, it must be reabsorbed into the formless if only for an instant; it must be restored to the primordial unity from which it issued. . . . What predominates in all these cosmico-mythological lunar conceptions is the cyclical recurrence of what has been before, in a word, eternal return . . . the motif of the repetition of an archetypal gesture, projected upon all planes—cosmic, biological, historical, human.

The Immortal Phoenix

For several milleniums, at least, the symbol of symbols for rebirth has been the phoenix, "a mythical bird of great beauty, the only one of its kind, fabled to live 500 or 600 years in the Arabian wilderness, to burn itself on a

[3] Britannica, 1959, article "Christmas."

[1] New York: Pantheon, 1954, pp. 86–89.

funeral pile and to rise from the ashes in the freshness of youth and live through another cycle of years." [1]

"The most familiar form of the legend," according to the *Britannica*,[2] "is that in the *Physiologus*,[3] where the phoenix is described as an Indian bird which subsists on air for 500 years, after which, lading his wings with spices, he flies to Heliopolis, enters the temple there, and is burned to ashes on the altar. Next day the young phoenix is already feathered; on the third day his pinions are full grown, he salutes the priest and flies away."

Some interesting facts are brought together by Dr. E. V. H. Kenealy in *The Book of God: The Apocalypse of Adam-Oannes*:[4]

Herodotus, as we have seen, mentions that the Phoenix was one of the sacred birds, or hieroglyphics of the Egyptians, and it is a curious circumstance that we find nations the most remote from each other well acquainted with this symbol. The ancient Irish ascribed a longevity of *six centuries* to their Phoenix, and considered *the production of the young bird as a restoration to life of the old one.* . . . By the Japanese the Phoenix is called *Kirin*, and by the Turks *Kerkes*. According to the latter it lives a thousand years. . . .

The Phoenix is also very plainly the same as the *Simorgh* of Persian romance; and the account which is given us of this last bird yet more decisively establishes the opinion that the death and revival of the Phoenix exhibit the successive destruction and reproduction of the world, which many believed to be effected by the agency of a fiery deluge. . . .

[The Rabbis speak of] an enormous Bird, sometimes standing on the earth, and sometimes walking in the ocean . . . while its head props the sky; and with the symbol, they have also adopted the doctrine to which it relates. They teach that there are to be seven successive renewals of the globe. . . . This opinion, which involves the doctrine of the pre-existence of each renewed creature, they may either have learned during their Babylonian captivity, or it may have been part of the primeval religion which their priests had preserved from remote times.

In a beautiful passage in his *Philosophy of History*, Hegel gives his interpretation of the phoenix myth as related to reincarnation. This will be quoted in Part Five, as will also Carlyle's similar use of the symbol. See also the poem of the Sufi poet, Hafiz, under "Islam" in Part Two.

The Serpent Reborn

[Nu, the deceased, triumphantly says:] I am the Serpent Sata whose years are many. I die and am born again each day. I am the Serpent Sata which

---

[1] *American College Dictionary*. New York: Random House, 1957.
[2] Eleventh edition.
[3] A collection of some fifty Christian allegories relating to the animal world. Though banned by the Church they were avidly read during the middle ages. (Eds.)
[4] London, undated, pp. 175–176.

dwelleth in the uttermost parts of the earth. I die and am born again, and . . .
grow young each day.

—*The Egyptian Book of the Dead* [1]

Dr. Henderson states in *The Wisdom of the Serpent*: [2] "The snake as a
symbol of rebirth following death is an ancient, yet ever-present conception
which can be traced through endless patterns of sculpture, painting, verse,
and the myths of gods, demi-gods, or heroic mortals. This is so because
during its yearly period of hibernation the snake sheds its skin and reappears as if renewed." It is this characteristic that has made the reptile such a
graphic symbol for reincarnation, as well as for psychological rebirth. Furthermore, to free itself from the constricting, seamless, outgrown encase-
ment, and function in its new skin, the snake must verily undergo the
throes of "death."

"The wisdom of the serpent," Henderson remarks, "is suggested by its
watchful lidless eye," and "lies essentially in mankind's having projected
into this lowly creature his own secret wish to obtain from the earth a
knowledge he cannot find in waking daylight consciousness alone. This is
the knowledge of death and rebirth forever withheld except at those times
when some transcendent principle, emerging from the depths, makes it
available to consciousness." [3] Westerners who find the serpent symbol repugnant because of the Garden of Eden story might well recall these words
of Jesus: "Be ye . . . wise as serpents, and harmless as doves." [4]

The eggs laid by the reptile are also indicative of rebirth, and it is
interesting that the famous 700-foot Serpent Mound in Ohio in the United
States bears an egg in its opened mouth.

The various positions assumed by this legless creature are reminders of
cyclic return, whether the snake, with wavelike motion, be slithering
through the grass, or is twined around a branch, coiled in repose, or ready
to strike. Sometimes the serpent is shown swallowing its tail. It is then
called the Circle of Eternity, symbolizing beginningless and endless life.
The tail running into the mouth would then signify the perpetual turning
of the circle, and the periodical coming forth and disappearing of the manifested universe. The word universe means, by derivation, "the turning of
the One."

[1] Trans. E. A. Wallis Budge. London: Kegan Paul, 1901, II, 278.
[2] Pp. 36–37.
[3] P. 36
[4] Matthew 10:16.

Psyche and the Butterfly

The goddess Psyche, to whom we are indebted for the root of our word psychology, was one of the names given by the Greeks to the soul. It was also the designation they gave to the butterfly. In fact, in early Greek art this goddess, as the soul, was represented as a butterfly or tiny winged creature.[1] The symbology involved here is too well known to go into detailed discussion. However, while everyone knows of the amazing metamorphic change from caterpillar to butterfly, few are aware that while in the caterpillar stage, the larva undergoes three or four complete sheddings of the skin—a characteristic that can be related to the serpent symbol just discussed. The newly clothed caterpillar is so different in marking from its "predecessor" that only a trained observer appreciates that the same species is involved in all these transformations. Then after the sleep of "death" in the tomblike chrysalis, form, function, and habit are all so changed that nothing but the evidence of direct testimony would convince us that the beautiful butterfly was the "re-embodiment" of the crawling, earthbound caterpillar.

Of course, metamorphosis and reincarnation are not identical processes, for metamorphosis usually means the transformation of the *same* form while rebirth involves the use of *new* forms. Yet Leibniz had grounds for believing that metempsychosis was actually a form of metamorphosis.[2] However, as symbols, both ideas have ever been inseparable. Ovid's celebrated volume, *The Metamorphoses*—from which our poets and scholars have recounted the myths of Greece and Rome appearing in Western literature—reveals that all these stories signify eternal transformation and re-embodiment. "My design leads me to speak of forms changed into new bodies." The reincarnation teaching of Pythagoras formed part of Ovid's design. These verses, in John Dryden's translation, may be found under "Ovid" in Part Five.

The Psyche myth itself has undergone radical metamorphosis in modern times. Western psychology, denying an eternal Self in man, was obliged to identify Psyche with the mind and mental processes alone. "Psychology," as Erich Fromm remarks, "became a science lacking its main subject matter, the soul."[3] But many psychologists, as we shall later see, are fast extending their horizons to include the insights of Eastern psychology, and

[1] *American College Dictionary*, under "Psyche."
[2] See under "Leibniz."
[3] *Psychoanalysis and Religion*. Yale University Press, 1950, p. 6.

if this trend continues, perhaps the goddess Psyche, as originally conceived, may incarnate again on earth.

The Transformations of Proteus

In classical mythology, Proteus, the old man of the sea, could change his form at will, and when pursued would escape by transforming himself into perhaps a dreadful beast, or into fire, or flood. (Our word "protean" has this derivative heritage.) One day a man made up his mind to catch Proteus and find out what he really was. The god at the time was sleeping heavily as a stone, but as soon as touched, he woke and turned himself into a plant. The man was about to pull up the plant, when, lo! a serpent coiled at his feet, and when he sought to kill the snake, a man stood laughing in his face. The man melted into thin air, a lightning-flash disclosing the outline of a wondrous spirit mounting ever higher until it was lost in the starry spaces of the sky. Here, it may be, we have described the universal Proteus —Life in its transmigratory journey through the kingdoms to man, and then to divine man, with power over all the cosmic forces. The old Hebrew Kabalistic aphorism tells the same story: "A stone becomes a plant, a plant an animal, an animal a man, and man a God."

Proteus was supposed to enjoy the gift of prophecy, a gift he exercised most reluctantly. Thus when humans wished to consult him, he would change his form with bewildering rapidity, and unless they clung to him through all the changes, no answer could be obtained to their questionings. Through recourse to Eastern philosophy this may find a ready explanation: all the forms through which life is constantly re-embodied are illusory or mayâvic. Only the man who clings to the Real within the form becomes the true sage and seer.

A number of the gods of the sea, of whom Proteus was one, were amphibious. They could live alternately on land and in the water. This characteristic has been related to rebirth, or alternate existence on earth and in the states of consciousness after death—the latter being aptly symbolized as the Great Sea and its mysterious, unfathomable depths. With the Greeks, amphibious meant simply "life on two planes," from amphi, "on both sides," and bios, life.[1]

The Wheel of Rebirth

In Buddhist art, sculpture, and architecture, the wheel is widely used to symbolize karma and reincarnation. Buddha's first sermon after attaining

[1] See p. 217.

enlightenment was called "Turning the Wheel of the Law." Later, the ceaselessly revolving wheel, which involves the unwary soul in the obligatory round of rebirths—as distinguished from will-chosen ones—signified the Twelve Nidanas, or Wheel of Causation. These twelve causes of existence, each dependent on its predecessor, belong to the most abstruse doctrines of the Buddhist metaphysical system.

The wheel of rebirth is also to be found in the Orphic mysteries of Greece. Dr. A. C. Pearson, Regius Professor of Greek at Cambridge, writes:

The prevalence of this mystical belief [of transmigration] and its religious potency are illustrated with remarkable clearness in certain inscriptions on golden tablets found in S. Italy, near Rome, and in Crete, which are chiefly attributed to the 4th or 5th centuries b.c. . . . One of these contains some words which form part of the appeal of the purified soul: "I have flown out of the sorrowful weary Wheel; I have passed with eager feet to the Circle desired." This refers to the mystical Wheel of Fortune which in its revolutions symbolizes the cycle of successive lives necessary to be traversed by the harassed soul before its final release. This specific cycle of progress, as well as the more general conception of a *Kuklos* [or cycle] in human affairs, is traditionally attributed to the Orphic-Pythagorean sphere of thought.[1]

The later Greeks continued the analogy. G. R. S. Mead states in *Orpheus*: [2] "The wheel of life, referred to by Pythagoras, is called by Proclus (*Tim.*, i. 32) the 'cycle of generation.' . . . Simplicius (*De Cælo*, ii. 91, C) says that it was symbolized by the wheel of Ixion, and adds, 'he was bound by God to the wheel of fate and of generation.' " Ixion, it will be recalled, was punished by Zeus for his love for Hera by being bound on an eternally revolving wheel in Tartarus.

W. R. Inge writes: "Even in that most Judaic of the epistles, that attributed to St. James, we are almost startled to find the Orphic phrase 'the wheel of birth.' . . ."[3]

Philosophically viewed, the whirling wheel and its ever motionless hub, can be a potent symbol of the human struggle for insight and harmony. Identification of consciousness with the rising and falling rim—or the body and personality—inevitably leads to an unbalanced outlook. Only in the still center of the imperishable Self, is true perspective achieved. Then the ups and downs of rebirth—even while experienced—disturb not. The Buddha therefore taught, as so beautifully expressed by Sir Edwin Arnold in *The Light of Asia*:

[1] Hastings' *Encyclopædia of Religion and Ethics*, XII, 432, article "Transmigration in Greek Religion."
[2] London, John Watkins, 1965, p. 192.
[3] *The Platonic Tradition in English Religious Thought*. London: Longmans, Green, 1926, p. 11.

If ye lay bound upon the wheel of change,
And no way were of breaking from the chain,
The Heart of boundless Being is a curse,
The Soul of Things fell Pain.
Ye are not bound! the Soul of Things is sweet,
The Heart of Being is celestial rest;
Stronger than woe is will: that which was Good
Doth pass to Better—Best.

◆ * ●

PART II

Reincarnation
in the World's Religions

If I were asked under what sky the human mind has most fully developed some of its choicest gifts, has most deeply pondered on the greatest problems of life, and has found solutions of some of them which well deserve the attention of those who have studied Plato and Kant—I should point to India. And if I were to ask myself from what literature we, here in Europe, we who have been nurtured almost exclusively on the thoughts of Greeks and Romans, and of one Semitic race, may draw that corrective which is most wanted in order to make our inner life more perfect, more comprehensive, more universal, in fact more truly human, a life, not for this life only, but a transfigured and eternal life—again I should point to India.

F. MAX MÜLLER
India, What Can It Teach Us?
(Cambridge University Lectures, 1882)

Through her connection with Great Britain, India is once again brought into relationship with the Western world. The interpenetration of the two great currents of human effort at such a crisis in the history of the human race is not without meaning for the future. With its profound sense of spiritual reality brooding over the world of our ordinary experience . . . Indian thought may perhaps wean us moderns from a too exclusive occupation with secular life or with the temporary formulations in which logical thought has too often sought to imprison spiritual aspiration.

We do not seem to be mentally or spiritually prepared for the increasing intimacy into which remote peoples are drawn by the force of physical and economic circumstances. The world which has found itself as a single body is feeling for its soul. May we not prepare for the truth of the world's yet unborn soul by a free interchange of ideas and the development of a philosophy which will combine the best of European humanism and Asiatic Religion, a philosophy profounder and more living than either, endowed with greater spiritual and ethical force, which will conquer the hearts of men and compel peoples to acknowledge its sway?

S. RADHAKRISHNAN
"The Religion of the Spirit and the World's Need"
The Philosophy of Sarvepalli Radhakrishnan

◆ ✳ ●

Hinduism

THE VEDAS

What extracts from the Vedas I have read fall on me like the light of a higher and purer luminary, which describes a loftier course through a purer stratum,—free from particulars, simple, universal.

—Thoreau[1]

"If we wish to learn to understand the beginning of our own culture," writes Winternitz, "if we wish to understand the oldest Indo-European culture, we must go to India, where the oldest literature of an Indo-European people is preserved. For whatever view we may adopt on the problem of the antiquity of Indian literature, we can safely say that the oldest monument of the literature of the Indians is at the same time the oldest monument of Indo-European literature which we possess." [2] This is the generally accepted view of the Western oriental scholars.[3]

What is this oldest monument? Of the thousands of volumes of Indian literature which have survived, the Vedas are acknowledged to be the most ancient. This scripture "is earlier than that of either Greece or Israel and reveals a high level of civilization among those who found in it the expression of their worship." [4] It should then be of significance to learn what the Vedas say on reincarnation. Most Western orientalists deny outright that the Vedas teach reincarnation, and state that only in the Brâhmanas and Upanishads the doctrine appears. Albert Schweitzer thought similarly: "The hymns of the Rig-Veda knew nothing as yet of a cycle of rebirths." [5]

---

[1] *The Journal of Henry D. Thoreau.* Boston: Houghton, Mifflin, 1949, II, 3–4.
[2] M. Winternitz, *History of Indian Literature.* University of Calcutta, 1927, I, 6.
[3] F. Max Müller, *Ancient History of Sanskrit Literature,* 1859, p. 63; Z. A. Ragozin, *Vedic India,* 1895, p. 114; Maurice Bloomfield, *The Religion of the Veda,* 1908, p. 17.
[4] Nicol Macnicol, *Hindu Scriptures.* London: J. M. Dent, 1938, p. xiv.
[5] A. Schweitzer, *Indian Thought and Its Development.* Boston: Beacon Press, 1957, p. 47.

The renowned oriental philosopher and scholar, Radhakrishnan, President of India, presents evidence to the contrary. In his translation of *The Principal Upanishads*[6] he states that the *elements* of reincarnation are to be found even in the earliest of the Vedas, namely, the Rig: "The passage of the soul from the body, its dwelling in other forms of existence, its return to human form, the determination of future existence by the principle of Karma are all mentioned. Mitra is born again.[7] The Dawn (Usas) is born again and again (I.92.10). 'I seek neither release nor return.'[8] 'The immortal self will be reborn in a new body due to its meritorious deeds.' "[9]

Max Müller's translation of the 32nd Rik of the Rig Veda, I, 164, reads: "Taking many births he has entered upon misery." However, an exhaustive study of the early Aryans is not possible, for as this German orientalist remarks: "We have no right to suppose that we have even a hundredth part of the religious and popular poetry that existed during the Vedic age."[10]

Regarding the Brâhmanas—that portion of the Vedas intended for the guidance of the Brahmins in the use of the Vedic hymns—Radhakrishnan states that "rebirth on earth is sometimes looked upon as a blessing and not an evil to be escaped from. It is promised as a reward for knowing some divine mystery."[11]

THE UPANISHADS

[The Upanishads are regarded as esoteric interpretations of the Vedas, and form a portion of the Vedas, although composed much later. The term "Upanishad" is explained by the Hindu pundits as meaning that which destroys ignorance and thus produces liberation of the spirit through knowledge of hidden truth. The selections below are from the translations of Charles Johnston published in the volume *Selections from the Upanishads and The Tao Te King*.[1] The first extract is from the Katha Upanishad. A young man, by name Nachiketas, goes to the House of Death, and Yama, the god of death, grants him three wishes.]

NACHIKETAS SPEAKS   This doubt that there is of a man that has gone forth [died]: "He exists," say some; and "He exists not," others say. A

[6] New York: Harper and Row, 1953, pp. 43-44.
[7] X.85.19.
[8] V.46.1.
[9] I.164.30; see also I.164.38.
[10] *Six Systems of Indian Philosophy*, 1899, p. 41.
[11] Sat. Brâhmanas, viii. I.4.10; *Indian Philosophy*. London: Allen & Unwin, 1929, I, 133.

[1] Los Angeles: Cunningham Press, 1951.

knowledge of this, taught by thee, this of my wishes is the third wish.

DEATH SPEAKS . . . not easily knowable, and subtle is this law. Choose, Nachiketas, another wish; hold me not to it, but spare me this. . . . Choose sons and grandsons of a hundred years, and much cattle, and elephants and gold and horses. . . . Choose wealth and length of days. . . . Ask me not of death, Nachiketas.

NACHIKETAS SPEAKS Tomorrow these fleeting things wear out the vigour of a mortal's powers. Even the whole of life is short. . . . Not by wealth can a man be satisfied. Shall we choose wealth if we have seen thee? Shall we desire life while thou art master? . . . This that they doubt about, O Death, what is in the great Beyond, tell me of that. This wish that draws near to the mystery, Nachiketas chooses no other wish than that. . . .

DEATH SPEAKS Thou indeed, pondering on dear and dearly-loved desires, O Nachiketas, hast passed them by. Not this way of wealth hast thou chosen, in which many men sink. . . . Thou art steadfast in the truth; may a questioner like thee, Nachiketas, come to us. . . .

The knower is never born nor dies, nor is it from anywhere, nor did it become anything. Unborn, eternal, immemorial, this ancient is not slain when the body is slain. . . . Smaller than small, greater than great, this Self is hidden in the heart of man. . . . Understanding this great lord the Self, bodiless in bodies, stable among unstable, the wise man cannot grieve.

Know that the Self is the lord of the chariot, the body verily is the chariot; know that the soul is the charioteer, and emotion the reins. They say that the bodily powers are the horses, and that the external world is their field. When the Self, the bodily powers and emotion are joined together, this is the right enjoyer; thus say the wise. But for the unwise, with emotion ever unrestrained, his bodily powers run away with him, like the unruly horses of the charioteer. . . . He whose charioteer is wisdom, who grasps the reins—emotion—firmly, he indeed gains the end of the path, the supreme resting-place of the emanating Power. . . . This is the hidden Self; in all beings it shines not forth; but is perceived by the piercing subtle soul of the subtle-sighted. . . .

He is released from the mouth of Death, having gained the lasting thing which is above the great, which has neither sound nor touch nor form nor change nor taste nor smell, but is eternal, beginningless, endless.

This is the immemorial teaching of Nachiketas, declared by Death. Speaking it and hearing it the sage is mighty in the eternal world.

Whosoever, being pure, shall cause this supreme secret to be heard in the assembly of those who seek the Eternal . . . he indeed builds for endlessness, he builds for endlessness.

[In the Brihad Aranyaka Upanishad, the daily "reincarnation" cycle of sleeping and waking, leads to a consideration of the alternations of death and rebirth:]

What is the Soul? It is the Consciousness in the life-powers. It is the Light within the heart. This Spirit of man wanders through both worlds, yet remains unchanged. . . .

The Spirit of man has two dwelling-places: both this world and the other world. The borderland between them is the third, the land of dreams. . . . Leaving the bodily world through the door of dream, the sleepless Spirit views the sleeping powers. . . . Soaring upward and downward in dreamland, the god makes manifold forms; now laughing and rejoicing with fair beauties, now beholding terrible things. . . . Then clothed in radiance, returns to his own home, the gold-gleaming Genius, swan of everlasting. . . . [From this state of *Sushupti* when the body is in deepest sleep and the soul completely free] the Spirit of man returns again by the same path hurrying back to his former dwelling-place in the world of waking. . . .

Then as a wagon heavy-laden might go halting and creaking, so the embodied soul goes halting . . . when it has gone so far that a man is giving up the ghost. When he falls into weakness, whether it be through old-age or sickness he falls into weakness, then like as a mango or the fruit . . . of the holy fig-tree is loosened from its stem, so the Spirit of man is loosed from these bodily members. . . . When he falls into a swoon, as though he had lost his senses, the life-powers are gathered in round the soul; and the soul, taking them up together in their radiant substance, enters with them into the inner heart. . . . Then the point of the heart grows luminous, and when it has grown luminous, it lights the soul upon its way. . . . The soul becomes conscious and enters into Consciousness. . . . As a worker in gold, taking an ornament, moulds it to another form newer and fairer; so in truth the soul, leaving the body here, and putting off unwisdom, makes for itself another form newer and fairer: a form like the forms of departed souls, or of the seraphs, or of the gods. . . .

Through his past works he shall return once more to birth, entering whatever form his heart is set on. When he has received full measure of reward in paradise for the works he did, from that world he returns again to this, the world of works. . . . According as were his works and walks in [another] life, so he becomes. He that does righteously becomes righteous. He that does evil becomes evil. He becomes holy through holy works and evil through evil. As they said of old: Man verily is formed of desire; as his desire is, so is his will; as his will is, so he works; and whatever work he does, in the likeness of it he grows.

THE BHAGAVAD-GITA

["In 1785," writes Radhakrishnan, "Charles Wilkins published an English translation of The Bhagavad-Gita, to which Warren Hastings (the first British Governor-General of India) wrote a preface in which he said that works like The Bhagavad-Gita 'will survive when the British dominion in India shall have long ceased to exist and when the sources which it once yielded of wealth and power are lost to remembrance.' "[1]

Three years later a Russian translation was published at the Moscow University Press through the agency of Nikolai Novikov, the eminent Russian journalist and writer.[2] The first German rendition is dated 1802, and August von Schlegel, who studied Sanskrit, edited the work in Bonn in 1823. Schlegel's glowing tribute is quoted later. The poem made a remarkable impression on Wilhelm von Humboldt, who said that "this episode of the Mahabharata was the most beautiful, nay perhaps, the only true philosophical poem which all the literatures known to us can show."[3] He devoted a long treatise to it in the Proceedings of the Academy of Berlin (1825–26). The interest in the Gita of such American authors as Emerson, Thoreau, and Whittier, is considered in Part Five.

In July, 1945, upon witnessing the first explosion of the atom bomb, atomic scientist Robert Oppenheimer found himself repeating a verse from Chapter 11 of the Gita. He had learned Sanskrit in order to read this and other Hindu works in the original.[4]

"When disappointments stare me in the face," wrote Gandhi, "and when I see not one ray of light . . . I turn to The Bhagavad-Gita . . . and I immediately begin to smile in the midst of overwhelming sorrow. My life has been full of external tragedies and if they have not left any visible and indelible effect on me, I owe it to the teaching of The Bhagavad-Gita."[5]

The Gita is in the form of a dialogue between Krishna, the great spirit-

[1] *Eastern Religions and Western Thought.* New York: Oxford University Press, 1940, pp. 247–248.
[2] N. V. Guberti, *Materials for Russian Bibliography.* Moscow: 1878, II, 309–13.
[3] Letter to Fr. von Gentz, 1827.
[4] *Time,* Nov. 8, 1948.
[5] *Young India,* August 6, 1925.

ual teacher of India, and his disciple Arjuna. While the background of the story is a war between two branches of a tribe in northern India, the poem is regarded in the East as a psychological study of the hidden conflicts raging within the mind and heart of man. At Arjuna's request, Krishna becomes his charioteer on the field of battle, and instructs him in philosophy so that he may fight and conquer. Esoterically, Krishna is viewed as the Supreme Self "seated in the heart of all beings," while Arjuna represents any man, dissatisfied with the confused, disoriented life he has been leading, who resolves to achieve emancipation through self-knowledge.]

ARJUNA   Now, O Krishna, that I have beheld my kindred thus standing anxious for the fight, my members fail me, my countenance withereth, the hair standeth on end upon my body, and all my frame trembleth with horror! Even Gandiva, my bow, slips from my hand, and my skin is parched and dried up. I am not able to stand; for my mind, as it were, whirleth round, and I behold on all sides adverse omens. When I shall have destroyed my kindred,[6] shall I longer look for happiness? . . .

KRISHNA   Whence, O Arjuna, cometh upon thee this dejection in matters of difficulty, so unworthy of the honorable, and leading neither to heaven nor to glory? It is disgraceful, contrary to duty, and the foundation of dishonor. Yield not thus to unmanliness, for it ill-becometh one like thee. Abandon, O tormentor of thy foes, this despicable weakness of thy heart, and stand up. . . . I myself never was not, nor thou, nor all the princes of the earth; nor shall we ever hereafter cease to be. As the Lord of this mortal frame experienceth therein infancy, youth, and old age, so in future incarnations will it meet the same. One who is confirmed in this belief is not disturbed by anything that may come to pass. . . . As a man throweth away old garments and putteth on new, even so the dweller in the body, having quitted its old mortal frames, entereth into others which are new. . . .

This perishable body, O son of Kunti, is known as Kshetra; those who are acquainted with the true nature of things call the soul who knows it, the Kshetrajna. . . . That knowledge which through the soul is a realization of both the known and the knower is alone esteemed by me as wisdom. . . . Know, O chief of the Bharatas, that whenever anything, whether animate or inanimate, is produced, it is due to the union of the Kshetra and Kshetrajna—body and the soul. . . . The

[6] "Kindred" in this context is supposed to represent the lower elements in man. When any Arjuna seriously determines to live a higher life, these tendencies—fighting for their very existence—throw up clouds of doubt and despair to deter him from proceeding further. (Eds.)

deluded do not see the spirit when it quitteth or remains in the body, nor when, moved by the qualities, it has experience in the world. But those who have the eye of wisdom perceive it, and devotees who industriously strive to do so see it dwelling in their own hearts. . . .

This exhaustless doctrine of Yoga[7] I formerly taught unto Vivaswat; Vivaswat communicated it to Manu and Manu made it known unto Ikshwaku; and being thus transmitted from one unto another it was studied by the Rajarshees (Royal Sages), until at length in the course of time the mighty art was lost. . . . It is even the same exhaustless, secret, eternal doctrine I have this day communicated unto thee because thou art my devotee and my friend.

ARJUNA   Seeing that thy birth is posterior to the life of Ikshwaku, how am I to understand that thou wert in the beginning the teacher of this doctrine?

KRISHNA   Both I and thou have passed through many births! Mine are known unto me, but thou knowest not of thine. . . . I produce myself among creatures, O son of Bharata, whenever there is a decline of virtue and an insurrection of vice and injustice in the world; and thus I incarnate from age to age for the preservation of the just, the destruction of the wicked, and the establishment of righteousness. . . .

ARJUNA   O slayer of Madhu, on account of the restlessness of the mind, I do not perceive any possibility of steady continuance in this yoga of equanimity which thou hast declared. For indeed, O Krishna, the mind is full of agitation, turbulent, strong, and obstinate. I believe the restraint of it to be as difficult as that of the wind.

KRISHNA   Without doubt, O thou of mighty arms, the mind is restless and hard to restrain; but it may be restrained, O son of Kunti, by practice and absence of desire. . . .

ARJUNA   What end, O Krishna, doth that man attain who, although having faith, hath not attained to perfection in his devotion because his unsubdued mind wandered from the discipline? Doth he . . . become destroyed, O strong-armed one, being deluded in the path of the Supreme Spirit? . . .

KRISHNA   Such a man, O son of Pritha, doth not perish here or hereafter. For never to an evil place goeth one who doeth good. The man whose devotion has been broken off by death goeth to the regions of the righteous, where he dwells for an immensity of years and is then born

[7] Raja Yoga, the "Great" Yoga, which purports to reveal how man's lower self may be united with his divine Immortal Self. Hatha or body Yoga, a far lower practice, recommends physical disciplines—postures, breathing exercises, etc.—to gain personal ends. (Eds.)

again on earth in a pure and fortunate family; or even in a family of those who are spiritually illuminated. But such a rebirth into this life as this last is more difficult to obtain. Being thus born again he comes in contact with the knowledge which belonged to him in his former body, and from that time he struggles more diligently towards perfection, O son of Kuru. For even unwittingly, by reason of that past practice, he is led and works on. Even if only a mere enquirer, he reaches beyond the word of the Vedas. But the devotee who, striving with all his might, obtaineth perfection because of efforts continued through many births, goeth to the supreme goal.

Trans. William Q. Judge[8]

All the worlds, and even the heavenly realm of Brahma, are subject to the laws of rebirth. . . . There is day, also, and night in the universe. . . . [When a new world is born] Day dawns, and all those lives that lay hidden asleep come forth and show themselves, mortally manifest. Night falls, and all are dissolved into the sleeping germ of life. Thus they are seen, O Prince, and appear unceasingly, dissolving with the dark, and with day returning back to the new birth, new death. . . .[9] But behind the manifest and the unmanifest, there is another Existence, which is eternal and changeless. This is not dissolved in the general cosmic dissolution. It has been called the unmanifest, the imperishable. To reach it is said to be the greatest of all achievements.

Trans. Prabhavananda and Isherwood [10]

THE ANUGITA

[The Anugita forms a portion of The Mahabharata.]

Hear how a man . . . enters a womb. Within the womb of a woman, he obtains as the result of action a body good or bad. . . . [The Soul] is the seed of all beings; by that all creatures exist. That soul, entering all the limbs of the foetus, part by part, and dwellng in the seat of the life-wind (i.e. the heart), supports them with the mind. Then the foetus, becoming possessed of consciousness, moves about its limbs. As liquefied iron being poured out assumes the form of the image, such you must know is the entrance of the soul into the foetus. As fire entering a ball of iron, heats it,

[8] Los Angeles: Theosophy Co., 1947, pp. 5, 9, 11, 30–31, 49–51, 93, 97, 107.
[9] The translators explain: "When, at the end of a time-cycle, or kalpa, the universe is dissolved, it passes into a phase of potentiality, a seed-state, and thus awaits its next creation." (Append. I.)
[10] New York: Harper and Row, 1944, Chap. 8.

such too, you must understand, is the manifestation of the soul in the foetus. And as a blazing lamp shines in a house, even so does consciousness light up bodies.[1] And whatever action he performs, whether good or bad, everything done in a former body must necessarily be enjoyed or suffered. . . .

The mind said: The nose smells not without me, the tongue does not perceive taste, the eye does not take in color, the skin does not become aware of any object of touch. Without me, the ear does not in any way hear sound. I am the eternal chief among all elements. Without me, the senses never shine, like an empty dwelling, or like fires the flames of which are extinct. Without me, all beings . . . fail to apprehend qualities or objects, even with the senses exerting themselves. . . . [The Self] is not to be grasped by the eye, nor by any of the senses. Only by the mind used as a lamp is the great Self perceived.

Trans. K. T. Telang[2]

KAPILA

Founder of the School of Sankhya Philosophy

[Tradition ascribes the authorship of the Sankhya system to the great sage Kapila, an almost legendary figure in Indian history. There apparently was a line of Kapilas. The Sankhya philosophy may have been taught originally by the first, and written down by the last. The following aphorisms are taken from the volume *The Sankhaya Philosophy of Kapila* translated by Jag Mohan Lawl.] [1]

Because the Soul exists in all times, therefore time is not the cause of the bondage [of the Soul]. Because the Soul can exist in any country or anywhere, therefore locality cannot be the cause of the bondage. Because age is the property of the body, and not of the Soul, therefore age cannot be the cause of the bondage. . . . Because the Soul is independent of matter, therefore matter cannot be the cause of bondage. . . . Because the Soul which is by nature free is subject to so many desires, even that is not the cause of bondage. . . . The transmigration of Souls is not the cause of bondage. . . . Bondage is not caused even by the conjunction of the body and the Soul, but by the wrong knowledge as to the nature of their con-

[1] The three similes, says Nîlakantha, show that the soul pervades the whole body, is yet imperceptible, and also unattached to the body. (Trans.)
[2] *Sacred Books of the East*, ed. F. Max Müller, VIII, 241–242, 253, 268.

[1] Edinburgh: Orpheus Publishing House, 1921, pp. 11–19, 33, 35–38, 211–212, 238, 251.

junction and the proper functions of body and Soul. . . . The real cause of bondage is non-discrimination or misunderstanding the nature of the Soul and the body, and not finding the true purpose of life. Just as darkness is removed by its natural opposite, light, so non-discrimination is removed by true discrimination. . . . The seat of bondage is in the mind; it is [only] by way of expression we call it the bondage of the Soul. . . .

Emancipation [does not] consist in going to a special spot, for the soul is motionless and all-pervading. . . . Nor does it consist in destroying everything, for that cannot be the soul's aim. . . . The soul's aim cannot be to destroy its own creation. Emancipation does not consist in the acquisition of property and wealth, for they are all perishable and non-eternal. Emancipation does not imply the absorption of the part in the whole. . . . Emancipation does not consist in getting superhuman powers. . . . Nor does emancipation consist in obtaining the rank of Indra. . . . The destruction of non-discrimination and its effects is emancipation. . . . Not even by the teachings of superhuman teachers is obtained emancipation. . . . It is only by discrimination and self-knowledge that emancipation is obtained.

PATANJALI
Ancient Founder of the School of Yoga Philosophy

[From the Yoga Aphorisms of Patanjali:]

The soul is the Perceiver; is assuredly vision itself pure and simple; unmodified; and looks directly upon ideas. For the sake of the soul alone, the Universe exists. . . .

A knowledge of the occurrences experienced in former incarnations arises in the ascetic from holding before his mind the trains of self-reproductive thought and concentrating himself upon them. . . . By concentrating his mind upon the true nature of the soul as being entirely distinct from any experiences, and disconnected from all material things . . . a knowledge of the true nature of the soul itself arises in the ascetic. . . .

The modifications of the mind are always known to the presiding spirit, because it is not subject to modification. The mind is not self-illuminative, because it is an instrument of the soul, is colored and modified by experiences and objects, and is cognized by the soul. . . . When the understanding and the soul are united, then self-knowledge results. . . .

The knowledge that springs from this perfection of discriminative power is called "knowledge that saves from rebirth." [1] . . . When the

1 Such an ascetic as is referred to . . . is a *Jivanmukta* and is not subject to reincar-

mind no longer conceives itself to be the knower, or experiencer, and has become one with the soul—the real knower and experiencer— . . . the soul is emancipated.

Trans. William Q. Judge[2]

SANKHARÂCHÂRYA (510–478? B.C.)
Founder of the Adwaita School of Vedanta Philosophy

[The Vedanta philosophy, of which Sankharâchârya is probably the greatest exponent, does not encourage escape from rebirth. As stated in the *Vedanta Dictionary* of Ernest Wood:[1] "The idea of rebirth is a cardinal one in Vedanta, since a series of improving lives provides for an increase in the capacity to be aware of one's essential freedom in all circumstances. Indeed, the realization of one's freedom has to be gained in those circumstances, not by any escape or release, in which there would be no overcoming."

Sankhara is regarded by some to be a reincarnation of the Buddha. He came at a period when an iconoclastic form of Buddhism overran India, and a return to an appreciation of India's Vedic heritage seemed important —hence the name Vedanta. In modern times owing to the missionary efforts of *Swami Vivekananda* and others, the Vedanta movement has had an effective influence in the West. The following selections are taken from Sankhara's renowned work *The Crest Jewel of Wisdom*, translated by Charles Johnston.[2]]

For living beings, human birth is hard to gain, then manhood, then holiness; harder is perfection in the path of the law of wisdom; hardest to gain is illumination. Discernment between the Divine Self and that which is not the Self, fully realized union with the Eternal Self, liberation—this is not to be attained without holiness perfected through a hundred myriad lives. . . .

The food-formed vesture is this body, which comes into being through food, which lives by food, which perishes without food. It is formed of cuticle, skin, flesh, blood, bone, water; this is not worthy to be the Self, eternally pure. The Self was before birth or death, and now is; how can it be born for the moment, fleeting, unstable of nature, not unified, inert,

---

nation. He, however, may live yet upon earth but is not in any way subject to his body, the soul being perfectly free at every moment. (Trans.)
[2] *The Yoga Aphorisms of Patanjali.* Los Angeles: Theosophy Co., 1951, pp. 26, 44, 51, 60–61, 68–69.

[1] New York: Philosophical Library, 1964, p. 149.
[2] London: John M. Watkins, 1964, pp. 13, 32, 67–68.

beheld like a jar? For the Self is the witness of all changes of form. The body has hands and feet, not the Self; though bodiless, yet because it is the Life, because its power is indestructible, it is controller, not controlled. Since the Self is witness of the body, its character, its acts, its states, therefore the Self must be of other nature than the body. . . . Of this compound of skin, flesh, fat, bone and water, the man of deluded mind thinks, "This is I"; but he who is possessed of judgment knows that his true Self is of other character, is nature transcendental. . . . Therefore, O thou of mind deluded, put away the thought that this body is the Self . . . discern the universal Self, the Eternal, changeless, and enjoy supreme peace. . . .

In whom this wisdom is well established . . . he is said to be free even in life. . . . In whom the circle of birth and death has come to rest, who is individual though without separateness, whose imagination is free from imaginings, he is said to be free even in life. Even though the body remains, he regards it as a shadow; he is without the thought of "I" and "my": this is the hall mark of him who is free even in life. . . . Whether good or evil fortune come, he regards it as equal in the Self, remaining unchanged by either: this is the hall mark of him who is free even in life.

The Crest Jewel of Wisdom

Once a Man, Always a Man?

In the Orient the belief in regression of human souls to subhuman levels is prevalent and is based usually on a literal interpretation of certain scriptures. The earliest sacred writings, the Vedas, make no mention of regression, while the Upanishads have only one or two casual references thereto. The dead letter interpretation of later texts has served the special interests of the orthodox Brahmin priests, for rigid caste practices are easily enforced when the penalty for violation is declared to be rebirth as an animal or insect!

The Western reincarnationist asks: is it conceivable that a human being with his remarkable mental powers could be "encased" in an insect or bird? Would not the mere contact cause instant disintegration, just as high-voltage power shatters a lamp? Furthermore, how could precipitation into an animal frame be in the least effective as a remedial or punitive measure, for a nonthinking animal would have little awareness of the loss of status and karmic lesson? Aristotle states on regression: "For any soul to be clothed with any body is . . . as absurd as to say that the art of carpentry could embody itself in a musician's flutes; each art must use its tools, each soul its body." [1]

[1] *De Anima*, I, 3, 407 22–25.

Radhakrishnan believes that the Hindu idea of regression "may have been derived from the beliefs of the aboriginal tribes," when the ancient Aryans descended into the Indian peninsula from their original home in northern Asia. "In almost all regions of the world," he states, "the untutored savage thought that human souls could pass into animal bodies." [2] Sir Edward Tylor, the father of anthropology, interestingly adds:

As it seems that the first conception of souls may have been that of the souls of men, this being afterwards extended by analogy to the souls of animals, plants, etc., so it may seem that the original idea of transmigration was the straightforward and reasonable one of human souls being reborn in new human bodies, where they were recognized by family likenesses in successive generations. This notion may have been afterwards extended to take in rebirth in bodies of animals. . . . The half-human features and actions and characters of animals are watched with wondering sympathy by the savage, as by the child. The beast is the very incarnation of familiar qualities of man; and such names as lion, bear, fox, owl, parrot, viper, worm, when we apply them as epithets to men, condense into a word some leading feature of a human life. Consistently with this, we see in looking over details of savage transmigration that the creatures often have an evident fitness to the character of the human beings whose souls are to pass into them, so that the savage philosopher's fancy of transferred souls offered something like an explanation of the likeness between beast and man.[3]

Under "Pythagoras" and "Proclus," in Part Five, will be discussed the use of human regression stories as allegorical warnings that while still a man in mind and form a person can sink morally "lower than the worm or gnat." Plato apparently employs this method in the *Phædo* (82), and the *Timæus* (42, 91–92). But in his *Republic* (Book X), animal types appear to be used entirely symbolically. At the close of *The Republic* several famous Greeks are shown on the eve of a new incarnation. Orpheus very appropriately chooses the life of a swan—the symbol of song and music—to signify perhaps that he was returning as a great poet and musician. Similarly Thamyras, an ancient Thracian bard renowned as a harpist and singer, selects the life of the nightingale. Ajax, the Homeric hero, who, next to Achilles, was the bravest of the Greeks, most fittingly chooses the life of a lion. Agamemnon selects the life of an eagle, for he was regarded as an incarnation of Zeus, whose symbol that was. As to the jester Thersites, who supposedly puts on the form of a monkey, comment is unnecessary. It seems inconceivable that Plato desired readers to believe that the noblest of his countrymen were to be demoted to the level of birds and beasts—yet he has been frequently accused of so teaching.

[2] *Indian Philosophy*, London: Allen & Unwin, 1929, I, 251.
[3] *Primitive Culture*. London: 1871, II, Chap. 12.

The history of the regression idea is probably worth investigating. It is on this subject that Western prejudice against reincarnation often centers, and the stories missionaries and travelers relate serve only to increase the prejudice. When it is observed, for example, that the Jain and the Buddhist act very carefully as to animals and insects, it is hastily concluded that this is done because dead friends or relatives are thought to exist therein. On the contrary, such care is usually exercised out of reverence for life. Applying the reincarnationist philosophy to the lower kingdoms, the Buddha enunciated this general commandment: "Kill not—for pity's sake—and lest ye slay the meanest thing upon its upward way." [4] Whether this injunction applies to harmful insects and dangerous animals has always been an open question.

[4] Edwin Arnold, *The Light of Asia*, Book the Eighth.

Jainism

[The Jains constitute a large religious body in India, closely resembling Buddhism, but preceding it by long centuries according to some authorities. They claim that Gautama, the Buddha, was a disciple of one of their Tirtankaras, or Mahatmas. In *Jaina Psychology*[1] Dr. Mohan Lal Mehta presents the views of the Jains on karma and rebirth:]

Our present life is nothing more than a link of the great chain of transmigratory circuit. The doctrine of karma is meaningless in the absence of a fully developed doctrine of transmigration. . . . The soul that runs through various stages of birth and death is not to be understood in the shape of a collection of habits and attitudes. It is in the form of an independent entity to which all these habits and attitudes belong. It is a spiritual and immaterial entity which is permanent and eternal in the midst of all changes. . . . To put it in psychological form, personal immortality is indeed an impossibility. But individual immortality is one of the deepest truths of life.

[1] Amritsar, India: 1955, pp. 173–174.

Sïkhism

The Sikhs reside in northern India and are renowned for their superb physical strength, beauty and gigantic stature. In Arnold Toynbee's foreword to *The Sacred Writings of the Sikhs*[1] he states that the principal meeting-ground between the Indian and Judaic religions—which are notoriously different in spirit and have sometimes behaved like oil and vinegar—has been in India, where Islam has come in violent contact with Hinduism. The Sikh religion, he thinks, has achieved the spiritual triumph of discovering the fundamental harmony underlying the discord. Toynbee believes that the living higher religions are going to influence each other more than ever, and that in the coming debate the doctrines of the Sikhs will have a special contribution to make.

Radhakrishnan, who wrote the introduction to the foregoing work, remarks that the Sikhs and their founder Nânak (1469–1539) hold that beings are caught in the whirling wheel of *samsâra*—of involuntary births and deaths—because of self-identification with the body and its environment. "The aim of liberation," writes Radhakrishnan, "is not to escape from the world of space and time but to be enlightened, wherever we may be. It is to live in this world knowing that it is divinely informed. . . . For those who are no longer bound to the wheel of *samsâra*, life on earth is centred in the bliss of eternity. Their life is joy and where joy is, there is creation. They have no other country here below except the world itself. They owe their loyalty and love to the whole of humanity."

[1] Trans. Trilochan Singh, *et al.* New York: Macmillan, 1960.

◆ * ●

Buddhism

*It is easy to see that we could not have any "Buddhism" unless a
Buddha had revealed it. We must, however, bear in mind that
"Buddha" is not the name of a person, but designates a type.
"Buddha" is Sanskrit for someone who is "fully enlightened" about
the nature and meaning of life. Numerous "Buddhas" appear successively at suitable intervals. Buddhism sees itself not as the record
of the sayings of one man who lived in Northern India about 500
B.C. His teachings are represented as the uniform result of an often
repeated irruption of spiritual reality into this world. . . . The state
of a Buddha is one of the highest possible perfection.[1] It seems self-
evident to Buddhists that an enormous amount of preparation over
many lives is needed to reach it.*

Edward Conze[2]

THE DHAMMAPADA

[The Dhammapada is the most popular and influential of the Buddhist
canonical literature. *Dhamma* means discipline, law, religion; *pada* is path.
The verses selected are from the Cunningham Press edition.[3] This is not a
new translation but a compilation from the best renditions. The foreword
states that a student under Freud's personal tutelage reported that his
teacher called Buddha the greatest psychologist of all time. In the verses
that follow Buddha is speaking:]

All that we are is the result of what we have thought: all that we are is
founded on our thoughts and formed of our thoughts. . . .

Who shall overcome this earth? And who the sphere of Yama, the god
of death? And who the world of the happy gods? And who shall choose the
steps on the Path of Law even as the gardener culls the choicest blooms?
The disciple will overcome this earth. Also Yamaloka. Also the sphere of
the gods. The disciple chooses to take steps on the Path of Law. He is the
expert gardener who culls the choicest blooms.

Knowing that this body is like froth, knowing that its nature is that of
a mirage, and breaking the flowery shafts of Mara, the disciple passes un-

[1] Highest possible on *this* earth. Perfection being a relative not an absolute condition,
higher goals are supposedly possible in higher worlds. (Eds.)
[2] *Buddhist Scriptures*, trans. Edward Conze. Penguin Classics, 1959, pp. 19–20.
[3] Los Angeles: 1955, pp. 1, 11, 37, 64, 78, 96–97.

touched by death. Death bears off the man whose mind is intent on pluck-
ing the flowers of sense, as a flood sweeps away a sleeping hamlet. . . . The
craving of a thoughtless man grows like the *Maluva* creeper that eats up the
tree on which it fastens. From life to life he is like a monkey seeking fruits
in a forest. . . .

You yourself must strive; Buddhas are but signposts. . . . The SELF
is the Lord of self; what higher Lord could there be? When a man subdues
well his self, he will find a Lord very difficult to find. . . . Him I call a
Brahamana who knows the mystery of death and rebirth of all beings, who
is free from attachment, who is happy within himself and enlightened.
. . . Him I call a Brahamana who knows his former lives, who knows
heaven and hell, who has reached the end of births, who is a sage of perfect
knowledge and who has accomplished all that has to be accomplished.

[From the *Dhammapada Commentary*, translated by F. L. Woodward [1]:]

Although the Master [Buddha] was preaching, yet, of five laymen
who sat there in His presence, one, being drowsy, fell asleep; another sat
grubbing in the ground with his finger; the third idly shook a tree to and
fro; the fourth sat gazing at the sky and paid no heed to what was said;
while the fifth was the only one of them who gave heed to the teaching.

So the Elder Ananda, who stood there fanning the Master, observing
the behaviour of these men, said to Him: "Lord, Thou art teaching the
Truth to these men even as the voice of the thunder when the heavy rains
are falling. Yet, behold! they sit doing this and that. . . . Thy teaching
cleaveth even through the skin and reacheth unto bones and marrow. How
can it be that when Thou preachest the Law these men pay no heed
thereto?"

"Ananda, such things as The Buddha, or The Law, or The Order of
Brethren, through countless hundred thousand cycles of time have never
been heard of by these beings. Therefore they cannot listen to this Law. In
this round of births and deaths, whose beginning is incalculable, these
beings have come to birth hearing only the talk of divers animals. They
spend their time in song and dance, in places where men drink and gamble
and the like. Thus they cannot listen to the Law."

"But what, Lord, is the actual reason, the immediate cause why they
cannot?"

The Master replied: "Ananda, owing to hatred, owing to delusion,

---

[1] *Buddhist Stories*, trans. F. L. Woodward. Madras: Theosophical Pub. House, 1925,
pp. 64–68.

owing to lust, they cannot do so. There is no such fire as the fire of lust. It burns up creatures, nor even leaves an ash behind. . . . But this one, who, sitting, hears the Law attentively, for many, many times successively was a master of the Vedas three, a brahmana who could repeat the Sacred Texts. So now also he pays good heed unto my words."

SAMANNAPHALA SUTTA

[Buddha speaks:] With his heart thus serene, made pure, translucent, cultured, devoid of evil, supple, ready to act, firm and imperturbable, he [the saint] directs and bends down his mind to the knowledge of the memory of his previous temporary states. He recalls to his mind . . . one birth, or two or three . . . or a thousand or a hundred thousand births, through many an aeon of dissolution, many an aeon of both dissolution and evolution.

Trans. T. W. Rhys Davids[1]

"THE LIGHT OF ASIA"

[These selections are from Book the Eighth of Sir Edwin Arnold's *The Light of Asia*, published in 1879 and written "to depict the life and character and indicate the philosophy of that noble hero and reformer, Prince Gautama of India, the founder of Buddhism." It is no exaggeration to say that the popularity Buddhism has enjoyed in the West owes more to this memorable poem than to anything that has been written before or since. Scholars may question its correctness in minor details, but as a whole it admirably portrays the Buddhistic teachings. At the instance of the Boston clergyman William Henry Channing, whose daughter married Edwin Arnold, Bronson Alcott zealously promoted the volume in the United States. According to the *Dictionary of National Biography*, "the poem aroused the animosity of many pulpits, but there were sixty editions in England and eighty in America, and translations were numerous." [1] In the twenty-six page review from the pen of Oliver Wendell Holmes,[2] he wrote that "its tone is so lofty there is nothing with which to compare it but the New Testament." [3]]

The Books say well, my Brothers! each man's life
The outcome of his former living is;

[1] *Sacred Books of the Buddhists*, ed. F. Max Müller. London: 1899, II, 90.

[1] Second Supplement. Article "Edwin Arnold." Oxford University Press.
[2] *The International Review*, October, 1879.
[3] See Arthur Christy, *The Orient in American Transcendentalism*. New York: Columbia University Press, 1932, pp. 248–258.

The bygone wrongs bring forth sorrows and woes
The bygone right breeds bliss. . . .

I, Buddha, who wept with all my brother's tears,
Whose heart was broken by a whole world's woe,
Laugh and am glad, for there is Liberty!
Ho! ye who suffer! know

Ye suffer from yourselves. None else compels
None other holds you that ye live and die,
And whirl upon the wheel, and hug and kiss
Its spokes of agony. . . .

Before beginning, and without an end,
As space eternal and as surety sure,
Is fixed a Power divine which moves to good,
Only its laws endure. . . .

That is its painting on the glorious clouds,
And these its emeralds on the peacock's train;
It hath its stations in the stars; its slaves
In lightning, wind, and rain. . . .

This is its work upon the things ye see,
The unseen things are more; men's hearts and minds,
The thoughts of peoples and their ways and wills,
Those, too, the great Law binds. . . .

It will not be contemned of any one;
Who thwarts it loses, and who serves it gains;
The hidden good it pays with peace and bliss,
The hidden ill with pains. . . .

It knows not wrath nor pardon; utter-true
Its measures mete, its faultless balance weighs;
Times are as nought, tomorrow it will judge,
Or after many days.

By this the slayer's knife did stab himself;
The unjust judge hath lost his own defender;
The false tongue dooms its lie; the creeping thief
And spoiler rob, to render.

Such is the Law which moves to righteousness,
Which none at last can turn aside or stay;
The heart of it is Love, the end of it
Is Peace and Consummation sweet. Obey! [4]

Southern and Northern Buddhism

Southern Buddhism—the Buddhism of Ceylon, Burma, Thailand, Cambodia, and Vietnam—bears the name Theravada, the doctrine of the Elders. It is also called Hinayana, or the lesser path or vehicle, a belittling name never used by Southern Buddhists. Northern Buddhism—the Buddhism of China, Japan, and Tibet—is known as Mahayana—the greater path or vehicle. As stated by Christmas Humphreys, President-Founder of The Buddhist Society (London), and author of numerous works on Buddhism, "the Buddha gave his deeper teaching to the Arhats; to the people he gave a limited yet magnificent way of life, which, at first transmitted orally, was written down as remembered in the first century B.C. [400 years after Buddha's death], and is now available to all as the Pali Canon of the Theravada school." "When the Mahayana school arose it was a blend of the esoteric tradition and of doctrines developed from the earlier teaching by minds which, if not of the Buddha's calibre, were some of the greatest yet to appear in the history of mankind. Within a thousand years the various forms of the teaching had spread over a large part of the earth, and today at least a third of mankind accepts in one form or another the noble message of the All Enlightened One." [1]

The selections already presented clearly suggest that Buddha taught the existence in man of an immortal, reincarnating individuality. However, as so many Westerners have gained the opposite impression, we quote the following from an illuminating essay on Buddha's thought contained in the translation of The Dhammapada already quoted:

It is a mistake to attempt a final estimate of the views of either Buddha, Plato, Jesus, or any other teacher of religious philosophy, by means of a literal analysis of the printed record of what they taught. In the case of Buddha, there is reason to think that, like Jesus, he taught an inner, higher doctrine to his immediate disciples. What may be called "popular" Buddhism is generally conceded to have been preserved by the Southern or Ceylonese School, and it is from the scriptures of Southern Buddhism that Western scholars have gained the impression that Buddha denied the possibility of immortality. Rhys Davids, the Orientalist whose interpretations are best known to the West, has written:

[4] London: Routledge & Kegan Paul, 1959.

[1] London: *The Middle Way*, November, 1957.

"there is no passage of a soul or I in any sense from the one life to the other."
. . . Davids also concludes that "death, utter death," is the sequel to Nirvana.
[There is, of course, no doubt that Rhys Davids reports accurately the beliefs of
the Theraveda School.] Edmond Holmes is convinced that this is a mutilation,
a complete misreading, of Buddhist philosophy, and his chapter in *The Creed of
Buddha* to correct the mistake seems a well-reasoned discussion of the central
implication of Buddhist teachings. The Southern version, briefly, is that at
death a man's tendencies and traits of character are [by a chain reaction of
cause and effect] reborn in some other person or individual, but without any
connecting link of continuing egoity.[1]

Northern Buddhism, on the other hand, while exuberantly metaphysical in
form, is said to have preserved the teaching given by Buddha to his arhats, or
initiated disciples, and here one finds unmistakably taught the doctrine of a
permanent identity which unites all the incarnations of a single individual. This
latter is the view adopted by Holmes: "The question which we have to ask
ourselves with regard to the Buddhist conception is a simple one: Is the identity
between me and the inheritor of my Karma . . . as real as the identity between
the me of today and the me of 20 years hence . . . ? If it is not as real, the
doctrine of reincarnation is pure nonsense." Holmes continues, showing that the
doctrine of Karma, the key teaching of Buddhism, becomes almost senseless
when divorced from the idea of a reincarnating ego.

Von Hartmann points out further that "the practical power of the
transmigration theory as *motive* stands and falls with belief in the essential
identity of the person of my successor with me, and is not preserved by the
mere continuance of the hypostasized sum of merit," as apparently taught
in Southern Buddhism.[2]

The disputes among the philosophers, however, leave the masses pretty
much untouched. As Alan Watts states in *Psychotherapy, East and West:*[3]
"The vast majority of Asian Buddhists continue to believe that reincarnation is a fact," and that there is a permanent soul in man.

The mission of Buddha was evidently not to teach metaphysical truths
to the people at large. He again and again turns attention to the individual,
his suffering, and his search for the path toward moral and spiritual freedom. In the Pali text of the Majjhima-Nikâya, the Buddha speaks in typical
fashion:

Mâlunkyâputta, bear always in mind what it is that I have not elucidated
and what it is that I have elucidated. . . . I have not elucidated that the world
is eternal, I have not elucidated that the world is not eternal. . . . I have not

---

[1] As the Theraveda School explains, the old personality gives rise to the new as a
candle burning low may be used to light another candle and so continue the series.
(Eds.)

[2] Eduard von Hartmann, *Das Religiose Bewusstein*, p. 344. Cited by Carl du Prel in
The Philosophy of Mysticism, London, 1889, II, 253.

[3] New York: Mentor, 1963, p. 49.

elucidated that the saint exists after death, I have not elucidated that the saint does not exist after death. I have not elucidated that the saint both exists and does not exist after death. . . . And what, Mâlunkyâputta, have I elucidated? Misery . . . the origin of misery . . . the cessation of misery . . . the path leading to the cessation of misery.[4]

An important problem remains to be discussed: does Buddha, himself, now exist? The Japanese philosopher, D. T. Suzuki, relates that as the decades and centuries passed after Buddha's departure, "Nirvana as the ideal of Buddhist life engaged the serious attention of Buddhist philosophers. . . . [They asked:] Did the Buddha really enter into a state of utter extinction leaving all sentient beings to their own fate? Did the love he showed to his followers vanish with his passing? Would he not come back among them in order to guide them, to enlighten them, to listen to their spiritual anguish? The value of such a grand personality as the Buddha could not perish with his physical existence, it ought to remain with us forever as a thing of eternal validity." [5]

The Southern School, consistent with the ideas already mentioned, believes that Buddha exists not; the chain of Karma was severed at his death; and the goal of Nirvanic absorption took place. The Mahayana school affirms, to use the words of Radhakrishnan, "that Buddha standing on the threshold of Nirvana took the vow never to make the irrevocable crossing so long as there was a single undelivered being on earth." [6] A similar pledge is said to have been made by the Chinese Buddhist goddess, Kwan-Yin, who vowed: "Never will I seek nor receive private individual salvation. Never will I enter into final peace alone; but forever and everywhere will I live and strive for the redemption of every creature throughout the world."

To the Northern Buddhist, furthermore, Nirvana is not a state of extinction of consciousness and individuality.[7] In Eitel's *Handbook of Chinese Buddhism*[8] he states that even the popular exoteric systems of Chinese Buddhism "define Nirvana as the highest state of spiritual bliss, as absolute immortality through absorption of the soul into itself, but preserving individuality. . . . This view is based on the Chinese translations of ancient sutras and confirmed by traditional sayings of Sakyamuni [Gautama, the Buddha] who, for instance, said in his last moments 'the spiritual body is immortal.' "

---

[4] Majjhima-Nikaya Sutta 63; H. C. Warren, *Buddhism in Translations*. Harvard Oriental Series, ed. C. R. Lanman, 1909, p. 122.
[5] *Essays in Zen Buddhism*, First Series. London: Luzac, 1927, p. 45.
[6] *A Source Book in Indian Philosophy*, ed. Radhakrishnan and Moore. Princeton University Press: 1957, p. 636.
[7] This point is elaborated later on. See Index under "Nirvana."
[8] Hongkong, 1888, pp. 109–110.

Zen Buddhism

Zen was first introduced into China in A.D. 527 by Bodhidharma, an Indian Arhat, and in the twelfth century reached Japan. It has been described as the revolt of the Chinese mind against the Buddhism of India. The Chinese wished above all else to apply Buddhism to everyday life, asserting that Enlightenment could be found as much by working in the world as in withdrawing from it in the Indian manner. Zen, and related forms of Buddhism, have therefore had profound influence on Far-Eastern culture, especially in the arts. Lafcadio Hearn states: "Architecture, painting, sculpture, engraving, printing, gardening—in short, every art and industry that helped to make life beautiful—developed first in Japan under Buddhist teaching." [1]

Zen—or Ch'an as it is called in China—declares the reality of a truth beyond conceptualization. Its war on concepts, on all "names and forms," has been called a "shock" technique of instruction. The Zen teacher is intent upon a single point—to free the inquirer from the delusion that knowledge is contained in words. This has led some to believe that Zen has no doctrine, no teaching. Charles Luk indicates otherwise in his three-volume Ch'an and Zen Teaching.[2] The study of the Buddhist Sutras, he says, has always been encouraged by the Zen Masters as a preliminary training, and upon reaching enlightenment the more renowned Masters commented on these Sutras. An important Zen doctrine, Luk states, is: "firm belief in the (law of) causality. If one wishes to know the causes formed in a previous life, one can find them in how one fares in the present life; if one wishes to know the effects in the next life, one can find them in one's deeds in the present life. . . . When one sows melon (seeds) one will gather melons (and) when one sows beans, one will gather beans. This is the plain truth."

Examples of reincarnation teaching of the great Zen masters, Bodhidharma, Lin-chi, and Huang-Po, may be found in D. T. Suzuki's Manual of Zen Buddhism and in his Essays in Zen Buddhism, Third Series.[3] Dr. Suzuki, probably the foremost Zen Buddhist philosopher of our time, will be quoted directly on karma and rebirth in Part Six.

Erich Fromm writes in Zen Buddhism and Psychoanalysis: [4]

[1] Japan—an Attempt at Interpretation. New York and London: Macmillan, 1904, p. 208.
[2] London: Rider, 1960, I, 29–30.
[3] Manual of Zen Buddhism. London: Rider, 1950, pp. 73–74, 118–119; Essays in Zen Buddhism, Third Series. London: Rider, 1953, pp. 51–52.
[4] New York: Harper and Row, 1960, pp. vii, 77–78, 80.

There is an unmistakable and increasing interest in Zen Buddhism among psychoanalysts. . . . Cf. Jung's introduction to D. T. Suzuki's *Zen Buddhism*,[5] [and] the French psychiatrist Benoit's work on Zen Buddhism, *The Supreme Doctrine*.[6] The late Karen Horney was intensely interested in Zen Buddhism during the last years of her life. The conference held in Cuernavaca, Mexico [with Dr. Suzuki], at which the papers published in this book were presented, is another symptom of the interest of psychoanalysts in Zen. . . . Any psychologist, even twenty years ago, would have been greatly surprised—or shocked—to find his colleagues interested in a "mystical" religious system such as Zen Buddhism. He would have been even more surprised to find that most of the people present were not just "interested" but deeply concerned, and that they discovered that the week spent with Dr. Suzuki and his ideas had a most stimulating and refreshing influence on them, to say the least. . . .

The study of Zen Buddhism has been of vital significance to me and, as I believe—is significant for all students of psychoanalysis. . . . [It] helps man to find an answer to the question of his existence, an answer which is essentially the same as that given in the Judaeo-Christian tradition, and yet which does not contradict the rationality, realism, and independence which are modern man's precious achievements. Paradoxically, Eastern religious thought turns out to be more congenial to Western rational thought than does Western religious thought itself.

Buddhism and Shintoism

[The relationship of Shintoism to Buddhism is very interestingly discussed by Lafcadio Hearn in his volume *Japan—An Attempt at Interpretation*.[1] Quoting therefrom:]

In Shinto there was no doctrine of metempsychosis. . . . The spirits of the dead, according to ancient Japanese thinking, continued to exist in the world: they mingled somehow with the viewless forces of nature, and acted through them. . . . Those who had been wicked in life remained wicked after death; those who had been good in life became good gods after death; but all were to be propitiated. . . . With these ancient beliefs Buddhism attempted to interfere only by expanding and expounding them,— by interpreting them in a totally new light. . . . In most Japanese houses today, the "god-shelf" and the Buddhist shrine can both be found; both cults being maintained under the same roof. . . .[2]

One particular attraction of Buddhist teaching was its simple and ingenious interpretation of nature. Countless matters which Shinto had never

[5] London: Rider, 1949.
[6] New York: Pantheon, 1955.

---

[1] Pp. 204–216.
[2] The combining of both religions is still prevalent in Japan. See *Information Please Almanac*, New York: Simon & Schuster, 1967, p. 445. (Eds.)

attempted to explain . . . Buddhism expounded in detail. . . . Its explanations of the mysteries of birth, life, and death were at once consoling to pure minds, and wholesomely discomforting to bad consciences. It taught that the dead were happy or unhappy not directly because of the attention or the neglect shown them by the living, but because of their past conduct while in the body. . . . To die was not to melt back into nature, but to be reincarnated. . . .

A man . . . was now sickly and poor, because in some previous existence he had been sensual and selfish. This woman was happy in her husband and her children, because in the time of a former birth she had proved herself a loving daughter and a faithful spouse; this other was wretched and childless, because in some anterior existence she had been a jealous wife and a cruel mother. . . . The girl whom you hoped to marry has been refused you by her parents,—given away to another. But once, in another existence, she was yours by promise; and you broke the pledge then given. Painful indeed the loss of your child; but this loss is the consequence of having, in some former life, refused affection where affection was due. Maimed by mishap, you can no longer earn your living as before. Yet this mishap is really due to the fact that in some previous existence you wantonly inflicted bodily injury. . . .

Life was expounded as representing but one stage of a measureless journey, whose way stretched back through all the night of the past, and forward through all the mystery of the future,—out of eternities forgotten into the eternities to be. . . . Even the Shinto doctrine of conscience—the god-given sense of right and wrong—was not denied by Buddhism. But this conscience was interpreted as the essential wisdom of the Buddha dormant in every human creature,—wisdom darkened by ignorance, clogged by desire, fettered by Karma, but destined sooner or later to fully awaken, and to flood the mind with light.

Japan—An Attempt at Interpretation

Tibetan Buddhism

A distinctive feature of Tibetan religion is belief in the successive rebirths of the highest Lamas, the Dalai, the Panchen or Teshu, and some others. Westerners are accustomed to think of all Tibetan monks as lamas. This title, however, is formally allowed only to such high ranking "Incarnations" and to monks who have lived unusually saintly lives. Heinrich Harrer, once tutor to the present (fourteenth) Dalai Lama, observes in *Seven Years in Tibet:*[1]

[1] New York: Dutton, 1954, pp. 291, 293.

Birthdays are unimportant dates in Tibet. They are generally not known and never celebrated. For the people the date of their King's birth [the Dalai Lama] is quite without interest. He represents in his person the return to earth of Chenrezi, the God of Grace, one of the thousand Living Buddhas who have renounced Nirvana in order to help mankind. . . . With us it is generally, but mistakenly, believed that each rebirth takes place at the moment of the predecessor's death. This does not accord with Buddhist doctrine, which declares that years may pass before the god once more leaves the fields of Heaven and resumes the form of man.

Chapter 16 of Harrer's book provides an eyewitness account of the long search for and final identification of the now living Dalai Lama. Sir Basil Gould, the former British agent in Lhasa, gives his firsthand account of the installation in his work *The Jewel in the Lotus*,[2] and tells why he was personally convinced of the genuineness of the incarnation. The late Bradford Smith of Columbia University states:

When the previous Dalai Lama died, wise men had gone forth to seek the new holy one, had found a little boy who recognized things that had belonged to his predecessor and could pick them out unerringly from among similar objects. . . . So here is a religion where an infant is born obscurely, recognized by wise men and worshipped; where a holy man prophesies that he will return from the dead. Does this make me suspect Christianity? Good—face the doubt. Virgin birth, infant god, the holy one violently killed, yet resurrected—these are repeated themes in the history of world religions. . . . These repetitions do not palliate or cancel the strength of the Christian story. Rather they are reinforcing examples of the universal religious impulse and of the way man seeks to represent the cycle of death and rebirth that runs through all of nature. In Tibetan Buddhism, with its firm faith in the rebirth of the soul, not only of Dalai Lamas but of all, and of a progress based upon behaviour during past lives, this impulse is dramatically present.

Meditation: The Inward Art [3]

THE FOURTEENTH DALAI LAMA

[In his memoirs *My Land and My People*,[1] the Dalai Lama writes: "I must give a brief explanation of our beliefs . . . because these beliefs had a most profound influence on all that I did and all that our people did when our time of trouble came"—the Chinese invasion of Tibet. After indicating the Buddhist teachings of karma and reincarnation, the Dalai Lama comments:]

[2] London: Chatto & Windus, 1957.
[3] Philadelphia: Lippincott, 1963, pp. 166–167.

[1] New York: McGraw-Hill, 1962, pp. 50–52, 236–237.

Belief in rebirth should engender a universal love [because] all living beings and creatures, in the course of their numberless lives and our own, have been our beloved parents, children, brothers, sisters, friends. And the virtues our creed encourages are those which arise from this universal love —tolerance, forbearance, charity, kindness, compassion. . . . If belief in afterlife is accepted, religious practice becomes a necessity, which nothing else can supplant, in the preparation for one's future incarnation. . . . By whatever name religion may be known, its understanding and practice are the essence of a peaceful mind and therefore of a peaceful world. If there is no peace in one's mind, there can be no peace in one's approach to others, and thus no peaceful relations between individuals or between nations. . . .

How do we know that there is an afterlife? According to Buddhism, although the nature of cause and effect may be different, they must have the same essential properties, they must have a definite connection. . . . For example, the human body can be perceived—it has form and color— and therefore, its immediate source or cause must also have these qualities. But mind is formless, and hence its immediate source or cause must also be formless. . . . Both mind and body begin in this life as soon as conception occurs. The immediate source of a body is that of its parents. But physical matter cannot produce mind, nor mind matter. The immediate source of a mind must, therefore, be a mind which existed before the conception took place; the mind must have a continuity from a previous mind. This we hold to prove the existence of a past life. It has been demonstrated by the accounts of adults and children who remember their past lives. . . . On this basis, we can conclude that past life existed, and thence that future life will exist also. . . .

Incarnations [called *Rimpoche*] are beings who have either achieved various stages of Nirvana or have achieved the highest stage below Nirvana —the Buddhas, Bodhisattvas and Arahats. They are reincarnated in order to help other beings to rise toward Nirvana, and by doing so the Bodhisattvas are themselves helped to rise to Buddhahood, and the Arahats also reach Buddhahood finally. Buddhas are reincarnated solely to help others, since they themselves have already achieved the highest of all levels.

THE BOOK OF THE GOLDEN PRECEPTS

[William James, writing of mysticism, and using as a frame of reference several quoted passages from H. P. Blavatsky's translation, *The Voice of the Silence*—or "The Book of the Golden Precepts," as it is known in the

East—remarked in *The Varieties of Religious Experience:* [1] "There is a verge of the mind which these things haunt; and whispers therefrom mingle with the operations of our understanding, even as the waters of the infinite ocean send their waves to break among the pebbles that lie upon our shores. . . . We recognize the passwords to the mystical region as we hear them, but we cannot use them ourselves; it alone has the keeping of 'the password primeval.' "

Christmas Humphreys refers to Madame Blavatsky's rendition as "that exquisite Tibetan scripture, accepted as such by many [a] Tibetologist, as well as by His Holiness the Dalai Lama who signed my copy in 1956." [2] D. T. Suzuki calls it "the real Mahayana Buddhism." [3] A facsimile of the original 1889 edition was published in Peking in 1927 at the instigation of the then Tibetan Panchen Lama and under the auspices of the Peking Buddhist Research Society.

In the preface Madame Blavatsky wrote: "The original Precepts are engraved on thin oblongs; copies very often on discs. These discs, or plates, are generally preserved on the altars of the temples attached to centres where [the] Mahayana Schools are established. They are written variously, sometimes in Tibetan but mostly in ideographs. . . . Some of them are pre-Buddhistic while others belong to a later date." Quoting from the rendition:]

Have perseverance as one who doth for evermore endure. Thy shadows live and vanish;[4] that which in thee shall live for ever, that which in thee knows, for it is knowledge, is not of fleeting life: it is the Man that was, that is, and will be, for whom the hour shall never strike. . . .

Learn that no efforts, not the smallest—whether in right or wrong direction—can vanish from the world of causes. E'en wasted smoke remains not traceless. "A harsh word uttered in past lives is not destroyed, but ever comes again." The pepper plant will not give birth to roses, nor the sweet jessamine's silver star to thorn or thistle turn. Thou canst create this "day" thy chances for thy "morrow." [5] In the "Great Journey," causes sown each hour bear each its harvest of effects, for rigid Justice rules the World. With mighty sweep of never erring action, it brings to mortals lives of weal or woe, the karmic progeny of all our former thoughts and deeds. . . .

Behold the Hosts of Souls. Watch how they hover o'er the stormy sea

[1] New York: Longmans, Green, 1925, pp. 421–422.
[2] *The Middle Way*, November, 1963.
[3] *The Middle Way*, August, 1965, p. 90.
[4] "Personalities" or physical bodies called "shadows" are evanescent.
[5] "Tomorrow" means the following rebirth or reincarnation.

of human life, and how, exhausted, bleeding, broken-winged, they drop one after other on the swelling waves. Tossed by the fierce winds, chased by the gale, they drift into the eddies and disappear within the first great vortex. . . . The moth attracted to the dazzling flame of thy night-lamp is doomed to perish in the viscid oil. The unwary Soul that fails to grapple with the mocking demon of illusion, will return to earth the slave of Mara. . . . Alas, alas, that all men should possess Alaya, be one with the Great Soul, and that possessing it, Alaya should so little avail them! Behold how like the moon, reflected in the tranquil waves, Alaya is reflected by the small and by the great, is mirrored in the tiniest atoms, yet fails to reach the heart of all. Alas, that so few men should profit by the gift, the priceless boon of learning truth, the right perception of existing things, the knowledge of the non-existent! [6] . . .

Help Nature and work on with her; and Nature will regard thee as one of her creators and make obeisance. And she will open wide before thee the portals of her secret chambers, lay bare before thy gaze the treasures hidden in the very depths of her pure virgin bosom. Unsullied by the hand of Matter, she shows her treasures only to the eye of Spirit—the eye which never closes, the eye for which there is no veil in all her kingdoms. . . .

The Path is one Disciple, yet in the end two-fold. . . . The Open Path leads to the changeless change—Nirvana, the glorious state of Absoluteness, the Bliss past human thought. . . . Know, O beginner, this is the way to selfish bliss, shunned by the Buddhas of Compassion. . . . The "Secret Way" leads also to Paranirvanic bliss—but at the close of Kalpas [cycles] without number; Nirvanas gained and lost from boundless pity and compassion for the world of deluded mortals. . . .

Now bend thy head and listen well, O Bodhisattva—Compassion speaks and saith: "Can there be bliss when all that lives must suffer? Shalt thou be saved and hear the whole world cry?" Now thou hast heard that which was said. . . . If thou would'st be Tathagata [Buddha], follow upon thy predecessor's steps, remain unselfish till the endless end. Thou art enlightened—choose thy way.[7]

[6] That which is beyond the manifested or existing. (Eds.)
[7] Los Angeles: Theosophy Co., 1928, pp. 9, 15, 26–27, 34, 36–37, 44–47, 78.

◆ * ●

Taoism

CHUANG TZU (FL. C. 300 B.C.)

[From the books of Chuang Tzu, the illustrious disciple of Lao Tzu, the extracts below are taken concerning the Great Sage and his teaching. Save for the last three sentences, the selections are from *Musings of a Chinese Mystic*, H. A. Giles translation.[1]]

To have attained to the human form must be always a source of joy. And then, to undergo countless transitions, with only the infinite to look forward to—what incomparable bliss is that! Therefore it is that the truly wise rejoice in that which can never be lost, but endures always. . . .

The Master [Lao Tzu] came, because it was his time to be born; he went, because it was his time to die. For those who accept the phenomena of birth and death in this sense, lamentation and sorrow have no place. . . . The ancients described death as the loosening of the cord on which the Tao is suspended. What we can point to are the faggots that have been consumed; but the fire is transmitted, and we know not that it comes to an end. . . .

Birth is not a beginning; death is not an end. There is existence without limitation; there is continuity without a starting-point. . . . There is birth, there is death, there is issuing forth, there is entering in. That through which one passes in and out without seeing its form, that is the Portal of the Heavenly Tao.

[In explaining the nature of Tao, Lao Tzu wrote in The Tao Te King: "There is something . . . which existed before Heaven and Earth. Oh

[1] London: John Murray, 1955, pp. 82–83, 104.

how still it is, and formless, standing alone without changing, reaching ev-
erywhere without suffering harm. It must be regarded as the Mother of the
Universe. It appears to be everlasting. Its name I know not. To designate it,
I call it Tao." [2]]

[From Joseph Campbell's The Masks of God: Oriental Mythology: [3]]

There is an anecdote recounted of the Taoist sage Chuang Tzu; that
when his wife died, the logician Hui Tzu came to his house to join in the
rites of mourning but found him sitting on the ground with an inverted
bowl on his knees, drumming upon it and singing. "After all," said Hui Tzu
in amazement, "she lived with you, brought up your children, grew old
along with you. That you should not mourn for her is bad enough; but to
let your friends find you drumming and singing—that is really going too
far!"

"You misjudge me," Chuang Tzu replied. "When she died, I was in
despair, as any man well might be. But soon, pondering on what had happened, I told myself that in death no strange new fate befalls us. In the
beginning [of the world] we lack not life only, but form; not form only,
but spirit. We are blent in the one great featureless, undistinguishable
mass. Then a time came when the mass evolved spirit, spirit evolved form,
form evolved life. And now life in its turn has evolved death. For not
nature only but man's being has its seasons, its sequence of spring and
autumn, summer and winter. If someone is tired and has gone to lie down,
we do not pursue him with shouting and bawling. She whom I have lost has
lain down to sleep for a while in the Great Inner Room. To break in upon
her rest with the noise of lamentation would be to show I knew nothing of
nature's Sovereign Law."

"This attitude toward death," writes Mr. Waley . . . "exemplified
again and again in Chuang Tzu, is but part of a general attitude toward the
universal laws of nature, which is one not merely of resignation nor even of
acquiescence, but a lyrical, almost ecstatic acceptance, which has inspired
some of the most moving passages in Taoist literature." [4]

[From The Self in Transformation, by Herbert Fingarette.] [5]

Chuang Tzu tells an anecdote which is often quoted in Western literature—but, no doubt because of our Western bias, almost always with the

[2] Selections from the Upanishads and Tao Te King, trans. Lionel Giles. Los Angeles:
Cunningham Press, 1951, p. 91.
[3] New York: Viking Press, 1962, p. 427.
[4] The Way and Its Power, by Arthur Waley, pp. 54–55.
[5] New York: Basic Books, 1963, p. 222.

omission of the crucial last two sentences. I add these, in Giles's translation and italicized, to Waley's text: "Once Chuang Chou dreamt that he was a butterfly. He did not know that he had ever been anything but a butterfly and was content to hover from flower to flower. Suddenly he woke and found to his astonishment that he was Chuang Chou. But it was hard to be sure whether he really was Chou and had only dreamt that he was a butter- fly, or he was really a butterfly and was only dreaming that he was Chou. *Between a man and a butterfly there is necessarily a barrier. The transition is called metempsychosis.*"

PO CHÜ-I (A.D. 772–846)
Taoist Poet

If I depart, I cast no look behind
Still wed to life, I still am free from care.
Since life and death in cycles come and go,
Of little moment are the days to spare.
Thus strong in faith I wait, and long to be
One with the pulsings of Eternity.

"Peaceful Old Age"
Trans. Lionel Giles [1]

[1] *Musings of a Chinese Mystic*, p. 33.

Confucianism

Doctrines regarding immortality and reincarnation are neither preached nor denied in Confucianism. Confucius, who was born 551 B.C., avoided discussion on these subjects. His mission was clearly not one of a religious reformer. "I only hand on; I cannot create new things; I believe in the ancients, and therefore I love them," he says in the Analects (Book VII, No. 1). That Confucius was a great ethical teacher is undeniable, and even today Confucianism is a code of morals and manners rather than a metaphysical religion. However, Confucius had the highest respect for Lao Tzu (though their respective followers have at times been at loggerheads), and in China one may be simultaneously a Confucian, a Taoist, and a Buddhist —a fact which complicates the tabulating of the religious populations of the oriental world, as statisticians confess.[1] Thus through Taoism or Buddhism, a Confucian may be an embracer of the philosophy of reincarnation.

[1] *Information Please Almanac*. New York: Simon & Schuster, 1967, p. 445.

Egyptian

Herodotus, Plato, Plutarch, and other ancient writers spoke of reincarnation as the general belief of the Egyptians. Nineteenth-century Egyptologists leaned toward this view. See, for example, Wilkinson's *The Manners and Customs of the Ancient Egyptians*.[1] However, in the early twentieth century writers were decisively emphatic that the Egyptians were not reincarnationists. Sir Flinders Petrie took a somewhat more flexible position:

The question of transmigration [as an Egyptian tenet] has been disputed. The Greek authors refer to it as an undoubted belief [of the Egyptians]; but there seems to be no Egyptian text which refers to the idea. . . . The Greek testimony is so strong that it seems unlikely to have all been derived from the metamorphoses [section of The Book of the Dead]. As all the [Greek] authors are post-Persian, it is possible that the idea really did blend with Egyptian belief during the Persian occupation, when other Indian ideas came into Egypt, such as asceticism. Transmigration is plainly stated in the Korē Kosmou, of the Persian period, probably about 500 B.C.[2] After that it is natural that the Greek writers, Herodotus [ii, 123], Plato, Theophrastus, Plutarch [*De Iside* 31, 72], and others, should ascribe the belief to the Egyptians of their times, unconscious that it was a new importation.[3]

New opinions and testimony are coming to the fore. Dr. Margaret Murray, a distinguished Egyptologist who worked for many years with Petrie, writes in *The Splendour That Was Egypt*:[4]

[1] London, 1878, III, 462.
[2] W. M. Flinders Petrie, *Personal Religion in Egypt before Christianity*. London and New York: 1909, pp. 43, 47.
[3] *Hastings' Encyclopædia of Religion and Ethics*, XII, 431.
[4] New York: Philosophical Library, 1949, pp. 210–211.

[One theory of the Hereafter held by the Egyptians] which has received little attention from Egyptologists, is the theory of reincarnation. Herodotus is very definite on this subject [and his statement] is fully borne out by the Egyptian evidence. . . . The ka-names of the first two kings of the xx-th dynasty show this belief clearly; Amonemhat I's name was "He who repeats births," and Senusert I's name was "He whose births live." In the xix-th dynasty the ka-name of Setekhy I was "Repeater of births," and it was by this epithet that he was addressed by the god Amon at Karnak.

Already, however, in the xviii-th dynasty the theory of reincarnation had been so far developed as to include lesser folk, and in that great storehouse of the later religion, the Book of the Dead, there are about a dozen chapters giving the proper spells to be recited in order to incarnate in various forms. . . . Pythagoras is usually credited with having invented the theory of reincarnation, but it was already hoary with age before the Greeks had emerged from barbarism.

The periods Dr. Murray refers to are, of course, long anterior to the Persian Invasion mentioned by Petrie.

The Book of the Dead

[The Book of the Dead is found in ancient tombs throughout Egypt. Hermes, the God of Wisdom, is its supposed author. Bunsen revered it as "that precious and mysterious book," but it is the Book of Immortal Life, rather than a funereal volume. The scenes depict the journey of the soul through the after-death conditions, called collectively Amenti. Amenti means literally the dwelling of the God Amen. This "dwelling" was also called the Kingdom of Osiris, and the "Good Father's House" in which there are "many mansions," or states of consciousness. When the higher states are reached, the defunct is Osirified, and exclaims: "I am Osiris, the Lord of Eternity!"

James Bonwick's *Egyptian Belief and Modern Thought*, published in 1878 and reissued in 1956, states regarding The Book of the Dead, in his chapter entitled "Reincarnation; or Transmigration of Souls":

The Ritual is full of allusions to the doctrine. Chapters 26 to 30 relate to the preservation of the heart or life for this purpose. . . . [Dévéria, the French Egyptologist] shows how this esoteric doctrine was revealed in that portion of Egyptian sacred Scripture, known as the "Book of that which is in the Lower Hemisphere." He admits that "the funeral books show us clearly that resurrection was, in reality, but a renovation, leading to a new existence, a new infancy, and a new youth." He says further, "The *sahou* was not truly the mortal body. It was a *new being* formed by the re-union of corporeal elements elaborated by nature, and in which the soul was reborn in order to accomplish a new terrestrial existence under many forms."

The following passages from The Book of the Dead seem suggestive of either reincarnation or pre-existence, the translation being that of E. A. Wallis Budge:]

Thou king of Right and Truth, thou lord of eternity, thou prince of everlastingness, thou sovereign of all the gods, thou god of life. . . . The company of the gods rejoice at thy rising, the earth is glad when it beholdeth thy rays; *the peoples that have been long dead* come forth with cries of joy to see thy beauties every day. . . .

May I perform all the transformations according to my heart's desire in every place wheresoever my *ka* (double) pleaseth so to do. . . .

Their divine souls come forth upon earth to do the will of their *kas*, let therefore the soul of Osiris Ani come forth to do the will of his *ka*. . . .

Nebseni, the lord of reverence, saith: "I am Yesterday, To-day, and To-morrow, [and I have] the power to be born a second time; [I am] the divine hidden Soul who createth the gods. . . .

Homage to thee [Osiris], O Governor of those who are in Amenti, who maketh mortals to be born again, who renewest thy youth. . . .

[Osiris asks:] How long . . . have I to live? [Answer:] It is decreed that thou shalt live for millions of millions of years. [Osiris:] May it be granted unto me that I pass on unto the holy princes, for indeed, I am doing away with all the wrong which I did, from the time when this earth came into being.[1]

[Commenting on the last selection, J. B. Priestley writes: "I agree that it could be argued . . . that what the god Thoth [Hermes] was offering his questioner was not the false eternity of popular Christianity but the innumerable incarnations . . . accepted by the Buddhists. This Egyptian, it could be said, would live for millions of years because he would return again and again and again to Time, in one shape and personality after another, until finally purged of all desire for any further existence on this earth." [2]]

"POPULAR STORIES OF ANCIENT EGYPT"

In the book of the above name Sir G. Maspero, the French Egyptologist, translates a tale concerning Horus, a magician, son of Panishi, who, realizing that Egypt was being menaced by an Ethiopian invader, caused himself

[1] Chicago and London, 1901, I, 16, 46, 145, 211; III, 598, 623.
[2] J. B. Priestley, *Man and Time*. New York: Doubleday, 1964, pp. 147–148.

to be reborn as Senosiris, the son of Princess Mahituaskhit, in order to save his country. According to the story, Horus had lived in Egypt fifteen hundred years prior, and so had the Ethiopian invader. In this new incarnation Horus retained the acquirements and consciousness of his former life, and returns to the heavenly region after victoriously accomplishing his self-imposed task.[1]

The Hermetic Works

The Soul passeth from form to form; and the mansions of her pilgrimage are manifold. . . . Thou puttest off thy bodies as raiment; and as vesture dost thou fold them up. Thou art from old, O Soul of man; yea, thou art from everlasting.

Hermetic Fragments

[At the beginning of the Christian era the chief religious movements that vied with Christianity for the spiritual mastery of the world were Mithraism, the Egyptian mysteries, and Alexandrian theology.[1] The Egyptian mysteries included what has been called the great Hermetic tradition. The word Hermetic in this connection refers to any doctrine or writing associated with the esoteric teachings of Hermes, who, whether as the Egyptian Thoth-Hermes, or the Greek Hermes, was the God of Wisdom with the ancients. The Books of Thoth-Hermes, renowned throughout antiquity, have been lost for at least two milleniums. The Neoplatonist, Iamblichus, remarks in his volume *The Egyptian Mysteries* (Part VIII) that the Egyptian priest, Manetho, attributed to Hermes 36,525 treatises. As already indicated, Hermes is the reputed author of The Book of the Dead. It appears likely, however, that there was a line of Great Teachers in Egypt who assumed this name, just as in Persia there was a line of Zoroasters. The Egyptians called Hermes by the name Tahuti, "thrice great." The Greek equivalent was Trismegistus. Hermes Trismegistus was also a generic name used by a number of Greek writers on philosophy and alchemy, but we are not here concerned with their works.

The selections to follow are from the Hermetic Fragments which have come down through the Greeks and Romans and were probably altered to some degree by them. The references to reincarnation are fairly frequent. In his French translation, Dr. Louis Ménard states that in the early days of Christianity the Fragments enjoyed a high repute among the Church Fa-

[1] New York: Putnam, 1915, p. 144.

[1] S. Radhakrishnan, *Eastern Religions and Western Thought*. Oxford University Press, 1942, p. 190.

thers, Augustine, Clement, Origen, and others, who invoked their testimony on behalf of the Christian mysteries, and considered them as genuine monuments to that ancient Egyptian theology in which Moses had been instructed. Lost to Europe during the Dark Ages, the Fragments reappeared prior to the Renaissance, having meanwhile been preserved and studied by the Arabians and the Moors. In Part Five of the present work, the Hermetic revival of the Renaissance will be considered.

About the middle of the seventeenth century religious writers began labeling the Fragments as forgeries and as plagiarisms from Christian teachings, dating the works as among the later productions of Greek philosophy. The controversy raged for several centuries. G. R. S. Mead in his three-volume history and translation *The Thrice-Greatest Hermes*,[2] analyzes the theories and concludes with this summary: [3]

Why did the early Church Fathers accept the Trismegistic writings as exceedingly ancient and authoritative, and in their apologetic writings quote them in support of the main impersonal dogmas of Christianity? . . . Why during the last two centuries and a half has a body of opinion been gradually evolved, infinitesimal in its beginnings, but well-nigh shutting out every other view, that these writings are Neoplatonic forgeries?

The answers to these questions are simple:—The Church Fathers appealed to the authority of antiquity and to a tradition that had never been called in question, in order to show that they taught nothing fundamentally new.[4] . . . They lived in days too proximate to that tradition to have [themselves] ventured bringing any charge of plagiarism and forgery against it without exposing themselves to a crushing rejoinder from men who were still the hearers of its "living voice" and possessors of its "written word." . . . [Toward the close of the Renaissance] it was perceived that, if the old tradition were accepted, the fundamental originality of general Christian doctrines . . . could no longer be maintained. It, therefore, became imperatively necessary to discredit the ancient tradition by every possible means. With what success this policy has been attended we have already seen; we have also reviewed . . . its baseless character and the straits to which its defenders have been put.

From the clouds of this obscurantism the sun of Thrice-greatest Hermes and the radiance of his Gnosis have once more shone forth in the skies of humanistic enquiry and unprejudiced research. He is no longer to be called bastard, and plagiarist, and thief of other people's property, but must be regarded as a genuine teacher of men, handing on his own, and giving freely of his substance to all who will receive the gift.

[2] London, 1906, reprinted 1964.
[3] I, pp. 44–46.
[4] St. Augustine wrote: "That which is called the Christian religion existed among the ancients, and never did not exist, from the beginning of the human race until Christ came in the flesh, at which time the true religion which already existed began to be called Christianity." (*Epis. Retrac.*, Lib. I, xiii. 3.) (Eds.)

Mead states, however, that the old unsubstantiated theories still persist as facts in current encyclopedias and are "trotted out with complacency and with the impressive air of official knowledge . . . Unfortunately these *ex cathedra* encyclopædic pronouncements are all the general reader will ever hear." [5]

Quoting now from several of the Fragments:]

From one Soul of the Universe are all Souls derived. . . . Of these Souls there are many changes, some into a more fortunate estate, and some quite contrary. And they which are of creeping things are changed into those of watery things, and those of things living in the water to those of things living on the land; and airy ones into men. Human souls that lay hold of immortality are changed into holy powers. And so they go on into the sphere of the Gods. . . . And this is the most perfect glory of the soul. . . .

Not all human souls but only the pious ones are divine. Once separated from the body, and after the struggle to acquire piety, which consists in knowing God and injuring none, such a soul becomes all intelligence. The impious soul, however, punishes itself by seeking a human body to enter into, for no other body can receive a human soul; it cannot enter the body of an animal devoid of reason. Divine law preserves the human soul from such infamy.

The Key (Corpus Hermeticum X) (XI), 7, 19 [6]

HORUS   How are souls born male or female?

ISIS   Souls, my son Horus, are all equal in nature. . . . There are not among them either males or females; this distinction exists only between bodies, and not between incorporeal beings. . . . (Part II.)

HORUS   Thou hast given me admirable instruction, O my most powerful Mother Isis . . . but thou hast not yet shown me whither souls depart when set free from bodies. . . .

ISIS   O great and marvellous scion of the illustrious Osiris, think not that souls on quitting the body mix themselves confusedly in the vague immensity and become dispersed in the universal and infinite spirit, without power to return into bodies, to preserve their identity, or to seek again their primeval abode. Water spilt from a vase returns no more to its place therein, it has no proper locality, it mingles itself

[5] Mead, *op. cit.*, pp. 33–34.
[6] Eva Martin, *The Ring of Return* (London: Philip Allan, 1927), p. 34. American ed. *Reincarnation, The Ring of Return* (New York: University Books, 1963). G. R. S. Mead, *The Thrice-Greatest Hermes*, II, 145, 153.

with the mass of waters; but it is not thus with souls, O most wise Horus. I am initiated into the mysteries of the immortal nature; I walk in the ways of the truth, and I will reveal all to thee without the least omission. . . .

Souls do not, then, return confusedly [to the after death states], nor by chance, into one and the same place, but each is despatched into the condition which belongs to her. And this is determined by that which the soul experiences while yet she is in the tenement of the body, loaded with a burden contrary to her nature. . . . The law of equity presides over the changes which take place above, even as upon earth also it moulds and constructs the vessels in which the souls are immured. (Part III.)

The Virgin of the World [7]

[In his *Treatise on Providence*, the Church Father, Synesius, is probably quoting a Hermetic work when he records the instructions received by Osiris concerning the periodical rebirth among men of wise benefactors—a doctrine taught to this day in the East. The translation is Thomas Taylor's, contained in *The Select Works of Plotinus*,[8] but is omitted in the 1912 reprint edited by Mead.]

Yet you must not think that the gods are without employment, or that their descent to this earth is perpetual. For they descend according to orderly periods of time, for the purpose of imparting a beneficent impulse in the republics of mankind. . . . But this happens when they harmonize a kingdom and send to this earth for that purpose souls who are allied to themselves. For this providence is divine and most ample, which frequently through one man pays attention to countless multitudes of men. . . . For there is indeed in this terrestrial abode the sacred tribe of heroes who pay attention to mankind, and who are able to give them assistance even in the smallest concerns. . . . This heroic tribe is, as it were, a colony [from the gods] established here in order that this terrene abode may not be left destitute of a better nature.

[The American Transcendentalists were interested in the Hermetic Fragments. Bronson Alcott published extracts in volume I of *The Dial*

---

[7] Trans. Anna Kingsford and Edward Maitland, Madras: 1885, pp. 25, 30–31, 34. In the Hermetic translation of Mead, Part III above is included under "The Sermon of Isis to Horus" (Mead, *op. cit.*, III, 189).
[8] London, 1817.

(1841). The last poem of Longfellow was a lyrical ode in honor of Hermes. Dated January, 1882, it reads in part:

Was he one or many, merging
Name and fame in one,
Like a stream, to which, converging,
Many streamlets run? . . .

Who shall call his dreams fallacious?
Who has searched or sought
All the unexplored and spacious
Universe of thought? . . .

Trismegistus! Three times greatest!
How thy name sublime
Has descended to this latest
Progeny of time!]

Persian

*

Zoroastrianism

[Zarathustra—or Zoroaster as he is called in Greek—was the great lawgiver of the Persians, and the founder of the religion variously called Mazdaism, Magism, Parseeism, and Zoroastrianism. Like Manu and Vyâsa in India, and Hermes in Egypt, Zarathustra appears to be a generic name for great teachers and reformers. Thirteen are mentioned in *The Dabistan*. The hierarchy began with the divine Zarathustra in the Vendidad or Zend-Avesta, and ended with the great, but mortal man, bearing that title, and now lost to history. Bunsen describes him as "one of the mightiest intellects and one of the greatest men of all time." [1] Only fragments of the immense body of Zoroastrian literature remain. More would exist if Alexander the "Great" had not destroyed so many sacred and precious works. Under Islamic rule the Zoroastrians were evicted from Persia, and their modern successors are the Parsis of India, a highly respected community living chiefly in Bombay.

Even as late as 1892 we find James Darmesteter, the translator of the Vendidad in the *Sacred Books of the East* series edited by Max Müller, asking in effect: "How is one to accept that a man who lived at least six centuries before our era, far away from Greece, could have expressed views on God and the world in philosophical language, using abstract notions which recall those of the Gnostics and the Neoplatonists? These discourses must, therefore, be forgeries composed seven or eight centuries after the time of the prophet to whom they are attributed." [2] Most modern scholars

[1] *God in History*, I, Book iii, Chap. vi, p. 276.
[2] *The Hymns of Zarathustra*, trans. Jacques Duchesne-Guillemin. London: John Murray, 1952, p. 3.

now believe that the latest Zoroaster lived about 6,000 to 6,500 B.C. The Greek writers Xanthus, Plato, Aristotle, and Theopomotes also held to this view.

In a radio broadcast delivered at Karachi, Pakistan, in 1964 on the occasion of Zoroaster's birthday, Gool K. Minwalla stated:

> There is much confusion and error in minds of people of other faiths regarding the pure monotheism of Zarathustra, because the Prophet also expounded the Doctrine of Dualism. This however is different from the doctrine of duality which speaks of two mighty Beings distinct from and always opposed to each other. In the Gathas, the Prophet speaks of "those two primeval spirits which are *twins.*" . . . These two . . . have been spoken of in connection with "anghu," that is human existence. . . . Because man is free to exercise his will for good or evil, he often oscillates between the two during his lifetime, not being wholly good nor wholly evil. Zarathustra has not conceived of evil as something permanent in man's constitution; he does not believe . . . in an original sin which cannot be conquered by man by his own exertions. On the contrary, he affirms over and over again the triumph of the good and the possibility of perfectibility. . . .
>
> The outer symbol that represents the living spirit of this great religion is fire. Here again those who seek to belittle the religion designate the Parsis as "Fire-Worshippers," as against the worshippers of the true God. Not the fire but the Immortal Holy Spirit symbolised by the fire is worshipped. As the fragrant sandalwood is offered to the fire so man is reminded to offer to the highest the fragrance of his pure and sacrificial life.

Shea and Troyer, in the preface to their translation of The Dabistan, summarize as they understand them, the views of the ancient Iranians on immortality and rebirth: "Human souls are eternal and infinite; they come from above, and are spirits of the upper spheres. If distinguished for knowledge and sanctity while on earth, they return above, are united with the sun, and become empyreal sovereigns; but if the proportion of their good works bore a closer affinity to any other star, they become lords of the place assigned to that star; their stations are in conformity with the degrees of their virtue; perfect men attain the beatific vision of the light of lights. . . . Vice and depravity, on the contrary, separate souls from the primitive source of light, and chain them to the abode of the elements: they become evil spirits. The imperfectly good migrate from one body to another, until, by the efficacy of good words and actions, they are finally emancipated from matter, and gain a higher rank."

The modern Parsis do not now teach reincarnation as part of their creed, although it is quite common for individual Parsis to speculate on a prior life.

Selections from various Zoroastrian scriptures now follow, the first two being particularly authoritative:]

Souls whose Inner Light continues dim,
Who have not yet beheld the Light of Truth,
Unto this Home of Falsehood shall return,
Surrounded by false Leaders, Egos false,
By those who think and speak and act untrue.
            Gatha Spenta-Mainyu (Yasna 49.11)[3]

ZARATHUSTRA   "Creator of the material world, Pure One! If a (female) dog that has ceased to bear, or a (male) dog whose seed is dried up, happens to die, where does its consciousness (*baodhangh*) go?"

AHURA-MAZDA   "Oh holy Zarathustra! it goes into a stream of water, where, from a thousand male, and a thousand female dogs, a pair—one male and one female—of the Udra,[4] that reside in the waters, comes into being."

                          The Vendidad (fargard XIII, 50, 51)

Mezdam separated man from the other animals by the distinction of a soul, which is a free and independent substance, without a body or anything material, indivisible and without position, by which he attaineth to the glory of the Angels.

And everyone who wisheth to return to the lower world [the earth] and is a doer of good shall, according to his knowledge and conversation and actions, receive something, either as a King or a Prime Minister, or some high office or wealth, until he meeteth with a reward suited to his deeds. . . . Those who, in the season of prosperity, experience pain and grief, suffer them on account of their words or deeds in a former body, for which the Most Just now punisheth them.

                                          The Desatir[5]

*

Mithraism

The excavation in this century of the ruins of a Mithraic Temple in the City of London[1] revived an age-old mystery concerning the disappearance from

[3] Iruch J. S. Taraporewalla, *The Divine Songs of Zarathustra*. Bombay: 1951, p. 727.
[4] Among the ancient Iranians the *Udra* or water dog (probably the seal, or walrus) was considered of greater value than even the dog, of which they took the greatest care.
[5] Trans. Mulla Firuz bin Kaus. Bombay: 1818, pp. 10–12.

[1] Robert C. Cowen, "Ruin Peeks into Past of Britain," *Christian Science Monitor*, Oct. 14, 1954.

the face of the earth and the memory of man of a religion, beloved of Roman Emperors and legions alike, that had been Christianity's chief rival for the first three centuries of our era.

In *The Gnostics and Their Remains*,[2] C. W. King states that Mithraism "was the theology of Zoroaster in its origin, but greatly simplified so as to assimilate it to the previously existing systems of the West. . . . Under this form it took its name from Mithras, who in the Zoroastrian creed is not the Supreme Being (Ormuzd) but the chief of the subordinate Powers, the seven Amhaspends. Mithras is the Zend name for the sun. . . ."

The Neoplatonist philosopher, Porphyry, in this extract from his *De Abstinentia* (iv, 16),[3] speaks first of Zoroastrianism and then of Mithraism:

Among the Persians those who are wise in divine concerns, and worship divinity, are called Magi. . . . But so great and so venerable are these men thought to be by the Persians, that Darius [558?–486 B.C.], the son of Hystaspes, had among other things this engraved on his tomb, that he had been the master of the Magi. They are divided into three genera, as we are informed by Eubulus, who wrote the history of Mithra, in a treatise consisting of many books. In this work he says . . . the dogma with all of them which ranks as the first is this, that there is a transmigration of souls; and this they also appear to indicate in the mysteries of Mithra.

The Belgian historian, Franz Cumont, also confirms that reincarnation was "accepted by the mysteries of Mithras."[4]

Cumont, the foremost authority in this field, remarks in the preface to his work *The Mysteries of Mithra*[5] that while the civilization of the Greeks and Romans was unsuccessful in establishing itself among the Persians, the religion of the Magi exercised a deep influence on Occidental culture at three different periods. It made a very distinct impression on Judaism in its formative stage. Later the influence of Mazdaism on European thought was still more direct when Asia Minor was conquered by the Romans. But at the beginning of our era, this religion, as Mithraism, suddenly emerged and pressed forward rapidly and simultaneously into the valleys of the Danube and the Rhine, and into the heart of Italy itself. Remains of its temples are to be found in Germany, France, Switzerland as well as in Britain. The Mithraists admitted members of all religions to their meetings. Cumont further states:[6]

[2] London: 1864, p. 47.
[3] *Porphyry on Abstinence from Animal Food*, trans. Thomas Taylor, ed. Esmé Wynne-Tyson. New York and London, 1965, pp. 166–167.
[4] *After Life in Roman Paganism*. New York: Dover Paperback, 1959, p. 178.
[5] Chicago: 1910, p. iv.
[6] Pp. v-vii.

In the heyday of its vigor, it exercised [a] remarkable influence on the society and government of Rome. Never perhaps, not even in the epoch of the Mussulman invasion, was Europe in greater danger of being Asiaticized than in the third century of our era.[7] . . . When the flood subsided it left behind in the conscience of the people a deep sediment of oriental beliefs, which have never been completely obliterated. . . . The defeat of Mithraism did not utterly annihilate its power. It had prepared the minds of the Occident for the reception of a new faith, which like itself, came also from the banks of the Euphrates. . . . Manicheism appeared as its successor and continuator. This was the final assault made by Persia on the Occident.

*

Manicheism

This religion, which eventually comprised as many as seventy sects, was founded by a Babylonian named Mani, who was born about A.D. 215. His seat of proselytizing was in Persia, but he journeyed into China and India, and westward into Christian lands. He gave himself out to be the expected "Comforter," the Messiah and Christ, and taught that there were two eternal principles of good and evil; the former furnishing mankind with souls, and the latter with bodies. Mani opposed Catholic Christianity but was influenced by the Christian Gnostics, particularly the Basilidians and Marcionites. He also borrowed from older Oriental faiths, especially from Babylonian and Zoroastrian sources, and even Buddhist ethics.

Cumont calls the Manicheans reincarnationists.[1] Beausobré in *Histoire Critique de Manichée et du Manicheisme*[2] considers the reincarnation views of these groups, as does St. Augustine in *Contra Faust*; *De Hæres*; and *De Quantitate Animæ*. Addressing the Manichees, Augustine states: "You do not promise Resurrection to your Disciples, but a return to a mortal body; in order that born again, they will live the life of the Elect."[3] In some of the just-cited accounts, the Manichees are shown embracing the most ridiculous notions on rebirth, and Sir Edward Tylor remarks: "These details come to us from the accounts of bitter theological adversaries, and the question is, how much of them did the Manichaeans really and soberly believe?"[4]

[7] Radhakrishnan states: "Julian the Apostate was an ardent votary of Mithra. The worship of Mithra proved the most dangerous rival to the Christian Church before its alliance with Constantine. No wonder Renan observed: 'If Christianity had been stopped in its growth by some deadly disease, the world would have been Mithraist.' " (*Eastern Religions and Western Thought*. Oxford University Press: 1940, p. 121.)

[1] *After Life in Roman Paganism*, p. 178.
[2] I, 245–247; II, 495–499.
[3] Beausobré, II, 298.
[4] *Primitive Culture*, Chap. XII.

The rapid growth of this movement until "it became one of the great religions," is summarized in a lengthy *Britannica* article. It gained "secret support even among the clergy," and St. Augustine was a member for nine years. Subsequent to A.D. 330 Manicheism spread rapidly in the Roman Empire, its adherents being recruited from the Gnostics, and from "the large number of the 'cultured' who were striving after a 'rational' and yet in some manner Christian religion." [5]

The Christian Byzantine and Roman emperors, from Valens onwards, enacted strict laws against the religion, and Justinian decreed punishment of death for being a member. "But it still continued to exist elsewhere, both in the Byzantine Empire and in the West, and in the earlier part of the middle ages it gave an impulse to the formation of new sects, which remained related to it. It is at least undoubted that the Paulicians and Bogomils, as well as the Catharists and the Albigenses are to be traced back to Manichaeism (and [Gnostic] Marcionitism). . . . Even after the conquests of Islam the Manichaean Church continued to maintain itself, indeed it seems to have become still more widely diffused by the victorious campaigns of the Mohammedans, and it frequently gained secret adherents among the latter themselves." [6]

The reincarnation beliefs of the Gnostics, the Paulicians, Bogomils, Catharists, and Albigenses will be considered in various subdivisions under "Christianity." As will be shown, the Christian Catharists and Albigenses grew to such proportions in Western Europe in late medieval times that they almost unseated ecclesiastical Christianity itself.

[5] Britannica, 1959 edition.
[6] *Ibid.*

◆ * ●

Judaism

*

The Old Testament

[The esoteric interpretation of the Old Testament, according to the Kabalists, is to be found in the Kabala, which will shortly receive treatment, and there reincarnation is plainly set forth. In the Old Testament itself very little can be pointed to directly inferring rebirth. As we will see, the New Testament has considerably more passages. From the questions asked of Jesus by his Hebrew disciples, it is evident how prevalent was the belief among the Jews of that time. (See pp. 94–96.)

The word "return" in the Old Testament verses that follow is usually interpreted: "return to the path of righteousness." If, as some hold, "return" means "returning to incarnation 'in a thousand years,'" the analogies Moses employs seem particularly appropriate.]

Thou turnest man to destruction;[1] and sayest, Return, ye children of men. For a thousand years in thy sight are but as yesterday when it is past, and as a watch in the night. Thou carriest them away as with a flood, they are as asleep; *in the morning* they are like grass which groweth up. In the morning it flourisheth, and groweth up; in the evening it is cut down, and withereth.

Psalms 90:3–6

The Lord possessed me in the beginning of his way, before his works of old. I was set up from everlasting, from the beginning, or ever the earth

---

[1] "To dust," according to the Revised Standard Version. New York: Thomas Nelson, 1952.

was. When there were no depths, I was brought forth; when there were no fountains abounding with water. Before the mountains were settled, before the hills was I brought forth: While as yet he had not made the earth, nor the fields, nor the highest part of the dust of the world. When he prepared the heavens, I was there. . . . When he established the clouds above . . . when he appointed the foundations of the earth: Then I was by him, as one brought up with him: and I was daily his delight, rejoicing always before him; Rejoicing in the habitable part of his earth; and my delights were with the sons of men.

Book of Proverbs 8:22–31

[In the above verses, who is the "I" that is speaking? From the context the "I" is Wisdom itself. Yet can wisdom exist divorced from some being whose wisdom it is? Reincarnationists usually interpret the lines as King Solomon soliloquizing upon his previous lives, inasmuch as the entire Book of Proverbs is supposed to be by the wise Solomon, whose very name is a synonym for Wisdom. The *Scofield Reference Bible*, which is authoritative in many Christian circles, likewise does not define the "I" as abstract Wisdom, but links it to the pre-existence of Christ, and concludes: "Prov. 8. 22–36, with John 1. 1–3; Col. 1.17, can refer to nothing less than the Eternal Son of God."]

Then the word of the Lord came unto me [Jeremiah] saying, Before I formed thee in the belly I knew thee; and before thou camest forth out of the womb I sanctified thee, and I ordained thee a prophet unto the nations.

Jeremiah 1:4–5

The thing that hath been, it is that which shall be . . . and there is no new thing under the sun. Is there any thing whereof it may be said, See, this is new? it hath been already of old time, which was before us. There is no remembrance of former things.

Ecclesiastes 1:9–11

[Does the above verse apply only to *things*, or to beings too? The translation is that of the King James Bible. The last sentence is translated "There is no remembrance of *them* of former times," in The Jewish Bible; The Holy Scriptures according to the Masoretic Text (Jewish Publication Society of America, 1955).]

[The Lord said:] And I took your father Abraham from the other side of the flood, and led him throughout all the land of Canaan, and multiplied his seed, and gave him Isaac.

Joshua 24:3

[Was the other side of the flood the time previous to the flood? If so, would this indicate that Abraham had incarnated before as well as after the flood? Joshua was leading the children of Israel to the land of Canaan; and the flood was long before that.]

*

The Essenes and the Pharisees

In one of A. Dupont-Sommer's books on the Dead Sea Scrolls, *The Essene Writings from Qumran*[1] he states: "The Jewish historian Flavius Josephus . . . has written two justly famous accounts of the Essenes, one in *The Jewish War*, and the other in *Jewish Antiquities*. . . . [He] must have known personally, in Palestine, the Essenes whom he describes, and must have recorded personal observations in his picture of them." Josephus states that there were three chief schools of philosophy among the Jews: the Essenes, the Pharisees, and the Sadducees. The Pharisees "believe that souls have an immortal vigour in them [and that the virtuous] shall have power to revive and live again [on earth]: on account of which doctrines they are able greatly to persuade the body of the people."[2] In *The Jewish War*,[3] Josephus writes further respecting the Pharisees' belief in reincarnation: "They say, that all the souls are incorruptible, but that the souls of good men only, are removed into other bodies, but the souls of bad men are subject to eternal punishment."

As to the Essenes, who have now become famous owing to the discovery of the Dead Sea Scrolls, Josephus states:

They contemn the miseries of life, and are above pain, by the generosity of their mind. And as for death . . . our war with the Romans gave abundant evidence what great souls they had in their trials. . . . They smiled in their very pains and laughed to scorn those who inflicted torments upon them, and resigned up their souls with great alacrity, as expecting to receive them again. For their doctrine is this, that bodies are corruptible, and that the matter they are made of is not permanent; but that the souls are immortal, and continue for ever: and that they come out of the most subtile air, and are united to their bodies as to prisons, into which they are drawn by a certain natural enticement; but that when they are set free from the bonds of flesh, they then, as released from a long bondage, rejoice and mount upward. . . . These are the divine doctrines of the Essenes about the soul, which lay an unavoidable bait for such as have once had a taste of their philosophy.[4]

[1] New York: Meridian Books, 1962, p. 26.
[2] Trans. William Whiston, *The Antiquities of the Jews*, Book 18, Chap. 1, Nos. 2–4.
[3] Book 2, Chap. 8, No. 14.
[4] Trans. William Whiston, *The Jewish War*, Book 2, Chap. 8, Nos. 10–11.

In *Die Christliche Mystik*, J. v. Görres writes: "The Kabala was held in high esteem particularly by the Essenes and even more so by the mystic Therapeutae among the Hellenizing Jews in Egypt." [5]

*

The Kabala

["In the Jewish Kabala . . . metempsychosis is an essential part of the system," states G. F. Moore in his Ingersoll Lecture on reincarnation at Harvard University.[1] The Kabala is said to represent the hidden wisdom behind the Old Testament, derived by the rabbis of the middle ages from still older secret doctrines. The first Jews to call themselves Kabalists were the Tanaiim who lived in Jerusalem about the beginning of the third century B.C. Two centuries later three important Kabalists appeared: Jehoshuah ben Pandira; Hillel, the great Chaldean teacher; and Philo Judæus, the Alexandrian Neoplatonist.

In *A Talmudic Miscellany*[2] Paul Isaac Hershon states: "The Hebrew word Kabbal, means 'to receive,' and its derivative Kabbalah, signifies 'a thing received,' viz., 'tradition,' which, together with the written law, Moses received on Mount Sinai, and we are distinctly told in the Talmud, Rosh Hashanah, fol. 19, col. I . . . 'the words of the Kabbalah are just *the same* as the words of the law.' In another part of this work we find that the Rabbis declare the Kabbalah to be *above* the law." (Italics in original.)

Pico della Mirandola, the Italian Renaissance Humanist, Kabalist, and Neoplatonist, explained in his *Conclusiones* and *Apologia* that the great teachers such as Moses had transmitted many of their ideas orally through the seventy wise men in unbroken tradition until they had been embodied in the Kabala.[3]

During medieval times there were many celebrated Kabalists, Spain being one of the important seats of their activity. Rabbi Isaac Luria founded a Kabalistic school around 1560, and Rabbi Chajim Vital, the great exponent of his teachings, wrote a renowned work *Otz Chiim*, or *The Tree of Life*, from which the Christian Kabalist Baron Knorr von Rosenroth (1636–1689) wrote *The Book on the Rashith ha Gilgalim*, revolutions of souls or scheme of reincarnations.

As will be seen later, Kabalists, among other groups, were instrumental

[5] Regensburg, 1840, III, p. 27.

[1] *Metempsychosis*. Cambridge: Harvard University Press, 1914, p. 54.
[2] London: Trubner's Oriental Series, 1880, p. 318.
[3] Lewis W. Spitz, *The Religious Renaissance of the German Humanists*. Cambridge: Harvard University Press, 1963, p. 67.

in bringing to birth the Italian Renaissance and the German Reformation. Milton and Blake are among some Western authors who made abundant use of the Kabala.[4]

The selections from the Kabala that follow are from Hershon's *Talmudic Miscellany:*[5]]

Most souls being at present in a state of transmigrations, God requites a man now for what his soul merited in a bypast time in another body, by having broken some of the 613 precepts. . . . Thus we have the rule:—No one is perfect unless he has thoroughly observed all the 613 precepts. If this be so, who is he and where is he that has observed all the 613 precepts? For even the lord of the prophets, Moses our Rabbi—peace be on him!—had not observed them all. . . . He who neglects to observe any of the 613 precepts, such as were possible for him to observe, is doomed to undergo transmigration (once or more than once) till he has actually observed all he had neglected to do in a former state of being.

Kitzur Sh'lu, p. 6, col. I and II

The sages of truth (the Kabbalists) remark that Adam, contains the initial letters of Adam, David, and Messiah; for after Adam sinned his soul passed into David, and the latter having also sinned, it passed into the Messiah.

Nishmath Chaim, fol. 152, col. 2

Know thou that Cain's essential soul passed into Jethro, but his spirit into Korah, and his animal soul into the Egyptian. This is what Scripture saith. "Cain . . . shall be avenged sevenfold" (Gen. iv. 24) . . . i.e. the initial letters of the Hebrew word rendered "shall be avenged," form the initials of Jethro, Korah, and Egyptian. . . . Samson the hero was possessed by the soul of Japhet, and Job by that of Terah.

Yalkut Reubeni, Nos. 9, 18, 24

Cain had robbed the twin sister of Abel, and therefore his soul passed into Jethro. Moses was possessed by the soul of Abel, and therefore Jethro gave his daughter to Moses.

Yalkut Chadash, fol. 127, col. 3

If a man be niggardly either in a financial or a spiritual regard, giving nothing of his money to the poor or not imparting of his knowledge to the

[4] Denis Saurat, *Milton Man and Thinker*. New York: Dial Press, 1925, Chap. "The Zohar and the Kabbalah." Denis Saurat, *Blake and Modern Thought*. New York: MacVeagh, 1929.
[5] Pp. 323–326.

ignorant, he shall be punished by transmigration into a woman.[6] . . .
Know thou that Sarah, Hannah, the Shunammite (2 Kings iv.8), and the
widow of Zarepta were each in turn possessed by the soul of Eve. . . . The
soul of Rahab transmigrated into Heber the Kenite, and afterwards into
Hannah; and this is the mystery of her words, "I am a woman of a sorrowful spirit" (I Sam. i.15), for there still lingered in her soul a sorrowful sense
of inherited defilement. . . . Eli possessed the soul of Jael, the wife of
Heber the Kenite. . . . Sometimes the souls of pious Jews pass by metem-
sychosis into Gentiles, in order that they may plead on behalf of Israel
and treat them kindly.

Yalkut Reubeni, Nos. 1, 8, 61, 63

[Turning now to the Zohar, tradition assigns the authorship of this Kabalistic classic to Rabbi Simeon ben Jochai, A.D. 80, although additions were
made by medieval Hebrew scholars. Rabbi Moses de Leon, of Guadalajara
in Spain, edited and first published the work as a whole in 1280. Quoting
from Volume II, fol. 99, et seq.:]

All souls are subject to the trials of transmigration; and men do not
know the designs of the Most High with regard to them; they know not
how they are being at all times judged, both before coming into this world
and when they leave it. They do not know how many transformations and
mysterious trials they must undergo; how many souls and spirits come to
this world without returning to the palace of the divine king.

The souls must re-enter the absolute substance whence they have
emerged. But to accomplish this end they must develop all the perfections,
the germ of which is planted in them; and if they have not fulfilled this
condition during one life, they must commence another, a third, and so
forth, until they have acquired the condition which fits them for reunion
with God.

The Zohar

*

Karaism and Hasidism

The Universal Jewish Encyclopedia states under "Souls, Transmigration of
(gilgul hanefesh):" "The doctrine of transmigration of souls . . . was es-

---

[6] Hinduism has also perpetuated this arrogant error regarding the inferiority of woman,
although in Vedic times women were the equal of men, as was also the case in Egypt.
In early Buddhism women were likewise highly regarded. (See *Women Under Primitive Buddhism*, I. B. Homer, London: Routledge, 1930.)

pecially accepted by the Karaites . . . and in Hasidism it becomes a universal belief."

The Karaites were a Jewish group which rejected Rabbinism and Talmudism, basing its tenets on interpretation of the scriptures. It was founded in Bagdad about A.D. 765 by Anan ben David, was formerly widespread, but in recent years has numbered some 12,000 adherents, chiefly in southern Russia.

Hasidism was an influential movement among Polish Jews of the eighteenth century that spread to the Ukraine, Galicia, and Lithuania, and still persists. The renowned philosopher, Martin Buber, devoted much of his life to spreading its teachings and way of life.

An article in *The New York Times* (Oct. 16, 1966) by Irving Spiegel reports:

> A group of Jewish scholars, working in cooperation with the Harvard University Press, will undertake the publication of a comprehensive 10-volume work embracing 37 Hasidic texts that reflect the thinking, sermons, commentaries and exegesis of Hasidism—the colorful Jewish religious movement. It will be the first English translation of this rich literature of Hasidism. . . .
>
> Hasidism exerted marked influence for roughly two centuries as a major force in Judaism. The Nazis destroyed its great centers of learning during World War II. But there still exist Hasidic sects in this country, particularly in Brooklyn, and throughout the free world. . . .
>
> Prof. Maurice Friedman of Sarah Lawrence College . . . noted the influence that Hasidism had had on the contemporary Jew. "It calls him," he said, "to a realization of the covenant through which the Jews became and have remained a people—a reminder that to become a 'Holy People' means not just becoming a collection of well-meaning individuals but a never-ending realization of righteousness, justice, and loving kindness in true community."

A few pages hence extracts on reincarnation will be presented from *The Dybbuk*, a celebrated story by S. Ansky, based on Hasidic life.

*

Rabbis, Philosophers, and Writers

PHILO JUDÆUS (20 B.C.–A.D. 54)
Alexandrian Philosopher

The air is full of souls; those who are nearest to earth descending to be tied to mortal bodies return to other bodies, desiring to live in them.

De Somniis I:22

The company of disembodied souls is distributed in various orders. The law of some of them is to enter mortal bodies and after certain prescribed periods be again set free. But those possessed of a diviner structure are absolved from all local bonds of earth. Some souls choose confinement in mortal bodies because they are earthly and corporeally inclined. . . . All such as are wise, like Moses, are living abroad from home. For the souls of such formerly chose this expatriation from heaven, and through curiosity and the desire of acquiring knowledge came to dwell in earthly nature. While they dwell in the body they look down on things visible and mortal around them, and urge return to the original source, calling that heavenly region . . . their citizenship, fatherland, but this earthly region in which they live, foreign.

De Gigantes, 2 et seq.

FLAVIUS JOSEPHUS (A.D. 37–100)
Historian

[The extract below is from an address of Josephus to some Jewish soldiers who desired to kill themselves rather than be captured by the Romans. Josephus at the time was a general in the campaign against the Roman commander Vespasian, and was one of the few survivors of a bloody siege.]

The bodies of all men are, indeed mortal, and are created out of corruptible matter; but the soul is ever immortal, and is a portion of the divinity that inhabits our bodies. . . . Do not you know, that those who depart out of this life according to the law of nature, and pay that debt which was received from God, when he that lent it [to] us is pleased to require it back again, enjoy eternal fame: that their houses and their posterity are sure; that their souls are pure and obedient, and obtain a most holy place in heaven, from whence, in the revolutions of ages, they are again sent into pure bodies; while the souls of those whose hands have acted madly against themselves are received by the darkest place in Hades.

The Jewish War (Book 3, Chap. 8, No. 5)
Trans. William Whiston

RABBI ISAAC LURIA (1534–1572)

[In an article "The Lion of the Cabbalah," appearing in the April, 1935 issue of *The Aryan Path*, a vivid picture is portrayed of Rabbi Luria and his times. The author, Cecil Roth, is a distinguished historian, and former President of the Jewish Historical Society of England. He writes:]

It was the darkest hour in Jewish history. The crowning tragedy of the expulsion from Spain had just taken place, in 1492, turning tens of thousands of homeless wanderers into an unfriendly world. As today, many of the exiles directed their footsteps towards Palestine, the Holy Land, there reëstablishing the settlement which had been all but extinct since the period of the Crusades. From the crushing vicissitudes of this world, they sought refuge in the contemplation of the mysteries of the next.

With greater singleness of purpose than ever before, they turned their attention to the study of the Zohar and the kindred esoteric literature. Gradually, the choicer spirits became concentrated in the "Holy City" of Safed in Upper Galilee—the scene of the terrestrial activity, fourteen centuries before, of Rabbi Simeon ben Jochai, reputed author of the Zohar, "The Book of Splendour." Here there grew up the strangest, strictest, maddest, most amazing community in Jewish history: a veritable Congregation of the Saints, recruited by eager mystics from every corner of Asia and Europe, passing twenty-four hours of every day in the study of the Holy Cabbalah, and maintaining in perpetuity the spirit of a revivalist camp. This was the scene of the activity of the Lion of the Cabbalah . . . Rabbi Isaac Luria. . . .

The new teacher's fame rapidly spread. Pupils came from as far afield as Italy or Bohemia, and filled the courts of Safed with their mystical chants. . . . The Master [Luria] differentiated between the five different aspects of the human soul, and taught not only metempsychosis, or the migration of souls, but also the "impregnation" of two souls, under certain circumstances, in one body. . . .

[His teaching] speedily permeated the Jewish world through and through, giving fresh life to old observances. . . . It was the most vital movement that had come from Palestine since the days of the Second Temple. The modern rationalists who sneer at the tendency do not realise what comfort it brought to their fathers in the long nightmare of the Ghetto, how it consoled them for the vicissitudes of daily life, how it made mechanical observances instinct with beauty, with hope, even with divinity.

RABBI MANASSEH BEN ISRAEL (1604–1657)
Theologian and Statesman

[History informs us that owing to the efforts of this revered son of Israel, Oliver Cromwell removed the legal prohibition of Jews from England that had existed for three hundred fifty years since the reign of Edward I. In his book *Nishmath Hayem*, Rabbi Manasseh wrote:]

The belief or the doctrine of the transmigration of souls is a firm and infallible dogma accepted by the whole assemblage of our church with one accord, so that there is none to be found who would dare to deny it. . . . Indeed, there are a great number of sages in Israel who hold firm to this doctrine so that they made it a dogma, a fundamental point of our religion. We are therefore in duty bound to obey and to accept this dogma with acclamation . . . as the truth of it has been incontestably demonstrated by the Zohar, and all books of the Kabalists.

Nishmath Hayem

S. ANSKY (1863–1920)

[Ansky, whose real name was Solomon Judah Lob Rapoport, was, as stated in The Universal Jewish Encyclopedia, "a unique figure in Yiddish literature. . . . His masterpiece is the dramatic legend Tzvishen Tzvei Velten, better known as the Dybbuk; it is mystical and symbolical, yet taken from actual Hasidic life."]

It's not only the poor it pays to be careful with. You can't say for a certainty, who any man might have been in his last existence, nor what he is doing on earth. . . . Through many transmigrations, the human soul is drawn by pain and grief, as the child to its mother's breast, to the source of its being, the Exalted Throne above. But it sometimes happens that a soul which has attained to the final state of purification suddenly becomes the prey of evil forces which cause it to slip and fall. And the higher it has soared, the deeper it falls.

The Dybbuk[1]

SHOLEM ASCH (1880–1957)
Yiddish Novelist and Playwright

Not the power to remember, but its very opposite, the power to forget, is a necessary condition of our existence. If the lore of the transmigration of souls is a true one, then these, between their exchange of bodies, must pass through the sea of forgetfulness. According to the Jewish view we make the transition under the overlordship of the Angel of Forgetfulness. But it sometimes happens that the Angel of Forgetfulness himself forgets to remove from our memories the records of the former world; and then our senses are haunted by fragmentary recollections of another life. They drift like torn clouds above the hills and valleys of the mind, and weave them-

[1] New York: Boni & Liveright, 1926, pp. 71–72, 101.

selves into the incidents of our current existence. They assert themselves, clothed with reality, in the form of nightmares which visit our beds. Then the effect is exactly the same as when, listening to a concert broadcast through the air, we suddenly hear a strange voice break in, carried from afar on another ether-wave and charged with another melody.

The Nazarene[1]

[1] New York: Putnam, 1939, p. 3.

◆ ✱ ●

Christianity

✱

The New Testament

As we have seen, many of the ancient Jews believed in the periodical return of their great prophets. Moses was in their opinion Abel, the son of Adam; and their Messiah was to be the reincarnation of Adam himself, who had already come a second time as David. According to the Samaritans the reincarnation sequence was: Adam, Seth, Noah, Abraham, Moses.[1] It is not strange then that the closing words of the Old Testament (Malachi 4:5) recorded this prophecy: "Behold, I will send you Elijah the prophet before the coming of the great and dreadful day of the Lord." Elijah had already lived among the Jews. Now the first book of the New Testatment refers to this prophecy on three occasions, and the remaining Gospels seven additional times, thus linking the Old and New Testament on the idea of rebirth. (In the King James version of the New Testament, the Greek form of "Elijah," namely "Elias," is used.) Quoting first from Matthew:

> When Jesus came into the coasts of Caesarea Philippi, he asked his disciples, saying, Whom do men say that I the Son of man am? And they said, Some say that thou art John the Baptist; some, Elias; and others, Jeremias, or one of the prophets.
>
> *Matthew 16:13–14*

> And as they came down from the mountain, Jesus charged them, saying, Tell the vision to no man, until the Son of man be risen again[2] from the dead. And his disciples asked him, saying, Why then say the scribes that Elias must

[1] Hastings' Encyclopædia of Religion and Ethics, XII, 437.
[2] The word "again" is interesting. Does it mean that in a former time Jesus had also "risen from the dead?"

first come? And Jesus answered and said unto them, Elias truly shall first come, and restore all things. But I say unto you, That Elias is come already, and they knew him not, but have done unto him whatsoever they listed. Likewise shall also the Son of man suffer of them. Then the disciples understood that he spake unto them of John the Baptist [who had already been beheaded by Herod].

Matthew 17:9–13

Verily I say unto you, Among them that are born of women there hath not risen a greater than John the Baptist. . . . And if ye will receive it, this is Elias, which was for to come.[3] *He that hath ears to hear, let him hear.* (Italics added.)

Matthew 11:11, 14–15

The foregoing statement from Matthew 16 is repeated almost word for word in Mark 8:27–28 and Luke 9:18–19. The statement from Matthew 17 is also made in Mark 9:9–13, but the name of John is omitted.

In John 1:19–23, John the Baptist is approached by priests and others from Jerusalem. "And they asked him . . . Art thou Elias? And he saith, I am not. Art thou that Prophet? and he answered, No. Then said they unto him, Who art thou? that we may give an answer to them that sent us." John replied in the words of Isaiah (Isaiah 40:3): "I am the voice of one crying in the wilderness, Make straight the way of the Lord." Does this imply that John did not know (as Jesus supposedly did) that he was a reappearance of Elias? Whatever the answer, here as in the foregoing verses we have strong evidence that the Jews of this period were expecting the rebirth not only of Elias but other of their prophets.

Another reference is to be found in Luke 9:7–9: "Now Herod the tetrarch heard of all that was done by [Jesus], and he was perplexed, because that it was said of some, that John was risen from the dead; and of some, that Elias had appeared; and of others, that one of the old prophets was risen again. And Herod said, John have I beheaded; but who is this of whom I hear such things?" The same incident is related in Mark 6:14–16.

Tertullian, as quoted in the section, "Church Fathers on Reincarnation," gives the view which some orthodox people take concerning all these verses from the New Testament. In brief, Tertullian's reasoning is that Elias never died in the first place. God translated him directly to heaven. Thus his subsequent redescent was not a rebirth, but merely a return visit. Tertullian probably bases this on the statement in II Kings 2:11: "Behold there appeared a chariot of fire, and horses of fire . . . and Elijah went up by a whirlwind into heaven," and was seen no more. However, if this

---

[3] In *The New English Bible*, Oxford and Cambridge Universities Press, 1961, this reads: "John is the destined Elijah, if you will but accept it."

Church Father's reasoning is to be logically sustained, Elijah's return to earth as John the Baptist should have been in the same miraculous way he left: he should have been precipitated on earth as a mature man. Yet the Scriptures indicate that John was born in the ordinary way. In Luke 1:13–17 an angel makes this prophecy to Zacharias: "And thy wife Elisabeth shall bear thee a son, and thou shalt call his name John . . . and he shall go before him in the spirit and power of Elias."

Incidentally, this last clause is made much of by some to show that John was merely overshadowed by Elias. Yet, as translated in *The New English Bible* published jointly in 1961 by Oxford and Cambridge Universities, this part now reads: "*possessed* by the spirit and power of Elijah." At any rate, Christ, as just quoted, states without qualification: "THIS IS ELIAS, which was for to come. He that hath ears to hear, let him hear."

The nineteenth century American philosopher, Francis Bowen of Harvard, after citing a number of the Gospel passages already quoted, remarked in his article "Christian Metempsychosis":[4] "That the commentators have not been willing to receive, in their obvious and literal meaning, assertions so direct and so frequently repeated as these, but have attempted to explain them away in a non-natural and metaphorical sense, is a fact which proves nothing but the existence of an invincible prejudice against the doctrine of the transmigration of souls."

When there was brought into the presence of Jesus a man who was born blind, the disciples naturally wondered why he had been thus punished, and asked Jesus: "Who did sin, this man, or his parents" (John 9:1–3). The disciples must have had the idea of reincarnation in mind, for obviously if the man had been born blind, his sin could not have been committed in this life. If the doctrine was wrong and pernicious, Jesus had the opportunity to deny the whole theory. He did not do so, although in the instant case he said the blindness was for other reasons.

Reincarnation is possibly taken for granted by Jesus in Mark 10:28–31: "Peter began to say unto him, Lo, we have left all, and have followed thee. And Jesus answered and said, Verily I say unto you, There is no man that hath left house, or brethren, or sisters, or father, or mother, or wife, or children, or lands, for my sake, and the gospel's, But he shall receive an hundredfold now in this time [in this age[5]] houses, and brethren, and sisters, and mothers, and children, and lands, with persecutions; and in the world to come eternal life. But many that are first shall be last; and the last first." Certainly the enumerated rewards could not possibly be fulfilled

---

[4] *Princeton Review*, May, 1881.
[5] "In this age," according to *The New English Bible*, Oxford and Cambridge Universities Press, 1961.

in one incarnation. Reincarnationists translate the last quoted verse thusly: "But many that are first in this incarnation, shall be last or in lowly positions in the next rebirth; while the last or least esteemed may be first in their future life." This would be similar to Buddha's teaching: "Who toiled a slave may come anew a prince, for gentle worthiness and merit won. Who ruled a king may wander earth in rags, for things done, and undone." [6]

In Galatians 4:19, St. Paul possibly speaks of his returning to earthlife until mankind is finally redeemed: "My little children, *of whom I travail in birth again* until Christ be formed in you, I desire to be present with you now, *and to change my voice*; for I stand in doubt of you." (Italics added.) Paul also speaks of the previous existence of Jacob and Esau, saying that the Lord loved the one and hated the other before they were born. (Romans 9:10–13.)

St. John in Revelation 3:12 states: "Him that overcometh will I make a pillar in the temple of my God, *and he shall go no more out.*" (Italics added.) Evidently he had gone out into incarnation before, otherwise the words "no more" could have no place or meaning. It may have been the old idea of the exile of the soul and the need for it to be purified by long wandering before it could be admitted as a "pillar in the temple of God."

*

The Apocrypha

[The Apocrypha, or Non-Canonical Books of the Protestant Bible, are considered by the majority of Christians to be divinely inspired. The fourteen books of The Apocrypha are appended to the Vulgate (Roman Catholic), and to the Septuagint (Greek Catholic), versions of the Old Testament, although the Jews themselves do not include them in their Bible. "Apocrypha" comes from the verb "crypto," meaning "to hide." Thus originally it simply meant a *secret* book. The following verses are from the King James translation:]

[King Solomon speaks:] Now I was a child good by nature, and a good soul fell to my lot. Nay, rather, being good, I came into a body undefiled.

The Wisdom of Solomon 8:19–20

Woe be unto you, ungodly men, which have forsaken the law of the most high God! for if ye increase, it shall be to your destruction: *and if ye*

[6] Sir Edwin Arnold, *The Light of Asia*, Book the Eighth.

be born, ye shall be born to a curse: and if ye die, a curse shall be your portion. (Italics added.)

Ecclesiasticus 41:11–12

*

Church Fathers on Reincarnation

JUSTIN MARTYR (A.D. 100?–C. 165)

This Church Father was a student of philosophy and a teacher of Platonic doctrines. He opened the first Christian School at Rome, and was supposedly scourged and martyred there. Under "Pre-Existence" in the *Britannica*,[1] it is stated that in the Christian era supporters of this doctrine, who called themselves "the Pre-existants or Pre-existiani, are found as early as the 2nd century, among them being Justin Martyr and Origen." In his "Dialogue with Trypho," a Jewish person he meets in his travels, Justin speaks of the soul inhabiting more than once a human body, but that it cannot remember previous experiences. Souls who have become unworthy to see God, he says, are joined to the bodies of wild beasts. Thus he defends the grosser conception of transmigration. Trypho opposes Justin's views, and it is not clear whether Justin finally accedes to the arguments raised.[2]

ST. CLEMENT OF ALEXANDRIA (A.D. 150?–220?)
Greek Theologian

In his "Exhortation to the Heathen," [1] Clement wrote: "Before the foundation of the world were we, who, because destined to be in Him, pre-existed in the eye of God before—we the rational creatures of the Word of God, on whose account we date from the beginning; for 'in the beginning was the Word.' . . . The Saviour, who existed before, has in recent days appeared. . . . He did not now for the first time pity us for our error; but He pitied us from the first, from the beginning."

In the foregoing, Clement appears to posit the pre-existence of both Christ and man, but in his *Eclogæ ex Scripturis Propheticis* he states: "God created us when we did not exist before. For if we had existed before, we would know where we had been, and we would know in what way and for what reason we had come into this world." [2] In *Stromata* (IV, 12), Clem-

[1] 1959 edition.
[2] Clark's Ante-Nicene Christian Library, Edinburgh, 1867, II, 92–93.

---

[1] *Ibid*, IV, 22.
[2] *Patrologiæ-Græca*, IX, 706.

ent postpones discussion as to whether "the soul is changed to another body." A contemporary says that this Church Father wrote "wonderful stories about metempsychosis and many worlds before Adam." [3] These stories have not survived.

Clement was a Platonist and headed the famous catechetical school in Alexandria (A.D. 190–203). The Reverend W. R. Inge stated that Clement "admits frankly that he does not write down all that he thinks; there is an esoteric Christianity which is not for everybody. But it is plain that he leans towards the doctrines which [his pupil] Origen develops more boldly." [4] Origen's views on pre-existence and reincarnation will shortly be considered.

TERTULLIAN (A.D. 160?–230)

[This Latin Father of the early Church was converted to Christianity about 190, and wrote many works in its defense. Around the year 207 he withdrew from the orthodox Church and became head of a small Montanist group in Carthage. In *De Anima*, Chapters 28 through 35, he devotes a number of pages to refuting reincarnation. The familiar objections raised today were current then: reincarnation does not account for the then alarming increase in the world's population;[1] if previous lives are not remembered they might as well not have been lived; human transmigration into animal forms is a ridiculous notion. Tertullian regarded Pythagoras as a deceitful fabricator of stories when he claimed to remember former lives. As to the Elias-John the Baptist "reincarnation," Tertullian wrote:]

I apprehend that heretics . . . seize with especial avidity the example of Elias, whom they assume to have been so reproduced in John [the Baptist] as to make our Lord's statement sponsor for their theory of transmigration, when He said, "Elias is come already, and they knew him not;" and again, in another passage, "And if ye will receive it, this is Elias, which was for to come." Well, then, was it really in a Pythagorean sense that the Jews approached John with the inquiry, "Art thou Elias?" and not rather in the sense of the divine prediction, "Behold, I will send you Elijah" the Tisbite? The fact, however, is, that their metempsychosis, or transmigration theory, signifies the recall of the soul which had died long before, and its return to some other body. But Elias is to come again, not after quitting life [in the

[3] E. D. Walker, *Reincarnation, a Study of Forgotten Truth*. Boston: Houghton, Mifflin, 1888, p. 232.
[4] W. R. Inge, *The Philosophy of Plotinus*. London: Longmans, Green, 1948, II, 17.

[1] The population question will be discussed later. See Index under "Population."

way of dying], but after his translation [or removal without dying];[2] not for the purpose of being restored to the body, from which he had not departed, but for the purpose of revisiting the world from which he was translated; not by way of resuming a life which he had laid aside, but of fulfilling prophecy,—really and truly the same man, both in respect of his name and designation, as well as of his unchanged humanity.

De Anima[3]

ORIGEN (A.D. C. 185–C. 254)

[Origen was "the most distinguished and most influential of all the theologians of the ancient church, with the possible exception of Augustine," writes the German theologian, Adolf Harnack, in his article on Origen in the *Britannica*.[1] "He is the father of the church's science; he is the founder of a theology which was brought to perfection in the fourth and fifth centuries, and which still retained the stamp of his genius when in the sixth century [the church] disowned its author." (*Ibid.*) At one time St. Jerome considered Origen "the greatest teacher of the Church after the apostles," while St. Gregory of Nyssa called him "the prince of Christian learning in the third century."

An instructive summary of Origen's philosophy is to be found in *The Philosophy of Plotinus*, by W. R. Inge, the late Dean of St. Paul's, London:

Origen takes the step which to every Greek seemed the logical corollary of belief in immortality—he taught the pre-existence of Souls. The Soul is immaterial, and *therefore* has neither beginning of days nor end of life. . . . So convincing is this Platonic faith to him, that he cannot restrain his impatience at the crude beliefs of traditionalists about the last day and resurrection of the dead. The predictions in the Gospels cannot have been intended literally. How can material bodies be recompounded, every particle of which has passed into many other bodies? To which body do these molecules belong? So, he says scornfully, men fall into the lowest depths of absurdity, and take refuge in the pious assurance that "everything is possible with God." . . .

As for the "conflagration" [at the end of the world], Origen, as is well known, follows the Stoics in teaching . . . that there will be a series of world-orders. But whereas Greek [Stoic] philosophy could admit no prospect except a perpetual repetition of the same alternate evolution and involution, a never-ending systole and diastole of the cosmic life, Origen holds that there is a constant upward progress. Each world-order is better than the last. . . . The con-

---

[2] The bracketed insertions are those of the translator.
[3] Clark's *Ante-Nicene Christian Library*, XV, 496–497.

---

[1] Eleventh edition.

flagration is really a purifying fire. . . . All Spirits were created blameless, all must at last return to their original perfection. The education of Souls is continued in successive worlds. (II, 17, 19.)

It is interesting to observe how St. Jerome viewed these articles of Origen's creed after Pope Theophilus' crusade against Origen. In A.D. 402, Jerome wrote in his "Apology against Rufinus":

Now I find among many bad things written by Origen the following most distinctly heretical: . . . that there are innumerable worlds, succeeding one another in eternal ages; that angels have been turned into human souls; that the soul of the Saviour existed before it was born of Mary; . . . that in the restitution . . . Archangels and Angels, the devil, the demons and the souls of men whether Christians, Jews or Heathen, will be of one condition and degree [i.e., they too will be saved]; and when they have come to their true form . . . and the new army of the whole race returning from the exile of the world presents a mass of rational creatures with all their dregs left behind, then will begin a new world from a new origin . . . so that we may have to fear that we who are now men may afterwards be born women, and one who is now a virgin may chance then to be a prostitute. These things I point out as heresies in the books of Origen.[2]

That Origen taught the pre-existence of the soul in past world-orders of this earth and its reincarnation in future worlds is beyond question. An occasional dispute has arisen as to whether he taught pre-existence and reincarnation on this earth as presently constituted. According to *The Catholic Encyclopedia*[3] he did so teach. Beausobre—who himself regarded reincarnation teaching as an error—stated: "It is certain that Origen believed that souls animate several bodies successively, and that these transmigrations are regulated according to the souls' merits or demerits."[4] G. F. Moore mentions that "Origen is accused by Theophilus of teaching that the soul was frequently re-embodied and repeatedly experienced death (See Jerome, Ep. 98, 10 f.)."[5] St. Jerome similarly believed that Origen so taught. (See extracts from Jerome's "Epistle to Avitus," which concludes this item.)

It is not strange, of course, that Origen should teach reincarnation, for he was an ardent Platonist and also had strong Gnostic tendencies. As Dr. Harnack states:

[2] *A Select Library of the Nicene and Post-Nicene Fathers of the Christian Church*, Second Series, eds. Philip Schaff and Henry Wace. New York: Scribner, 1900, III, 508.
[3] Article "Metempsychosis," 1913 edition.
[4] *Op. cit.*, II, 492.
[5] *Metempsychosis*. Harvard University Press, 1914, p. 50.

The science of faith, as expounded by him bears unmistakably the stamp both of Neo-Platonism and of Gnosticism. . . . He regularly attended the lectures of [the great Neoplatonist] Ammonius Saccas, and made a thorough study of the books of Plato and Numenius, of the Stoics and the Pythagoreans. . . . As a philosophical idealist, however, he transmutes the whole contents of the faith of the church into ideas which bear the mark of Neo-Platonism, and were accordingly recognized by the later Neo-Platonists as Hellenic.[6]

Clement and Augustine were also Platonists. (See *Christian Platonists of Alexandria* by the Reverend Charles Bigg.[7]) The Reverend William Fairweather states that half a century after Origen's death, Neoplatonism "became the prevailing philosophy in Christian as well as in pagan circles." [8] Neoplatonism will receive special treatment in Part Five.

The supposed condemnation of Origen by the Fifth Ecumenical Council in A.D. 553 will be considered in the section "The Anathemas Against Pre-Existence." Because of this "condemnation" very few, until recent times, have ventured to raise their voice for him, although during the Renaissance, for a brief time, Origen "rose from the dead." After reading a great part of his extant works, Erasmus wrote to Colet: "Origen opens the fountains of theology." [9]

The scant references that follow from Origen's writings probably do not do justice to his convictions. Many of his works have been allowed to perish. Dr. Harnack states: "Origen was probably the most prolific author of the ancient church. 'Which of us,' asks Jerome, 'can read all that he has written?' The number of his works was estimated at 6,000, but that is certainly an exaggeration. Owing to the increasing unpopularity of Origen in the church, a comparatively small portion of these works have come down to us in the original. We have more in the Latin translation of Rufinus; but this translation is by no means trustworthy, since Rufinus, assuming that Origen's writing had been tampered with by the heretics, considered himself at liberty to omit or amend heterodox statements." [10]

The first selection is from Origen's *Contra Celsum*, the second from his *De Principiis*, or *The First Principles*, called by Robert Payne "the most important and the most wide-reaching of Origen's works. . . . What survives is the wreck of an original text, in which we can discern the true voice of Origen at intervals, when Rufinus was either too lazy or too engrossed in the task of translation to alter Origen's theology.[11]]

[6] *Encyclopædia Britannica*, 1959 ed., article "Origen."
[7] Oxford University Press, 1886.
[8] *Origen and Greek Patristic Theology*. New York: 1901, p. 215.
[9] W. R. Inge, *The Platonic Tradition in English Religious Thought*. London: Longmans, Green, 1926, p. 100.
[10] *Encyclopædia Britannica*, 1959 ed.
[11] *The Holy Fire*. New York: Harper and Row, 1957, p. 49.

Is it not more in conformity with reason, that every soul, for certain mysterious reasons (I speak now according to the opinion of Pythagoras, and Plato, and Empedocles, whom Celsus frequently names), is introduced into a body, and introduced according to its deserts and former actions? It is probable, therefore, that this soul also which conferred more benefit by its [former] residence in the flesh than that of many men (to avoid prejudice, I do not say "all"), stood in need of a body not only superior to others, but invested with all excellent qualities.

Contra Celsum (Book I, Chap. 32)[12]

I am, indeed, of opinion that, as the end and consummation of the saints will be in those [ages] which are not seen, and are eternal, we must conclude (as frequently pointed out in the preceding pages), from a contemplation of that very end, that rational creatures had also a similar beginning. And if they had a beginning such as the end for which they hope, they existed undoubtedly from the very beginning in those [ages] which are not seen, and are eternal.

And if this is so, then there had been a descent from a higher to a lower condition, on the part not only of those souls who have deserved the change by the variety of their movements, but also on that of those who, in order to serve the whole world, were brought down from those higher and invisible spheres to these lower and visible ones . . . [and as] to those souls which, on account of their excessive mental defects, stood in need of bodies of a grosser and more solid nature . . . this visible world was also called into being. . . . The hope indeed of freedom is entertained by the whole of creation—of being liberated from the corruption of slavery—when the sons of God, who either fell away or were scattered abroad, shall be gathered together into one, or when they shall have fulfilled their other duties in this world.

De Principiis[13]

[During Jerome's life the Greek *De Principiis* was still in existence and it just happens that we have a translation therefrom made by him on the very point of reincarnation. It was made for his friend Avitus who appreciating that Rufinus' translation was unreliable, desired to know what Origen really taught. The extract is from Jerome's lengthy "Epistle to Avitus" (written about A.D. 410), and is to be found in *A Select Library of Nicene and Post-Nicene Fathers of the Christian Church.*[14]]

[12] Clark's *Ante-Nicene Christian Library*, X, 432.
[13] Book III, Chap. 5, No. 4. Clark's *Ante-Nicene Christian Library*, X, 256–258.
[14] Second Series, VI, Letter CXXIV, Part 15, p. 244.

[Jerome:] The following passage is a convincing proof that [Origen] holds the transmigration of souls and annihilation of bodies. "If it can be shown that an incorporeal and reasonable being has life in itself independently of the body and that it is worse off in the body than out of it; then beyond a doubt bodies are only of secondary importance and arise from time to time to meet the varying conditions of reasonable creatures. Those who require bodies are clothed with them, and contrariwise, when fallen souls have lifted themselves up to better things, their bodies are once more annihilated. They are thus ever vanishing and ever reappearing."

ST. GREGORY OF NAZIANZUS (A.D. 329?–389)
Bishop of Constantinople

[Some hold] that the soul exchanges one man for another man, so that the life of humanity is continued always by means of the same souls. . . . As for ourselves, we take our stand upon the tenets of the Church, and assert that it will be well to accept only so much of these speculations as is sufficient to show that those who indulge in them are to a certain extent in accord with the doctrine of the Resurrection. Their statement, for instance, that the soul after its release from this body insinuates itself into certain other bodies is not absolutely out of harmony with the revival which we hope for. For our view, which maintains that the body, both now, and again in the future, is composed of the atoms of the universe, is held equally by these heathens. In fact, you cannot imagine any constitution of the body independent of a concourse of these atoms. But the divergence lies in this: we assert that the same body again as before, composed of the same atoms, is compacted around the soul; they suppose that the soul alights on other bodies. . . .

On the Soul and the Resurrection (Chap. 32)[1]

ST. AUGUSTINE (354–430)
Bishop of Hippo

[Augustine was a "strangely divided genius," remarks Dean Inge.[1] In The Story of the Faith, the Reverend William Alva Gifford supplies some interesting facts regarding his career:

Unable to rest in Catholicism [in which he was raised] Augustine [became] a Manichaean for nine years. . . . Still restless and falling into skepti-

[1] A Select Library of the Nicene and Post-Nicene Fathers. . . . Second Series, VII, 453–454.

[1] W. R. Inge, The Platonic Tradition in English Religious Thought, p. 28.

cism, Augustine removed to Rome. . . . Very fortunately [he] now came upon the writings of [the Neoplatonist] Plotinus. . . . They were medicine for his skepticism. . . . Augustine never . . . ceased to be a Neoplatonist; but his early confidence in the power of reason steadily gave way to reliance on divine revelation. . . . In the authoritative Church and its authoritative Scriptures . . . he found certitude. . . .

Augustine's system, in fact is a curious combination of mystical piety, Neoplatonic philosophy, allegorical interpretation of the Scriptures, and Catholic tradition, all handled with rigorous logic, but often inconsistent with each other. . . . Augustine's logic led him [to] the doctrine of predestination [which] was as yet no part of the Catholic tradition. . . . [He] is as vivid as Tertullian when he pictures the joys of eternal life and the torments of the damned. . . . He was to become the most influential theologian of the West, and the father of much that is characteristic of both mediaeval Catholicism and Protestantism.[2]]

Say, Lord to me . . . say, did my infancy succeed another age of mine that died before it? Was it that which I spent within my mother's womb? . . . and what before that life again, O God my joy, was I anywhere or in any body? For this I have none to tell me, neither father nor mother, nor experience of others, nor mine own memory.

The Confessions of St. Augustine[3]

The message of Plato, the purest and most luminous in all philosophy, has at last scattered the darkness of error, and now shines forth mainly in Plotinus, a Platonist so like his master that one would think they lived together, or rather—since so long a period of time separates them—that Plato is born again in Plotinus.

Contra Academicos[4]

That noble philosopher Plato endeavored to persuade us that the souls of men lived even before they bore these bodies; and that hence those things which are learnt are rather remembered, as having been known already, than taken into knowledge as things new. . . . But we ought rather to believe, that the intellectual mind is so formed in its nature as to see those things, which by the disposition of the Creator are subjoined to things intelligible in a natural order, by a sort of incorporeal light of a unique kind; as the eye of the flesh sees things adjacent to itself.

On the Trinity[5]

[2] New York: Macmillan, 1958, pp. 212–215, 217.
[3] Book I. Trans. Edward B. Pusey, *Harvard Classics*. New York: P. F. Collier, 1909, VII, 9.
[4] Eva Martin, *The Ring of Return*, p. 80.
[5] Book XII, Chap. 15, No. 24. *A Select Library of the Nicene and Post-Nicene Fathers.* Ed. Philip Schaff. Buffalo, N.Y.: 1886, First Series, III, 164.

[The Neoplatonist, Porphyry] was of opinion that human souls return indeed into human bodies [and not into animal bodies]. He shrank from the other opinion, lest a woman who had returned into a mule might possibly carry her own son on her back. He did not shrink, however, from a theory which admitted the possibility of a mother coming back into a girl and marrying her own son.[6] How much more honorable a creed is that which was taught by the holy and truthful angels, uttered by the prophets who were moved by God's Spirit, preached by Him who was foretold as the coming Savior by His forerunning heralds, and by the apostles whom He sent forth, and who filled the whole world with the gospel,—how much more honorable, I say, is the belief that souls return once for all to their own bodies [at the resurrection], than that they return again and again to divers bodies?

The City of God [7]

SYNESIUS (C. 370–430)
Bishop of Ptolemais

This Church Father and Neoplatonist is most familiar to English readers as the convent patriarch in Charles Kingsley's *Hypatia*. When the citizens of Ptolemais invited him to their bishopric, he declined that dignity at first because he cherished certain opinions which they might not approve, but which after mature reflection had struck deep roots in his mind. Foremost among these he mentioned the doctrine of pre-existence.[1]

Beausobré[2] states: "Nicephorus Gregoras was right in attributing [metempsychosis] to Synesius. It is to be found in several passages of the works of this Father, and especially in the following prayer which he addresses to God: 'Father, grant that my soul, mingling in the Light, may no more be plunged in the delusion of Earth.'" Beausobré continues: "Let us add to Synesius another Christian philosopher Chalcidius of an earlier date who gives his unqualified consent to the same error, when writing: 'Souls who have failed to unite themselves with God, are compelled, by the law of destiny, to begin a new kind of life, entirely different from their former, until they repent of their sins. . . . Thus, it was not only the . . . Gnostics who accepted the error of Metempsychosis; it was the Christian Philosophers of high merit, of great virtue—the error being very attractive because

---

[6] The Platonists and their successors did not believe that the soul returned immediately after death. See p. 163.
[7] Book X, Chap. 30. *A Select Library of the Nicene and Post-Nicene Fathers.* . . . First Series, II, 200.

---

[1] Walker, *Reincarnation.* . . . p. 236.
[2] *Op. cit.,* II, 493.

of its antiquity, its universality, and its Principles, of which they believed it was a consequence."

Under "The Hermetic Works" in the Egyptian section, Synesius' *Treatise on Providence* is quoted on the periodical incarnation among men of wise benefactors and heroes. That section is pertinent to a treatment of the periods in early church history under consideration inasmuch as the Hermetic Fragments, which enjoyed a high repute with Clement, Origen, Augustine, and other early Christians, frequently mention and take for granted reincarnation.

Synesius wrote in his *Treatise on Dreams:*

Philosophy speaks of souls being prepared by a course of transmigrations. . . . When first it comes down to earth, it [the soul] embarks on this animal spirit as on a boat, and through it is brought into contact with matter. The soul's object is to take this spirit back with her; for if she were to abandon it and leave it behind on earth . . . the manner of her return would bring disgrace on her. . . . The soul which did not quickly return to the heavenly region from which it was sent down to earth had to go through many lives of wandering.[3]

NEMESIUS (LATE FOURTH CENTURY)
Philosopher, Bishop of Emesa

In his work *De natura hominis*, Nemesius wrote: "Plato asserts that there is one soul and many souls, the one soul being the soul of the universe and the other being the souls of particular things. . . . All Greeks, then, who represent the soul as immortal agree in believing in transmigration." [1] G. F. Moore states that in that same work Nemesius "agrees with Porphyry and Iamblichus that human souls migrate only into human bodies." [2]

OTHER CHURCH FATHERS

Irenaeus in his *Against Heresies*[1] discounts rebirth because the individual does not remember previous existences.[2] The Church Fathers listed below confine their remarks on reincarnation to ridiculing the improbable notion that men "become flies, gnats, and bushes" in a future life—a subject which is discussed elsewhere in this work.[3]

[3] Eva Martin, *The Ring of Return*, pp. 79–80.

[1] *Library of Christian Classics*. Philadelphia: Westminster Press, 1955, IV, 287–288.
[2] *Metempsychosis*, p. 82, note 62.

[1] Book II, Chap. 33.
[2] Clark's *Ante-Nicene Christian Library*, V, 247–250.
[3] See Index under "Animals."

St. John Chrysostom (345?–407): *Homily II, Nos. 3 and 5.*[4]
St. Basil the Great (330?–379?): *The Hexaemeron, Homily VIII.*[5]
St. Gregory of Nyssa (331?–396?): *On the Making of Man, Chap.* XXVIII.[6]
St. Ambrose (340?–397): Book II, n. 130.[7]

*

Gnosticism

The word "Gnostic" comes from the Greek "gnose," meaning knowledge. The Christian Gnostics were all reincarnationists, and included, among others, the followers of Basilides, Valentinus, and Marcion; the half-Gnostic Manicheans comprising more than seventy sects; the Simonists or disciples of that much-maligned personage Simon Magus;[1] and the Priscillians of Spain. According to Radhakrishnan, "Gnosticism was one of the most powerful currents of thought which influenced Christian doctrine and practice. [It] remained a power down to the fifth century through its alliance with Neoplatonism." [2]

In orthodox circles Gnosticism is usually regarded as an adventitious pseudo-Christian religious philosophy running parallel to the mainstream of Christianity. Modern scholars are beginning to reverse this picture. In the Reverend A. A. F. Lamplugh's introduction to his translation of the Gnostic work Codex Brucianus, published as *The Gnosis of the Light*,[3] he writes: "Recent investigations have challenged . . . the traditional 'facts.' With some today, and with many more tomorrow, the burning question is, or will be—not how did a peculiarly silly and licentious heresy rise within the Church—but how did the Church rise out of the Great Gnostic movement, how did the dynamic ideas of the Gnosis become crystallized into Dogmas?" In recent years, owing to the discovery of ancient scrolls and manuscripts—some of which will presently be mentioned—Lamplugh's burning question is being raised again and again.

A growing number of writers consider the possibility that the Gnostics

---

[4] *A Select Library of the Nicene and Post-Nicene Fathers* . . . , First Series, XIV, 5–6.
[5] *Ibid.*, Second Series, VIII, 95–96.
[6] *Ibid.*, Second Series, V, 419.
[7] *Ibid.*, Second Series, X, 196.

---

[1] Simon's reincarnation views are indicated in *Hastings' Encyclopædia of Religion and Ethics*, XI, 517; XII, 437.
[2] *Eastern Religions and Western Thought*, p. 200.
[3] London: John M. Watkins, 1918.

may have been the descendants of the original Christians and the inheritors of the esoteric teachings of Christ. Jesus said to his disciples: "Unto you it is given to know the mystery of the Kingdom of God; but unto them that are without, all these things are done in parables." (Mark 4:11. See Matthew 13:10–16.) In the New Testament we have the parables, but what happened to the inner teaching? St. Clement and Origen both testified to an esoteric lining to Christianity.[4] St. Paul is still another witness: "And I, brethren, could not speak unto you as unto spiritual, but as unto carnal, as unto babes in Christ. I have fed you with milk, and not with meat; for hitherto ye were not able to bear it, neither yet now are ye able." (I Corinthians 3:1–2.) Smith and Wace's *Dictionary of Christian Biography*[5] states regarding the Gnostics:

We have no reason to think that the earliest Gnostics intended to found sects separated from the Church and called after their own names. Their disciples were to be Christians, elevated above the rest as acquainted with deeper mysteries, and called *Gnostikoi* because possessed of a Gnosis superior to the simple faith of the multitude.[6]

They also boasted to be in possession of genuine apostolical traditions, deriving their doctrines, some from St. Paul, others from St. Peter, and others again from Judas, Thomas, Philip, and Matthew. In addition moreover, to the secret doctrine which they professed to have received by oral tradition, they appealed also to alleged writings of the apostles themselves or their disciples.[7]

Basilides, who taught in Alexandria about A.D. 125, and around whom the founders of the various Gnostic schools grouped themselves, maintained that he had all his doctrines from the Apostle Matthew and from Peter, through Glaucus, his disciple. The orthodox Eusebius reports that Basilides published twenty-four volumes of *Interpretations of the Gospels*, which were later burned by the Church.[8] Such a loss seems incalculable in the light it would throw upon Christian beginnings, for these works were written long before the so-called canonical bible was officially sanctioned at the Council of Nicea in 325.

In 1900 appeared G. R. S. Mead's volume on the Gnostics entitled *Fragments of a Faith Forgotten*. Kenneth Rexroth states in his introduction to the 1960 reprint:[9] "After sixty years Mead is still the most reliable

---

[4] W. R. Inge, *The Philosophy of Plotinus*, II, p. 17. Origen's *Contra Celsum*, I, vii; *Clark's Ante-Nicene Christian Library*, X, 403–404.
[5] London: John Murray, 1882.
[6] Article "Gnosticism," II, 679.
[7] Article "Irenaeus," III, 269.
[8] *Hist. Eccles.*, iv. 7.
[9] New York: University Books.

guide to the corpus of Gnosticism that we have." Quoting from the volume itself:

The whole of [Gnosticism] revolved round the conception of cyclic law for both the universal and individual soul. Thus we find the Gnostics invariably teaching the doctrine not only of the pre-existence but also of the rebirth of human souls. . . . They held rigidly to the infallible working out of the great law of cause and effect. It is somewhat curious that these two main doctrines [of reincarnation and karma] which explain so much in Gnosticism and throw light on so many dark places, have been either entirely overlooked or, when not unintelligently slurred over, despatched with a few hurried remarks in which the critic is more at pains to apologise for touching on such ridiculous superstitions as "metempsychosis" and "fate," than to elucidate tenets which are a key to the whole position. (P. 142.)

Mead is also the translator of the important Gnostic scripture the Pistis Sophia—a name which means "knowledge-wisdom." In his introduction, Mead writes: "Our Gnostics . . . found no difficulty in fitting [transcorporation or reincarnation] into their plan of salvation, which shows no sign of the expectation of an immediate end of all things—that prime article of faith [of the orthodox Christian] of the earliest days. So far from thinking that reincarnation is alien to gospel-teaching, they elaborately interpret certain of the most striking sayings in this sense, and give graphic details of how Jesus, as the First Mystery, brought to rebirth the souls of John the Baptizer and of the disciples, and supervised the economy of his own incarnation. In this respect the Pistis Sophia offers richer material for those interested in this ancient and widespread doctrine than can be found in any other old-world document in the West.[10]

In the first extracts from this translation the Saviour, Christ, is relating what chastisements will befall various souls when they enter upon a new incarnation:

[THE SAVIOUR:]   This is the chastisement of the curser . . . Yaluham . . .
bringeth a cup filled with the water of forgetfulness and handeth it to the soul, and it drinketh it and forgetteth . . . all the regions to which it hath gone. And they cast it down into a body which will spend its time continually troubled in its heart. . . .
This is the chastisement of the arrogant and overweening man. . . . Yaluham . . . cometh and bringeth the cup with the water of forgetfulness and handeth it to the soul; and it drinketh and forgetteth all things and all the regions to which it hath gone. And they cast it up into a lame and deformed body, so that all despise it persistently. . . .
[JOHN SAID:]   A man who hath committed no sin, but done good persistently, but hath not found the mysteries . . . what will happen unto him? . . .

[10] London: John M. Watkins, rev. ed. 1921, p. xlv.

[THE SAVIOUR:]   Thereafter there cometh a receiver of the little Sabaōth, the Good, him of the Midst. He himself bringeth a cup filled with thoughts and wisdom, and soberness is in it; he handeth it to the soul. And they cast it into a body which can neither sleep nor forget because of the cup of soberness which hath been handed unto it; but it will whip its heart persistently to question about the mysteries of the Light until it finds them, through the decision of the Virgin of Light, and inherit the Light for ever. . . .

I have turned Elias and sent him into the body of John the Baptizer, and the rest [of the prophets] also I turned into righteous bodies, which will find the mysteries of the Light, go on high and inherit the Light-kingdom.[11]

All outward manifestations of Gnosticism and Gnostic Manicheism were eventually suppressed by Emperors and Popes alike—the death penalty often being inflicted for belief. Yet these movements long maintained a secret existence even in the West. In the Byzantine empire where the eastern half of the Catholic Church prevailed, they withdrew ostensibly to the boundaries of the empire, but still maintained hidden relations with kindred groups scattered throughout the provinces and even in Constantinople itself. The subsequent widespread Gnostic revival of medieval times will receive treatment in the section "Reincarnation in the Dark Ages."

In the Spring, 1959, issue of the University of Chicago quarterly *Diogenes*, an article appeared entitled "The Gnostic Manuscripts of Upper Egypt" by Eva Meyerovitch (translated from the French by James H. Labadie). Several paragraphs therefrom seem particularly pertinent to our discussion:

Our epoch . . . has in recent years seen several discoveries which hold extraordinary interest for history in general and for the history of religions in particular. Around 1930 seven volumes of Manichean writings were discovered at Fayum; in 1941, a few miles outside Cairo, near Tura, unpublished works of Origen and his disciple Didymus the Blind were found; the discovery of the Dead Sea Scrolls occurred around 1945; and in Egypt, at roughly this same time, an equally fortuitous find was made of a considerable body of Coptic manuscripts dating perhaps from the third century A.D. Although these last have not been entirely deciphered, they are considered by specialists to be prodigiously rich; such a find, says one, "does not merely enrich or renew our previous knowledge of the literature, the genealogy, or the history of Gnosticism: it revolutionizes this knowledge, and opens to research in the field a path absolutely distinct from all those which criticism has previously followed." [12] . . .

In the Acts and in the Epistles we find trace of the struggle which primitive

---

[11] Pp. 293, 315, 320, 322–323.
[12] H. Charles Puech, Professor at the Collège de France, *Les nouveaux écrits gnostiques découverts en Haute-Égypte.*

Christianity had to wage against Gnostic tendencies, a struggle which became more and more intensified and no doubt reached its apogee in the second century. The works of Christian writers of that time bear witness to the bitterness of the struggle. However, they all look upon the Gnose . . . as a phenomenon to be considered uniquely *in relation to* Christianity, as a heresy within the church. We cannot view it in this light today. The comparative history of religions shows us that the term must be given a much wider meaning; it is essentially concerned, as a matter of fact, with a specific religious attitude in regard to the problem of salvation. . . . There exist pagan Gnoses, such as Hermetism; extra-Christian Gnoses such as Mandeism;[13] oriental Gnoses like Ishmaelism.[14] . . .

The Gnostics constructed for themselves a universe in which they might finally find life from the moment they believed themselves able to answer the questions which tormented them concerning the origin of man, his reason, and his purpose. Escaping from ignorance and oblivion, conscious that in reality he is not of this world, that he is "foreign" to it, that he is "a fallen god who remembers the heavens," man, thanks to a knowledge, a saving Gnose, "in the course of an illumination which is both regeneration and divinization, regrasped himself in his truth, remembered himself anew, thus achieving with the possession of his veritable 'self' . . . the explanation of his destiny." [15] . . . This conception of man's liberation through knowledge is to be found as well in Hermetism, Manicheism, Catharism, the Jewish Cabala, as well as in the Islamic Gnoses.

Inasmuch as each of these five movements taught reincarnation as an intrinsic part of its philosophy, a close relationship may exist between the pursuit of what the Hindus call *Atma Vidyâ*, or Spiritual Knowledge, and the doctrine of many lives.

*

The Anathemas against Pre-Existence

For fourteen long centuries the dialogue on reincarnation was silenced in orthodox Christendom because it was generally believed that in the year 553 an important church council anathematized (cursed) the doctrine of the pre-existence of the soul. While reincarnation and pre-existence (in the limited sense the latter term is used by some churchmen) are not synonymous terms, obviously if pre-existence is false, previous lives on earth are impossible, and by inference future lives also. Evidence advanced by Catholic scholars now throws new light on what acutally occurred at this council, as shall shortly be seen.

[13] An ancient Gnostic sect still surviving in southern Mesopotamia. (Eds.)
[14] See under 'Islam.'
[15] H. Charles Puech, article cited in *Annuaire du Collège de France*, 1953.

In the early centuries of Christian history, many battles were waged over issues of doctrine, church councils being convened to settle disputes. In the sixth century Emperor Justinian declared war against the followers of Origen. At Justinian's instigation it appears that a local synod, which convened in Constantinople in the year 543, condemned the teachings of Origen, and ten years later, in 553, Justinian issued his anathemas against Origen, possibly submitting them for final ratification at an extra-conciliary or unofficial session of the Fifth Ecumenical Council—also called the Second Council of Constantinople. The anathemas cursed, among other teachings of Origen, the doctrine of the pre-existence of the soul.

The Catholic Encyclopedia[1] gives some rather astonishing information concerning this Fifth Ecumenical Council, permitting the conclusion, on at least technical grounds, that there is no barrier to belief in reincarnation for Catholic Christians.[2] With the exception of six Western bishops from Africa, the council was attended entirely by Eastern bishops, no representative from Rome being present. Although Pope Vigilius was in Constantinople at the time, he refused to attend. In fact, the Pope was Justinian's prisoner since November of 545, when he had been kidnaped from Rome.[3] The president of the Council was Eutychius, Patriarch of Constantinople. "From the time of Justinian the emperor controlled the patriarch absolutely." [4]

There apparently had been intense conflict between Justinian and Pope Vigilius for several years. Violating previous agreements, Justinian in 551 issued an edict against what was known as "The Three Chapters," the teachings of three supposed heretics. "For his dignified protest Vigilius thereupon suffered various personal indignities at the hands of the civil authority and nearly lost his life." [5] Later, to bring peace between the Eastern and Western branches of the church, this Fifth Ecumenical Council was called. Justinian, however, refused Pope Vigilius' request for equal representation of bishops from East and West, and summarily convened the council on his own terms; hence the Pope's refusal to attend. When we learn that as many as 165 bishops were present at the final meeting on June 2, only six of whom could possibly be from the West, it can safely be concluded that the voting during all the sessions was very much in Justinian's hands. The Council's "decrees were received in the East, but long contested in the

[1] 1913 edition, IV, 308–309; XI, 311.
[2] There has never been a papal encyclical explicitly against reincarnation. See Mentor Religious Classic, *The Papal Encyclicals in Their Historic Context*, by the Catholic religious scholar, Anne Fremantle.
[3] *The Cambridge Medieval History*, II, 47.
[4] *The Columbia Encyclopedia*, 2d ed., "Orthodox Eastern Church."
[5] *Catholic Encyclopedia*, IV, 309.

Western Church, where a schism arose that lasted for seventy years." [6]

Of this period, the Reverend William Alva Gifford wrote in *The Story of the Faith* (p. 178):

Justinian assumed the headship of the Church. Imperial edicts regulated public worship, directed ecclesiastical discipline, and even dictated theological doctrines. The Church had to submit for a time to "Caesaro-papism," a papacy of the Emperor. . . . One education centre of paganism remained, the University of Athens [the last stronghold of Neoplatonism]. It was closed in 529 by the Emperor Justinian, in the interest of the Christian schools at Constantinople. That was the death-knell of paganism. As for the scholars of Athens, they fled to Persia, where their descendants became leaders of the literary and scientific life of Islam, at Bagdad and other centres.[7]

Thomas Whittaker writes in *The Neo-Platonists*[8] that up to this time "in spite of the formal prohibition of the ancient religion, the philosophers at Athens had retained some freedom to oppose Christian positions on speculative questions. This seems clear from the fact that Proclus had been able to issue a tractate in which he set forth the arguments for the perpetuity of the world against the Christian doctrine of creation. Justinian, who was desirous of a reputation for strictness of orthodoxy, resolved that even this freedom should cease; and in 529 enacted that henceforth no one should teach the ancient philosophy. . . . The liberty of philosophising was now everywhere brought within the limits prescribed by the Christian Church." [9]

Quoting directly from *The Catholic Encyclopedia* regarding the Fifth Ecumenical Council:[10]

Were Origen and Origenism anathematized? Many learned writers believe so; an equal number deny that they were condemned; most modern authorities are either undecided or reply with reservations. Relying on the most recent studies on the question it may be held that:

1. It is certain that the fifth general council was convoked exclusively to deal with the affair of the Three Chapters, and *that neither Origen nor Origenism were the cause of it.*

2. It is certain that the council opened on 5 May, 553, in spite of the protestations of Pope Vigilius, who though at Constantinople refused to attend it, and that in the eight conciliary sessions (from 5 May to 2 June), the Acts of which we possess, *only the question of the Three Chapters is treated.*

3. Finally it is certain that *only the Acts concerning the affair of the Three*

[6] *Britannica*, 9th ed., XIII, 796.
[7] See under "Islam."
[8] Cambridge University Press, 1928.
[9] P. 182.
[10] XI, 311. The section on Origen was written by Father Ferdinand Prat, S.J., member of the Biblical Commission, College St. Michel, Brussels.

Chapters were submitted to the pope for his approval, which was given on 8 December, 553, and 23 February, 554.[11]

4. It is a fact that Popes Vigilius, Pelagius I (556–61), Pelagius II (579–90), Gregory the Great (590–604), in treating of the fifth council deal only with the Three Chapters, make no mention of Origenism, and speak as if they did not know of its condemnation.

5. It must be admitted that *before the opening of the council*, which had been delayed by the resistance of the pope, the bishops already assembled at Constantinople had to consider, by order of the emperor, a form of Origenism that had practically nothing in common with Origen, but which was held, we know, by one of the Origenist parties in Palestine. . . .

6. The bishops [at this extra-conciliary session referred to in No. 5 above] certainly subscribed to the fifteen anathemas proposed by the emperor [against Origen]; an admitted Origenist, Theodore of Scythopolin, was forced to retract; but there is no proof that the approbation of the pope, who was at that time protesting against the convocation of the council, was asked.

7. It is easy to understand how this *extra-conciliary sentence was mistaken at a later period* for a decree of the actual oecumenical council. (Italics added.)

However, one far-reaching result of the mistake still persists, namely, the exclusion from consideration by orthodox Christianity of the teaching of the pre-existence of the soul and, by implication, reincarnation.

In the light of the references to reincarnation in the Bible, and of statements by some of the early Church Fathers, and now of the position of Catholic scholars in disclaiming the crusade against Origen, it is not remarkable that a growing number of the clergy are speaking favorably of the new interest in reincarnation,[12] and are even hoping that this "lost chord of Christianity" may once more vibrate in harmony with Christ's teaching of hope and responsibility.

Now what do Protestant scholars and theologians say about the supposed condemnation of Origen? Dr. Henry R. Percival writes in *A Select Library of Nicene and Post-Nicene Fathers*:[13]

Did the Fifth synod examine the case of Origen and finally adopt the XV. Anathemas against him which are usually found assigned to it? It would seem that with the evidence now in our possession it would be the height of rashness

---

[11] Some further significant details are furnished by Joseph Campbell in *The Masks of God: Occidental Mythology* (New York: Viking, 1964), p. 418. When Pope Vigilius refused to attend the Council, although he was Justinian's prisoner at the time, the Pope produced his own document, the *Constitutum ad Imperatoreum*, in which he condemned only sixty passages of one of the three "heretics," and not the author himself, on the ground that it was not customary to condemn the dead. Nor would he condemn the works of the other two. The Ecumenical Council thereupon condemned not only the works and authors in question but the captive Pope himself; and, thoroughly undone, the poor man finally joined his name to theirs and, permitted to return to his see, died in Syracuse on the way.

[12] See pp. 126–130, 133–137.

[13] Second Series, XIV, 316.

to give a dogmatic answer to this question. Scholars of the highest repute have taken, and do take today, the opposite sides of the case. . . . To my mind the chief difficulty in supposing these anathematisms to have been adopted by the Fifth Ecumenical is that nothing whatever is said about Origen in the call of the council, nor in any of the letters written in connection with it; all of which would seem unnatural had there been a long discussion upon the matter, and had such an important dogmatic definition been adopted as the XV. anathemas.

According to *The Oxford Dictionary of the Christian Church*, metempsychosis "was implicitly condemned by the Council of Lyons (1274) and Florence (1439), which affirmed that the souls go immediately to heaven, purgatory, or hell." [14] This does not nullify rebirth, for most reincarnationists teach that after death the soul undergoes a purgatorial condition before it is pure enough to "experience" heaven. They merely deny that these states of consciousness last forever. Commenting on the *Oxford Dictionary* statement, the Reverend Patrick Blakiston, Rector of the Episcopal Church in Alvechurch, Worcester, England, wrote in his monthly letter to parishioners (May, 1963): "The Church of England is not bound by the decisions of the mediaeval Roman Catholic Councils and, even if it could be shown that the undivided ancient Church officially forbade belief in reincarnation the 21st of our Articles of Religion says 'General Councils may err and sometimes have erred, even in things pertaining unto God.' "

Whatever the truth of this obscure phase of early church history, the anathemas themselves are most revealing. They are reprinted in *Reincarnation, an East-West Anthology*, pp. 321–325.[15] The anathema aimed at preexistence and reincarnation is the first: "If anyone assert the fabulous preexistence of souls, and shall assert the monstrous restoration which follows from it: let him be anathema." Origen and six others are anathematized at the close of the document, which concludes with these words: "If anyone does not anathematize [these heretics] as well as their impious writings, as also all other heretics already condemned and anathematized by the Holy Catholic and Apostolic Church, and by the aforesaid four Holy Synods and (if anyone does not equally anathematize) all those who have held and hold or who in their impiety persist in holding to the end the same opinion as those heretics just mentioned: let him be anathema."

To curse! To commit to eternal damnation all who disagree with a particular interpretation of sacred writ! How unlike the spirit and example of the Prince of Peace who admonished his disciples: "love your enemies, bless them that curse you." (Matthew 5:44.)

[14] Ed. F. L. Cross. Oxford University Press: 1957, "Metempsychosis."
[15] Taken from *A Select Library of Nicene and Post-Nicene Fathers of the Christian Church*, Second Series, eds. Philip Schaff and Henry Wace. New York: Scribner, 1900, XIV, 318–320.

*

Reincarnation in the Dark Ages

The Cathari and Albigenses

We now approach a chapter of Western history concerning which the educated world in general is almost completely uninformed. Who, for example, is aware that the Inquisition first came into being in the thirteenth century to destroy the Cathari? Who is aware that in the latter part of the Middle Ages this movement "spread so rapidly and resisted so stubbornly the sternest efforts of suppression that at one time it may be fairly said to have threatened the permanent existence of Christianity itself"? This statement by Henry Lea appears in his monumental three volume *History of the Inquisition of the Middle Ages*—the definitive work in this field.[1]

No adequate picture of religious thought through the centuries and of the forces that ultimately brought about the Renaissance and Reformation can be had without considering the part played by these numerous Christian Gnostic groups, branded as heretics by their fellow Christians. According to the British educator, Edmond Holmes, "Catharism overran southern and western Europe from Constantinople to the Pyrenees and from the Mediterranean to the North Sea."[2] In all there were about seventy-two groups,[3] among these being the Albigenses of southern France, the Italian Paterins, the German Cathari, the Bogomils of Bulgaria and the Paulicians of Armenia.

The Cathari were reincarnationists and together with such Christian groups as the Knights Templar, the Troubadours of southern Europe, and some of the Hermetic philosophers, Alchemists and Rosicrucians, kept embers of reincarnation philosophy burning during the night of Western civilization. These movements will receive brief treatment in Part Five. To the list of reincarnationists must of course be added the Christian and Hebrew Kabalists (see under "Judaism"), and also the Taborites, a branch of the Hussites.[4] How and through whom reincarnation teaching was preserved in the Middle East will be considered under "Islam."

[1] New York, Harper and Row, 1888, I, 89. Reprinted (1955) in the Scholar's Classic Series published by Russell & Russell, New York.
[2] *The Holy Heretics.* London: Watts, 1948, p. 2.
[3] *Webster's New International Dictionary*, 2d. ed., under "Cathari."
[4] M'Clintock and Strong's *Cyclopædia of Biblical, Theological and Ecclesiastical Literature*, under "Transmigration." Howard Kaminsky in his *History of the Hussite Revolution* of Bohemia indicates that only in the Taborite communities was the full promise of the original Hussite aspirations fulfilled. (University of California Press, 1967.)

A few introductory words seem appropriate as to the term "heretic"—a fearful, destestable word to those of pious faith. By derivation it means one who is "able to choose." Thus all who choose to think for themselves rather than blindly believe are heretics, and they have a noble predecessor in St. Paul, who, in his first epistle to the Thessalonians (5:21), counseled: "PROVE ALL THINGS: HOLD FAST THAT WHICH IS GOOD."

The thread of our narrative must be picked up where it was dropped a few pages back in the chapter on Gnosticism, for as stated in the *Britannica*,[5] "it is at least undoubted that the Paulicians and Bogomils, as well as the Catharists and the Albigenses are to be traced back to [Gnostic] Manichaeism and [Gnostic] Marcionitism."

Now about the middle of the fifth century, Gnosticism and Manicheism reappeared as Paulicianism in Syrian Armenia. "The Paulicians . . . inherited certain doctrines of eastern origin, such as . . . a theory of metempsychosis."[6] During the eighth century the movement spread through Asia Minor, and gained still more adherents when, rejuvenated by Sergius, it even partly enjoyed the favor of the Byzantine emperors. In the ninth century, being warred upon and defeated, it turned its attention westward, slowly infiltrating into central Europe.

The Reverend Mandell Creighton of Cambridge University states that the presence in Europe proper of these Gnostic Cathari, now also called the Bogomils,

". . . can first be traced in Bulgaria soon after its conversion [to Christianity] in 862, where the struggle between the Eastern and Western churches for the new converts opened a way for the more hardy speculations of a system which had never entirely disappeared, and [had] found a home amongst the Paulicians of Armenia. The name of Cathari, taken by the adherents of this new teaching, sufficiently shows the Oriental origin of their opinions, which spread from Bulgaria amongst the Slavs, and followed the routes of commerce into central Europe. The earliest record of their presence there is the condemnation of ten canons of Orleans [in northern France] as Manichees in 1022, and soon after this we find complaints of the prevalence of heresy in northern Italy and in Germany."[7]

However, Görres states[7a] that even before the year 1000, they had reached Italy gaining many followers, especially in Milan.

As to the reincarnation ideas of the Cathari, Lea states:[8] "Human souls are all fallen spirits passing through probation, and this was very gen-

[5] 1959 edition, "Manichaeism."
[6] *Britannica*, 9th ed., article "Albigenses."
[7] *Ibid.*, article "Waldenses."
[7a] J. v. Gorres, *Die Christliche Mystik*, Regensburg, 1840, III, p. 31.
[8] *Op. cit.*, I, 98.

erally the belief of all the sects of Cathari, leading to a theory of transmigration very similar to that of Buddhism, though modified by the belief that Christ's earthly mission was the redemption of these fallen spirits." In the scholarly volume, *Massacre at Montésequr; a History of the Albigensian Crusade,*[9] Zoé Oldenbourg adds: "The Cathars, generally speaking, acknowledged the doctrine of metempsychosis as held by the Hindus, with the same precise calculations governing posthumous retribution for the individual. A man who had led a just life would be reincarnated in a body better suited for his further spiritual development; whereas the criminal was liable, after his death, to be reborn in a body full of flaws and hereditary vices. . . ."

"In Italy, Catharism found a soil prepared for its reception," writes Holmes in *The Holy Heretics.*[10] "There the Manichaean heresy had maintained itself for many centuries in spite of all the efforts of Popes and Emperors to extirpate it. . . . And, with the awakening of the humanistic spirit in Italy at the end of the eleventh century, came a readiness to welcome and propagate ideas which had the charm of novelty, besides being free from the odious associations which orthodox Catholicism had contracted. . . . The ignorance, the avarice, and the immorality of the Italian clergy[11] exposed them to the contempt of the laity and inclined the latter to lend willing ears to anti-orthodox doctrine. . . . Catharism [was] the religion of *catharsis*, or purification. . . . Membership of the Church was confined to those who had received the Holy Spirit and were leading pure and sinless lives."

The historian, F. C. Conybeare, writes: "The influence of Catharism on the Catholic Church was enormous. To counteract it celibacy was finally imposed on the clergy, and the great mendicant orders evolved. . . . The sacrament of 'extreme unction' was also evolved by way of competing with the death-bed *consolamentum* of the Catharists." [12] As to the Albigenses of southern France, their industry, morality, and general sweetness of character led to their being known proverbially as "the good people." [13] They actually practiced the New Testament precepts, it is said, and were greatly beloved by their neighbors, but their enemies have frequently accused them

[9] New York: Pantheon, 1961, p. 35.
[10] Pp. 15, 26.
[11] Lea, I, 52, 61. "The highest authorities in the church admitted that its scandals were the cause, if not the justification of heresy. . . . No more unexceptionable witness as to the Church of the twelfth century can be had than St. Bernard, and he is never weary of denouncing the pride, the wickedness, the ambition, and the lust that reigned everywhere."
[12] *Britannica*, 11th ed., under "Cathars."
[13] Harold Bayley, *A New Light on the Renaissance*. London: J. M. Dent, 1909, p. 12.

and other Gnostics of the grossest forms of licentiousness and devil worship. The aim of the Cathari, says Schmidt, "was to restore the primitive purity of the Church, to understand the Church in its spiritual meaning, and to represent it in its ideal sanctity and perfection." [14]

Industry, art, and science, says Lea,[15] were far in advance of the age in twelfth-century southern France. The cities had won virtual self-government, and citizens, both men and women, boasted a degree of education and enlightenment unknown elsewhere. "The Albigenses," Dr. Gifford informs us, "were protected by the powerful Count Raymond of Toulouse, and had enjoyed religious freedom so long that the local clergy feared to discipline them. Pope Innocent III discerned in their individualism a menace to the Catholic Church. The essence of heresy is that one chooses doctrine for oneself. Innocent therefore summoned the faithful of Europe to a crusade against the Albigenses. Men came from everywhere. Simon de Montfort, Earl of Leicester, gave leadership. The Albigenses were crushed; Count Raymond submitted; and out of the crusade arose the Holy Tribunal of the Inquisition, whose sole business was to deal with heresy." [16] Not only was the civilization of the Albigenses destroyed but entire populations (men, women, and children) put to the sword by soldiers and armed clerics, mostly from northern France. At the taking of Beziers (July 22, 1209), the Abbot Arnold, being asked how the heretics were to be distinguished from the faithful, replied: "Slay all; God will know his own." [17]

Soon the iron hand of the "Holy" Inquisition was to descend over most of Europe, and for several centuries heretic-hunting on the part of the masses and clergy alike raged with an unparalleled fury, sending to the stake, as sons of Satan, hundreds of thousands of these brave, free-thinking Christians. Gradually the night of enslavement over the human mind came to an end. But as to reincarnation, the supposed curse against pre-existence of A.D. 553, followed later by the indefatigable work of the Inquisitors, proved exceedingly effective. Reincarnation was now dead to the masses of people in the West. Henceforth, and until the latter half of the nineteenth century, only among philosophers, writers, and a few daring theologians, was the doctrine to be quietly welcomed.

Let us conclude this historical survey with a quick glance at some of the religious beliefs of the Middle Ages, and then ask ourselves if it is conceivable that the philosophy of karma and rebirth could obtain a hearing

[14] C. Schmidt, *Histoire et Doctrine de la Secte des Cathares ou Albigeois*. Paris: 1858, II, 171.
[15] I, 67; II, 110.
[16] *The Story of the Faith*, pp. 282–283.
[17] *Britannica*, 9th ed., article "Albigenses."

among the orthodox of this time. St. Paul had affirmed the law of karma when he said: "Be not deceived; God is not mocked: for whatsoever a man soweth, that shall he also reap." (Galatians 6:7.) Jesus taught similarly: "With what measure ye mete, it shall be measured to you again." (Matthew 7:2.) But this was opposed to the dominant belief of the Dark Ages—the Old Testament teaching of original sin. Humanity for countless generations reaped what someone else—Adam—had sown. Belief in salvation by proxy, or vicarious atonement, was one escape; forgiveness of sins via the confessional another. An unconfessed sin could reap everlasting torture. The scales of justice did not, and were not expected to, balance.

How could people steeped in these beliefs entertain the idea of many lives? Karma and reincarnation imply individual responsibility; each man his own saviour and redeemer; each enjoys or suffers in exact proportion to thoughts and deeds in this or a former incarnation. It was the dead letter rendering of the Old Testament teachings that obviously prevailed during medieval times, not the spirit of the New Testament. "Be ye perfect, even as your Father which is in heaven is perfect," said Christ. (Matthew 5:48.) In this latter view man was not a weak, miserable sinner, but a being of dignity and power. "Ye shall know the truth, and the truth shall make you free." (John 8:32.)

*

Churchmen and Religious Writers

JOSEPH GLANVILL (1636–1680)
British Divine

[Glanvill, Chaplain to King Charles II, was one of the leading lights of the movement known as "The Cambridge Platonists" (see Part Five), although Glanvill himself was from Oxford. The extracts are from his *Lux Orientalis*, which bears the subtitle: "An Inquiry into the Opinions of the Eastern Sages concerning the Præexistence of Souls. Being a Key to Unlock the Grand Mysteries of Providence in Relation to Man's Sin and Misery." Glanvill argues for rebirth as well as pre-existence.]

Christ and His Apostles spoke and writ as the condition of the persons, with whom they dealt, administered occasion. . . . Therefore doubtless there were many noble theories which they could have made the world acquainted with. . . . Few speculative truths are delivered in Scripture but such as were called forth by the controversies of those times; and Pre-existence was none of them, it being the constant opinion of the Jews. . . .

Every soul brings a kind of sense with it into the world, whereby it tastes and relisheth what is suitable to its peculiar temper. . . . What can we conclude but that the soul itself is the immediate subject of all this variety and that it came prejudiced and prepossessed into this body with some implicit notions that it had learnt in another? To say that all this variety proceeds primarily from the mere temper of our bodies is methinks a very poor and unsatisfying account. For those that are the most like in the temper, air, and complexion of their bodies, are yet of a vastly differing genius. . . . What then can we conjecture is the cause of all this diversity, but that we had taken a great delight and pleasure in some things like and analogous unto these in a former condition?

Lux Orientalis[1]

CHEVALIER RAMSAY (1686–1743)
Scottish Author

[Coleridge's interest in reincarnation has been thought to stem, in part, from reading Ramsay's *Philosophical Principles*, from which the selection below is taken. (See under "Coleridge.") The edition used is the 1748, Edinburgh one (II, 236–246).]

The holy oracles always represent Paradise as our native country, and our present life as an exile. How can we be said to have been banished from a place in which we never were? This argument alone would suffice to convince us of pre-existence, if the prejudice of infancy inspired by the schoolmen had not accustomed us to look upon these expressions as metaphorical, and to believe, contrary to Scripture and to reason, that we were exiled from a happy state, only for the fault of our first parents. . . .

St. Paul seems to confirm this when he says: For the children being not yet born, having neither done good nor evil, it was said unto Rebecca, "Jacob have I loved, but Esau have I hated." [Romans 9:13.] God's love and hatred depend upon the moral dispositions of the creature. Since God says that he loved Jacob and hated Esau ere they were born, and before they had done good or evil in this mortal life, it follows clearly that they must have pre-existed in another state.

If it be said that these texts are obscure; that pre-existence is only drawn from them by induction, and that this opinion is not revealed in

1 London, 1662, pp. 51–52, 99, 101–103. Republished, with annotations by Dr. Henry More, in 1682.

Scripture by express words, I answer, that the doctrines of the immortality of the soul are nowhere revealed expressly in the sacred oracles of the Old or New Testament, but because all their morals and doctrines are founded upon these great truths. We may say the same of pre-existence. The doctrine is nowhere expressly revealed, but it is evidently supposed, as without it original sin becomes not only inexplicable, but absurd, repugnant, and impossible.

The Philosophical Principles of Natural and Revealed Religion

The Doctrine of Pre-Existence

"The pre-existence of the soul, whether taught by Pythagoras, sung by Empedocles, dreamed by Fludd, or contended for by Beecher is the principal foundation of the belief in metempsychosis." Thus writes the Reverend William R. Alger in *A Criticial History of the Doctrine of a Future Life*.[1] From the seventeenth century onward, many ministers and religious writers taught the pre-existence of the soul. However, they usually confined the soul's incarnation on earth to one visit, to be followed by an eternal stay in heaven. In *Reincarnation, an East-West Anthology* (Parts One and Two), a number of these writers were quoted, but in the present work Chevalier Ramsay and Sir Thomas Browne, are the sole representatives of this school of thought.

In the Gospel of John the pre-existence of Christ is mentioned again and again. "I am the living bread which came down from Heaven." (6:51.) "Ye shall see the Son of man ascend up where he was before." (6:62.) "Glorify thou me with thine own self with the glory which I had with thee before the world was." (17:5.) In John 8:56–59, we find Jesus taunted by the Jews that he was setting himself up as being greater than their father Abraham. Jesus replied: "Your father Abraham rejoiced to see my day; and he saw it, and was glad." "Then said the Jews into him: Thou art not yet fifty years old, and hast thou seen Abraham? Jesus said unto them, verily, verily, I say unto you, Before Abraham was, I am." Again quoting the fourth gospel (1:14–15): "And the Word was made flesh, and dwelt among us . . . full of grace and truth. John [the Baptist] bare witness of him, and cried, saying, 'This was he of whom I spake, He that cometh after me is preferred before me: for he was before me.' " St. Paul in Ephesians 1:4 includes mankind (or at least Christians) as having pre-existed with Christ: "According as he [God] hath chosen us in him [Christ] before the foundation of the world, that we should be holy and without blame before him in love."

[1] New York: 1878, p. 476.

As applied to men generally, two reasons made the teaching of pre-existence popular: First, as David Hume and many a philosopher before and after him has pointed out, only the beginningless can be endless; a soul created in time must end in time. The *Britannica* therefore calls pre-existence "the natural correlative of a belief in immortality." [2] Second, pre-existence explains "original sin," and thus exonerates deity of the crime of supposedly cursing all the generations after Adam simply because Adam ate of the forbidden fruit.

However, a little thought will reveal that those who believe in immortality but deny a special creation of souls at birth come very close to reincarnation thinking. Wherever the soul existed previously it must have had some vesture through which to manifest its powers and communicate with others. On earth it acquires a body of flesh. In the after life it must there, too, have its appropriate vehicle. Therefore, as McTaggart states, "a belief in pre-existence and post-existence is itself a belief in a plurality of lives, since it is a belief in three at least." [3]

The question at issue then becomes, "WHERE is the soul to be reborn?" A farmer reaps his harvest in the field where he casts the seed. It is natural for souls to do likewise, says the reincarnationist. St. Paul's words "As ye sow so shall ye reap" would then connote: "Where you sow and with whom you sow, there too shall you reap." The reincarnationist further suggests that to allow human beings but one sojourn on an earth which has been evolving for millions of years and which affords almost illimitable opportunities for growth of intelligence, talents, and moral powers, would be an inconceivable waste of valuable resources.

They will come back, come back again, as long as
the red Earth rolls.
He never wasted a leaf or a tree. Do you think He
would squander souls?

Rudyard Kipling

JOHANN PETER HEBEL (1760–1826)
Swiss-Born German Poet and Prelate

[From notes for a sermon at Karlsruhe where Hebel was prelate (published in Volume II of Hebel's works), the theme being "Have We Lived Before?":]

[2] 1959 ed., article "Pre-existence."
[3] J. M. E. McTaggart, *The Nature of Existence*. Cambridge University Press, 1927, II, 383 fn.

(a) Yes, it is possible; here or elsewhere. . . . We drank from Lethe's sweet bowl and a sweeter one, Mneme's [Memory's] is awaiting us. How much we forget in this life!

(b) Multiplicity of experience; wisdom is the fruit of experience; but how little one life has to offer!

(c) And have we really no memories at all? Do we not observe: easy developments, certain talents. What if we had possessed those once before? . . . Inexplicable sympathy. Preference for the history of special periods, men, countrysides. Have we been there before . . . ?

(d) How attractive the thought: I have lived in the period of the mammoths, the patriarchs, have been an Arcadian herdsman, a Greek adventurer, partaken in Hermann's battle. . . .

Some day, having drunk from the golden cup of Mneme, having finished with many wanderings, preserved my "I" through so many forms and conditions, become acquainted with joys and sorrows, and purified through both; what memories, what bliss, what gain!

"Have We Lived Before?"

FRIEDRICH SCHLEIERMACHER (1768–1834)
German Theologian and Philosopher

[Of his *Reden Ueber Die Religion* ("Talks on Religion"), published in 1799, it is said the whole Western world sat up and took notice, although Schleiermacher was then a relatively unknown chaplain. He became a major reformer of Protestant theology, eventually to become one of the greatest theologians of the Evangelical Church. His *Talks on Religion* are now esteemed as a classic of theological as well as German literature. Quoting from the Second Talk:]

History, in its essential meaning, is the highest aspect of religion. . . . For here you observe the return of Spirits and Souls ordinarily regarded as mere tender, poetic imaginings. In more than one sense we have [in this conception of metempsychosis] a wonderful arrangement of the universe, enabling us to compare the different periods of mankind on the basis of a reliable measure. For after a long interval, during which nature could not produce anything comparable, an excellent individual will return, recognized only by the Seers, and from the effect this individual produces they alone can judge the signs of the different cycles. A single moment of mankind's history will return, and from the various causes leading thereto, you shall discern the course of the universe and the formula of its laws. A genius

. . . will awaken from his slumber, appearing on a new scene. His speedier growth, his broader exertions, his more beautiful and powerful body, shall then indicate by how much the climate of mankind has improved, and is better adapted to the nourishing of noble growths.

Reden Ueber Die Religion

WILLIAM R. ALGER (1822–1905)
American Minister and Scholar

[To appreciate Alger's remarks on reincarnation, the following background information from E. D. Walker's *Reincarnation, a Study of Forgotten Truth* (p. 100) is of particular interest:

The noblest work of modern times, and probably of all time, upon immortality, is a large volume by the Rev. William R. Alger, entitled "A Critical History of the Doctrine of a Future Life." [1] It was published in 1860 and still remains [1888] the standard authority upon that topic throughout Christendom. . . . The author is a Unitarian minister, who devoted half his lifetime to the work, undermining his health thereby. In the first edition (1860) the writer characterizes reincarnation as a plausible delusion, unworthy of credence. For fifteen years more he continued studying the subject, and the latest edition (1878) gives the final result of his ripest investigations in heartily endorsing and advocating reincarnation. . . . That a Christian clergyman, making the problem of the soul's destiny his life's study, should become so overpowered by the force of this pagan idea as to adopt it for the climax of his scholarship is extremely significant.

A few extracts will suffice here; others may be found elsewhere in the present work.]

The argument [for reincarnation] from analogy is especially strong. It is natural to argue from the universal spectacle of incarnated life that this is the eternal scheme everywhere, the variety of souls finding in the variety of worlds an everlasting series of adventures in appropriate organisms.

It must be confessed that of all the thoughtful and refined forms of the belief in a future life none has had so extensive and prolonged prevalence as this. It has the vote of the majority, having for ages on ages been held by half the human race with an intensity of conviction almost without a parallel. Indeed, the most striking fact at first sight about the doctrine of the repeated incarnations of the soul . . . is the constant reappearance of the faith in all parts of the world, and its permanent hold on certain great nations. . . .

---

[1] It includes a bibliography, comprising 4,894 books relating to the nature, origin, and destiny of the soul, compiled by Ezra Abbot, Librarian of Harvard University. (Eds.)

It is not propounded with the slightest dogmatic animus. It is advanced solely as an illustration of what may possibly be true, as suggested by the general evidence of the phenomena of history and the facts of experience. The thoughts embodied in it are so wonderful, the method of it so rational, the region of contemplation into which it lifts the mind is so grand, the prospects it opens are of such universal reach and import, that the study of it brings us into full sympathy with the sublime scope of the idea of immortality, and of a cosmopolitan vindication of providence uncovered to every eye. It takes us out of the littleness of petty themes and selfish affairs, and makes it easier for us to believe in the vastest hopes mankind has ever known.

A Critical History of the Doctrine of a Future Life[2]

WILLIAM R. INGE (1860–1954)
Philosopher; Dean of St. Paul's Cathedral, London (1911–1934)

The doctrine of transmigration offers us "chains of personalities linked together by impersonal transitions" [quoting Bosanquet]. Nothing survives except the bare being of the Soul, and, we may add, its liabilities. But Plato does not hold the doctrine in an uncompromising form: Souls do not all drink enough of the waters of Lethe to forget everything; the importance of "recollection" in his writings is well known. Leibnitz thought that "immortality without recollection is ethically quite useless"; and many others profess that such an immortality would have no attraction for them. But others would be satisfied to know that they will live on in the great spiritual interests with which they identified themselves; they could say with Browning, "Other tasks in other lives, God willing." It is not continuity of consciousness which they prize, but perpetuity of life amid the eternal ideas.

The Philosophy of Plotinus[1]
Gifford Lectures, 1917–18

Has an ex-dignitary of the Anglican Church any business to dabble in these heathen beliefs? Well, they are not so alien as we think. Rebirth is plainly asserted in the Wisdom of Solomon (viii, 19, 20,) which the Roman Church rightly accepts as canonical.[2] It is implied in St. John's Gospel, where the disciples ask whether the blind man is punished for his sins in a former life. Herod thought that Jesus might be one of the old prophets, or even John the Baptist, whom he had beheaded himself. The belief was widely held among the Jews. . . . I believe there is an element

[2] New York: 1878, pp. 736, 739.

[1] London: Longmans, Green, 1948, II, 30.
[2] See Index under "Apocrypha."

of truth in this belief about our personality, which is common to India and all the mystics. Practically it amounts to disinterestedness, which is the core of all higher religion.

London Evening Standard, March 23, 1944

RICHARD WILHELM (1873–1930)

[From an article on reincarnation by this eminent German Sinologue, Theologian, Missionary, and collaborator of C. G. Jung:]

Let us consider what attitude to take toward this idea. In the first place we must insist that, from the viewpoint of Christianity, it is absolutely feasible. Christianity, it is true, lays stress only on the law of Karma, though it remains silent as to the working of its operations; looking only to its ultimate consummation, it does not touch upon the intervening stages. . . .

Unprejudiced observation and reasonable reflection lead us to the conviction that this law [of Karma] actually exists. However, in one life, bounded by birth and death, we can only experience a part of the whole of existence. We live through certain occurrences in which one tangled skein of Karmic effects is unraveled, while at the same time new threads of Karma are spun that cannot be worked out in this life, because their disentanglement is cut short by death. On the other hand we see results come to fruition, the causes of which are not to be found in this life. These are the great problems with which a Job battles, and to which—in spite of all faith in a hereafter—only the words "and yet?" of the Psalmist must be uttered, if the Wisdom of the East is not called to our aid. And so it is easy to understand that many of our deepest and clearest thinkers, as for instance Lessing and Goethe, look upon reincarnation as a theory well worthy of consideration. . . .

The following is an important point: heredity evidently plays a part in the life of man, but does not adequately account for every phase of the question. Children of the same parents, in spite of family likenesses, show entirely different traits of character that cannot be accounted for by heredity alone. Indeed, the fact is irrefutable that in one and the same family more and less advanced souls are born. It is Karmic law undoubtedly that plays the most decisive part.

"Reincarnation" [1]

[1] *The Theosophical Path.* Point Loma, California, January, 1924, pp. 37–45. Translation printed in said periodical with the permission of Dr. Wilhelm.

NICOLAS BERDYAEV (1874-1948)
Russian Christian Philosopher

[The translated selection that follows is from an essay of Berdyaev's appearing in the volume *Pereselienye Doosh—Transmigration of Souls*.[1] The volume bears the subtitle: "The Problem of Immortality in Occultism and Christianity." It contains the reincarnation views, pro and con, of such well-known Russian writers as Father O. Boulgakov, B. Vysheslavtchev, B. B. Zenkovsky, O. G. Florovsky, and S. Frank.]

The popularity of Theosophy and Anthroposophy is due precisely to the teaching of reincarnation. And the weakness and unreasonableness of theologic teachings concerning the genesis of the soul and its final destiny are responsible for this popularity. It is difficult to reconcile oneself to the traditional teaching according to which the soul is created at the moment of conception and at this moment the primordial sin is communicated as if it were a communicable disease. Also it is difficult to accept the other teaching, according to which the soul is a product of a hereditary process and receives the primordial sin as it would receive an hereditary disease. Neither of these teachings . . . supply any justification whatsoever for human sufferings and the injustices of individual destiny. But most intolerable is the teaching of eternal suffering in Hell. . . . Any attempt to construct a sensible teaching about Hell awakens moral protest. . . .

The teaching of reincarnation is simple. It makes rational the mystery of human destiny and . . . reconciles man to the [apparent] unjust and incomprehensible sufferings of life . . . man stops comparing his destiny with the happier destiny of other people and accepts it.

"The Teaching of Reincarnation and the Problem of Man"

ALBERT SCHWEITZER (1875-1965)
Philosopher, Physician, Clergyman, Musician

By reason of the idea of reincarnation Indian thought can be reconciled to the fact that so many people in their minds and actions are still so engrossed in the world. If we assume that we have but one existence, there arises the insoluble problem of what becomes of the spiritual ego which has lost all contact with the Eternal. Those who hold the doctrine of reincarnation are faced by no such problem. For them that non-spiritual atti-

[1] Paris; YMCA Press, undated.

tude only means that those men and women have not yet attained to the purified form of existence in which they are capable of knowing the truth and translating it into action. So the idea of reincarnation contains a most comforting explanation of reality by means of which Indian thought surmounts difficulties which baffle the thinkers of Europe.

Indian Thought and Its Development[1]

[In an article appearing in the Schweitzer memorial issue of *The Saturday Review*,[2] Emory Ross writes:]

In 1959, Robert Hutchins persuaded Albert Schweitzer to come to America. Many had tried previously, with no success. But the Goethe bicentennial commemoration that Hutchins and his colleagues were planning at Aspen, Colorado, won his consent. He and his wife came by ship, and my wife and I went to meet them when they docked. Sixty-five men and women of the American and world press, radio, and television were also there, pencils and cameras poised. The first thing Schweitzer did was to bow deeply and say in French, "Ladies and gentlemen, in my youth I was a stupid young man. I learned German and French, Latin, Greek, Hebrew— but no English. In my next incarnation, English shall be my first language."

"Schweitzer in America"

ARTHUR P. SHEPHERD (1 8 8 5 –   )
Canon of Worcester Cathedral, England

If we take into our unprejudiced thinking the picture of reincarnation as the process of human evolution, we shall find in it the answer to the problems of the new world situation. . . . So too, the vast picture of the meaningless masses and movements of the [starry] nebulae resolves itself into a universe of spirit beings, in infinite creative relationships to one another and to man. The perplexity of history, with its procession of rising and falling civilizations, is seen as mankind's pilgrimage of spiritual descent and ascent, in which we all have taken part, and in which recurring individual reincarnation is the principle of unification and progress. So too, the apparent inadequacy of a single earth life, or its bondage to physical or mental or moral or circumstantial deficiency, is given new hope and understanding in the realization of the process of reincarnation.

"Christ and the Modern Man" [1]

[1] Boston: Beacon Press, 1952, pp. 222–223.
[2] September 25, 1965.

[1] "The Second Maurice Elliott Memorial Lecture," November 30, 1961. London: Churches' Fellowship for Psychical Study, pp. 8–9.

PAUL TILLICH (1886–1965)
Theologian and Philosopher

[In *Reincarnation, An East-West Anthology*, published in December, 1961, selections were given from a talk, "Symbols of Eternal Life," delivered by Dr. Tillich at the University of California. This address in somewhat modified form was presented on February 1, 1962 at Harvard University as the Ingersoll Lecture on the Immortality of Man. The sentences below in parentheses were not in the earlier lecture and this is mentioned because they now clarify Dr. Tillich's views on reincarnation.]

The Nirvana as a symbol of eternal life indicates the life of absolute fullness, not the death of absolute nothingness. The life of Nirvana is beyond all distinction of subject and object; it is everything because it is nothing definite. . . . But in order to reach this, many reincarnations are necessary. They are continuations of temporal existence and consist of punishment and suffering. Only the end of temporal existence brings full participation in eternal life. In it individualization is transcended by participation. A full recession to the "Ground" has taken place. (But, we may ask critically, how can the One be abundance if there is no differentiation within it? And what does reincarnation of the same subject mean, if there is no awareness of the identity of the subject in each reincarnation?). . .

The doctrine of the immortality of the soul in its [Greek] classical form . . . describes the fall of the soul from the realm of the eternal essences to which it belongs into the realm of existence, matter, temporality, genesis and decay. It also describes the return of the soul to its former state, through a process of individual salvation. The eternal life of the soul which it anticipates in its bodily prison and to which it returns is individual participation in the supra-temporal world. . . . The individual is preserved, but only in its reunion with the eternal.

The history of these ideas, their amalgamation with the Christian tradition, their transformation by the philosophers of the Enlightenment into the idea of moral progress after death, their criticism by Hume and Kant, the attempts to restate the idea—all this shows the difficulties immanent in the symbols of immortality. The danger becomes clear in its use in contemporary American Protestantism, especially in secularized Protestantism. There it is understood as a desirable continuation of life after death indefinitely. . . . The "life hereafter" is imagined as a bodiless continuation of the experiences and activities of this life. The classical doctrine of immortality has become a popular Christian superstition. . . . One continues to live after one has died in almost the same way, but without a body—blessed spirits, walking on beautiful meadows.

[After considering further difficulties concerning the nature of life after death, Dr. Tillich concludes:] The question remains, what about the differences, not only between men, but between all beings and parts of the universe? How to solve the riddle of the unequal capacities for the reception of the light coming from the dimension of the eternal? The answer is given in [the symbol of] the Kingdom of God. The symbol of the Kingdom of God implies universal fulfillment, a new heaven and a new earth, but not in terms of receding of the universe into its Ground, but in a reunion of all separated and heterogeneous elements of being in the unity and clarity of the divine life. More than this cannot be said. God will be "all in all," as Paul expresses it. In this ecstatic symbol of fulfillment the contrast of the types is lessened but not completely obliterated.

Here a decision cannot be avoided. The Western world, even if it does not use the phrase, has decided for the symbol of the Kingdom of God because in the significance of the individual person the ideas of social justice and the valuation of history are implied. The future history of religion will be largely an encounter of the two central symbols of eternal life: Nirvana and the Kingdom of God.

"Symbols of Eternal Life" [1]

[Dr. Tillich raises important and deep-probing questions regarding Nirvana. It needs emphasizing, however, that the wide range of opinion existing among Christians as to the nature of Heaven, also exists in the East regarding Nirvana. It would hardly be correct to assume that in all oriental schools the Nirvanic state implies loss of individuality. Eitel's *Sanskirt-Chinese Dictionary* has already been quoted to show that Northern Buddhism does not so teach. The great Vedantic sage, Sankarâchârya, taught: "Having got rid of ignorance the wise man enjoys the bliss of Nirvana even while on this earth." [2] The Theosophists have some interesting things to say about the preservation of conscious awareness throughout Nirvana. (See p. 157.) One would imagine that the separative form of individuality man experiences here could hardly be preserved in a state of absoluteness where the unit expands its consciousness to embrace the WHOLE. The much misunderstood Buddhist simile, "the Dewdrop slips into the Shining Sea," implies a state of supreme identification with the Parent Source. A drop of

[1] *Harvard Divinity Bulletin*, April, 1962.
[2] *Crest Jewel of Wisdom*, Sloka 72.

oil can only float on the universal waters. At-one-ness becomes impossible.

The British explorer and author, Sir Francis Younghusband, remarks: "Western writers refer to Nirvana as if it were a state of blank emptiness, when the man's mind would be devoid of all intelligence and all feeling—a complete vacuum. The truth is the precise opposite. One who has attained the state of Nirvana may indeed be motionless and regardless of all sights and sounds. Yet inwardly his soul may be in a condition of intensest activity. . . . This is the goal of Buddhism. Not nothingness, but superlative activity. So Buddha urged each to become what he is—what he really is down in his deepest foundations—what in moments of loftiest exaltation he discovers himself to be." [3]

In contrasting the symbols for eternal life, one needs of course to appreciate that the Nirvanic condition—though it may continue for millions of years—is not regarded as enduring forever. In a new solar system, reborn from the old, the same entities are believed to go on with their evolutionary pilgrimage.]

LESLIE D. WEATHERHEAD (1893–   )
British Clergyman and Author

[Quoting from an article "Leslie Weatherhead . . . A bit of a Saint":[1] Dr. Weatherhead, "a former president of the Methodist Conference of Great Britain, was minister of London's historic City Temple—'the cathedral of nonconformism'—for 28 years until his retirement in 1960. In a country where fewer than 10 per cent regularly attend church, it was standing room only at The City Temple during the Weatherhead ministry. . . . He is a genuine intellectual, a Ph.D. in psychology, whose 37 books have sold over a half-million copies. [He] was a pioneer in the area of pastoral psychology. Nearly 30 years ago he set up a religio-psychological clinic which combined the insights of faith and psychiatry to help disturbed people."

The extracts below are from Dr. Weatherhead's lecture "The Case for Reincarnation," delivered at the opening session of the 1957–58 season of The City Temple Literary Society, of which he was then President. The lecture has been published in pamphlet form, some 50,000 copies being now in print.[2]]

[3] *Some Sayings of the Buddha,* trans. F. L. Woodward, Oxford University Press, 1939, Introduction, pp. xviii–xix.

[1] *Toronto Daily Star,* Oct. 16, 1965.
[2] Available from the publisher, M. C. Peto, 16 Kingswood Rd., Tadworth, Surrey, England.

The intelligent Christian asks not only that life should be just, but that it shall make sense. Does the idea of reincarnation help here? I think it does. Let us suppose that a very depraved or entirely materialistic person dies. Let us suppose that from a religious point of view he has entirely misused his earth-life. Will his translation to a spiritual plane do all that needs doing? Will it not be like putting a person who has never given himself any chance to understand music, into an everlasting concert . . . ? Can a man who has entirely neglected spiritual things be happy in a spiritual environment? If you say, "Oh well, he can learn in the next phase"— can he? Doesn't such a speculation make the earth-life meaningless? . . . I don't think we shall be able to skip the examinations of life like that. It would be as incongruous and unsound as telling a medical student who failed his qualifying examination, not to bother, but to go on treating people as if he had qualified. If I fail to pass those examinations in life which can only be taken while I dwell in a physical body, shall I not have to come back and take them again? . . .

If every birth in the world is the birth of a new soul, I don't see how progress can ever be consummated. Each has to begin at scratch. . . . How then can there be progress in the innermost things of the heart? We can pass on some wisdom and, in outward circumstance, those who follow us can in some ways go on where we left off. They will not have to re-discover electricity or atomic energy. But they will have to discover, for example, each for himself, the vital supremacy of love. Each child is born a selfish little animal . . . not able in character to begin where the most saintly parent left off. . . . How can a world progress in inner things—which are the most important—if the birth of every new generation fills the world with unregenerate souls full of original sin? There can never be a perfect world unless gradually those born into it can take advantage of lessons learned in earlier lives instead of starting at scratch.

"The Case for Reincarnation"

[In chapter "Reincarnation and Renewed Chances," in Dr. Weatherhead's book *The Christian Agnostic*,[3] he considers this familiar argument:]

"But," says the objector, "I should lose my identity in a number of incarnations." I don't think you will, any more than you have lost it already half a dozen times. You are William Tompkins, let us suppose. All right. You are the little, runny-nosed Willie Tompkins who got punished for being late at school. Do you want to keep your identity with him? You are

[3] London: Hodder & Stoughton, 1965; Nashville, Tenn,: Abingdon-Cokesbury Press.

the Will Tompkins who wrote those wet verses and slipped them into the hand of that girl of sixteen with blonde plaits. Do you want to assert your identity with him? You are the William Tompkins who got sacked for being unable to account for money received on behalf of the firm. Do you feel robbed if he passes out of your sense of identity? You are W. Tompkins, with rheumatic joints and poor hearing and peering sight, whose body is now a nuisance. Try this experiment: Say "William Tompkins, William Tompkins, William Tompkins" over to yourself aloud a hundred times. Imagine a hundred thousand angels all round you doing the same thing. . . . Is it really important that the whole personality of Tompkins should go on for a hundred, a thousand, ten thousand, a hundred thousand years? Still William Tompkins . . . !

Our true identity will not be lost, the pure gold of the ego will be maintained, purified, and strengthened. But why this emphasis on separateness? . . . We may lose our separateness in a new context of closer relationship . . . I don't want to be one note sounding on alone. . . . If I could be one note in a glorious symphony, would it not be well for separateness to be lost in symphony?

The Christian Agnostic

Roman Catholic Clerics on Reincarnation

ARCHBISHOP PASSAVALLI (1820–1897)

[Wincenty Lutoslawski, a noted Platonic scholar, and former Professor of Philosophy at the University of Wilno, Poland, wrote in his book *Pre-Existence and Reincarnation:*[1]]

For those who are interested in the relation of the Church to the dogma of palingenesis, an Italian book, published in 1911, is of the greatest importance: *Monsignor Arcivescovo L. Puecher Passavalli*, [by] Attilio Begey e Allessandro Favero.[2] Here we find the life and letters of a pious and learned Roman Catholic archbishop who at the age of sixty-four accepted the truth of pre-existence and reincarnation from two disciples of the Polish seer Towianski, namely Stanislaw Falkowski and Tancredi Canonico. Archbishop Passavalli admitted that reincarnation is not condemned by the Church, and that it is not at all in conflict with any Catholic dogma. . . . He lived up to the age of seventy-seven, unshaken in his conviction

1 London: Allen & Unwin, 1928, pp. 28–29.
2 Milano: Fratelli Bocca, 1911.

that he had already lived many times on earth and that he was likely to return.[3] [He remained archbishop until his death.]

Another Catholic priest, who also after long discussion gave up the prejudice against reincarnation . . . was Edward Dunski, whose *Letters*, edited by Attilio Begey and Jozef Komenda, were published by Bona in Torino in 1915. Many other priests in Poland and Italy believe in reincarnation, being influenced by the great mystic Andrzej Towianski (1799–1878) whose works were printed privately in three large volumes at Torino in 1882.

CARDINAL MERCIER (1851–1926)
Belgian Cardinal and Scholastic Philosopher

Under the term Wiedermenschwerdung, metempsychosis, or the transmigration of souls, a great variety of ideas may be understood: either a series of repetitions of existence under the twofold condition that the soul maintains consciousness of its personality and that there is a final unit in the series of transmigrations; or a series of repetitions of existence without any final unit, and yet with the presupposition that the soul maintains consciousness of its personality; or, finally, an endless series of repetitions of existence with the loss of consciousness of personal identity. . . . So far as concerns the first assumption, we do not see that reason, if left to itself, would declare this to be impossible or certainly false.

Psychologie[1]

THE CATHOLIC ENCYCLOPEDIA

[The *Catholic Encyclopedia*[1] states in its article on Metempsychosis:]

It was a tenet common to many systems of philosophic thought and religious belief widely separated from each other both geographically and historically. . . . There is evidence that at one period or another it has flourished in almost every part of the world. . . . This universality seems to mark it as one of those spontaneous or instinctive beliefs by which man's nature responds to the deep and urgent problems of existence. . . .

St. Jerome tells us that metempsychosis was a secret doctrine of certain sectaries in his day, but it was too evidently opposed to the Catholic doc-

[3] The Catholic theologian, Baron Friedrich von Hügel, also speaks of the Archbishop's "acceptance of a doctrine of successive earthly lives for human souls." See *Essays and Addresses on the Philosophy of Religion*. New York: Dutton, 1921, p. 232.

[1] Quoted in *Reincarnation as a Phenomenon of Metamorphosis*, Guenther Wachsmuth. New York: Anthroposophic Press, 1937, p. 7.

[1] 1913 edition.

trine of Redemption ever to obtain a settled footing. It was held, however, in a Platonic form by the Gnostics, and was so taught by Origen in his great work Περὶ ἀρχῶν [*De Principiis*].

In the face of a belief at first sight so far-fetched and yet at the same time so widely diffused, we are led to anticipate some great general causes which have worked together to produce it. A few such causes may be mentioned: (1) The practically universal conviction that the soul is a real entity distinct from the body and that it survives death; (2) connected with this, there is the imperative moral demand for an equitable future retribution of rewards and punishments in accordance with good or ill conduct here. The doctrine of transmigration satisfies in some degree both these virtually instinctive faiths; (3) As mentioned [previously], it offers a plausible explanation of the phenomena of heredity. . . . The world thus seems to become, through and through, moral and human. Indeed, where the belief in a personal Providence is unfamiliar or but feebly grasped, some form of metempsychosis understood as a kind of ethical evolutionary process, is almost a necessary makeshift.

Other Clergymen Favoring Reincarnation

Rev. Columbus Bradford, Methodist Episcopal clergyman of Illinois: *Birth a New Chance*. Chicago: 1901.

Rev. A. Henderson, Vicar of St. John of the Sepulchre, Norwich, England: *The Wheel of Life*. London: Rider, 1931.

Rev. Emmet Fox, Church of the Healing Christ, New York, N. Y.: *Power Through Constructive Thinking*. New York: Harper and Row, 1932, Chap. "Reincarnation."

Rev. Ernest C. Wilson, Christ Church, Los Angeles, California: *Have We Lived Before?* New York: Prentice Hall, 1956.

Rev. Robert G. Katsunoff, United Church of Canada, Montreal. "Does the Bible Teach Reincarnation and Karma?" (Pamphlet, undated).

Rev. Patrick Blakiston, Rector of the Anglican Church in Alvechurch, Worcester, England: *Parish Magazine*, May, 1963.

Rev. Harold Boon, Rector of Episcopal Church, Philadelphia, Pennsylvania: *Toronto Daily Star*, Oct. 5, 1964. Report of his lecture on reincarnation.

*

Statistics of Reincarnation Belief

In the 1940's, Mass-Observation, a British fact-finding organization, conducted "A Study in popular attitudes to religion, ethics, progress and politics in a London Borough." The results of the survey were disclosed in a book, Puzzled People,[1] from which the following is taken:

The conception of life after death was explored at various levels—by long informal conversations and through the written comments of Mass-Observation's National Panel. Perhaps the least expected, and in some ways the most significant fact which came to light was the extent of belief in reincarnation. Among the interview sample about one person in twenty-five spontaneously went into enough detail to show that they held some such belief. That amounts to about one in ten of those who have any definite belief in an afterlife at all, and is almost certainly an underestimate, since no attempt was made by direct questioning to go into the details of people's conception.

A decade later, the British anthropologist, Geoffrey Gorer, wrote in Exploring English Character—a volume based on a survey of 5,000 people living in a London borough:

A quarter of all those who believe in an after-life (an eighth of the population) do not appear to believe that this after-life will be eternal. Eleven per cent believe in future lives just like their present life, 2 per cent believe in life on another planet, and 11 per cent believe in reincarnation, either implicitly or explicitly on this earth. [In other words, 24 per cent of those believing in an after-life accepted some form of reincarnation.]
The relative prevalence of the belief in reincarnation (explicit statements come from 252 individuals out of a population of 5,000) is perhaps the most surprising single piece of information to be derived from this research. Reincarnation is a belief of the major Asiatic religions, but it is contrary to the creeds of all the established religions of Europe and the Near East. The Theosophists imported it into Europe at the end of the last century, but they comprise a minute portion of my sample; and, apart from the Presbyterians, some members of every denomination subscribe to this belief, though many of its holders must be "undenominational." . . . By and large the believers in reincarnation are very evenly distributed throughout the population.[2]

The London Daily Telegraph for August 6, 1960, reported: "There is a strong preoccupation among senior schoolchildren with some form of rein-

[1] London: Victor Gollancz, 1948.
[2] London: Cresset Press, 1955, pp. 259–260, 262.

carnation, judged on informal talks among them on religious education in secondary modern schools." This study—a survey of the relationship between contemporary Christianity and the youth of Great Britain—was subsequently published as a paperback entitled *Teenage Religion*.[3] The research had been organized by Harold Loukes, Reader in Education at Oxford University, and was published under the auspices of the Study and Research Committee of the Institute of Christian Education. The method chosen was simply to report, through tape recordings, the actual replies of students to questions concerning religious belief.

Mr. Loukes, himself a Christian, noted the frequent emergence in teenage thought of "the curious streak of reincarnation, respectable in the east, odd, yet morally attractive, in the west." His own objection is mentioned politely in one of the closing chapters:[4] "Reincarnation cannot be disproved; but it is open to the objection that it makes *this* life of less importance because it gives us further chances. We do not need to listen to a history lesson if we know we shall get the same thing tomorrow. And our conviction is that this life does matter, in a once-for-all kind of way." This argument would appear to divorce reincarnation from karmic law. The wages of procrastination are heavy enough within one life, and if humans have future lives, the karma of postponing obligations is likely to be increasingly burdensome. C. S. Lewis, writing on rebirth, remarks: "I believe that if a million chances were likely to do good, they would be given." [5] But what if *not* likely to do good? The reincarnationist holds that if life after life and age after age an individual persists in the path of inertia, he eventually becomes a "drop-out"—a failure for that world-period. The evolutionary ascent must some day be recommenced on a new earth, reborn from the old, but at the lowest rungs of the ladder of human development.

Here are sample statements made by the students regarding rebirth:[6]

I'm not struck on saying there is a heaven. I think you come back to life again.

I think when I die I will come back as someone else and carry on like that. I don't believe in heaven and hell because millions of people are dying every day, and there wouldn't be enough room for us all, we would be meeting stone age men and so on.

I think that you kind of come back into the world again, to live and lead a better life, and you go on coming back until you're perfect, and then, well, there isn't a place, but I think you go to God when you're perfect.

[3] London: SCM Press, 1961.
[4] P. 137.
[5] *The Problem of Pain.* London: Geoffrey Bles, 1941, p. 112.
[6] Pp. 62, 65.

◆ * ●

Islam

*

Reincarnation in Early Islam

We return now to the Middle Ages. The persecution of scholars by the medieval church had gradually driven most students of science and philosophy out of Europe. These people found refuge in Arabia, the land of liberty in those days. The Christian Gnostics gave the Arabs a knowledge of Greek philosophy and Gnosticism; the Nestorians made them acquainted with the Neoplatonic philosophers; and the exiled Jews instructed them in the Kabala. Fragments of the teachings of the Egyptian Hermes found their way into the Middle East. Alberuni accompanied Sultan Mahmud of Ghazni to India and acquired a knowledge of Hindu religious classics. A number of these were translated into Arabic. All these influences combined to make Islamic thinkers natural heirs to the philosophy of rebirth.

Among the various groups who took sanctuary in Arabia, the Nestorians were at first the most powerful. Nestorius, the founder of the Order, was the Alexandrian Christian Bishop and Neoplatonist who in the fifth century refused to accept the Virgin Mary as the Mother of God, had been excommunicated and exiled to an African oasis where he died of thirst. After his death his followers emigrated to Asia Minor, China, Tartary, and India, where they soon outnumbered all the Christians of the Greek and Roman churches combined. Many of the Nestorians were students of the Hermetic philosophy and the Kabala. Many, like Nestorius, were Neoplatonists, while others followed the Gnostic teachings. The thirteenth-century Franciscan missionary and traveler, Rubruquis (also known as William of Ruysbroeck), wrote that the idea of souls passing from body to body was general among the medieval Nestorians.[1]

[1] Gul. de Rubruquis, *Rec. des Voy. Soc. de Géographie de Paris*, IV, 356. Cited by

Mohammed (A.D. 570–632) as a boy came in contact with a Nestorian monastery in Busra, and grew deeply interested in the religious and philosophical views of the monks. Upon reaching manhood, some say he came more and more under Nestorian influence.

In his monumental work, *Literary History of Persia*,[2] E. G. Browne indicates in the chapters on the Ismailis and other esoteric schools of Islam how widely prevalent was the belief in reincarnation in the early centuries of the Mohammedan era. Three aspects of rebirth were accepted: *hulul*, the periodical incarnation of the Perfect Man or the Deity; *rij'at*, the return of the Imam or spiritual leader after death; and *tanasukh*, reincarnation of the soul of ordinary men. The author shows that in addition to the Ismailis, the Shiites known as "Ghulat," as well as the Caramthians, Bātinis, Hurufis, and other Islamic groups all held to these doctrines. As to the Sufis, this authority states that the prince of Sufi masters, Mansur-al-Hallāj, "certainly held all the cardinal doctrines of the Ghulat—*hulul*, *rij'at* and the like." An extract from Mansur's writings on rebirth will be presented a few pages hence, together with selections from the works of other leading Sufis.

In the eighth century, Neoplatonic thought gained new life from the great Arabian philosopher Al-Kindi, and in the ninth century from Al-Ferabi, who in turn taught the Persian-born physician and philosopher, Avicenna. Spain had been conquered by the Muslims in the eighth century and under Islamic influence the Iberian Peninsula became a great center of civilization and enlightenment. An important link in the Neoplatonic succession was the Kabalist Ibn Gebirol, a Spanish Jew, known to medieval scholastics as Avicebron (1021?–1058). It was through him that the long-exiled teachings of Plato returned to Europe via Spain, where, during the Dark Ages, adventurous Christian scholars and monks traveled in search for knowledge. However, the real revival in Europe did not take place until the Renaissance.

Dr. W. Y. Evans-Wentz, well known for his works on Eastern religion, stated in his lecture, "The Christian Doctrine of Rebirth": "During the Dark Ages of Europe, when the Moors of Spain almost alone in the Western world kept alight the sacred Torch of Learning . . . , the doctrine of rebirth was being taught by the great Saracenic philosophers—Al Ghazali and Al Batagni—in the Schools of Bagdad in the East and of Cordova [Spain] in the West. And in Europe, the disciples of these great teachers were Paracelsus and the martyred Bruno. It was due chiefly to Moslem scholars of those days that to Europe was restored the classical culture of

---

E. B. Tylor in *Religion in Primitive Culture*. New York: Harper Torchbook, 1958, 101 fn.
[2] London, 1902.

Greece, and that the Light from the Orient was re-lit in the Occident." [3]
(Paracelsus and Giordano Bruno are considered in Part Five.)

*

The Koran

This sacred scripture of Islam is regarded as having been revealed to the
Prophet Mohammed by Allah himself. It is largely ethical in character. In
the work, honor is rendered to Issa Ben Yussuf, or Jesus, son of Joseph.

The existence of an esoteric foundation to the Koranic teaching is indicated in these statements from The Sayings of Mohammed: "The Koran
was sent in seven dialects; and in every one of its sentences there is an
external and an internal meaning. . . . I received from the messenger of
God two kinds of knowledge: One of these I taught to others and if I had
taught them the other it would have broken their throats." [1]

In a letter, dated October 8, 1963, Mikhail Naimy, the renowned Leb-
anese mystic and friend and biographer of Kahlil Gibran, wrote to Joseph
Head: "In Al Koran clear hints [on rebirth] are found which orthodox
Islam brushes aside as meaning something else than reincarnation. . . . In
Al Koran occurs the following verse which I give in my own translation:
'And you were dead, and He brought you back to life. And He shall cause
you to die, and shall bring you back to life, and in the end shall gather you
unto Himself' [Sura 2:28]. The words 'you were dead' mean that they had
lived before becoming dead. That is the clear implication of the phrase.
Then the whole sentence would clearly indicate that it had reference to
more than one life and one death."

Quoting now from other parts of the Koran:

> As the rains turn the dry earth into green thereby yielding fruits, similarly
> God brings the dead into life so that thou mayest learn. (Chapter 8—Sura
> Iraf—Meccan Verses 6–6–13.)
> And He sent down rains from above in proper quantity and He brings back
> to life the dead earth, similarly ye shall be reborn. (Chapter 25—Sura Zakhraf
> —Meccan Verses 5–10–6.)
> [Those who doubt immortality] are dead and they do not know when they
> will be born again. Your God is peerless and those who have no faith in the
> ultimate have perverse hearts and they want to pose as great men. (Chapter
> 14—Sura Nahel—Verses 2–12–8.)

[3] Pamphlet No. 2 in the Buddhist Chronicle Series. Ceylon: Maha Bodhi Press, 1921.

[1] Nadarbeg K. Mirza, Reincarnation and Islam. Madras: 1927, pp. 4–5.

In a series of articles entitled "Reincarnation—Islamic Conceptions," Murtuza Husain Abdi, a Moslem scholar, states: "Commentator Ayashi on the authority of Imam Baqer says that the ultimate referred to in the fore-going verse really means Rajat [reincarnation] or going up and down and he further says that Rajat means rebirth in this world of great Holy Beings as well as of well known kafirs before Qiyamat (resurrection). . . . Kafir means the perverse. Clearer still are the following verses: [The Kafirs] have sworn by the strongest oath that one who dies shall not be reborn. Surely they will be reborn and this law is perfect but people who do not possess wisdom do not comprehend it. (Chapter 14—Sura Nahel Verses 4–0–10.) Commentator Qummi quoting Imam Jafer, the well known authority in the Islamic world, says that [this] means rebirths to be undergone before entering the Heaven world." [2]

In the last of his articles Mr. Abdi has some interesting things to say on how reincarnation gradually lost popularity in Islam:

> The position adopted by the successive luminaries who followed the Prophet, was to affirm the belief in reincarnation but not to propagate it as a teaching for the masses. This attitude was due to psychological reasons. The emphasis in Islamic teachings has throughout been on the purity of action. Another factor to remember is that the defensive wars, which have been described as Jehad or holy wars, which the Muslims fought in the early days and the wars of conquests (therefore not holy) which the Muslims fought in later days . . . gave a different shift to Islamic teachings. Philosophical, mystical and ethical teachings received an impetus in the first phase but they had subdued existence in the later phase. During this phase the republican character of the State was changed into monarchy and the supremacy no more belonged to the saints and philosophers. A subject like reincarnation demands a subtle mental attitude. It entails understanding of the higher planes of consciousness, the laws of cause and effect and the working of the laws of evolution. The monarchs had no interest in such subjects. Like so many other teachings, reincarnation was confined to the study and attention of the outer and inner students of Sufism. . . . [However] there is no danger for a Muslim being called a heretic if he believes and expresses himself in favour of reincarnation. [3]

*

The Sufis

"It is a well known historical fact," states Abdi, "that Muslims were divided on the question of succession of the Prophet, which ultimately re-

---

[2] *Theosophy in Pakistan*, Oct.-Dec., 1964; Jan.-Mar., 1965.
[3] *Ibid.*, Oct.-Dec., 1965.

sulted in the establishment of the two main sects of the Sunnis and the Shias." "The significant fact has however been that there has always existed a cementing class that brought the two sects and their sub-sects together and that was the class known as Sufis. . . . The soul of Islam always yearned after them. . . . Even now Rumi, Hafiz, Jami, Ibne Sina and a host of other Sufis command universal respect." [1]

As already indicated, and as will shortly be shown, it was among the Sufis (from Sophia, wisdom), that the teaching of reincarnation was more especially preserved. The Sufis claimed to possess the esoteric philosophy of Islam and to have preceded Mohammed by several thousand years. Saadi, Rumi, Hafiz, and other celebrated Sufi poets apparently concealed many of their ideas behind the symbolism of "the Beloved," a practice later adopted by the Troubadours, and by Dante and Raymond Lully. (See pp. 227–228.) Avicenna became a Sufi in later life. Some of his biographers claim him as the real author of the *Rubaiyat* of Omar Khayyam, a poem which makes abundant use of "the Beloved" symbolism.

The enormous though largely unacknowledged impact of Sufism on Western as well as Eastern thought is disclosed in Idries Shah's book *The Sufis*.[2] Robert Graves, who writes the introduction, states:

> Instances abound in all European literature of the debt to the Sufis. The legend of Wilhelm Tell is found in Attar's *Parliament of the Birds* (twelfth century) long before its appearance in Switzerland. . . . Although Don Quixote (pronounced "Kishotte" by the Aragonese and Provençals) seems the most Spanish of all Spaniards, Cervantes himself acknowledges his indebtedness to an Arabic source. This attribution has been dismissed as a quixotic joke by scholars, but Cervantes' stories often closely follow those of Sidi Kishar, a legendary Sufi teacher sometimes equated with Nasrudin, including the famous incident of mistaking mills . . . for giants. (Pp. xvii–xviii.)

Mr. Shah, who indicates that the Sufis believe in *conscious* evolution and the limitless perfectability of man, reveals further influences on the West:

> The Eastern impact in the dark ages was absorbed on several levels. Of these the most important are the theological and the occultist. Lully, Assisi, Scot [Duns Scotus] and dozens of others passed on the theological version. But we have only to glance at the list of the famous names of occult illuminati of Europe to see what was the nature of the secret doctrine which they were passing down, in however garbled a form.

Raymond Lully, according to the occultists, was an alchemist and illumi-

---

[1] *Ibid.*
[2] New York: Doubleday, 1964.

nate. According to the devout, he was a Christian missionary. According to his own writings, he was an adapter of Sufi books and exercises. Roger Bacon, another hierophant of occultism, wrote on Sufi illuminism. Paracelsus, who tried to reform Western medicine, presents Sufi ideas. . . . Geber the alchemist was one of the best-known Sufis of Iraq. He is known as a master of occultism [and the father of chemistry]. Also in the occult tradition is Albertus Magnus, both scholastic and magician, who studied in Arab schools and inspired St. Thomas Aquinas. Numerous Popes supposed to be magicians or transmitters of a secret doctrine . . . were graduates of Arab schools—such as Gerbert, Pope Silvester II. . . . In organizations it is the same story. If the Franciscan Order bears the stamp of Sufi origins, so do the Rosicrucians and the Masons. (Pp. 242–243.)

The seventeenth-century oriental treasure-house, *The Dabistan,* states that the eastern school of Sufis was derived from certain ancient Zoroastrian mystics. These Sufis taught: "When the souls not yet come forth from the pit of the natural darkness of bodily matter, are nevertheless in a state of increasing improvement, then, in an ascending way, they migrate from body to body, each purer than the former one, until the time of climbing up to the steps of the wished-for perfection of mankind . . . after which, purified of the defilement of the body, they join the world of sanctity . . .[3] In Chapter 12, entitled "Religion of the Sufis," (III, 277–278), the Sufi master, Sáid Muhammed Nurbakhsh, is shown distinguishing between *tanāsukh,* or ordinary reincarnation, and *burūz,* the reincarnation of a perfect soul "for the sake of perfecting mankind." Selections from the writings of other renowned Sufis now follow.

MANSUR AL-HALLĀJ (10TH CENTURY)

[This Sufi poet was executed on the cross because of his claim of *Inal Haq,* or being one with deity. One of his couplets reads, as translated by a Moslem lawyer, Nadarbeg K. Mirza, in his small work, *Reincarnation and Islam:*[1]]

Like the herbage I have sprung up many a time on the banks of flowing rivers. For a hundred thousand years I have lived and worked and tried in every sort of body.

[3] Trans. Shea and Troyer, London: 1843, III, 149–150. For later information on *The Dabistan* and its author, see A. V. Williams Jackson's introduction to the abridged edition published in the Universal Classics Library, ed. A. P. C. Griffin, Washington, D.C., M. Walter Dunne, 1901.

[1] Madras, 1927, pp. 57–58.

IBN 'ARABI (1164–1240)
Spanish-Born Sufi Philosopher and Poet

[Ibn 'Arabi is said to have exercised considerable influence upon Dante and the Spanish mystic Raymond Lully. (See p. 228.) Owing to his profound metaphysical views, especially concerning an absolute impersonal Deity, his teachings have only recently become known in the West.]

There is some difference of opinion among the Muslim learned men as regards the method of Resurrection. Some of them say that Resurrection will be by reincarnation and quote passages from the Koran and authenticated sayings of the Prophet in support of their contention.

Al Futūhat Al-Makkiyyah

JALALU'L-DIN RUMI (1207–1273)

[Rumi was the greatest of the Persian Sufi mystical poets. His *Mathnawi* comprises six books of about 25,000 couplets. It is considered next in rank to the Koran, and in fact is called "the Koran in Persian" because the views therein are based on the writings and sayings of the Prophet. Idries Shah writes in *The Sufis*:[1]

The extent of Rumi's influence can hardly be calculated; though it can be glimpsed occasionally in the literature and thought of many schools. Even Doctor Johnson, best known for his unfavorable pronouncements, says of Rumi, "He makes plain to the Pilgrim the secrets of the Way of Unity, and unveils the Mysteries of the Path of Eternal Truth." His work was well enough known within less than a hundred years of his death in 1273 for Chaucer to use references to it in some of his works, together with material from the teachings of Rumi's spiritual precursor, Attar the Chemist (1150–1229/30). From the numerous references to Arabian material which can be found in Chaucer, even a cursory examination shows a Sufi impact of the Rumi school of literature.

The first selection offered from the *Mathnawi* is contained in *Rumi, Poet and Mystic*,[2] by R. A. Nicholson. The remaining selections are to be found in *Reincarnation and Islam*.[3]]

I died as mineral and became a plant,
I died as plant and rose to animal,
I died as animal and I was Man.

[1] Pp. 115–116.
[2] London: Allen & Unwin, 1950, p. 103.
[3] Pp. 55–56.

Why should I fear? When was I less by dying?
Yet once more I shall die as Man, to soar
With angels blest; but even from angelhood
I must pass on. . . .

For a million years I floated in ether, even as the atom floats uncontrolled. If I do not actually remember that state of mine, I often dream of my atomic travels.

I am but one soul but I have a hundred thousand bodies. Yet I am helpless, since Shariat (exoteric religion) holds my lips sealed. Two thousand men have I seen who were I; but none as good as I am now.

There have been thousands of changes in form and each has always been better than the previous. Look always to the form in the present; for, if you think of the forms in the past, you will separate yourself from your true Self. These are all states of the permanent which you have seen by dying. Why then do you turn your face from death? As the second stage has always been better than the first, then die happily and look forward to taking up a new and better form. Remember, and haste not. You must die before you improve. Like the sun, only when you set in the West can you rise again with brilliance in the East.

Mathnawi

HAFIZ (14TH CENTURY)

[In the verses below, taken from *Persian Lyrics*[1] Hafiz figures the soul as the phoenix alighting on Tuba, the Tree of Life, and periodically descending to earth.]

My phoenix long ago secured
His nest in the sky-vault's cope;
In the body's cage immured
He was weary of life's hope.

Round and round this heap of ashes
Now flies the bird amain,
But in that odorous niche of heaven
Nestles the bird again.

Once flies he upward he will perch
On Tuba's golden bough;

[1] London: 1800.

His home is on that fruited arch
  Which cools the blest below. . . .

Either world inhabits he,
  Sees oft below him planets roll;
His body is all of air compact,
  Of Allah's love, his soul.

"The Sufis of Syria"

This group, known popularly as the Druses of Mt. Lebanon, came to prominence in the eleventh century. They exist today mainly in Syria, Lebanon,
and Jordan. Many theories of their origin have been suggested, and their
religion is described as a blending of Mohammedanism, Judaism, and
Christianity, strongly tinged with Gnosticism, Tibetan Lamaism, and the
Magian system of Persia. They are thought to be the descendants of the
persecuted mystics of all nations who found refuge in the mountains of
Syria during the early years of the Christian era. Some of them trace their
order back to Hemsa, the uncle of Mohammed who in 625 went to Tibet in
search of secret wisdom. He is said to have incarnated again in the eleventh
century as H'amsa, the founder of the Order. From that time he is supposed to have reincarnated successively in the body of the chief Hierophant
(or Okhal) in the same way that some of the Buddhas are said to incarnate
in the Tibetan Lamas. Lawrie in his *History of Freemasonry* claims that the
original Knights Templar, founded in 1118, inherited their knowledge from
the Druses. Reincarnation is one of their fundamental teachings.[1]

[1] Laurence Oliphant, *The Land of Gilead, with Excursions in the Lebanon*. London:
1880, pp. 381, 389. Ian Stevenson, *Twenty Cases Suggestive of Reincarnation*. New
York: American Society for Psychical Research, 1966, pp. 243–245.

PART III

Reincarnation
in Theosophy and Masonry

Less than a century has passed since [Indian teachings] became known to the West. Although all sorts of miraculous tales had come to Europe two thousand years before from the fabled land of India, with its wise men . . . yet no real knowledge of Indian philosophy and philosophical practices can be said to have existed until, thanks to the efforts of the Frenchman, Anquetil du Perron, the Upanishads were transmitted to the West. A general and more profound knowledge was first made possible by Max Müller, of Oxford, and the Sacred Books of the East edited by him. To begin with, this knowledge remained the preserve of Sanskrit scholars and philosophers. But it was not so very long before the theosophical movement inaugurated by Mme. Blavatsky possessed itself of the Eastern traditions and promulgated them among the general public.

C. G. JUNG
Psychology and Religion: West and East

◆ ✳ ●

Theosophy

The first widespread movement in the modern Western world to investi-
gate and study reincarnation and related concepts was begun by the Theosophical Society, founded in New York City in 1875 by Mme. H. P. Blavatsky, Colonel H. S. Olcott, William Q. Judge, and others. The movement,
of course, is not limited to a study of Eastern religions. It aims rather for a
synthesis of religion, philosophy, science, and psychology. "The most important" of our objects, said Mme. Blavatsky, "is to revive the work of
Ammonius Saccas"—the founder of the Neoplatonic School of 1,700 years
ago.[1] (See Part Five.) The work of that School, she stated, was "to reconcile all religions, sects and nations under a common system of ethics, based
on eternal verities." The aim of Ammonius was "to induce Gentiles and
Christians, Jews and Idolators, to lay aside their contentions and strifes,
remembering only that they were all in possession of the same truth under
various vestments. . . ."[2] Ammonius and his disciples called their work
the Eclectic Theosophical School, the word "theosophy"—which means
godlike wisdom—being first used by them.

    Present-day Theosophists have an approach to the reincarnation theory
that is quite different from that commonly found in the East, or among the
early Jews and Christians. In the Orient, as previously mentioned, the great
hope has often been to escape as quickly as possible from the wheel of
rebirth and to attain Moksha or Nirvana. Western religions usually viewed

---

[1] H. P. Blavatsky, "What are the Theosophists," *The Theosophist*, October, 1879,
p. 5.
[2] H. P. Blavatsky, *The Key to Theosophy*. Los Angeles: Theosophy Co., 1930, pp. 3, 5.

return to earth life as a penance, or as a means of purging oneself of impurities. The Theosophists, however, regard re-embodiment as the universal law of evolutionary progress, holding that in an infinite universe there must be infinite possibilities for growth and development. Hence one would never outgrow the need for fresh experience and new cycles of incarnations, although a long period of rest, assimilation, and reunion with the Supreme Source may separate one life, as well as one great world-period of activity, from another.

To the old teaching of the periodical reincarnation of great spiritual teachers—taught by the Jews, the early Moslems, the Egyptians, and all the peoples of the East[3]—the theosophists add that these beings form a living fraternity of perfected adepts who continually help mankind to the degree its karma and evolutionary development permit.

A letter to the writer, Sean O'Faolain, written in 1935 by George Russell (Æ), the well-known Irish poet, painter, and editor, tells of the interest in literary and scholarly circles evoked by Mme. Blavatsky's writings (in which reincarnation is a frequent theme):

You dismiss H. P. Blavatsky rather too easily as "hocus pocus." Nobody ever affected the thought of so many able men and women by "hocus pocus." The real source of her influence is to be found in *The Secret Doctrine*, a book on the religions of the world suggesting or disclosing an underlying unity between all great religions. It was a book which Maeterlinck said contained the most grandiose cosmogony in the world, and if you read it merely as a romantic compilation, it is one of the most exciting and stimulating books written for the last hundred years. It is paying a poor compliment to men like Yeats, Maeterlinck, and others, to men like Sir William Crookes, the greatest chemist of modern times, who was a member of her society, to Carter Blake, F.R.S., the anthropologist, and the scholars and scientists in many countries who read H. P. Blavatsky's books, to assume that they were attracted by "hocus pocus."

If you are ever in the National Library, Kildare Street, and have a couple of hours to spare, you might dip into "The Proem" to *The Secret Doctrine*, and you will understand the secret of the influence of that extraordinary woman on her contemporaries. . . . You should not be misled by popular catchwords . . . but try to find out the real secret of H. P. Blavatsky's influence, which still persists strong as ever, as I have found over here [in London] among many intellectuals and well-known writers.[4]

Strangely enough, the Theosophical Movement, though Western in origin, brought about a revival of interest in reincarnation in the Orient as well as the Occident. The influence of the missionaries and of materialistic

---

[3] Jews, pp. 87, 94–96; Islam, pp. 143, 145, 148; Egyptians, pp. 70, 71, 106; Hindus, p. 41; Buddhists, pp. 51, 57, 60–61, 62. See also Index under "Reincarnation of Great Men."

[4] John Eglinton, A *Memoir of Æ*. London: Macmillan, 1937, pp. 164–165.

science had caused many Hindus to lose faith in their religious heritage, and the Indian youths in particular were fast becoming atheists. Take, for example, Gandhi. The book that was to have the greatest effect on his life was The Bhagavad-Gita. This jewel of Eastern philosophy was not read by him until as a young man in his twenties he lived in England. He writes in his *Autobiography*:[5]

> Towards the end of my second year in England I came across two Theosophists, brothers. . . . They talked to me about the *Gita*. . . . They invited me to read the original with them. I felt ashamed, as I had read the divine poem neither in Sanskirt nor in Gujarati. . . . I began reading the *Gita* with them. . . . They also took me on one occasion to the Blavatsky Lodge and introduced me to Madame Blavatsky and Mrs. Besant. . . . I recall having read, at the brothers' instance, Madame Blavatsky's *Key to Theosophy*. This book stimulated in me the desire to read books on Hinduism, and disabused me of the notion fostered by the missionaries that Hinduism was rife with superstition.

HELENA PETROVNA BLAVATSKY (1831–1891)

[From Mme. Blavatsky's first work, *Isis Unveiled:*[1]]

When, years ago, we first travelled over the East, exploring the penetralia of its deserted sanctuaries, two saddening and ever-recurring questions oppressed our thoughts: *Where, WHO, WHAT, is GOD? Who ever saw the IMMORTAL SPIRIT of man, so as to be able to assure himself of man's immortality?*

It was while most anxious to solve these perplexing problems that we came into contact with certain men, endowed with such mysterious powers and such profound knowledge that we may truly designate them as the sages of the Orient. To their instructions we lent a ready ear. They showed us that by combining science with religion, the existence of God and immortality of man's spirit may be demonstrated like a problem of Euclid. For the first time we received the assurance that the Oriental philosophy has room for no other faith than an absolute and immovable faith in the omnipotence of man's own immortal self. We were taught that this omnipotence comes from the kinship of man's spirit with the Universal Soul—God! The latter, they said, can never be demonstrated but by the former. Man-spirit proves God-spirit, as the one drop of water proves a source from which it must have come. Tell one who had never seen water, that there is an ocean of water, and he must accept it on faith or reject it altogether. But

[5] *Gandhi's Autobiography*, Washington, D.C., Public Affairs Press, 1948, pp. 90–91.

[1] New York: 1877.

let one drop fall upon his hand, and he then has the fact from which all the rest may be inferred. After that he could by degrees understand that a boundless and fathomless ocean of water existed. Blind faith would no longer be necessary; he would have supplanted it with KNOWLEDGE. When one sees mortal man displaying tremendous capabilities, controlling the forces of nature and opening up to view the world of spirit, the reflective mind is overwhelmed with the conviction that if one man's spiritual *Ego* can do this much, the capabilities of the FATHER SPIRIT must be relatively as much vaster as the whole ocean surpasses the single drop in volume and potency. . . . Prove the soul of man by its wondrous powers. . . .

The doctrine of *Metempsychosis* has been abundantly ridiculed by men of science and rejected by theologians, yet if it had been properly understood in its application to the indestructibility of matter and the immortality of spirit, it would have been perceived that it is a sublime conception. . . . If the Pythagorean metempsychosis should be thoroughly explained and compared with the modern theory of evolution it would be found to supply every "missing link" in the chain of the latter. . . . There was not a philosopher of any notoriety who did not hold to this doctrine of metempsychosis, as taught by the Brahmans, Buddhists, and later by the Pythagoreans. . . .

The esoteric doctrine teaches, like Buddhism and Brahmanism, and even the *Kabala*, that the one infinite and unknown Essence exists from all eternity, and in regular and harmonious successions is either passive or active. In the poetical phraseology of Manu these conditions are called the "day" and the "night" of Brahma. The latter is either "awake" or "asleep." . . . Upon inaugurating an active period an expansion of this Divine essence, *from within outwardly,* occurs in obedience to eternal and immutable law, and the phenomenal or visible universe is the ultimate result of the long chain of cosmical forces thus progressively set in motion. In like manner, when the passive condition is resumed, a contraction of the Divine essence takes place, and the previous work of creation is gradually and progressively undone. The visible universe becomes disintegrated, its material dispersed; and "darkness," solitary and alone, broods once more over the face of the "deep." To use a metaphor which will convey the idea still more clearly, an outbreathing of the "unknown essence" produces the world; and an inhalation causes it to disappear. *This process has been going on from all eternity, and our present universe is but one of an infinite series which had no beginning and will have no end.*

Isis Unveiled [2]

[2] Los Angeles: Theosophy Co., 1931 (facsimile of original 1877 edition), I, vi, 8–9, 12; II, 264–265.

[From Mme. Blavatsky's chief work, *The Secret Doctrine*, original 1888 edition:]

Nature is no better than "a comely mother, but stone cold" . . . is true only so far as regards *external* physical nature. . . . To the superficial observer, she is no better than an immense slaughterhouse wherein butchers become victims, and victims executioners in their turn. It is quite natural that the pessimistically inclined profane, once convinced of Nature's numerous shortcomings and failures, and especially of her autophagous propensities, should imagine this to be the best evidence that there is no deity *in abscondito* within Nature, nor anything divine in her. Nor is it less natural that the materialist and the physicist should imagine that everything is due to blind force and chance, and to the survival of the *strongest*, even more often than of the *fittest*. But the Occultists, who regard physical nature as a bundle of most varied illusions on the plane of deceptive perceptions; who recognise in every pain and suffering but the necessary pangs of incessant procreation: a series of stages toward an ever-growing perfectibility . . . , the Occultists, we say, view the great Mother otherwise. . . .

The Secret Doctrine teaches the fundamental identity of all Souls with the Universal Over-Soul . . . and the obligatory pilgrimage for every Soul . . . through the Cycle of Incarnation (or "Necessity") in accordance with Cyclic and Karmic Law, during the whole term. . . . The pivotal doctrine of the Esoteric philosophy admits no privileges or special gifts in man, save those won by his own Ego through personal effort and merit throughout a long series of metempsychoses and reincarnations. . . .

Those who believe in *Karma* have to believe in *destiny*, which, from birth to death, every man is weaving thread by thread around himself, as a spider does his cobweb. . . . This LAW, whether Conscious or Unconscious—predestines nothing and no one. . . . Karma creates nothing, nor does it design. It is man who plans and creates causes, and Karmic law adjusts the effects; which adjustment is not an act but universal harmony, tending ever to resume its original position, like a bough, which, bent down too forcibly, rebounds with corresponding vigor. If it happens to dislocate the arm that tried to bend it out of its natural position, shall we say that it is the bough which broke our arm, or that our own folly has brought us to grief?

Karma has never sought to destroy intellectual and individual liberty. . . . It has not involved its decrees in darkness purposely to perplex man, nor shall it punish him who dares to scrutinize its mysteries. On the contrary, he who unveils through study and meditation its intricate paths, and throws light on those dark ways, in the windings of which so many men perish owing to their ignorance of the labyrinth of life, is working for the good of his fellow-men. . . .

Believers in Karma cannot be regarded as Atheists or materialists—still less as fatalists. . . . Karma is a highly philosophical truth, a most divine noble expression of the primitive intuition of man concerning Deity. It is a doctrine which explains the origin of Evil, and ennobles our conceptions of what divine immutable Justice ought to be, instead of degrading the unknown and unknowable Deity by making it the whimsical, cruel tyrant, which we call Providence. . . .

Nor would the ways of Karma be inscrutable were men to work in union and harmony, instead of disunion and strife. . . . Were no man to hurt his brother, Karma-Nemesis would have neither cause to work for, nor weapons to act through. It is the constant presence in our midst of every element of strife and opposition, and the division of races, nations, tribes, societies and individuals into Cains and Abels, wolves and lambs, that is the chief cause of the "ways of Providence." We cut these numerous windings in our destinies daily with our own hands, while we imagine that we are pursuing a track on the royal high road of respectability and duty, and then complain of those ways being so intricate and dark. We stand bewildered before the mystery of our own making, and the riddles of life that we will not solve, and then accuse the great Sphinx of devouring us. But verily there is not an accident in our lives, not a misshapen day, or a misfortune, that could not be traced back to our own doings in this or in another life. . . .

The suppression of one single bad cause will suppress not one, but a variety of bad effects. And if a Brotherhood or even a number of Brotherhoods may not be able to prevent nations from occasionally cutting each other's throats—still unity in thought and action, and philosophical research into the mysteries of being, will always prevent some . . . from creating additional causes in a world already so full of woe and evil. Knowledge of Karma gives the conviction that if—"virtue in distress, and vice in triumph make atheists of mankind," (Dryden), it is only because that mankind has ever shut its eyes to the great truth that man is himself his own saviour as his own destroyer. . . .

Intimately, or rather indissolubly, connected with Karma, then, is the law of rebirth, or of the reincarnation of the same spiritual individuality in a long, almost interminable, series of personalities. The latter are like the various costumes and characters played by the same actor, with each of which that actor identifies himself and is identified by the public, for the space of a few hours. The *inner*, or real man, who personates those characters, knows the whole time that he is Hamlet for the brief space of a few acts, which represent, however, on the plane of human illusion the whole life of Hamlet. And he knows that he was, the night before, King Lear, the transformation in his turn of the Othello of a still earlier preceding night; but the outer, visible character is supposed to be ignorant of the fact.

In actual life that ignorance is, unfortunately, but too real. Nevertheless, the *permanent* individuality is fully aware of the fact, though, through the atrophy of the "spiritual" eye[3] in the physical body, that knowledge is unable to impress itself on the consciousness of the false personality. . . . "That which is part of our souls is eternal," says Thackeray . . . and though "the book and volume" of the *physical* brain may forget events within the scope of one terrestrial life, the bulk of collective recollections can never desert the divine soul within us. Its whispers may be too soft, the sound of its words too far off the plane perceived by our physical senses; yet the shadow of events *that were,* just as much as the shadow of the events *that are to come,* is within its perceptive powers, and is ever present before its mind's eye. . . .

"Pilgrim" is the appellation given to our *Monad* . . . during its cycle of incarnations. It is the only immortal and eternal principle in us, being an indivisible part of the integral whole—the Universal Spirit, from which it emanates, and into which it is absorbed at the end of the cycle. . . . Is this annihilation, as some think? . . . To see in Nirvana annihilation amounts to saying of a man plunged in a sound *dreamless* sleep . . . that he, too, is annihilated. . . . Re-absorption is by no means such a "dreamless sleep," but, on the contrary, *absolute* existence, an unconditioned unity, or a state, to describe which human language is absolutely and hopelessly inadequate. . . . Nor is the individuality . . . lost, because re-absorbed. For, however limitless—from a human standpoint—the paranirvanic state, it has yet a limit in Eternity. Once reached, the same monad will re-emerge therefrom, as a still higher being, on a far higher plane, to recommence its cycle of perfected activity. The human mind cannot in its present stage of development . . . reach this plane of thought. It totters here, on the brink of incomprehensible Absoluteness and Eternity. . . .

Sooner or later, all that now *seemingly* exists, will be in reality and actually in the state of [Paranirvana]. But there is a great difference between *conscious* and *unconscious* "being." The condition of [Paranirvana] without Paramârtha, the Self-analysing consciousness . . . is no bliss, but simply extinction (for Seven Eternities). Thus, an iron ball placed under the scorching rays of the sun will get heated through, but will not feel or

[3] The pineal gland. (Eds.)

appreciate the warmth, while a man will. It is only "with a mind clear and undarkened by personality, and an assimilation of the merit of manifold existences devoted to being in its collectivity (the whole living and sentient Universe)," that one gets rid of personal existence, merging into, becoming one with, the Absolute, and continuing in full possession of Paramârtha (Self-consciousness). . . .

There can be no possible conflict between the teachings of occult and so-called exact Science, where the conclusions of the latter are grounded on a substratum of unassailable fact. It is only when its more ardent exponents, over-stepping the limits of observed phenomena in order to penetrate into the arcana of Being, attempt to wrench the formation of Kosmos and its *living* Forces from Spirit, and attribute all to blind matter, that the Occultists claim the right to dispute and call in question their theories. Science cannot, owing to the very nature of things, unveil the mystery of the universe around us. Science can, it is true, collect, classify, and generalize upon phenomena; but the occultist, arguing from admitted metaphysical data, declares that the daring explorer, who would probe the inmost secrets of Nature, must transcend the narrow limitations of sense, and transfer his consciousness into the region of noumena and the sphere of primal causes. To effect this, he must develop faculties which are absolutely dormant—save in a few rare and exceptional cases—in the constitution of our Race. . . .

The reincarnationists and believers in Karma alone dimly perceive that the whole secret of Life is in the unbroken series of its manifestations. . . . This relates to the greatest problem of philosophy.

The Secret Doctrine[4]

HENRY STEEL OLCOTT (1832–1907)

[While residing in the Orient as International President of The Theosophical Society, Colonel Olcott rendered considerable assistance to the people of Ceylon. An article on this American Civil War colonel by Martin G. Berck of the United Nations[1] states: "Throughout the Island of Ceylon, from the ancient capital of Anuradhapura to the venerated peak of Shri Pada, polished brass lamps were lit yesterday as Buddhists paused to do religious honor to an American. . . . With such homage, Ceylonese Budd-

---

[4] The selections may be found in the facsimile reprint of the original 1888 edition published by Theosophy Co., Los Angeles, as distinguished from revised editions published after Mme. Blavatsky's death: I, 16–17, 48 fn, 53–54, 238, 266, 477–478, 639, 643–644; II, 304–306, 424, 475.

[1] *New York Herald Tribune*, February 18, 1962.

hists marked the death on Feb. 17, 1907, of Col. Henry Steel Olcott, whom they regard as a key and sainted figure in the renaissance of their religion and their national culture." For use in their Buddhist schools, and effectively to unite southern and northern Buddhism, Olcott prepared *A Buddhist's Catechism*, which was later widely circulated in the West and published in "The Wisdom of the East" series.[2] The book bears the imprimatur of the Ceylonese High Priest H. Sumangala, Principal of Widyodaya College.]

On this point [of reincarnation] the Western world is for the most part as far from understanding the Oriental conception as it is in mistaking Nirvana for "annihilation." . . . Much of the Western misconception is due to ignorance of the difference between [a man's] individuality and his personality at any given period. These two are only temporarily coincident and conjoined. . . . In each birth the personality differs from that of a previous or next succeeding birth. . . . But though personalities ever shift, the one line of life along which they are strung, like beads, runs unbroken; it is ever that *particular line*, never any other. It is therefore individual, an individual vital undulation, which began in Nirvana . . . and leads through many cyclic changes back to Nirvana.

A Buddhist's Catechism

WILLIAM Q. JUDGE (1851–1896)

[Mr. Judge, an Irish-American lawyer, was President of the Theosophical Society in America.]

How man has come to be the complex being that he is and why, are questions that neither Science nor Religion makes conclusive answer to. This immortal thinker having such vast powers and possibilities, all his because of his intimate connection with every secret part of Nature from which he has been built up, stands at the top of an immense and silent evolution. He asks why Nature exists, what the drama of life has for its aim, how that aim may be attained. But Science and Religion both fail to give a reasonable reply. Science does not pretend to be able to give the solution, saying that the examination of things as they are is enough of a task; religion offers an explanation both illogical and unmeaning. . . . The educated and enquiring mind knows that dogmatic religion can only give an answer invented by man while it pretends to be from God.

[2] London: John Murray.

What then is the universe for, and for what final purpose is man the immortal thinker here in evolution? It is all for the experience and emancipation of the soul, for the purpose of raising the entire mass of manifested matter up to the stature, nature, and dignity of conscious god-hood. The great aim is to reach [complete] self-consciousness; not through a race or a tribe or some favored nation, but by and through the perfecting, after transformation, of the whole mass of matter as well as what we now call soul. Nothing is or is to be left out. The aim for present man is his initiation into complete knowledge, and for the other kingdoms below him that they may be raised up gradually from stage to stage to be in time initiated also. This is evolution carried to its highest power; it is a magnificent prospect; it makes of man a god, and gives to every part of nature the possibility of being one day the same. . . .

Viewing life and its probable object, with all the varied experience possible for man, one must be forced to the conclusion that a single life is not enough for carrying out all that is intended by Nature to say nothing of what man himself desires to do. The scale of variety in experience is enormous. There is a vast range of powers latent in man which we see may be developed if opportunity be given. Knowledge infinite in scope and diversity lies before us, and especially in these days when special investigation is the rule. We perceive that we have high aspirations with no time to reach up to their measure, while the great troop of passions and desires, selfish motives and ambitions, war with us and among themselves, pursuing us even to the door of death. All these have to be tried, conquered, used, subdued. One life is not enough for all this. To say that we have but one life here with such possibilities put before us and impossible of development is to make the universe and life a huge and cruel joke. . . .

The persistence of savagery, the rise and decay of nations and civilizations, the total extinction of nations, all demand an explanation found nowhere but in reincarnation. . . . Great civilizations like those of Egypt and Babylon have gone because the souls who made them have long ago reincarnated in the great nations of Europe and the present American continents. As nations and races they have been totally reincarnated and born again for greater and higher purposes than ever. . . . Savagery remains because there are still Egos whose experience is so limited that they are still savage; they will come up into higher races when ready. Races die out because the Egos have had enough of the experience that sort of race gives. So we find the red Indian, the Hottentot, the Easter Islanders, and others as examples of races deserted by high Egos, and, as they are dying away, other souls who have had no higher life in the past enter into the bodies of the race to go on using them for the purpose of gaining such experience as the race body will give. . . . These lower Egos are not able to keep up to the limit of the capacity of the congeries of energies left by the other Egos, and so while the new set gains as much experience as is possible the race in time dies out after passing through its decay. . . .

Reincarnation being the great law of life and progress, it is interwoven with that of the cycles and karma. These three work together, and in practice it is almost impossible to disentangle reincarnation from cyclic law. Individuals and nations in definite streams return in regularly recurring periods to the earth, and thus bring back to the globe the arts, the civilization, the very persons who once were on it at work. And as the units in nation and race are connected together . . . , large bodies of such units moving slowly but surely all together reunite at different times and emerge again and again together into new race and new civilization as the cycles roll their appointed rounds. Therefore the souls who made the most ancient civilizations will come back and bring the old civilization with them in idea and essence, which being added to what others have done for the development of the human race in its character and knowledge will produce a new and higher state of civilization. . . .

And along this road are the points when the small and large cycles of Avatars bring out for man's benefit the great characters who mould the race from time to time. . . . In every age and complete national history these men of power and compassion are given different designations. They have been called Initiates, Adepts, Magi, Hierophants, Kings of the East, Wise Men, Brothers, Mahatmas. . . . The Elder Brothers of Humanity are men who were perfected in former periods of evolution. These periods of manifestation . . . when out of the Great Unknown there come forth the visible universes, are eternal in their coming and going, alternating with equal periods of silence and rest again in the Unknown. The object of these mighty waves is the production of perfect man, the evolution of soul, and they always witness the increase of the number of Elder Brothers. . . . The Theosophist agrees with Thomas Huxley[1] in the assertion that there must be beings in the universe whose intelligence is as much beyond ours as ours exceeds that of the black beetle, and who take an active part in the government of the natural order of things. . . .

Although reincarnation is the law of nature, the complete trinity [in man] of *Spirit-Soul-Mind*[2] does not yet fully incarnate in this race. They

---

[1] *Essays on Some Controverted Questions.* London, 1891. See quotation in Part Six of this anthology, under "Thomas Huxley."
[2] In the original text the author used the Sanskrit equivalents: *Atma-Buddhi-Manas.*

use and occupy the body by means of the entrance of Mind, the lowest of the three, and the other two shine upon it from "above." . . . This was symbolized in the old Jewish teaching about the Heavenly Man who stands with his head in heaven and his feet in hell. That is, the head, Spirit and Soul, are yet in heaven,[3] and the feet, Mind, walk in hell, which is the body and physical life. For that reason man is not yet fully conscious, and reincarnations are needed to at last complete the incarnation of the whole trinity in the body. When that has been accomplished the race will have become as gods. . . . It was so grand a thing in the case of any single person, such as Jesus or Buddha, as to be looked upon as a divine incarnation. . . .

It is because the trinity is not yet incarnate in the race that life has so many mysteries, some of which are showing themselves from day to day in all the various experiments made on and in man. The physician knows not what life is nor why the body moves as it does, because the spiritual portion is yet enshrouded in the clouds of heaven; the scientist is wandering in the dark, confounded and confused by all that hypnotism and other strange things bring before him, because the conscious man is out of sight . . . thus compelling the learned to speak of the "subconscious mind," the "latent personality," and the like; and the priest can give us no light at all because he denies man's god-like nature [and] reduces all to the level of original sin. . . . But this old truth solves the riddle and paints God and Nature in harmonious colors. . . .

As Mind is being evolved more and more as we proceed in our course along the line of the race development, there can be perceived underneath in all countries the beginning of the transition from the animal possessed of the germ of real mind to the man of mind complete. . . . The race mind is changing by enlargement. The old days of dogmatism are gone and the "age of inquiry" has come. The inquiries will grow louder year by year and the answers be required to satisfy the mind as it grows more and more, until at last, all dogmatism being ended, the race will be ready to face all problems, each man for himself, all working for the good of the whole, and that the end will be the perfecting of those who struggle to overcome the brute.

The Ocean of Theosophy[4]

ANNIE BESANT (1847–1933)

The Ancient Wisdom teaches, indeed, that the soul progresses through many worlds, but it also teaches that he is born in each of these worlds over

[3] Heaven is used as a state of consciousness, not a place. (Eds.)
[4] Original edition, 1893. Reprint, Los Angeles: Theosophy Co., 1962, pp. 2, 6, 50–51, 60–61, 66–67, 82–85, 119.

and over again, until he has completed the evolution possible in that world. . . . Other worlds . . . are not open to us until we have learned and mastered the lessons our own world has to teach.

The Ancient Wisdom[1]

[A question often asked is:] If the number of Egos [belonging to a given world] be a fixed number, how do you account for the increase of population? . . . Those who raise this objection generally take it for granted that the proportion of Egos out of incarnation to those in incarnation is about half and half, whereas the number out of incarnation is enormously greater than that of the Egos incarnated. The globe is as a small hall in a large town, drawing the audiences that enter it from the total population. It may be at one time half empty, at another crowded, without any change in the total population of the town. So our little globe may be thinly or thickly populated, and the vast number of Egos [out of incarnation] on which it draws to replenish its stock of inhabitants remains practically inexhaustible. . . . A very slight shortening of the period out of incarnation for some must vastly increase the incarnated population.

Reincarnation[2]

[Theosophists suggest that while some individuals, owing to causes self-engendered, may return immediately, or in say fifty or a hundred years, the majority may not incarnate for many centuries. Ancient scriptures like The Bhagavad-Gita (Chap. 6) speak of an "immensity of years" between lives. Plato's *Phædo* (107) states that "many revolutions of ages" ensue between incarnations, and his *Republic* X (615) indicates a thousand-year cycle of rebirth. Virgil does likewise in the *Aeneid* (vi, 758). However, sensualists were believed to return more quickly (*Phædo*, 81), as also—at the other pole—the great altruists, propelled by their ardent desire to benefit life.

Population as everything else in the universe is apparently subject to cycles of rise and fall. Tertullian, it will be recalled, spoke of the alarming increase of the birth rate in Roman times, and consequently argued against reincarnation on those grounds.

Although the world population of late has increased enormously, there are of course no means of comparison with any period of ancient history. Vast civilizations have disappeared in Central Asia, the Middle East, Africa, and ancient America, concerning which census figures are not even remotely available. The *Britannica*[3] states in its article on Population:

[1] London: Theosophical Pub. Society, 1897, p. 231.
[2] Adyar, Madras: Theosophical Pub. House, 1948, pp. 83-85.
[3] 1959 edition.

"Few reliable population figures exist [for individual countries] for any period before the 18th century." As to world population statistics they are nonexistent.]

CHARLES JOHNSTON (1867-1931)

[Johnston was founder of the Dublin Theosophical Society of which Yeats, George Russell and a number of other Irish writers were members. (See Index under "Ireland's Literary Renaissance.") He is particularly noted for his translations from The Upanishads and other Hindu scriptures. A few extracts bearing on rebirth have been chosen from Johnston's account of his first meeting with Mme. Blavatsky in London in 1887. Among questions he asked, was this one: How do theosophical teachings benefit humanity?]

H.P.B. "How does it benefit you to know the laws of life? Does it not help you to escape sickness and death? Well, there is a soul-sickness, and a soul-death. Only the true teaching of Life can cure them. The dogmatic churches, with their hell and damnation, their metal heaven and their fire and brimstone, have made it almost impossible for thinking people to believe in the immortality of the soul. And if they do not believe in a life after death, then they have no life after death. That is the law."

C.J. "How can what people believe possibly affect them? Either it is or it isn't, whatever they may believe."

H.P.B. "Their belief affects them in this way. Their life after death is made by their aspirations and spiritual development unfolding in the spiritual world. According to the growth of each, so is his life after death. It is the complement of his life here. All unsatisfied spiritual longings, all desires for higher life, all aspirations and dreams of noble things, come to flower in the spiritual life, and the soul has its day, for life on earth is its night. But if you have no aspirations, no higher longings, no beliefs in any life after death, then there is nothing for your spiritual life to be made up of; your soul is a blank. . . . You reincarnate immediately, almost without an interval, and without regaining consciousness in the other world. . . ."

C.J. "What else do you teach, as Theosophists?"

H.P.B. "We teach something very old, and yet which needs to be taught. We teach universal brotherhood."

C.J. "Don't let us get vague and general. Tell me exactly what you mean by that."

H.P.B. "Let me take a concrete case. . . . Take the English. . . . How badly they treat my poor Hindus!"

C.J.   "I have always understood that they had done a good deal for India in a material way."

H.P.B.   "What is the use of material benefits, if you are despised and trampled down morally all the time? If your ideals of national honor and glory are crushed in the mud, and you are made to feel all the time that you are an inferior race—a lower order of mortals—pigs, the English call them, and sincerely believe it. Well, just the reverse of that would be universal brotherhood. . . . No amount of material benefit can compensate for hurting their souls and crushing out their ideals. Besides there is another side of all that, which we as Theosophists always point out. There are really no 'inferior races,' for all are one in our common humanity; and as we have all had incarnations in each of these races, we ought to be more brotherly to them. . . ."

[At the conclusion of the account, Johnston gives these impressions of Mme. Blavatsky:]

There was something in her personality, her bearing, the light and power of her eyes, which spoke of a wider and deeper life. . . . That was the greatest thing about her, and it was always there; this sense of a bigger world, of deeper powers, of unseen might. . . . When the last word is said, she was greater than any of her works, more full of living power than even her marvellous writings. . . . Most perfect work of all, her will carried with it a sense and conviction of immortality. Her mere presence testified to the vigour of the soul.

"On H. P. Blavatsky" [1]

[1] H. P. Blavatsky, *Collected Writings*, ed. Boris de Zirkoff, Adyar, Madras, India: Theosophical Pub. House, 1960, VIII, 402, 404–406, 409.

◆ * ●

Masonry

In Part Five, consideration will be given to probable connections of Masonry with reincarnationist groups of the Middle Ages and Renaissance periods. A possible connection with the Sufis has already been indicated under "Islam."

The deeper students of Masonry have frequently shown a serious interest in rebirth, and in the nineteenth century many leading Masons were attracted to the Theosophical Movement. Mme. Blavatsky was accorded a high Masonic degree because of her book *Isis Unveiled*.[1] In years past, *The New Age*, the official Masonic organ of the Supreme Council 33d degree (Southern Jurisdiction, U.S.A.), has contained articles treating frankly and sympathetically of both reincarnation and karma. In the September, 1952 issue, under the title "Freemasonry and Reincarnation," C. I. Reynolds, a 32d degree Mason, considers why the founders of Masonry refused to doctrinalize the teaching:

[The criticism is made] that comparative research shows that masonry is the only esoteric system whose followers have endeavored to carry on their work without some clear-cut doctrine of reincarnation. They say that in every other esoteric organization in history it is taught that man lives on earth not once but many times, and that each being, in due course and according to his need, will eventually enter upon and be instructed in the secret teachings concerning the soul. This may be true, but the criticism completely overlooks in fact that the reason is that each and every member of the Craft, wherever he may be, is at liberty to decide for himself what he shall believe.

[1] H. P. Blavatsky, *Collected Writings*, ed. Boris de Zirkoff. Madras: 1966, I, pp. 307–312. Facsimile of diploma opposite p. 305.

In reviewing *Reincarnation, an East-West Anthology* in *The New Age*,[2] Aemil Pouler commented that many of the selections "bring vividly to mind the principles and precepts that are the basis of much that was written by Albert Pike and that is set forth in the ritual of the Scottish Rite Degrees."

Some fascinating passages on Masonry, with direct allusions to pre-existence and rebirth, are to be found in the novel *Bedford Village* by Hervey Allen, the author of *Anthony Adverse*, and are quoted in Part Five. Mr. Allen shows the important function of Masonry in America during frontier times. The formation of the United States and its early history was intimately associated with Freemasonry. George Washington, an active Mason, bore the title Grand Master of America. The Great Seal of the United States, displayed on the dollar bill, is largely Masonic in character. (See such works as *George Washington and His Masonic Compeers*,[3] by Sidney Hayden.)

William L. Wilmshurst, Past Master, Past Provincial Grand Registrar (West Yorks, England), writes in his illuminating work *The Masonic Initiation*:[4]

The observant Masonic student is made aware by the formula used at Lodge-closing, that by some great Warden of life and death each soul is called into this objective world to labour upon itself, and is in due course summoned from it to rest from its labours and enter into subjective celestial refreshment, until once again it is recalled to labour. For each the "day," the opportunity for work at self-perfecting, is duly given; for each the "night" cometh when no man can work at that task. . . .

The world-old secret teaching upon this subject, common to the whole of the East, to Egypt, the Pythagoreans and Platonists, and every College of the Mysteries, is to be found summed up as clearly and tersely as one could wish in the *Phædo* of Plato, to which the Masonic seeker is referred as one of the most instructive of treatises upon the deeper side of the science.

It testifies to the great rhythm of life and death above spoken of, and demonstrates how the soul in the course of its career weaves and wears out many bodies, and is continually migrating between objective and subjective conditions, passing from labour to refreshment and back again many times in its great task of self-fulfillment . . . until such time as its work is completed and it is "made a pillar in the House of God and no more goes out" [5] as a journey-man builder into this sublunary workshop.

[2] February, 1962.
[3] New York: 1866.
[4] London: John Watkins, 1927, pp. 123-124.
[5] Revelation 3:12.

PART IV

Reincarnation
Among Peoples of the World

Transmigration, dating back to a remote antiquity, and being spread all over the world, seems to be anthropologically innate, and to be the first form in which the idea of immortality occurred to man.

M'Clintock and Strong's Cyclopædia of Biblical,
Theological and Ecclesiastical Literature

The Aryan races, Italian, Celtic, and Scythic or Hyperborean tribes are mentioned as having entertained a faith in Metempsychosis, nay, traces of it have lately been discovered even among the uncivilised inhabitants of America, Africa, and Eastern Asia. And why not? In India certainly it developed spontaneously; and if this was so in India, why not in other countries?

F. MAX MÜLLER
The Six Systems of Indian Philosophy (Chap. 3)

Introduction

By consulting the following sources and similar works it will be found that
the peoples listed in this section hold (or if ancient, held) to some form of
reincarnation belief:

Sir Edward Tylor, *Primitive Culture*, Chapter XII.
Hastings' *Encyclopædia of Religion and Ethics*, art. "Transmigration," XII,
    pp. 425–29.
Encyclopædia Britannica, 1959 ed., article "Metempsychosis."
Sir J. G. Frazer, *The Golden Bough*, unabridged editions.
Sir J. G. Frazer, *The Belief in Immortality and the Worship of the Dead*,
    Vol. I, Australia, New Guinea, and Melanesian (Gifford Lectures,
    1911–13); Vol. II, Polynesians.

The above volumes by Sir James Frazer are recommended reading in
the *Britannica* article on metempsychosis, but modern anthropologists and
religious scholars are re-evaluating Frazer's entire approach to anthropology.
As was seen in Part One, "Reincarnation in Myth and Symbol," a remarkable revolution is taking place in the study of ancient religions, myths, and
symbolisms. Gone forever is the Victorian's simple faith in his own racial,
moral, and cultural superiority, and in the so-called comparative method
which was the application of these standards outside of their legitimate
context. Applying such criteria, "Sir James Frazer, in some 20,000 pages,
had discovered how all the thoughts, imaginings and yearnings of archaic
man, all his myths and rites, all his gods and religious experiences, are only a

monstrous mass of beastliness, cruelty and superstititon, happily abolished by scientific human progress." Thus speaks one of the most distinguished among contemporary scholars, Professor Mircea Eliade.[1] Lord Raglan, a past president of the Royal Anthropological Institute, adds that "the 'primitive man' of Frazer," was "always asking himself questions and giving himself the wrong answers." The word "primitive," this authority remarks, "has led to more muddled thinking than all the other words in the dictionary put together." It should be banished from our vocabulary.[2]

Whatever his interpretations and conclusions may have been, Frazer was unquestionably impressed by the prevalence of reincarnation belief. He wrote: "However it has been arrived at, this doctrine of the transmigration or reincarnation of the soul is found among many tribes of savages; and from what we know on the subject we seem to be justified in conjecturing that at certain stages of mental and social evolution the belief in metempsychosis has been far commoner and has exercised a far deeper influence on the life and institutions of primitive man than the actual evidence before us at present allows us positively to affirm." [3]

[1]Quoted in the broadcast lecture "The Author of 'The Golden Bough,'" delivered over BBC by the Reverend Victor White, and published in *The Listener*, Jan. 21, 1954, p. 137.
[2] Lord Raglan, *The Temple and the House*. London and New York: 1964, pp. 3-4.
[3] *The Belief in Immortality and the Worship of the Dead*, I, 29.

◆ * ●

Africans

East Africa:
Suks (Kenya); Wanikas; Akikiyus; Bari of the White Nile.
West Africa:
Mandingo; Edo; Ibo; Ewes; Yorubas; Kagoro; Akan; Old Calabar tribes.
South Africa:
Siena; Twi; Zulus; Bantus; Barotse; Ba-ila; Maravi tribes of Madagascar.

E. G. Parrinder of University College, Ibadan, Nigeria—the British author of *African Traditional Religion, West African Psychology,* the Penguin paperback, *Witchcraft,* and similar volumes—wrote in the *Hibbert Journal* [1] under the title "Varieties of Belief in Reincarnation":

In tropical Africa, belief in rebirth is deeply enrooted. The studies made by anthropologists and other serious writers in many different parts of Africa, especially in the last forty years, have revealed deep-seated beliefs in reincarnation held by many different African peoples. . . .
Reincarnation, to most Africans, is a good thing. It is a return to this sunlit world for a further period of invigorating life. There is little idea of an end to the number of incarnations, or a search for that as desirable. . . . On the contrary, it is bad not to be reborn, and childlessness is a great curse because it blocks the channel of rebirth. Hence the great attention devoted to fertility and the continuing popularity of polygamy, for the ancestor is only reincarnated in his own family. . . . It is a common practice for the diviner to be called in at the birth of a child to declare which ancestor is reincarnated, and family resemblances are explained as due to use of the same soul-stuff. . . .

[1] April, 1957.

Various phrases are used to describe reincarnation. One West African people calls it "the shooting forth of a branch," and another "a recurring cycle." In the latter case the same word is used to describe a vine which twines round a post, reappearing continually higher up. . . .

A further point worth noting is that African belief does not appear to suggest that evildoers will be born again in animal form. . . . The African, as we have pointed out, has a long history behind him. We can but affirm that today he does not believe in degradation to the animal level as a punishment for the sins of mortal life. This is not to say that Africans do not believe in metempsychosis (or metamorphosis) into animal form at all. They do; but not as a punishment for sin. It is indeed very widely held that certain people, notably sorcerers, have the special power of changing at will into animal form.

Tylor states in *Primitive Culture* (Chapter 12) that the Yorubas "greeting a new-born infant with the salutation, 'Thou art come!' look for signs to show what ancestral soul has returned among them." An interesting article on West African beliefs by K. Brakatu Ateko, a native of Ghana, outlines four main teachings:

I. God A maxim says *Obi Nkyere abofra Nyame*, literally, No one teaches a child God. Over and above the tutelary, tribal and family gods and goddesses is the Supreme Being to whom no sacrifices are made. . . . It is crystal clear that the African conception of the High God is not of recent growth. . . .

II. *Karma* There are proverbs which illustrate this law: (1) When Mr. Lizard eats pepper, it is he who perspires and not Mrs. Lizard. (2) When Akosua commits evil, Akua is not punished. . . .

III. *Reincarnation* The Yoruba and the Edo-speaking tribes, among whom I sojourned as a teacher half a century ago, have a strong belief in reincarnation. At that period the white man's influence had not affected the beliefs and the ways of life of the hinterlands of Nigeria. The Yorubas, for instance, name a boy Babatunde, meaning "Father has returned," and the girl, Yetunde (Iyantude) signifying "Mother has returned." In Ghana, the name Ababio "He has come again," carries the same meaning.

IV. *Death* Our traditional philosophy of death was grander than that acquired in the wake of Christianity. Death was not looked upon as an enemy to be feared and propitiated. If one died, he was believed to have been born on the other side of the veil and vice versa in the case of birth in our world.[2]

Writing of the Ba-ila of Rhodesia, Edwin Smith remarks in *Knowing the African*:[3] "My old friend Mungalo now sitting smoking his pipe with me, or sitting yonder under the eaves of his hut and carving a wooden spoon, is the Mungalo who lived here a hundred years ago and, furthermore,

[2] *The Canadian Theosophist*, Jan.-Feb., 1962.
[3] London: Lutterworth, 1947, p. 103.

Mungalo is his *musedi*, his guardian spirit, shall we say, always accompanying him, guarding him, warning him of danger."

Some additional works describing the reincarnation views of various African peoples are:

M. J. Field, *Religion and Medicine of the Ga People*. Oxford University Press: 1937, pp. 94, 174–175, 197, 202.

Eva L. R. Meyerowitz, *The Sacred State of the Akan*. London: Faber, 1951, pp. 86–88.

R. S. Rattray, *Religion and Art in Ashanti*. Oxford University Press, 1927, pp. 317–318.

R. E. Bradbury, *The Benin Kingdom*. London: International African Institute, 1957, pp. 40, 52, 57, 152, 160.

Edward G. Parrinder, *African Traditional Religion*. London: SPCK, 1962, pp. 138–140.

J. Olumide Lucas, *The Religion of the Yorubas*. Lagos, C.M.S. Bookshop, 1948, pp. 245, 247, 254.

Australians

Aruntas; Kadhirs; Warramunga; Binbinga; Anula; Urabunna; Tasmains.

Baldwin Spencer and F. J. Gillen state in *Northern Tribes of Central Australia:*[1] "In every tribe without exception there exists a firm belief in the reincarnation of ancestors. Emphasis must be laid on the fact that this belief is not confined to tribes such as the Arunta, Warramunga, Binbinga, Anula, and others, amongst whom descent is counted on the male line, but is found just as strongly developed in the Urabunna tribe, in which descent, both of class and totem, is strictly maternal."

Frazer commends the researches of Spencer and Gillen, and remarks: "We naturally ask . . . whether the belief in reincarnation of the dead, which prevails universally among the Central tribes, reappears among the tribes in other parts of the continent. It certainly does so, and although the evidence on this subject is very imperfect it suffices to raise a presumption that a similar belief in the rebirth or reincarnation of the dead was formerly universal among the Australian aborigines." [2] This seems particularly interesting, because scientists have suggested that the Australian native—coexisting as he does with an archaic fauna and flora to be found practically nowhere else on the globe—probably dates back to an enormous antiquity. Commenting upon the religion and mythology of the tribes, Gerland writes: "The statement that the Australian civilization indicates a [previous] higher grade, is nowhere more clearly proved than here, where every-

[1] London: Macmillan, 1904, p. 145.
[2] *The Belief in Immortality and the Worship of the Dead,* I, 127.

thing resounds like the expiring voices of a previous and richer age." [3]

Later research supports the presumption raised by Frazer. See *Ancient Religions* edited by Vergilius Ferm.[4]

[3] Cited in Schmidt's *Doctrine of Descent and Darwinism*, pp. 300–301.
[4] New York: Philosophical Library, 1950, pp. 283–284.

◆ * ●

Oceanians and Malaysians

Tahitians; Okinawans; Papuans of New Guinea; Melanesians; Marquesans; Indonesians; Solomon Islanders; Sandwich Islanders; Fijians; Dayaks; Kayans; and Bakongs of Borneo; Balinese; Poso-Alfures of Celebes; tribes of New Caledonia; New Zealand Maoris.

An American soldier, serving in Okinawa during World War II, interviewed the former chief librarian of the Okinawan Prefecture, Shimabuku Zenpatsu. As to the religious views of his people, the librarian stated:

According to the Okinawan God-idea, Deity is without shape and sexless. The majority of Okinawans believe in Reincarnation, *i.e.*, that the human being has a spirit which leaves his body at death and returns to earth in a new-born babe. This spirit can not occupy an animal body. The original Okinawan belief is this: After a man's death, the spirit stays in his home for 49 days; on the 49th day, when the memorial services are complete, the spirit enters *Gusho*—"after this present world." The period in the after-death state varies, but the Okinawans believe that the spirit will return within seven generations, producing an individual who strongly resembles its former embodiment. Not all spirits reincarnate. Some remain in *Gusho* indefinitely, and will greet new arrivals in that state. It should be understood that the Okinawan conception of *Gusho* is a spiritual state, where only the spirit of man exists. . . . Not mind, but *spirit*, reincarnates . . . mind being received by the individual through ancestral descent.[1]

[1] *Theosophy.* Los Angeles, Calif., Sept., 1946, pp. 437–438.

Time[2] reports that a United States psychiatrist has discovered that the psychic health of the Okinawans is superior to most other people. Of five hundred natives subjected to terrible bombardment—"a nerve-shattering ordeal that drove many a Jap to suicide and many a G.I. into the mental ward"—only one cracked up. The early training of the Okinawan child, the Navy psychiatrist said, is such that by the time he is five, "he has such a sense of security that his mental foundation is sturdy enough to survive catastrophe."

This of course raises the question of whether a person's conviction in reincarnation can be responsible for inner stability. The anthropologist, Margaret Mead, in her book *Male and Female*,[3] indicates how her own mind works in doing research along these lines:

If reincarnation seems relevant, I may think over the cultures known to have a belief in reincarnation, and then may add, "Of course it will be interesting to see what is the relationship between who you are when you are born and who you will be when you die." This may lead to comparing Esquimo and Balinese [who both accept reincarnation]; among both peoples infants are treated as having prophetic powers at birth, and in both of them children learn complex skills early. I may add a question here, "Is the relationship between learning and a theory of birth and immortality perhaps a key point?" and then compare the Balinese position—in which the individual is reincarnated over and over in the same family, so that the life-cycle . . . merely completes one of an endless set of circles between this world and the other—and the Manus position, where human beings are originally built from material from fathers' and mothers' bodies, reach their full powers at maturity, survive a little as strong ghosts immediately after death and then dribble off into lower and lower levels of sea-slugs and slime.

Then I may say: "The Balinese believe you can learn at any age—the very young and the old learn with great relative effortlessness, beauty lasts into old age—while among the Manus, people are finished at forty. Perhaps we may suggest that there is a relationship here which it would be worth while to explore further." From there I may go on to consider whether I know any instances of a group who believe in reincarnation but also have a sharply marked decline in vigor during the life-span—thus looking for negative instances to disprove my developing hypothesis. At the same time, I will be running over in my mind what we know about learning at different ages in different cultures. . . . Or I may turn back to two ethnological categories, like "belief in reincarnation" and "life-cycle," in which case it would be possible to go up to Yale University and pull out a card catalogue in which material on a great many societies has been arranged in such categories, so that it is possible to see how the two things fit together.

2 February 4, 1946.
3 New York: William Morrow, 1949, pp. 389–390.

Asians

◆ ✳ ●

India:

Andaman Islanders and Santals of Bengal; Dravidians and Nayars of southern India; Tukarams; Khonds of east India; Garos and Anagami Nagas of Assam; Changs of Naga Hills.

Other Places:

Lusheis of Indo-China; Karens of Burma; Semany of Malay Peninsula.

Giliaks, Yenisei Ostiaks and Buriats of Russian Siberia; and the Cheremiss of east central Russia.

What is particularly interesting about this list is that it largely represents aboriginal peoples. The Dravidians, for example, lived in southern India long before they were conquered by the invading Hindu Aryans, who descended into the Indian peninsula from their home in northern Asia.

◆ * ●

American Indians

Charles Eastman, whose Indian name was Ohiyesa, wrote in The Soul of the Indian:[2] "Many of the Indians [of the United States] believed that one may be born more than once; and there were some who claimed to have full knowledge of a former incarnation." Algic Researches[3] reports: It is believed by the American Indians that their great teacher Hiawatha "is again to reappear and to exercise an important power in the final disposition of the human race." In Myths of the New World, Daniel G. Brinton, Professor of American Archaeology and Linguistics at the University of Pennsylvania, stated:

This seemingly extraordinary doctrine [of reincarnation], which some have asserted was entirely unknown and impossible to the American Indians, was in

[1] Respecting the last six named tribes, see Ian Stevenson, Twenty Cases Suggestive of Reincarnation, pp. 191–192, 195–199.
[2] Boston: Houghton, Mifflin, 1911, p. 167.
[3] I, 172–173.

fact one of their most deeply-rooted and widespread convictions,[4] especially among the tribes of the eastern United States. It is indissolubly connected with their highest theories of a future life, their burial ceremonies, and their modes of expression. . . .

The Maryland Indians said the whites were an ancient generation who had come to life again, and had returned to seize their former land. . . . [That such legends existed] is almost proved by the fact that in Mexico, Bogota, and Peru, the whites were at once called from the proper names of the heroes of the dawn, Suas, Viracochas, and Quetzalcoatls. . . . The dawn heroes were conceived of as of fair complexion, mighty in war, and though absent for a season, destined to return and claim their ancient power. . . . Historians have marveled at the instantaneous collapse of the empires of Mexico, Peru, the Mayas, and the Natches, before a handful of Spanish filibusters. The fact was, wherever the whites appeared they were connected with these ancient predictions of the spirit of the dawn returning to claim his own.[5]

In an article, "Inca's Sun God," by H. J. Maidenberg,[6] it is stated that despite centuries of Christianizing, "today, many Christian Indians still look to their holy lake [Lake Titicaca] for the return of the Sun God and the restoration of the highly advanced civilization that was destroyed by Francisco Pizarro's expedition from Spain more than 400 years ago."

Some curious doctrines of the Eskimos are discussed by Vilhjalmur Stefansson, naturalist and explorer, in *Redbook*.[7] Stefansson, who lived with the Coronation Gulf Eskimos in northern Canada for ten years, discovered among his Eskimo friends "beliefs that resembled, in a way, the reincarnation theories that we associate with India."[8] The following excerpt justifies the title of his article, "Primitive People Are Far From Simple," and suggests that many so-called primitives may be descendants of once highly civilized races:

I know from experience that two men who speak English and Eskimo well are not going to converse in English unless what they are talking about is some particularly English subject, like the dramas of Shakespeare or the cotton-spinning of Lancashire. . . . You can say as much in one hour of Eskimo-speaking as you can in two hours with English, and you will say it more precisely as well as more concisely. . . . In Eskimo a single noun, like "man" or "house," can have more than a thousand forms, each different in meaning from any other, and the difference is so precise that no misunderstanding is possible. . . . If

---

[4] The anthropologist, Paul Radin, indicates similarly in his *Autobiography of a Winnebago Indian*. New York: Dover, 1963, p. 72 and fn. (Eds.)
[5] Philadelphia: David McKay, 1896, pp. 220–223, 295.
[6] *New York Times*, June 19, 1966.
[7] March, 1946.
[8] See also: *Mythology of All Races*, ed. John A. MacCulloch. New York: Cooper Square, 1964, Vol. 10: *North American Mythology*, p. 10.

you were to study in succession Latin, Greek, Hebrew and Russian, each till you could think in it and speak in it fluently and correctly, you would find those four languages combined easier to learn than Eskimo alone. . . . The most brilliant conversation I ever listened to has been among Stone Age Eskimos.

"What do we know of savage tribes beyond the latest chapter of their history?" asks Max Müller. "Their language proves indeed that these so-called heathens, with their complicated systems of mythology, their artificial customs, their unintelligible whims and savageries, are not the creatures of today or yesterday. . . . They may have passed through ever so many vicissitudes, and what we consider as primitive may be, for all we know, a relapse into savagery, or a corruption of something that was more rational and intelligible in former stages." [9]

[9] *Collected Works of The Right Hon. F. Max Müller.* London: Longmans, Green, 1919, XIII, 110 (*India, What Can It Teach Us?*)

Europeans

Finns; Lapps; Danes; Norse; Icelandic peoples; Early Saxons; Celts of Gaul, Wales, England, and Ireland; Old Prussians and Early Teutonics; Lithuanians; Letts; Lombards of Italy.

Teutonic

The northern European Caucasian stock (characterized by tall stature, blond hair, blue eyes, and elongated head), from which many of the German, Dutch, Scandinavian, and British peoples are descended, are known to ethnologists as the Old Teutons. Bruce Dickins, author of *Runic and Heroic Poems of the Old Teutonic Peoples*, states in his article on transmigration in *Hastings' Encyclopædia of Religion and Ethics:*[1] "It is clear that the doctrine of metempsychosis was held by the early Teutonic peoples. . . . Such evidence as exists is chiefly derived from Scandinavian records. The only reference in early poetry is to be found in *Siguroarkvipa kinn skamma*, 45, where Hogni refuses to hold Brynhild back from self-destruction: 'Let no man stay her from the long journey, and may she never be born again.'" It is interesting that Richard Wagner preserved this thought in his *Götterdämmerung*. (See Index under "Wagner.")

Dickins' article continues: "More striking evidence for the [reincarnation] belief is furnished by the prose passages contained in *Helgakvipa Hjorvarossonar* and *Helgakvipa Hundingsbana*, ii. At the end of the former it is said that Helgi and Sváva, the hero and heroine, were born again (en-

[1] XII, 440.

drborin); in the latter we are told that the heroine Sigrún was Sváva reincarnate, and later that both she and her husband Helgi Hundingsbani were born again as Kára and Helgi Haddingjaskati."

In *Viking Civilization*[2] Axel Olrik states: "A special form of family relationship was that in which one newly deceased was reborn in his descendants, and the latter were accordingly given the name of the deceased. This belief appears as late as the period of the Migration, first among the East Goths, from whom it spread far and wide. . . . It continued to exist as a current folk belief for many centuries. 'We shall come again' said the old people in Saetersdal [Norway], when death called them from the ancestral home."

Appian's *History of the Romans*[3] describes the Germans who followed Ariovistus as "scorning death because of their hope of rebirth."

Celtic

In his *Literary History of Ireland*, Douglas Hyde (former President of Ireland) stated that "the idea of rebirth, which forms part of a half-a-dozen existing Irish sagas, was perfectly familiar to the Irish Gael."[4] Dr. W. Y. Evans-Wentz, in his book *The Fairy-Faith in Celtic Countries*[5] quoted Alfred Nutt one of the foremost authorities on the subject: "In Greek Mythology as in Irish, the conception of rebirth proves to be a dominant factor of the same religious system in which Elysium is likewise an essential feature."[6] Chapters 7 and 12 of Evans-Wentz's book treat in detail of the Celtic doctrine of reincarnation, and also provide evidence that even to this day the idea is alive among some of these peoples.

The ancient Celts are today represented by the Irish Gaels, the Welsh, the Cornish of England, the Scotch of the Hebrides and Highlands, the Manx of the Isle of Man, and the Bretons of northwestern France, or Brittany. In early Roman times, however, their territory included in addition to Great Britain and Ireland: northern Italy, France, Belgium, western Switzerland, and Germany west of the Rhine.

Whence sprang their reincarnation views? The source was certainly pre-Roman, considering the statements of Julius Caesar, Valerius Maximus, and Lucan which will be quoted or cited later in this volume. For centuries

[2] New York: W. W. Norton, 1930, p. 23.
[3] IV, de Rebus Gallicia, 3.
[4] London: T. Fisher Unwin, 1901, pp. 95–96.
[5] Oxford University Press, 1911, p. 358.
[6] "The Celtic Doctrine of Rebirth," Alfred Nutt, *The Voyage of Bran*, ed. Kuno Meyer. London: 1895–1897, II. (Eds.)

the world has been intrigued by the "Atlantis theory," a widely held belief that there once existed in the Atlantic Ocean, opposite the mouth of the Mediterranean Sea, a large island, which was but the remnant of a vast Atlantic continent. From the mighty civilization which it is thought developed on that continent, colonizing parties went out to the Americas, Europe, Africa, and Asia. The Biblical story of the flood is supposed by some to be a fragmentary record of the sinking of Atlantis. Although the literature on this subject comprises some five thousand works in twenty different languages, the classic work is Ignatius Donnelly's *Atlantis: The Antediluvian World*, published by Harper in New York in 1882 (a revised 1949 edition is still in print). No other author since Plato's story of Atlantis in the *Timæus* and the *Critias* has influenced the minds of so many people to give serious consideration to this strange theory, which if proved would radically alter scientific views in anthropology, archaeology, and related fields, and push back the origin of civilization perhaps millions of years. Here is Donnelly's idea of how the Celts and their Druidic priests obtained their reincarnation beliefs:[7]

There are many evidences that the Old World recognized Ireland as possessing a very ancient civilization. In the Sanskrit books it is referred to as Hiranya, the "Island of the Sun," . . . The Greeks called Ireland the "Sacred Isle" and "Ogygia." "Nor can any one," says Camden, "conceive why they should call it Ogygia, unless, perhaps, from its antiquity; for the Greeks called nothing Ogygia unless what was extremely ancient." . . .

We would naturally expect, in view of the geographical position of the country, to find Ireland colonized at an early day by the overflowing population of Atlantis. And, in fact, the Irish annals tell us that their island was settled *prior to the Flood.* . . . We have seen their annals laying claim to an immigration from the direction of Atlantis prior to the Deluge. . . . Many analogies have been found to exist between the beliefs and customs of the Druids and the other religions which were drawn from Atlantis. . . . It would appear probable that the religion of the Druids passed from Ireland to England and France. The metempsychosis or transmigration of souls was one of the articles of their belief long before the time of Pythagoras; it had probably been drawn from the storehouse of Atlantis.

[7] pp. 251, 254–255, rev. ed.

◆ ✳ ●

_____

PART V

Western Thinkers
on Reincarnation

I cannot recite, even rudely, laws of the intellect, without remembering that lofty and sequestered class who have been its prophets and oracles, the high-priesthood of the pure reason, the Trismegisti, the expounders of thought from age to age. When, at long intervals, we turn over their abstruse pages, wonderful seems the calm and grand air of these few, these great spiritual lords, who have walked in the world—these of the old religion. . . . This band of grandees, Hermes, Heraclitus, Empedocles, Plato, Plotinus, Olympiodorus, Proclus, Synesius, and the rest, have somewhat so vast in their logic, so primary in their thinking, that it seems antecedent to all the ordinary distinctions of rhetoric and literature, and to be at once poetry, and music and dancing, and astronomy, and mathematics. I am present at the sowing of the seed of the world. With a geometry of sunbeams the soul lays the foundations of nature.

RALPH WALDO EMERSON
"Intellect"

Apollonius and Iamblichus held that it was not "in the knowledge of things without, but in the perfection of the soul within, that lies the empire of man, aspiring to be more than men." . . . But our philosophers, tightly shutting themselves up in their shells of flesh, cannot or dare not carry their timid gaze beyond the comprehensible. For them there is no future life; there are no godlike dreams, they scorn them as unscientific; for them the men of old are but "ignorant ancestors"; and whenever they meet during their physiological researches with an author who believes that this mysterious yearning after spiritual knowledge is inherent in every human being, and cannot have been given us utterly in vain, they regard him with contemptuous pity.

H. P. BLAVATSKY
Isis Unveiled, I, 64

*How can an educated person stay away from the Greeks? I have always been far more interested in them than in science. **** I maintain that cosmic religious feeling is the strongest and noblest incitement to scientific research.*

ALBERT EINSTEIN

Greek and Roman

ORPHEUS
Legendary Greek Teacher

Thomas Taylor writes in his *Mystical Hymns of Orpheus:*[1] "This alone may be depended upon, from general assent, that there formerly lived a person named Orpheus, who was the founder of theology among the Greeks . . . the first of prophets and the prince of poets . . . who taught the Greeks their sacred rites and mysteries, and from whose wisdom . . . the divine muse of Homer and the sublime theology of Pythagoras and Plato flowed." To use the words of Proclus, "all the theology of the Greeks comes from Orphic mystagogy," that is to say, initiation into the mysteries.[2] And although in modern times there have been disputes as to whether Orpheus ever existed, the great honor in which he was held by so many generations of the highest intellects of antiquity would suggest that the theology attributed to him came from a venerable and archaic source.

"The doctrine of metempsychosis," writes Professor Zeller, "seems really to have passed from the theology of the mysteries into Philosophy. . . . In the Orphic theology . . . transmigration is clearly to be found. . . . We have every reason to believe that it was taught in the Orphic mysteries prior to the date of Pythagoras. According to Herodotus, the Orphics obtained it from Egypt. But it is also conceivable that this belief, the affinity of which with Hindu and Egyptian doctrines indicates an Eastern source, may have originally emigrated from the East with the Greeks them-

[1] London, 1884, p. xliv.
[2] Lobeck, *Aglaophamus*, p. 723.

selves, and have been at first confined to a narrow circle becoming afterwards more important and more widely diffused." [3]

Alfred Bertholet, professor of theology at the University of Basle, remarks in his small work *The Transmigration of Souls:*[4] The Orphici teach that "the soul is divine, immortal, and aspires to freedom, while the body holds it in fetters as a prisoner. Death dissolves the compact, but only to reimprison the liberated soul after a short time: for the wheel of birth revolves inexorably. . . . The Orphic belief seems to have been widely current in the Greek colonies in Southern Italy and Sicily." The purified soul, of course, could achieve release from the need for periodic return.

PHERECYDES OF SYROS (6TH CENTURY B.C.)
Greek Philosopher

Pherecydes has been called one of the Seven Wise Men of Greece. Mead writes of him in *Orpheus:*[1] "Pherecydes is said to have been the master of Pythagoras, and to have obtained his knowledge from the secret books of the Phœnicians. . . . He is further stated to have been the pupil of the Chaldæans and Egyptians. . . . The most important subject he treated of, was the doctrine of metempsychosis and the immortality of the soul (Suidas, and Cicero, *Tusc.*, i. 16), and this he set forth in his great prose work *Theologia*, generally known as the 'Seven Adyta.' . . . He is said to have been the first who used prose for such a subject."

PYTHAGORAS (C. 582–507 B.C.)
Greek Philosopher and Mathematician

[Pythagoras] was accustomed to speak of himself in this manner: that he had formerly been Aethalides. . . . At a subsequent period, he passed into Euphorbus, and was wounded by Menelaus at the siege of Troy, and so died. In that life he used to say that he had formerly been Aethalides; and that he had received as a gift from Mercury [the god of Wisdom] the memory of his soul's transmigrations . . . also the gift of recollecting what his own soul and the souls of others had experienced between death and rebirth.

Diogenes Laertius
Life of Pythagoras[1]

---

[3] Edward Zeller, *History of Greek Philosophy*. London: Longmans, Green, 1880, pp. 67, 69, 71–72.
[4] London: Harper, 1909, pp. 79–81.

---

[1] London: John Watkins, 1965, p. 21.

---

[1] Diogenes Laertius, *The Lives and Opinions of Eminent Philosophers*, Book 8, Chap. 4.

What Pythagoras wished to indicate by all these particulars was that he knew the former lives he had lived, which enabled him to begin providential attention to others and remind them of their former existences.

Iamblichus
Life of Pythagoras (*Chap. XIV*)

[Pythagoras has frequently been accused of teaching that human souls could incarnate in animal forms. In *As You Like It* (III. ii) Shakespeare's Rosalind says: "I was never so be-rhymed since Pythagoras' time, that I was an Irish rat, which I can hardly remember." Pythagoras himself left no writings, but Dacier in his *Life of Pythagoras* points out: "A sure token that Pythagoras never held the opinion attributed to him lies in the fact that there is not the faintest trace of it in the symbols we have left of him, or in the precepts his disciple, Lysis, collected together and handed down as a summary of the Master's teaching." John Reuchlin, the great German humanist, was of similar opinion (see p. 235), while Sir Thomas Browne stated in *Religio Medici*: "I cannot believe the wisdom of Pythagoras did ever positively, and in a literal sense, affirm his Metempsychosis, or impossible transmigration of the Souls of men into beasts." (*Harvard Classics*.)[2] To a similar opinion, the *Britannica* adds that the many allusions to transmigration in the writings of the Greeks are generally of a playful character: "Thus Menander, in the play called *The Inspired Woman*, supposes some god to say to an old man Crato, 'When you die, you will have a second existence; choose what creature you would like to be, dog, sheep, goat, horse, or man.' To which he replies, 'Make me anything rather than a man, for he is the only creature that prospers by injustice.' "[3]

Hierocles, a Pythagorean, wrote in his *Commentary of the Golden Verses of Pythagoras*: "He who expects that after his death he shall put on the body of a beast, and become an animal without reason, because of his vices, or a plant because of his dullness and stupidity; such a man . . . is infinitely deceived, and absolutely ignorant of the essential form of our soul, which can never change; for being and continuing always man, 'tis only said to become god or beast by virtue or vice, though by its nature it cannot be either the one or the other, but only by its resemblance to the one or the other."[4] This view was shared by the Neoplatonists regarding Plato's remarks on regression.[5]]

---

[2] New York: P. F. Collier, 1909, III, 289.
[3] 9th ed., article "Metempsychosis."
[4] Verses LII and LIII, included in André Dacier's *The Life of Pythagoras*, London: 1707.
[5] See under "Proclus."

HERACLITUS OF EPHESUS (C. 540–C. 480 B.C.)
Greek Philosopher

[Heraclitus wrote:] This world which is the same for all, neither any god nor any man made; but it was always, is, and ever shall be, an ever-living fire. . . . The quick and the dead, the wakers and the sleepers, young and old; all are the same. For the last are moved about to be the first, and the first in turn become the last. They rise again and become watchful guardians of the quick and the dead.

[The foregoing is quoted in *The Dawn of Philosophy* by the German philosopher, George Misch.[1] Misch comments: "The 'everliving fire' subsists only in its transmigrations, as that which is perpetually changing, since it is not a fixed quantity that 'is,' but 'lives.' This dynamic principle accords very well with the idea of world-cycles of events; indeed periodicity was a self-evident fact to all thinking persons right down to modern times. In connection with these up-down cycles or the 'wheel of births,' to use the Indian term, he [Heraclitus] says, 'The way up and the way down are the same.' "]

PINDAR (522?–443 B.C.)
Greek Lyric Poet

[Speaking no doubt symbolically of the goal of incarnations, Pindar wrote:]

They who thrice on either side of death have refrained their souls from wickedness, travel on the road of Zeus to the tower of Cronus, where the ocean breezes blow around the island of the blest!

Odes (Olympia 2)

While the body of all men is subject to over-mastering death, [the soul] remaineth alive, for it alone cometh from the gods. But it sleepeth, while the limbs are active. . . . As for those from whom Persephone has exacted the penalty of their ancient sins, in the ninth year she once more restoreth their souls to the upper sunlight; and from these come into being

[1] Harvard University Press, 1951, pp. 233, 237.

august monarchs, and men who are swift in strength and supreme in wisdom; and, for all future time, men call them sainted heroes.[1]

Dirges[2]

EMPEDOCLES (C. 490–430 B.C.)
Greek Philosopher and Statesman

I was once already boy and girl,
Thicket and bird, and mute fish in the waves.
All things doth Nature change, enwrapping souls
In unfamiliar tunics of the flesh.
The worthiest dwellings for the souls of men.

The Purifications
Trans. Wm. Ellery Leonard

There is an oracle of Necessity, ancient decree of the gods, eternal and sealed with broad oaths: whenever one of those demi-gods, whose lot is long-lasting life, has sinfully defiled his dear limbs with bloodshed, or following strife has sworn a false oath, thrice ten thousand seasons does he wander far from the blessed, being born throughout that time in the forms of all manner of mortal things and changing one baleful path of life for another. . . . Of these I too am now one, a fugitive from the gods, who put my trust in raving strife.

Fragments[1]

The Greek Mysteries

In Greece, the doctrine of transmigration . . . appears to have been generally inculcated as one of the deepest doctrines of the mysteries. . . . The Greek mysteries were, in fact, not only a school in which metempsychosis was taught, but an indispensable grade or lodge through which all of the aspirants must pass before they could be purified and go on to higher stages of existence.

M'Clintock and Strong's Cyclædia of Biblical,
Theological and Ecclesiastical Literature[1]

"In all ages of which we have any literary records," writes William Kingsland, "we find the tradition of a recondite knowledge which could not be disclosed to any save to those who had undergone the severest tests as to

[1] This sentence is quoted in Plato's *Meno* (81).
[2] *The Odes of Pindar including the Principal Fragments.* London: Heinemann, 1915, p. 589. Two slight changes have been made in this translation of Sir John Sandys as a result of comparison with other translations.

[1] G. S. Kirk and J. E. Raven, *The Presocratic Philosophers.* Cambridge University Press, 1957, pp. 351–352.

[1] New York: Harper, 1881, article "Transmigration."

their worthiness to receive it. This knowledge was very generally known under the term of the *Mysteries*, and it was concerned with the deepest facts of Man's origin, nature, and connection with supersensual worlds and beings, as well as with the 'natural' laws of the physical world." [2]

The Greek Mystery Schools are believed to be copies of the more ancient Indian and Egyptian Mysteries. Herodotus stated that they were introduced into Greece by Orpheus. "It is only when we come to the first five or six centuries B.C., and to the palmy days of Greece and Alexandria," continues Kingsland, "that we obtain a definite knowledge of the existence of the Mystery Schools, and of some of their more detailed teachings. This period is associated with such names as Anaxagoras, Pythagoras, Socrates, Plato, Aristotle, and later on, before the dominance of ecclesiastical Christianity had suppressed the Gnosis . . . we have such names as Philo Judæus, Clement of Alexandria, Valentinus, Origen, Proclus, Basilides, Iamblichus, and Plotinus, all speaking openly of the existence of the *Mysteries* and Mystery Schools, claiming initiation therein, and openly teaching as much of it as it was permitted for them to make public." [3]

The most celebrated, and the last to be destroyed, were the Eleusinian Mysteries, whose center was located in a hamlet not far from Athens. Those initiated bound themselves by this promise: "I swear to give up my life for the salvation of my brothers, who constitute the whole of mankind, and, if called upon, to die in the defense of truth." For many centuries the Mysteries of Eleusis illuminated the land of Greece, but by the end of the second century A.D. anyone who had the price could become an "initiate." In 396 the vast Temple of Eleusis, one of the most renowned buildings of the ancient world, was reduced to ashes by the Goths.

In the various mystery dramas, nature's laws and processes were personified by the priests and neophytes, who assuming the role of various gods and goddesses, repeated scenes from their respective lives. These were explained in their hidden meaning to the candidates for initiation and incorporated into philosophical doctrines. The pre-existent condition of the spirit and soul was symbolized; the lapse of the latter into earth life and Hades; the long wanderings through many lives; the gradual purification of the soul and its eventual reunion with spirit.

At Eleusis the familiar story of Demeter and Persephone was portrayed, signifying, according to Sallust, the periodical descent of souls.[4] Thomas Taylor agrees with this interpretation in his *Eleusinian and Bacchic Mys-*

[2] *The Gnosis or Ancient Wisdom in the Christian Scriptures.* London: Allen & Unwin, 1937, p. 93.
[3] P. 97.
[4] *De Diis et Mundo,* iv.

teries.[5] The six months of Persephone's stay in the upper world of sunlight midst the beauties and glories of nature depicted the heavenly state of bliss after death, while the equal period in Hades, or the dark region of Pluto, symbolized incarnation on earth. (In Eastern tradition the earth is called Myalba, or Hell—the only hell that mortals have to endure.) In this context, the red pomegranate seeds which Persephone has eaten in the underworld and which condemn her to return periodically to that realm are suggestive of attachment to sensuous existence, making reincarnation obligatory.

In the Orphic Mysteries, Bacchus torn to pieces by the Titans and then made whole again, was dramatized. Plutarch calls this "a sacred narrative concerning reincarnation." [6]

PLATO (427?–347 B.C.)
Greek Philosopher

["The real weight and importance of metempsychosis" in the West, states the *Britannica* (11th ed.) "is due to its adoption by Plato." "Had he not embodied it in some of his greatest works it would be merely a matter of curious investigation for the anthropologist and student of folk-lore." The degree to which Plato's reincarnation ideas influenced Western literature and philosophy may be evaluated in a general way by consulting the index to the present work, under "Plato."

"Out of Plato come all things that are still written and debated among men of thought," wrote Emerson, and added: "Among secular books, Plato only is entitled to Omar's fanatical compliment to the Koran, when he said, 'Burn the libraries; for their value is in this book.' [His] sentences contain the culture of nations . . . , the corner-stone of schools . . . , the fountain-head of literatures." [1]]

SOCRATES   I have heard from certain wise men and women who spoke . . . of a glorious truth, as I conceive.

MENO   What was it? and who were they?

SOCRATES   Some of them were priests and priestesses, who had studied how they might be able to give a reason [for] their profession: there have been poets also, who spoke of these things by inspiration, like Pindar, and many others who were inspired. And they say—mark, now, and

[5] New York: 1875, p. 117.
[6] *De Esu Carn.*, Or. 1. 7, 240, T. xiii.

[1] Essay "Plato; or the Philosopher." *The Selected Writings of Ralph Waldo Emerson*, ed. Brooks Atkinson. New York: Modern Library, 1940, p. 471.

see whether their words are true—they say that the soul of man is immortal, and at one time has an end, which is termed dying, and at another time is born again, but is never destroyed. And the moral is, that a man ought to live always in perfect holiness. . . .

The soul, then, as being immortal, and having been born again many times, and having seen all things that exist, whether in this world or in the world below, has knowledge of them all; and it is no wonder that she should be able to call to remembrance all that she ever knew about virtue, and about everything; for as all nature is akin, and the soul has learned all things, there is no difficulty in her eliciting or as men say learning, out of a single recollection all the rest, if a man is strenuous and does not faint; for all enquiry and all learning is but recollection. . . .

MENO . . . if you can prove to me that what you say is true, I wish that you would.

SOCRATES It will be no easy matter, but I will try to please you to the utmost of my power. Suppose that you call one of your numerous attendants, that I may demonstrate on him.

[A young boy, a Greek slave, is introduced, from whom answers to certain mathematical problems are elicited by Socrates during a long series of questionings.]

SOCRATES Now, has any one ever taught him all this? You must know about him, if, as you say, he was born and bred in your house.

MENO I am certain that no one ever did teach him. . . .

SOCRATES But if he did not acquire the knowledge in this life, then he must have had and learned it at some other time?

MENO Clearly he must. . . .

SOCRATES And if there have been always true thoughts in him . . . which only need to be awakened into knowledge by putting questions to him, his soul must have always possessed this knowledge? . . .

MENO Obviously.

SOCRATES And if the truth of all things always existed in the soul, then the soul is immortal. Wherefore be of good cheer, and try to recollect what you do not know, or rather what you do not remember.

MENO I feel, somehow, that I like what you are saying.

SOCRATES And I, Meno, like what I am saying. Some things I have said of which I am not altogether confident. But that we shall be better and braver and less helpless if we think that we ought to enquire, than we should have been if we indulged in the idle fancy that there was no knowing and no use in seeking to know what we do not know;—that is a theme upon which I am ready to fight, in word and deed, to the utmost of my power.

Meno
Trans. Benjamin Jowett

[A few selections from the *Phædrus* follow. A detailed examination of certain aspects of Plato's discussion of rebirth in this dialogue appeared in the *American Journal of Philology*[2] under the title "The Phædrus and Reincarnation." The author, R. S. Bluck, philologist of the University of London, suggests that Plato's 10,000-year cycle of periodic rebirths is not meant to refer to the whole of the soul's history. He shows furthermore that when speaking of the soul's "fall" Plato explains it in the light of a difficult incarnation resulting from "bad training" by the ego of some of its instruments in a prior life. Therefore the "fall" has none of the connotations associated with the doctrine of original sin. As Dr. Bluck states: Plato "may be suggesting, rather, that the human soul may [by reincarnating] aspire to *promotion* which would enable it to enjoy such happiness as it has never known before. . . . How long it takes to achieve that will depend upon individual effort, and will not be fixed at all." [3]]

Every soul is immortal—for whatever is in perpetual motion is immortal. . . . All that is soul presides over all that is without soul and patrols all heaven, now appearing in one form and now in another. . . . Every man's soul has by the law of his birth been a spectator of eternal truth, or it would never have passed into this our mortal frame, yet still it is no easy matter for all to be reminded of their past by their present existence. . . . By making the right use of those things remembered from the former life, by constantly perfecting himself in the perfect mysteries, a man becomes truly perfect—an initiate into the diviner wisdom.

Phædrus[4]

[The *Phædo*, Plato's story of Socrates' last day on earth "is perhaps the greatest thing in the prose literature of Europe," writes A. E. Taylor in *Socrates, the Man and His Thought.*[5] "Socrates," Taylor continues, "finding that his young friends from Thebes, Cebes and Simmias, were much troubled with 'scientific' doubts that the soul may be no more than a perishable function of the body, devoted his last morning to reasoning with

[2] April, 1958.
[3] Pp. 160, 164.
[4] Josiah Wright is the translator, save for the final sentence.
[5] New York: Doubleday Anchor Book, 1954, p. 124.

them in his own justification, on the 'real distinction of the soul from the body,' and the grounds for believing that it is neither born with the body nor dies with it. . . . Through the whole discussion he showed himself free alike from depression by the prospect of imminent death, and from over-anxiety to cling to a comforting belief without giving full weight to all there might be to urge against it." Of the various evidences adduced by Socrates to support immortality, one is here selected bearing particularly on rebirth. The translation is Jowett's. Socrates also reviews all the arguments supporting his "favorite doctrine that knowledge is simply recollection," that this "implies a previous time in which we have learned that which we now recollect," and that "this is another proof of the soul's immortality." (See sections 73–77.)]

Suppose we consider the question whether the souls of men after death are or are not in the world below. There comes into my mind an ancient doctrine which affirms that they go from here into the other world, and returning hither, are born again from the dead. Now if it be true that the living come from the dead, then our souls must exist in the other world, for if not, how could they have been born again? . . .

Let us consider the whole question, not in relation to man only, but in relation to animals generally, and to plants, and to everything of which there is generation, and the proof will be easier. Are not all things which have opposites generated out of their opposites? . . . The state of sleep is opposed to the state of waking, and out of sleeping waking is generated, and out of waking, sleeping. [Other examples are furnished, such as pleasure and pain, heat and cold.] Then here is a new way by which we arrive at the conclusion that the living come from the dead, just as the dead come from the living; and this, if true, affords a most certain proof that the souls of the dead exist in some place out of which they come again. . . .

If generation were in a straight line only, and there were no compensation or circle in nature, no turn or return of elements into their opposites, then you know that all things would at last have the same form and pass into the same state, and there would be no more generation of them. . . . If all things which partook of life were to die, and after they were dead remained in the form of death, and did not come to life again, all would at last die, and nothing would be alive—what other result could there be? . . . Must not all things at last be swallowed up in death? . . . But I am confident that there truly is such a thing as living again, and that the living spring from the dead, and that the souls of the dead are in existence, and that the good souls have a better portion than the evil.

[The sensuous man was believed to return to earthlife more quickly than the good, for in the same dialogue—and this time Harry Cary's translation is used—Socrates states:]

The soul of the true philosopher . . . abstains as much as possible from pleasures and desires, griefs and fears . . . because each pleasure and pain, having a nail, as it were, nails the soul to the body, and fastens it to it, and causes it to become corporeal, deeming those things to be true whatever the body asserts to be so. For, in consequence of its forming the same opinions with the body, and delighting in the same things . . . it can never pass into Hades in a pure state, but must ever depart polluted by the body, and so quickly falls into another body . . . and consequently is deprived of all association with that which is divine, and pure, and uniform.

Phœdo

O youth or young man, who fancy that you are neglected by the Gods, know that if you become worse you shall go to the worse souls, or if better to the better, and in every succession of life and death you will do and suffer what like may fitly suffer at the hands of like. This is the justice of heaven, which neither you nor any other unfortunate will ever glory in escaping. . . . Take heed thereof, for it will be sure to take heed of you. If you say—I am small and will creep into the depths of the earth, or I am high and will fly up to heaven, you are not so small or so high but that you shall pay the fitting penalty. . . . And thinkest thou, bold man . . . that thou needest not to know this?—he who knows it not can never form any true idea of the happiness or unhappiness of life or hold any rational discourse respecting either.

Laws (Book X)
Trans. Benjamin Jowett

[We conclude with selections from the last part of Plato's celebrated work *The Republic*. In several of his dialogues Plato relates stories of humans entering animal forms. One such occurs in *The Republic*, and is discussed at page 47 of the present work, and also under "Proclus." The translation that follows is Josiah Wright's, save for the last paragraph which is Jowett's. The closing lines of the ten books of *The Republic* end on the note of rebirth.]

Well, I will tell you a tale . . . of what once happened to a brave man, Er, who, according to the story, was killed in battle [but his body would not disintegrate]. . . . On the twelfth day after his death, as he lay on the funeral pyre, he came to life again, and then proceeded to describe what he had seen in the other world. . . . Each soul, as it arrived, wore a travel-stained appearance . . . and those who had descended from heaven were questioned about heaven by those who had risen out of the earth; while the latter were questioned by the former about the earth. Those who were come from earth told their tale with lamentations and tears, as they bethought them of all the dreadful things they had seen and suffered in their subterranean journey . . . while those who were come from heaven described enjoyments and sights of marvellous beauty.

[The souls about to enter earth life are thus addressed:] "Ye short-lived souls, a new generation of men shall here begin the cycle of its mortal existence. Your destiny shall not be allotted to you, but you shall choose it for yourselves. . . . Virtue owns no master. He who honours her shall have more of her, and he who slights her less. The responsibility lies with the chooser. Heaven is guiltless." . . .

It was a truly wonderful sight, he said, to watch how each soul selected its life—a sight at once melancholy, and ludicrous, and strange. The experience of their former life generally guided the choice. . . . It so happened that the soul of Odysseus had drawn the last lot of all. When he came up to choose, the memory of his former sufferings had so abated his ambition that he went about a long time looking for a quiet retired life, which with great trouble he discovered lying about, and thrown contemptuously aside by the others. As soon as he saw it, he chose it gladly, and said that he would have done the same if he had even drawn the first lot. . . .

Now, when all the souls had chosen their lives . . . they all travelled into the plain of Forgetfulness . . . and took up their quarters by the bank of the river of Indifference. . . . each, as he drinks, forgets everything. When they had gone to rest, and it was now midnight, there was a clap of thunder and an earthquake; and in a moment the souls were carried up to their birth, this way and that, like shooting stars. Er himself was prevented from drinking any of the water; but how, and by what road, he reached his body, he knew not: only he knew that he suddenly opened his eyes at dawn, and found himself laid out upon the funeral pyre.

And thus, Glaucon, the tale has been saved and has not perished, and will save us if we are obedient to the word spoken; and we shall pass safely over the river of Forgetfulness and our soul will not be defiled. Wherefore my counsel is that we hold fast ever to the heavenly way and follow after justice and virtue always, considering that the soul is immortal and able to endure every sort of good and every sort of evil. Thus shall we live dear to one another and to the gods . . . and it shall be well with us both in this life and in the pilgrimage of a thousand years [between incarnations] which we have been describing.

The Republic (Book X)

ARISTOTLE (384–322 B.C.)
Greek Philosopher

[In the volume *Aristotle—Fundamentals of the History of His Development*,[1] one finds that Aristotle accepted pre-existence and reincarnation in his early dialogue *Eudemus or On The Soul*, but in his later works largely rejected these ideas. The author, the well-known classical scholar, Werner Jaeger, further shows that the historic split between Aristotle and his teacher Plato—which was to make of the former the father of materialism in philosophy, science, and religion of all subsequent eras of Western thought—occurred over Plato's teaching of immortality and pre-existence. Jaeger states[2]:]

In the *Eudemus* Aristotle follows the view of [Plato's] *Phædo* even in holding that "the whole soul" is immortal. This realistic view is the only one that can give religious comfort to the heart of man, which cares nothing for the eternity of the impersonal reason, without love and without memory of this life. But Aristotle has wrestled with doubts, and they have left traces in his notion of Platonic recollection. We know that in his psychology he rejects recollection along with the Idea-theory and the survival of "the whole soul." [3] The *Eudemus*, on the other hand, is still based on this theory. But at the time of writing it Aristotle had already put to himself, and attempted to answer by Plato's methods, the psychological question whether consciousness is continuous in the life after death. This is the question on which immortality in the sense meant in the *Phædo* later seemed to him to founder. [Aristotle held that] the continuity of consciousness depends on memory. Whereas he later denies that Nus [Nous or Spirit] possesses this, in the Eudemus he tries to save it for the soul that has returned to the other world. He does this by enlarging Plato's [theory of] recollection into a doctrine of the continuity of consciousness in all three phases of the soul's existence—its former existence, its life on this earth, and its life after death. Alongside the Platonic view that the soul remembers the other world he sets his thesis that [in the after life] it remembers this one.

He supports this by an analogy. When men fall ill they sometimes lose

[1] Oxford University Press, 1948.
[2] Pp. 50–52.
[3] *De Anima*, III. 5, 430ᵃ 23; *Metaphysics*, A 9, 993ᵃ I.

their memories, even to the extent of forgetting how to read and write; while on the other hand those who have been restored from illness to health do not forget what they suffered while they were ill. In the same way the soul that has descended into a body forgets the impressions received during its former existence, while the soul which death has restored to its home in the other world remembers its experiences and sufferings here. Life without a body is the soul's normal state; its sojourn in the body is a severe illness. Our Lethe of what we beheld in our previous lives is only a temporary interruption and obscuration of our memories and of the continuity of our consciousness. Since nothing of this kind is to be feared when we grow well again, i.e., when our souls are freed from their bodies, this view appears to guarantee the immortality of "the whole soul."

The validity of the proof depends on the correctness of its presupposition, that man's knowledge is a recollection of "the visions there." The personal immortality that the *Eudemus* teaches necessarily stands or falls along with this Platonic dogma. Plato had supported his great logical discovery, the *a priori*, with the myth of recollection. At first the young Aristotle followed along the lines of this myth, and we should not be justified in regarding this way of thinking . . . as a mere metaphor in the pupil. But the moment that he had clearly grasped the specifically logical nature of pure thought, and realized that memory is a psycho-physical phenomenon, he denied that Nus was capable of recollection and dropped pre-existence and immortality.

[The objections to rebirth on the basis of memory have been considered at length by C. J. Ducasse in our introduction. In Part Six another twentieth-century philosopher, John McTaggart, deals with the problem, as does also Gustave Geley, who speaks from the standpoint of modern psychology.[1]

In Aristotle's later dialogues he did not completely abandon the philosophy of pre-existence, for as the seventeenth century Cambridge Platonist, Henry More, points out in his treatise on the "Immortality of the Soul:"[2]]

We shall evince that Aristotle, who has the luck to be believed more than most authors, was of the same opinion [as to the pre-existence of the soul], in his treatise "De Anima," where he says . . . "for every art must use its proper instruments, and every soul its body." . . . He speaks some-

[1] See also Index under "Memory of Past Lives."
[2] *A Collection of Several Philosophical Writings of Dr. Henry More*, London, 1712, Book II, pp. 116–117.

thing more plainly in his "De Generatione Animae." "There are generated," saith he, "in the earth, and in the moisture thereof, plants and living creatures . . . and in the whole universe an animal warmth or heat; insomuch that in a manner all places are full of souls." . . .

We will add a third place still more clear, out of the same treatise, where he starts this very question of the pre-existency of souls, of the sensitive and rational especially . . . and he concludes thus: . . . It remains that the rational or intellectual soul only enters from without, as being only of a nature purely divine; with whose actions the actions of this gross body have no communication. Concerning which point he concludes like an orthodox scholar of his excellent master Plato; to whose footsteps the closer he keeps, the less he ever wanders from the truth. For in this very place he does plainly profess, what many would not have him so apertly guilty of, that the Soul of man is immortal, and can perform her proper functions without the help of this terrestrial body.

ENNIUS (239?–169 B.C.)
Roman Poet

This Calabrian poet is said to have introduced the doctrine of reincarnation to the Romans. He it is who tells in his *Annals* how Homer appeared to him in a dream and told him that their bodies had once been animated by the same soul. The *Annals* have been lost, but the dream has survived through repetition by the classical Roman authors.[1]

The Roman Renaissance

An informative though somewhat literal study of Roman views on immortality may be found in *After Life in Roman Paganism* by Franz Cumont. Professor Cumont's work, which has been reprinted as a Dover paperback,[1] was originally published by the Yale University Press, and constituted the Silliman Memorial Lectures at Yale in 1921. The author is considered an outstanding authority in the field of comparative religions of classical antiquity. The following summary is based mainly on these lectures, to be followed by direct quotations therefrom:

The "rationalistic" period of Greek thought inaugurated by Aristotle filled the Hellenistic and later Roman period for several centuries. Toward the end of the Roman Republic—marked by the assassination of Julius Caesar in 44 B.C.—faith in a future life reached its lowest ebb. The skepti-

[1] Britannica, 11th ed., XVIII, 260.

[1] New York: 1959.

cism or indifference of the Greek Alexandrians had infected the Romans, and Epicurus became very popular. As Plato deduced the persistence of the soul after death from its supposed previous existence, so Epicurus drew an opposite conclusion from man's ignorance of his earlier life. He glorified death as annihilation and the end of all men's troubles. This doctrine which the Roman Lucretius preached with the enthusiasm of a neophyte had a profound reaction in Rome. Its adepts in Cicero's circle were numerous, including Cassius, the chief conspirator against Caesar. The Roman historian, Sallust, goes so far as to make Caesar himself affirm, in full senate, that death, as rest from torment, dispels the ills which afflict mankind. Epicureanism also spread into the lowest strata of society, as can be proven from numerous epitaphs. One maxim was repeated so often on tombstones that it was sometimes expressed only by initials: "I was not; I was; I am not: I do not care."

The other system which shared the dominance of minds in Rome was Stoicism. The Stoics, Cumont informs us, held man to be a microcosm who reproduces in his being the constitution of the universe, and that he periodically reincarnates. The universe was thought to be governed by cycles, and after the destruction of each world, the individual souls returned to their divine home, the Soul of the World, from which they originally emanated. Cosmic life being conceived as formed of an infinite series of exactly similar cycles, so in a new world the same souls, endowed with the same qualities, found themselves in existence again.

The reincarnation beliefs of the Stoics are also attested to by the Christian writer, Hippolytus (martyred c. A.D. 235), in his chief work *Philosophumena*, a refutation of heresies. He states in Book I, Chapter 18 that the Stoics "acknowledge there is a transition of souls from one body to another." [2] The later Stoic philosophers like Epictetus and Marcus Aurelius concentrated on ethical ideas and did not mention reincarnation. Marcus Aurelius "had not the ready solution, of all the East, of Plato, and Pythagoras, in Metempsychosis, in the long training of the soul through different lives and fortunes," writes F. W. Bussell in *Marcus Aurelius and the Later Stoics*.[3]

When mysticism and the teachings of Plato and Pythagoras began to triumph in the Roman world, Epicureanism ceased to exist, and Stoicism—which by this time had become quite materialistic—was replaced by Neo-Stoicism. Quoting directly from *After Life in Roman Paganism*:[4]

[2] Clark's *Ante-Nicene Christian Library*, VI, 56.
[3] Edinburgh: 1910, p. 145.
[4] Pp. 20–22, 26–27.

In the first century B.C. the birth was seen, or rather the rebirth, of a mystic movement. . . . The chief preoccupation of philosophers began to be those capital questions as to the origin and end of man which the schools of the earlier [Aristotelian and Epicurean] period had neglected as unanswerable. It was above all the Neo-Pythagoreans who gave up pure rationalism, and thus brought Roman thought to admit new forms of immortality. . . . They claimed that they remained faithful to the wisdom of the sages who, at the dawn of [their] civilization, had received a divine revelation, which had been transmitted first to Pythagoras and then to Plato. . . .

The first to give new life to the Pythagorean school, which had died in Italy centuries before, was, according to Cicero, his friend, the senator Nigidius Figulus . . . a Roman magistrate, a man of singular erudition [who was] bitten with all the occult sciences. . . . This religious philosophy, which, by a symbolism transforming the meaning of the traditional beliefs, reconciled these with men's intelligence, did more than any other to revive faith in immortality. . . .[5]

[The belief in immortality and metempsychosis] of the Pythagoreans was to find a powerful interpreter in [Posidonius], a thinker who had a predominant influence over his contemporaries and the succeeding generation. . . . We know little of his life. Born at Apamea in Syria, about the year 135 [B.C.], he early left his native country . . . and as a young student in Athens he attended the lectures of the older Stoic Panaetius. The universal curiosity which was to make him a scholar of encyclopaedic knowledge soon impelled him to take long journeys. . . . Upon his return he opened a school in the free city of Rhodes and there numbered Cicero among his hearers. When he died at the age of eighty-four the prestige he enjoyed both in the Roman world and among the Greeks was immense.

He owed his intellectual ascendancy as much to the marvellous variety of the knowledge which he displayed, as philosopher, astronomer, historian, geographer and naturalist, as to his copious, harmonious and highly coloured style [of writing]. . . . He gave the support of his authority and his eloquence to the eclecticism which reconciled the principles of the ancient Greek Schools. Moreover, his Syrian origin led him to combine these doctrines with the religious ideas of the East. . . . Posidonius introduced into Stoicism momentous ideas derived at once from Pythagorism and from Eastern cults, and sought to establish them firmly by connecting them with a system of the world, which his vast intelligence had sought to understand in all its aspects.

After explaining Posidonius' views on reincarnation and the after life, Cumont comments:[6] "This theology attributed to man a power such as to satisfy his proudest feelings. It did not regard him as a tiny animalcule who had appeared on a small planet lost in immensity, nor did it, when he

[5] One of the main causes of skepticism had been that the gods "lost face" with the masses and the old mythological stories of the after-life, which had been taken literally, were now regarded as ridiculous fairytales. The new movement portrayed the myths as grand symbols of cosmic and psychological processes. (Eds.)
[6] Pp. 30–31.

scrutinised the heavens, crush him with a sense of his own pettiness as compared with bodies whose greatness surpassed the limits of his imagination. It made man king of creation." Cumont states further:

> [Posidonius] exerted a far-reaching action beyond the narrow circle of the school. . . . Seneca in particular . . . shows the imprint of the philosopher of Apamea. . . . The erudition of the antiquarian Varro, the poems of Virgil and Manilius and the biblical exegesis of Philo the Jew, all drew on [Posidonius] for inspiration. But the author in whom we can best discern his influence is his pupil Cicero, the abundance of whose writings allows us to follow the evolution of his thought, which is characteristic of the whole society of his time. Cicero was an agnostic for the greater part of his life [but] by his study of the writings of his master Posidonius and by his intercourse with the senator Nigidius Figulus, a fervent adept of Pythagorism, [Cicero] had been brought in contact with the stream of mystical ideas which was beginning to flow through the West.

To complete this brief survey of Roman thought in relation to reincarnation, the reader is referred first to the sections under Persian Religions entitled "Mithraism," and "Manicheism," two religions which had a powerful effect on Roman thought during the early centuries of our era, and second to the treatment of Neoplatonism which will be presented a few pages hence. As stated by Cumont:[7] "The mental evolution of Roman society was complete when Neo-Platonism took upon itself the office of directing minds. The powerful mysticism of Plotinus (A.D. 205–262) opened up the path which Greek philosophy was to follow until the world of antiquity reached its end."

CICERO (106–43 B.C.)

Roman Orator, Statesman, and Philosopher

[Regarding Orpheus and his successors, Cicero wrote:]

The ancients, whether they were seers or interpreters of the divine mind in the tradition of the sacred initiations, seem to have known the truth, when they affirmed that we were born into the body to pay the penalty for sins committed in a former life (*vita superiore*).

Hortensio, Fragments, p. 60[1]

The soul is of heavenly origin, forced down from its home in the highest, and, so to speak, buried in earth, a place quite opposed to its divine nature and its immortality. . . . Nor is it only reason and argument that

[7] P. 40.

[1] G. R. S. Mead, *Orpheus*. London: John Watkins, 1965, p. 189.

have brought me to this belief, but the great fame and authority of the most distinguished philosophers. I used to be told that Pythagoras and the Pythagoreans—almost natives of our country, who in old times had been called the Italian school of philosophers—never doubted that we had souls drafted from the universal Divine intelligence.

I used besides to have pointed out to me the discourse delivered by Socrates on the last day of his life upon the immortality of the soul—Socrates . . . the wisest of men. I need say no more. I have convinced myself, and I hold—in view of the rapid movement of the soul, its vivid memory of the past and its prophetic knowledge of the future, its many accomplishments, its vast range of knowledge, its numerous discoveries—that a nature embracing such varied gifts cannot itself be mortal. And since the soul is always in motion and yet has no external source of motion, for it is self-moved, I conclude that it will also have no end to its motion, because it is not likely ever to abandon itself. . . .

It is again a strong proof of men knowing most things before birth, that when mere children they grasp innumerable facts with such speed as to show that they are not then taking them in for the first time, but remembering and recalling them. . . .

No one, my dear Scipio, shall ever persuade me that your father, Paulus, and your two grandfathers . . . or the father of Africanus, or his uncle, or many other illustrious men not necessary to mention, would have attempted such lofty deeds as to be remembered by posterity, had they not seen in their minds that future ages concerned them.

On Old Age[2]
Trans. E. S. Shuckburgh

JULIUS CAESAR (100–44 B.C.)
Roman General and Statesman

[Caesar found the Celts to be remarkably fearless in battle. He apparently investigated the reason for this, and wrote in his volumes on the wars with the Gauls:]

They wish to inculcate this as one of their leading tenets, that souls do not become extinct, but pass after death from one body to another, and they think that men by this tenet are in a great degree excited to valor, the fear of death being disregarded.

Gallic War (Book VI, 14)
Trans. William A. MacDevitt

[2] *Harvard Classics.* New York: P. F. Collier, 1909, IX, 72–74.

[The well-known Roman author, Valerius Maximus, wrote that the Druids "would fain have us believe that the souls of men are immortal. I should be tempted to call these breeches-wearing gentry, fools, were not their doctrine the same as that of the mantle-clad Pythagoras." (Book II, vi.) The Greek historian, Diodorus of Sicily, wrote similarly of the reincarnation beliefs of the Celts in Book V, 28, of his works, as did Lucan, the Spanish-born Roman poet, in his *Pharsalia* I, 449–456.]

LUCRETIUS (96?–55 B.C.)
Roman Poet

[Lucretius was a Roman noble and an ardent follower of Epicurus. He supposedly took his life under the influence of a love potion given him by his wife. Lucretius has been celebrated as a poet's poet and is chiefly remembered for his *De Rerum Natura*, a philosophical poem on "The Nature of Things," the central theme being that the universe is ruled entirely by material laws and that mankind is free to work out its destiny, undisturbed by any supernal guidance. He hoped to liberate men from fear, particularly the fear of death, death being regarded as annihilation. His objections to reincarnation are indicated in the selections that follow:]

If soul immortal is, and winds its way
Into the body at the birth of man,
Why can we not remember something, then,
Of life-time spent before? why keep we not
Some footprints of the things we did of old?
. . . . Were mind
Immortal, were it wont to change its bodies,
How topsy-turvy would earth's creatures act!
The Hyrcan hound would flee the onset oft
Of antlered stag, the scurrying hawk would quake
Along the winds of air at the coming dove,
And men would dote, and savage beasts be wise. . . .
But should some say that always souls of men
Go into human bodies, I will ask:
How can a wise become a dullard soul?
And why is never a child's a prudent soul? . . .
And at the rites of Love, that souls should stand
Ready hard by seems ludicrous enough—
Immortals waiting for their mortal limbs
In numbers innumerable, contending madly
Which shall be first and chief to enter in!—

Unless perchance among the souls there be
Such treaties stablished that the first to come
Flying along, shall enter in the first,
And that they make no rivalries of strength! . . .
. . . . *Death to us*
Is nothing, nor concerns us in the least,
Since nature of mind is mortal evermore. . . . .
Nor yet if time our scattered dust re-blend,
And after death upbuild the flesh again,
Yea, and our light of life arise re-lit,
Can such new birth concern the self one whit,
When once dark death has severed memory's chain.
Naught reck we, then, our lives lived in the past,
Nor for their sorrows feel one pang of pain.

The Nature of Things (Book 3)[1]

VIRGIL (70–19 B.C.)
Roman Poet

[In Book the Sixth of Virgil's Aeneid, Aeneas is shown traveling through the Valley of Oblivion. This phase of the hero's journey is summarized by Gayley in Classic Myths in English Literature and Art:[1]]

Aeneas perceived before him a spacious valley, with trees gently waving to the wind, a tranquil landscape, through which the river Lethe flowed. Along the banks of the stream wandered a countless multitude, numerous as insects in the summer air. Aeneas, with surprise, inquired who were these. Anchises answered: "They are souls to which bodies are to be given in due time. Meanwhile they dwell on Lethe's bank and drink oblivion of their former lives."

"O father!" said Aeneas, "is it possible that any can be so in love with life as to wish to leave these tranquil seats for the upper world?" [Anchises replies by explaining the plan of evolution, and how man eventually became impure.] Thus the more earth predominates in the composition the less pure is the individual; and we see that men and women with their full-grown bodies have not the purity of childhood. So in proportion to the time which the union of body and soul has lasted, is the impurity contracted by the spiritual part. This impurity must be purged away after death. . . .

[1] Except for the last seven lines, the translator is William Ellery Leonard.

[1] Boston: Ginn & Co., 1939, pp. 359–360.

Some few, of whom Anchises intimates that he is one, are admitted at once to Elysium, there to remain. . . . Anchises, having explained so much, proceeded to point out to Aeneas individuals of his race who were hereafter to be born, and to relate to him the exploits they should perform in the world.

OVID (43 B.C.–A.D. 17)
Roman Poet

Pythagoras speaks:
Those I would teach; and by right reason bring
To think of death as but an idle thing.
Why thus affrighted at an empty name,
A dream of darkness, and fictitious flame? . . .
What feels the body when the soul expires,
By time corrupted, or consumed by fires?
. . . the spirit, but new life repeats
In other form, and only changes seats.
Ev'n I, who these mysterious truths declare,
Was once Euphorbus in the Trojan war;
My name and lineage I remember well,
And how in fight by Sparta's king I fell.
In Argive Juno's fane I late beheld
My buckler hung on high, and own'd my former shield.

Then death, so call'd, is but old matter dress'd
In some new figure, and a varied vest:
Thus all things are but alter'd, nothing dies;
And here and there the unbodied spirit flies. . . .
From tenement to tenement though toss'd,
The soul is still the same, the figure only lost:
And as the soften'd wax new seals receives,
This face assumes, and that impression leaves;
Now call'd by one, now by another name;
The form is only changed, the wax is still the same.
So death, so call'd, can but the form deface,
The immortal soul flies out in empty space;
To seek her fortune in some other place.

Metamorphoses (15th Book)
Trans. John Dryden[1]

[1] *The Poetical Works of John Dryden.* London: 1886, IV, 292–293.

APOLLONIUS OF TYANA (FIRST CENTURY A.D.)
Greek Philosopher

[The most renowned philosopher of the first century A.D. was Apollonius of Tyana. Born in the year 1, some biographers state he lived to be one hundred. Marcus Aurelius said: "From him I have learned freedom of will and understanding, steadiness of purpose, and to look to nothing else, not even for a moment, except to reason." [1] Apollonius journeyed extensively through Italy, Greece, Spain, Africa, Asia Minor, Persia, and India, teaching wherever he went. Thirteen years were spent with the sages in Kashmir. He was the author of a voluminous philosophical literature which was collected and preserved by the Emperor Hadrian. Tredwell says: "He speaks and acts as a reformer and lover of humanity everywhere. . . . He had no narrow notions of nationality, no local clique to serve; he came to no chosen people, but to all mankind." [2] The record of his life was written by Damis, his constant companion for more than fifty years. This was partially transcribed by the historian, Philostratus (170?–245), and published in A.D. 210 at the request of the Neoplatonist, Emperor Severus, and his wife, Julia Domna, one of the illustrious women of history and a philosopher of note. Philostratus reports a conversation—which we quote in part below—between Apollonius and Iarchas, a wise man of Kashmir, to whom Apollonius had traveled to be instructed in the higher philosophy. Although particulars are here given of Apollonius' former life, he was later to emphasize: "I never declared to the Greeks either from what body my soul has migrated, or into what it is to migrate." [3]]

And what view do you take of the soul?" [asked Apollonius]. "That which Pythagoras imparted to you, and which we imparted to the Egyptians." "Would you then say," said Apollonius, "that, as Pythagoras declared himself to be Euphorbus, so you yourself, before you entered your present body, were one of the Trojans or Achaeans or someone else?" And the Indian replied: "Those Achaean sailors were the ruin of Troy, and your talking so much about it is the ruin of you Greeks. For you imagine that the campaigners against Troy were the only heroes that ever were, and you forget other heroes both more numerous and more divine, whom your own

[1] Daniel M. Tredwell, *A Sketch of the Life of Apollonius of Tyana.* New York: 1886, p. 47.
[2] *Ibid.*, p. 57.
[3] *Ibid.*, p. 327.

country and that of the Egyptians and that of the Indians have produced. . . ."

[Iarchas related some incidents of a previous incarnation in India, and then remarked:] "You must not be surprised at my transformation from one Indian to another; for here is one," and he pointed to a stripling of about twenty years of age, "who in natural aptitude for philosophy excels everyone . . . yet in spite of all these advantages he detests philosophy." "What then," said Apollonius, "O Iarchas, is the matter with the youth? For it is a terrible thing you tell me, if one so well adapted by nature to the pursuit refuses to embrace philosophy, and has no love for learning. . . ."

"The truth is this stripling was once Palamedes of Troy, and he found his bitterest enemies in Odysseus and Homer; for the one laid an ambush against him of people by whom he was stoned to death, while the other denied him any place in his Epic; and because neither the wisdom with which he was endowed was of any use to him, nor did he meet with any praise from Homer . . . he has conceived an aversion to philosophy, and deplores his ill-luck. And he is Palamedes, for indeed he can write without having learned his letters." . . .

[Iarchas] asked Apollonius the question: "Will you tell us . . . about your earlier incarnation, and who you were before the present life?" And he replied: "Since it was an ignoble episode, I do not remember much about it." Iarchas therefore took him up and said: "Then you think it ignoble to have been the pilot of an Egyptian vessel, for I perceive that this is what you were?" "What you say," said Apollonius, "is true, Iarchas; for that is really what I was. . . ."

[The two men then proceed to a discussion of philosophical subjects, at the conclusion of which Damis comments that "he was transported with admiration and applauded loudly; for he could never have thought that a native of India could show such mastery of the Greek tongue, nor even that, supposing he understood that language, he could have used it with so much ease and elegance."]

Philostratus' Life of Apollonius of Tyana[4]

PLUTARCH (A.D. 46?–120?)
Greek Biographer and Philosopher

Sir Samuel Dill states in *Roman Society from Nero to Marcus Aurelius*[1] that Plutarch and Maximus as the leaders of the new Platonist school of the

[4] Trans. F. C. Conybeare. London: Wm. Heinemann, 1912, I, Book 3, Chaps. 19, 22, 23, 36.

[1] London: Macmillan, 1925, p. 520.

first century "were in this age, the great apostles of the hope of immortality. Platonists in their theory of mind and God, Neo-Pythagorean in their faith in the openness of the human spirit at its best to supernatural influences, they felt the doctrine of the coming life to be axiomatic." Radhakrishnan calls "Plutarch a cultivated Gnostic of a tolerant frame of mind. . . . Plutarch believes in the rebirth of souls. . . . In the development of his views he was influenced by Greek thought and Egyptian religion." [2]

The Neoplatonists

"Neoplatonic thought is, metaphysically, the maturest thought that the European world has seen," writes Thomas Whittaker in *The Neo-Platonists*.[1] According to the *Britannica*:[2] "Pagan Greek philosophy was Neoplatonist till it faded out in the sixth century A.D. Many of the greatest Christian thinkers of this period, the great formative period of Christian theology, were deeply influenced by Neoplatonism, as were later the great Moslem philosophers. The influence of Neoplatonism on the thought of the middle ages was thus very great; and it has continued, through very diverse channels, to influence men's minds down to our own day."

Ammonius Saccas was the founder in A.D. 193 of the famous Alexandrian School of Neoplatonism in Egypt. He was born of Christian parents but disavowed Church dogmas. Origen, Plotinus, Herennius, and Longinus—the counselor of Queen Zenobia—were among his immediate disciples. Iamblichus, Porphyry, Proclus, Eratosthenes (the astronomer), Hypatia (the virgin philosopher), the Emperor Julian, and numerous stars of second magnitude, all belonged at various times to this School, helping to make Alexandria with its incomparable library one of the greatest seats of learning the world has known.

With the revival of the teachings of Plato, the philosophy of reincarnation again came into prominence, as will be seen from the selections from the voluminous works of Ammonius' pupils, although he himself left no written record of his thought. The Neoplatonists, however, did not limit themselves to Plato. Known as the Philalethians, "the lovers of truth," and the eclectic theosophical school, they sought to reconcile all religions and philosophies under one system of truth, and restore to its purity the wisdom of the ancients. This they held to be the real object of Jesus. Ammonius received the cooperation of the two Church Fathers, Clement and Athen-

---

[2] *Eastern Religions and Western Thought*, p. 203.

[1] Cambridge University Press, 1918, p. 209.
[2] 1959, Article "Neoplatonism."

agoras, the learned Rabbis of the Synagogues, and the initiates of the various Mystery Schools.

The Neoplatonic movement reached its height of popularity in the fifth century. The leading Platonist then was Hypatia, the daughter of Theon—himself a celebrated philosopher and mathematician. After contacting the School in Athens, Hypatia went to Alexandria where she held lectures and classes in philosophy and mathematics at the famous Museum. Her eloquence, wisdom, youth, and extraordinary beauty soon attracted crowds of students, and among her champions and students were two of the most influential men of the day, Orestes, the Prefect of Alexandria, and the Christian philosopher Synesius, then Bishop of Cyrene. (See Part Two under "Synesius.")

In 412 St. Cyril became Bishop of Alexandria, and in 414 under his instigation a group of his monks led by Peter the Reader murdered Hypatia on the altar of a Christian church, dragged her naked body through the streets, later scraping the flesh from the bones. Clergyman-author, Charles Kingsley, tells the story in his two-volume novel, *Hypatia*, from which we shall later quote. With Hypatia's death the Neoplatonic School came to an end in Alexandria. Some of the philosophers removed to Athens but their school was closed by the Emperor Justinian in 529 and the last seven Neoplatonic philosophers fled to the east. It was not until the Renaissance that Platonism returned to Christian Europe, although meanwhile—as indicated under "Islam"—it was revived in Arabia, Persia and in Moorish Spain. The death of Hypatia has been called the beginning of the Dark Ages for Europe.

PLOTINUS (A.D. 205–270)
Greek Neoplatonic Philosopher

[Professor Elmer O'Brien (S.J.) of Loyola College, Montreal, writes in *The Essential Plotinus:*[1] "For the student of history of ideas there is to be had at first hand [in Plotinus' *Enneads*] the ideas that . . . molded Western thinking more than did those of a Plato or an Aristotle. . . . The doctrine of the *Enneads* . . . has always managed to overleap the usual confinement of time and space . . . the most varied minds down the ages have served from time to time as its native land; the most unpropitious of circumstances have seemingly brought about its successive reincarnations in an Augustine, a Hugh of St. Victor, a Meister Eckhart." Augustine, who attended the lectures of Plotinus, even went so far as to speculate that

[1] New York: Mentor, 1964, pp. vii, 13–14.

Plotinus was Plato reborn. (See Part Two, under "Augustine.") G. F. Moore calls Plotinus "the fountain head of the higher Christian mysticism," and states that "the bible of the mediaeval mystics, Dionysius Areopagita, is thoroughly Plotinian . . . but the transmigration of souls . . . was tacitly let fall." [2]

W. R. Inge in his Gifford Lectures is especially enthusiastic regarding this pupil of Ammonius:

Plotinus is generally regarded as the great philosopher of mysticism. . . . This kind of philosophy may not be in fashion just now; but when we see what havoc popular subjectivism has made of religious philosophy, and how it has encouraged a recrudescence of superstition, we may be glad to return to Plato and his successors. For them, mysticism involves and rests upon metaphysics. . . . No other guide on this pathway equals Plotinus in power and insight and spiritual penetration. He leaves us, it is true, much to do ourselves; but this is because the spiritual life cannot be described to those who are not living it. He demands of us a strict moral discipline as well as intellectual capacity for learning.

On the intellectual side, Neoplatonism sums up the results of 700 years of untrammelled thinking, the longest period of free speculation which the human race has enjoyed. The greater part of it passed over into Christian philosophy, which it shaped for all time. . . . The neglect of Plotinus, alike by students of Greek philosophy and of Christian dogma, is therefore much to be regretted. It makes a gap where no gap exists. . . . The lecturer has found Plotinus a most inspiring and fortifying spiritual guide, as well as a great thinker. In times of trouble like the present he has much to teach us, lifting us up from the miseries of this world to the pure air and sunshine of eternal truth, beauty, and goodness. (*The Philosophy of Plotinus.*[3])

The highlights of Plotinus' career are reviewed by Alice Zimmern in the introduction to her translation of *Porphyry, The Philosopher, to His Wife Marcella.*[4] She writes that after eleven years of instruction by Ammonius, Plotinus "set out for the East to study the wisdom of Persia and India. At the age of forty he settled in Rome, and there opened a school of philosophy. . . . In spite of the abstruse nature of his teaching, crowds flocked around Plotinus. Men of science, physicians, senators and lawyers came to hear him; even Roman ladies enrolled themselves among his disciples. . . . This popularity of an abstruse philosopher is a curious and perhaps unique phenomenon. . . ."

The translator of the first selections from the *Enneads* is Stephen

---

[2] *Op. cit.,* p. 41.
[3] London: Longmans, Green, 1948, pp. xiii–xiv.
[4] London: George Redway, 1896, p. 26.

Mackenna, a member of the Dublin circle of George Russell, Yeats, James Stephens, and other writers of Ireland's literary renaissance.]

The animals devour each other: men attack each other: all is war without rest, without truce: this gives new force to the question how Reason can be author of the plan and how all can be declared well done. . . . What does it matter when [beings] are devoured only to return in some new form? It comes to no more than the murder of one of the personages in a play; the actor alters his make-up and enters in a new role. The actor, of course, was not really killed; but if dying is but changing a body as the actor changes a costume, or even an exit from the body like the exit of the actor from the boards when he has no more to say or do, what is there so very dreadful in this transformation of living beings one into another? . . .

Murders, death in all its guises, the reduction and sacking of cities, all must be to us just such a spectacle as the changing scenes of a play; all is but the varied incident of a plot, costume on and off, acted grief and lament. For on earth, in all the succession of life, it is not the Soul within but the Shadow outside of the authentic man, that grieves and complains and acts out the plot on this world stage which men have dotted with stages of their own constructing. All this is the doing of man knowing no more than to live the lower and outer life, and never perceiving that, in his weeping and in his graver doings alike, he is but at play. . . .

Every man has his place, a place that fits the good man, a place that fits the bad: each . . . makes his way, naturally, reasonably, to the place, good or bad, that suits him, and takes the position he has made his own. There he talks and acts, in blasphemy and crime or in all goodness: for the actors bring to this play what they were before it was ever staged. . . .

But these actors, Souls, hold a peculiar dignity; they act in a vaster place than any stage; the Author has made them masters of all this world; they have a wide choice of place; they themselves determine the honor or discredit in which they are agents since their place and part are in keeping with their quality. . . . If a man were . . . nothing more than a made thing, acting and acted upon according to a fixed nature—he could be no more subject to reproach and punishment than the mere animals. But as the scheme holds, man is singled out for condemnation when he does evil; and this with justice. For he is no mere thing made to rigid plan; his nature contains a Principle apart and free.

Trans. Stephen Mackenna[5]

[5] *Plotinus: Psychic and Physical Treatises.* London: Philip Lee Warner, 1921, II, 28–30, 33–34, 39.

The soul . . . falling from on high, suffers captivity, is loaded with fetters, and employs the energies of sense. . . . She is reported also to be buried and to be concealed in a cave; but when she converts herself to intelligence she then breaks her fetters and ascends on high, receiving first of all from reminiscence the ability of contemplating real beings. . . . Souls therefore are necessarily of an amphibious nature, and alternately experience a superior and inferior condition of being; such as are able to enjoy a more intimate converse with Intellect abiding for a longer period in the higher world, and such to whom the contrary happens, either through nature or fortune, continuing longer connected with these inferior concerns. . . .

Thus the soul, though of divine origin, and proceeding from the regions on high, becomes merged in the dark receptacle of body. . . . By this means it receives a knowledge of evil, unfolds its latent powers, and exhibits a variety of operations peculiar to its nature, which, by perpetually abiding in an incorporeal habit, and never proceeding into energy, would have been bestowed in vain. . . . For the experience of evil produces a clearer knowledge of good. . . . Indeed, if it is proper to speak clearly what appears to me to be the truth . . . the whole of our soul does not enter into body, but something belonging to it always abides in the intelligible . . . world . . . . For every soul possesses something which inclines downwards to body, and something which tends upwards toward intellect . . . but the superior part of the soul is never influenced by fraudulent delights, and lives a life always uniform and divine.

Trans. Thomas Taylor[6]

PORPHYRY (A.D. 233–C. 304)
Greek Scholar and Neoplatonic Philosopher

[Esmé Wynne-Tyson writes in the introduction to the reprint of Thomas Taylor's translation of Porphyry's *On Abstinence from Animal Food*.[1] "In the present age Porphyry is renowned chiefly for having been the pupil of the great Neoplatonist, Plotinus . . . and for having edited *The Enneads* of his Master; but in earlier times he was considered to be one of the most erudite philosophers of the West. Augustine refers to him as 'the noble philosopher,' 'the great ethnic philosopher' and ranks him even above Plato. Eusebius, his implacable enemy, speaks of him as 'the wonderful theologian' and 'the great prophet,' while to Simplicius he was 'the most

[6] *Five Books of Plotinus*. London: 1794, pp. 268–269, 273–274, 280, 282–285.

[1] New York: Barnes & Noble, 1965.

learned of philosophers.' '" Porphyry was a Hellenized Hebrew. Some have thought that his works surpassed those of Plotinus, but there is no way to confirm this as his books were publicly burned by Constantine and by Theodosius, and only a few treatises are extant. That Porphyry taught reincarnation is, of course, beyond question, but his views thereon have come to us mainly through the reports of his adversaries. Augustine has been quoted earlier as to Porphyry's supposed ideas. Voltaire in his article "Viande" [2] wrote of Porphyry's De Abstinentia: "One might believe in reading him that this great enemy of the Church is a Father of the Church. He does not speak of the metempsychosis [in this treatise] but he regards other animals as our brothers. . . ." Porphyry does speak of reincarantion in De Abstinentia. One selection has been given under "Mithraism." Another appears to be the following:]

As long as any one injures another, though he should possess the greatest wealth, and all the acres of land which the earth contains, he is still poor. . . . He is unjust, without God, and impious, and enslaved to every kind of depravity, which is produced by the lapse of the soul into matter. . . . He wanders from the principle of the universe. . . . He likewise yields to the mortal part of his nature, while he remains ignorant of his real self. . . . However, in the choice of lives [that individual] is the more accurate judge who has obtained an experience of both [the better and the worse kind of life], than he who has only experienced one of them. . . . Hence, he who lives according to intellect, will more accurately define what is eligible and what is not, than he who lives under the dominion of irrationality. For the former has passed through the irrational life . . . but the latter, having had no experience of an intellectual life [acts] like a child among children.

De Abstinentia[3]
Trans. Thomas Taylor

IAMBLICHUS (A.D. C. 250–C. 330)
Greek Philosopher

[Iamblichus, the third member of the great Neoplatonic triad, was born in Chalsis in Coele-Syria. From the fragments of his life collected by impartial historians, it is evident that he was a man of great learning, renowned for his charity and self-denial. His mind was deeply impregnated with the Pythagorean doctrines, and in his famous biography of Pythagoras set forth

[2] Voltaire's *Philosophical Dictionary*.
[3] P. 143 of the New York: Barnes & Noble, and the London: Centaur Press, editions.

the philosophical, ethical, and scientific teachings of the Sage of Samos. In D. S. Merezhovsky's historical novel, *The Death of the Gods*—in which the Emperor Julian is the central figure—a truly breath-taking picture is given of the God-taught Iamblichus, as he was called.

Iamblichus was a profound student of the Egyptian Mysteries and was determined to make public what hitherto had been taught in secrecy. To accomplish this he founded a school of theurgy among the Neoplatonists. Porphyry at first opposed this project because the knowledge of practical theurgy is dangerous for most men. He therefore addressed a letter to an Egyptian initiate known as Anebo, asking for an explanation of certain points in the Egyptian system. The letter was answered by Iamblichus under the name of his teacher Abammon. The discussion between Porphyry and Iamblichus composes the book known as *The Egyptian Mysteries*, recorded by Iamblichus himself. The selections below are from the translation of Professor Alexander Wilder.[1] The opening paragraph is from the section "The Music at the Arcane Rites."]

What shall we say in regard to the question: "Why do the divinities that are invoked require the worshiper to be just, although they themselves when entreated consent to perform unjust acts?" In reply to this I am uncertain in respect to what is meant by "performing unjust acts," as the same definition may not appear right both to us and to the gods. We, on the one hand, looking to that which is least significant, consider the things that are present, the momentary life, what it is and how it originates. The beings superior to us, let me say, know for certain the whole life of the soul and all its former lives; and if they bring on a retribution from the supplication of those who invoke them, they do not increase it beyond what is just. On the contrary, they aim at the sins impressed upon the soul in former lifetimes, which men do not perceive, and so imagine that it is unjust that they fall into the misfortunes which they suffer.

The many are also generally accustomed to propose the same doubt in regard to Providence; that certain persons are suffering from wrong-doing, who had not wronged any one previously. For they are unable here to reason as to what the soul is, what its entire life has been, the magnitude of its great errors in former lives, and whether it is now suffering these things for what it did formerly. . . .

That condition about which thou utterest doubt, does not exist, namely: "*That all things are bound fast in the indissoluble bonds of Necessity, which they term Fate.* . . . All things in the world of Nature are not

[1] New York: Metaphysical Pub., 1911, pp. 122, 175, 259–260.

controlled by Fate. . . . For the soul has a principle of its own leading to the realm of Intelligence, and not only standing aloof from things of the world of generated existence, but also joining it to that which IS, even to the divine nature. . . . [This] principle of the soul . . . is superior to the whole realm of nature and generated existence. By it we can be united to the gods, rise above the established order of the world, and likewise participate in the life eternal and in the energy of the gods of the highest heaven. Through this principle we are able to set ourselves free. For when the better qualities in us are in activity, and the soul is exalted to those beings superior to itself, then it becomes separate altogether from every thing which held it fast in the realm of generated existence, keeps itself aloof from inferior natures, exchanges one life for the other, and gives itself to a different order, entirely abandoning the former.

The Egyptian Mysteries

EMPEROR JULIAN (A.D. 331–363)
Roman Neoplatonist

Julian, the nephew of the first Christian emperor, Constantine, was a pupil of Aedesius, who had been taught by Iamblichus. He was initiated at Ephesus, and later into the Eleusinian Mysteries. Succeeding the despotic Constantine, his reign lasted only 18 months, but it was noted for its enlightenment and religious tolerance. Exiled Christian bishops were returned to their posts, and pagan subjects were granted complete religious liberty. Few characters in history have been as unjustly maligned as Julian "the Apostate." This is mildly implied in Henry Fielding's reincarnation story of Julian.[1]

Julian was mortally wounded by an assassin. While dying he said: "I have learned from philosophy how much more excellent the soul is than the body, and that the separation of the nobler substance should be the subject of joy rather than affliction." (Marcellinus Ammianus' History, Book XXV.) Then, emulating Socrates, Julian turned to the two philosophers Priscus and Maximus and entered into a metaphysical discussion as to the nature of the soul. Incidentally, Julian appears to have had reason to believe himself the reincarnation of the unenviable Alexander the "Great." Ibsen dwelt on this theme in his play *The Emperor Julian.*[2]

[1] See Index under "Fielding."
[2] See under "Ibsen."

SALLUSTIUS (FOURTH CENTURY)
Roman Philosopher

Sallustius was Pretorian Prefect under Emperor Julian. Thomas Whittaker writes of him in *The Neo-Platonists:*[1] "Sallust, the friend of Julian, in setting forth . . . a creed for the reformed paganism, had put only in cryptic language his explanation of the change that had come over the world. The guilt, he says, that is now punished in some by total ignorance of the true divine order may be that of having deified their kings in a former life. Thus it appears that in Julian's circle Christianity was regarded as nemesis for the deification of the Emperors."

In her work *A Prison, a Paradise,*[2] Loran Hurnscot quotes Sallust's views on why atheism exists: "It is not unlikely that the rejection of God is a kind of punishment: we may well believe that those who knew the gods and neglected them in one life may in another be deprived of the knowledge of them altogether."

MACROBIUS (FOURTH–FIFTH CENTURY)
Roman Neoplatonist

[The spiritual amnesia, as well as loss of memory of prior lives, resulting from the soul's supposed drinking of the waters of Lethe, receives an illuminating explanation from Macrobius in the twelfth chapter of his *Commentary on The Dream of Scipio*. The extract, as translated, is to be found as a footnote in Thomas Taylor's *Select Works of Porphyry*.[1]]

As soon as the soul gravitates towards body . . . she begins to experience a material tumult, that is, matter flowing into her essence. And this is what Plato remarks in the *Phædo*, that the soul is drawn into body staggering with recent intoxication; signifying by this, the new drink of matter's impetuous flood, through which the soul, becoming defiled and heavy, is drawn into a terrene situation. . . . Hence oblivion, the companion of intoxication . . . begins silently to creep into the recesses of the soul. For if souls retained in their descent to bodies the memory of divine concerns, of which they were conscious in the heavens, there would be no dissension among men about divinity. But all, indeed, in descending, drink of obliv-

[1] P. 304.
[2] New York: Viking, 1959, p. 268.

---

[1] London: 1823, pp. 187–188.

ion; though some more, and others less. On this account, though truth is not apparent to all men on the earth, yet all exercise their opinions about it; because a defect of memory is the origin of opinion. But those discover most who have drunk least of oblivion, because they easily remember what they had known before in the heavens. . . .

The soul is drawn down to these terrene bodies, and is on this account said to die when it is enclosed in this fallen region, and the seat of mortality. Nor ought it to cause any disturbance that we have so often mentioned the death of the soul, which we have pronounced to be immortal. For the soul is not extinguished by its own proper death, but is only overwhelmed for a time. Nor does it lose the benefit of perpetuity by its temporal demersion. Since, when it deserves to be purified from the contagion of vice, through its entire refinement from body, it will be restored to the light of perennial life, and will return to its pristine integrity and perfection.

Commentary on the Dream of Scipio

PROCLUS (A.D. 410–485)
Greek Neoplatonic Philosopher

[Proclus is called "the last grand master of Neoplatonism." In his *Commentaries on the Phædrus* of Plato, Proclus endeavored to show by a multitude of arguments that man's soul can never incarnate in an animal, and in his *Commentaries* on Plato's *Timæus* summarized these views:]

It is usual to inquire how human souls can descend into brute animals. And some, indeed, think that there are certain similitudes of men to brutes, which they call savage lives: for they by no means think it possible that the rational essence can become the soul of a savage animal. . . . In his "Republic" Plato says, that the soul of Thersites assumed an ape, but not the body of an ape; and in the "Phædrus," that the soul descends into a savage life, but not into a savage body. For life is conjoined with its proper soul. And in this place he says it is changed into a brutal nature. For a brutal nature is not a brutal body, but a brutal life.[1]

[The following is from Proclus' *The Elements of Theology*, as translated by E. R. Dodds,[2] the statements being presented as propositions:]

The soul-order, originating from one primal Soul, descends to a manifold of souls and again carries back the manifold to the one. . . .

[1] Quoted in G. R. S. Mead's preface to *Select Works of Plotinus*, trans. Thomas Taylor. London: Rider, 1912, pp. xxix–xxx.
[2] Oxford University Press, 1963, pp. 25, 181.

Every particular soul can descend into temporal process and ascend from process to [spiritual] Being an infinite number of times. For if at certain times it is in the company of gods and at others falls away from its upward tension towards the divine . . . it is plain that by turns it comes-to-be in the world of process and [then] has true Being among the gods. For it cannot (have been for an infinite time in material bodies and thereafter pass a second infinite time among the gods, neither can it) have spent an infinite time among the gods and again be embodied for the whole time thereafter, since that which has no temporal beginning will never have an end, and what has no end cannot have had a beginning. It remains, then, that each soul has a periodic alternation of ascents out of process and descents into process, and that this movement is unceasing by reason of the infinitude of time. Therefore each particular soul can descend and ascend an infinite number of times, and this shall never cease to befall every such soul.

The Elements of Theology

[Commenting on the foregoing, Professor Dodds states:][3]

The question whether the human soul can attain a final release from the "circle of birth" . . . was one on which the Neoplatonists were not unanimous. . . . Porphyry . . . seems to have asserted in *de regressu animae* . . . that the soul, at any rate the soul of the philosopher, *will* eventually be released for ever. Later we find the contrary opinion, that souls cannot "leave the body once for all and remain through all time in idleness," maintained by Sallustius (who is very probably following Iamblichus here): he supports it (a) by the argument from function, that souls have their natural citizenship in the body; and (b) by the consideration that . . . the earth would on the Porphyrian theory eventually be depopulated.

Proclus takes the same view as Sallustius, but relies on the more general argument that an eternal life cannot start from, or finish at, a point in time. He holds with Syrianus that while self-will causes some human souls to descend more often than is necessary, cosmic law requires that each shall descend at least once in every world-period. Consistently with this, he rejects the . . . view that such descent is in itself sinful. . . . He definitely treats the descent as a necessary part of the soul's education or as a necessary cosmic service.

[3] Pp. 304–305.

◆ ✳ ●

Middle Ages

The following sections from Part Two are pertinent to this period:

TALIESIN (SIXTH CENTURY)
Welsh Bard

[Joseph Campbell writes in The Hero with a Thousand Faces:[1] "Taliesin, 'Chief of the Bards of the West,' may have been an actual historical personage of the sixth century A.D., contemporary with the chieftain who became the 'King Arthur' of later romance. The bard's legend and poems survive in a thirteenth-century manuscript, 'The Book of Taliesin,' which is one of the 'Four Ancient Books of Wales'. . . . Gwion Bach, who, having tasted three drops from the poison kettle of inspiration, was eaten by the hag Caridwen, reborn as an infant, and committed to the sea, was found next morning in a fishtrap. . . . When the men took up the leathern bag out of the trap and opened it and saw the forehead of the baby boy, they said . . . 'Behold a radiant brow (taliesin)!' 'Taliesin be he called.' . . . The larger portion of the bard's song is devoted to the Imperishable, which lives in him. . . . Those listening are oriented to the Imperishable in themselves. . . . Though he had feared the terrible hag, he had been

[1] New York: Pantheon, 1949, pp. 198 fn., 239, 241–242.

swallowed and reborn. Having died to his personal ego, he arose again established in the Self." The poems tell of actual reincarnation as well as psychological rebirth.]

I have been in many shapes before I attained a
*   congenial form . . .*
There is nothing in which I have not been. . . .
I was with my Lord in the highest sphere
On the fall of Lucifer into the depth of hell;
I have borne a banner before Alexander. . . .
I am a wonder whose origin is not known.
I have been in Asia with Noah in the ark,
I have seen the destruction of Sodom and Gomorrah.
I have been in India when Roma was built. . . .
I shall be until the doom on the face of the earth. . . .
I was originally little Gwion,
And at length I am Taliesin.[2]

Knowest thou what thou art
In the hour of sleep—
A mere body, a mere soul—
Or a secret retreat of light? . . .
I marvel that in their books
They know not with certainty
The properties of the soul;
Or what form are its members;
In what part, and when, it takes up its abode,
Or by what wind or stream it is supplied.[3]

The Grail Epics and the Troubadours

In reviewing the book *King Arthur's Avalon* by Geoffrey Ashe,[1] DeLancey Ferguson writes: "The Grail stories mostly grew up outside the Church. . . . Mr. Ashe suggests possible reasons why the Church fought shy of this cult. A wonder-working vessel is a recurrent theme in ancient religions; so is the idea of special knowledge to be achieved by an initiate who performs secret rituals. 'The Grail cult may well have been only the most complex codification of a bold strain of mysticism, persisting through the centuries but never openly unfolded.' To the Church, of course, the hint of spiritual

[2] Eva Martin, *The Ring of Return.* pp. 110–11.
[3] Lewis Spence, *Magic Arts in Celtic Britain.* London: Rider, undated, p. 128.

[1] New York: Dutton, 1958.

knowledge hidden even from the clergy was flat heresy." [2] One of the King Arthur legends made this prophecy: "He shall come again full twice as fair to rule over his people." [3]

The Grail stories are to be found also in France, Italy, and Germany. Harold Bayley in his remarkable work *A New Light on the Renaissance*[4] presents evidence that the Grail romances (amounting in bulk to a set of the *Britannica!*) were nothing less than the scriptures of the Albigenses, propagated during the age of chivalry by the Troubadour poets of southern France and northern Italy and Spain. These vast cycles of mystic literature, written and declaimed by the Troubadours, spread like wildfire over Europe, and were translated into many languages.

In the south of France where the Albigensian reincarnationists were so deeply rooted, the Troubadours for centuries exercised an enormous influence, and kept aflame the love of art and literature that was traditional to that region. At a time of almost total illiteracy in Europe and when the printing press was unknown, the Troubadours filled the role now occupied by the press, and also embraced the callings of poet, musician, chronicler, *littérateur*, and theologian. When between the years 1209 and 1226 the Church devastated the Albigensian provinces, the home of the Troubadours was demolished and its language (the *langue d'oc*) proscribed and extinguished. Finding asylum in all parts of Europe they continued their work of humanistic and mystical education, adding perpetual fuel to the smoldering fires of heresy and rebellion to Rome. Likewise small bands of Albigensian artisans penetrated to the remotest parts of the continent, some of them emigrating to England where history knows them as the Lollards.

Dante and the Fideli d'Amore

Dante's *Divine Comedy* gives a description in allegorical language of the drama of after-death conditions, of purification in purgatory, of sublimation in heaven, and at least one hint of the soul's return to earth. In Canto XX (Paradiso), Dante writes of meeting a Roman emperor in the Heaven of Jupiter and being told:

He from Hell came back into his bones, and this was the reward of living hope—the living hope which put power into the prayers made to God to raise him up, that his will might be moved. The glorious soul returning to flesh where

[2] *New York Herald Tribune*, June 8, 1958.
[3] *The Reader's Encyclopedia*, ed. Wm. Rose Benét. New York: Crowell, 1948, p. 50.
[4] London: J. M. Dent, 1909.

it abode awhile, believed in Him who had power to help, and believing, kindled into such a flame of Love that at the second death it was worthy to come into this Joy.

Writers of this time were compelled to veil unorthodox thinking in obscure symbolism. A favorite method was to clothe ideas in the garments of pure earthly love. Dante (1265–1321), one of the important forerunners of the Italian Renaissance, apparently exercised great caution in what he said. It has been shown by such scholars as Gabriele Rossetti, Luigi Valli, Francesca Perez, and Giovanni Pascoli that Dante and the group of poets known as the Fideli d'Amore, or the Faithful in Love, used this secret language.

At least thirty words commonly used by them were found to have one and sometimes two hidden meanings. Belonging to the cipher were love, madonna, death, life, women, nature, stone, rose, flower—all of which appear repeatedly, often confusing the surface meaning of the author. Characteristically, the "Beloved," be it Rosa, Beatrice, or Savage, always seems to represent Wisdom. Dante wrote: "I say and affirm that the lady of whom I was enamoured after my first love was the most beautiful and pure daughter of the Emperor of the Universe to whom Pythagoras gave the name Philosophy." [1] This symbolism of the Beloved was also used by the Sufi poets of Islam; the Spanish mystics of whom Raymond Lully was one; the Troubadours of France and Italy; and the Minnesingers or Love Singers of Germany, who have been immortalized in Wagner's *Tannhäuser*,[2] and *Der Meistersinger*.

The Troubadours were conspicuous as Pilgrims of Love, and Knights Errant in the service of a mysterious Lady. (Cervantes followed this traditional pattern in *Don Quixote*.) The Troubadours viewed their service as both an art and a science, their *"gai savoir,"* their *"gai science,"* and it is believed that under a well-recognized erotic jargon, matters and ideas of great moment were communicated to the scattered fidèles. Many of their love poems, which today are regarded as amatory trifles, may in reality be works of a recondite character, enshrining doctrines traditionally handed down from past ages. The Troubadours at times made little effort to dissemble the fact. "Thou can'st go whither thou wilt," says one of them, addressing his own love poem, "I have dressed thee so well that thou will be understood by those endowed with intelligence: of others thou need'st not be concerned." [3]

[1] Harold Bayley, *op. cit.*, p. 61.
[2] In *Tannhäuser* (Act II, Scene 3), the Landgrave, addressing the Minstrels, says: "Full oft within these walls your lays have sounded; in veiled wisdom or in mirthful measures."
[3] Harold Bayley, *op. cit.*, pp. 60–62.

In his two-volume work *Disquisitions on the Anti-Papal Spirit which produced the Reformation*, Gabriele Rossetti (the father of Christina and Dante Gabriel Rossetti) states that the art of speaking and writing in a language bearing a double interpretation is of great antiquity; it was in practice among the priests of Egypt, brought thence by the Manichees, from whom it passed to the Templars and Albigenses, spread over Europe, and aided in bringing about the Reformation. John Yarker, who mentions this in *Mysteries of Antiquity*,[4] comments that Boccaccio left several works, including parts of *The Decameron* "written in this jargon, which all refer to Dante, as to a great model," and that beyond doubt "Dante borrowed his style of figurative writings from the Templars and Albigenses."[5] In this connection it is worth reporting that in a work on Dante published in Paris in 1854, the Catholic writer, Eugene Aroux, called him a fountain of heresy and a leader of the Albigensian or Cathari "church" who had conceived the audacious project of employing ecclesiastical symbols to convey his Platonic teaching.

In *Il Mistero del Amore Platonico* (Vol. 3), Rossetti traces the movement first through the Provençals or the Troubadours of France; to the Sicilian poets (Frederic II, Pier della Vigna, Jacopo Lentini); from these to the Bolognese (Guinzelli); and eventually to the Toscans (Dante, Cavalcanti, Ceno). The French author, Maurice Magre, states "it was after the visit of Nicetas . . . the Bulgarian mystic and great propagator of Catharism . . . that the group of the Faithful in Love was formed, whose doctrine had so much in common with Catharism. It is said that Frederick II, the protector of heretics, was an initiate. One of the masters of this group was Guido Cavalcanti, the friend and initiator of Dante."[6]

Dante's use of symbolical language appears also to have been a deliberate borrowing from the Muslim Sufi mystics. In *The Philosophy of Ibn 'Arabī*—the Sufi philosopher and poet quoted in the Islam section—Rom Landau writes:

In the Western world, Dante provides one of the most conspicuous examples of Ibn 'Arabī's pervasive influence. Señor Asín y Palacios, the leading authority on the subject, has proved in his remarkable studies published in the volume *Islam and the Divine Comedy*[7] that not only were innumerable ideas in the *Divine Comedy* inspired by Ibn 'Arabī, but the entire geography of heaven and hell was taken over by Dante from Ibn 'Arabī (and other Muslim sources).

[4] New York: 1878, p. 41.
[5] P. 46.
[6] *Magicians, Seers, and Mystics*. New York: Dutton, 1932, pp. 49–50. Published in England as *The Return of the Magi*.
[7] London, John Murray, 1926.

And to mention but one other Western thinker whose work unmistakably shows Ibn 'Arabī's influence, there is Ramon Lull, the Spanish mystic.[8]

The Sufi connection of both the Troubadours and the Fideli d'Amore is considered in Idries Shah's history of the Sufis from which we have already quoted. He writes respecting the Troubadours:

Professor Hitti and others are fully persuaded of the Arab origins of the troubadours: "The troubadours . . . resembled Arab singers not only in sentiment and character but also in the very forms of their minstrelsy. Certain titles which these Provençal singers gave to their songs are but translations from Arabic titles." [9] . . . The correspondence between troubadour feeling, however diluted a form of the Sufi stream it became . . . , was noted even by people who had no specialist knowledge of the interior contact. Emerson equates the great Sufi love poet Hafiz and the troubadours, and claims for them the true essence of poetry: "Read Hafiz and the *trouvères*: fact books which all geniuses prize as raw material and as an antidote to verbiage and false poetry." . . .

Such was the vitality of the inner Sufic theme of this [troubadour] poetry that it laid the foundation of a great deal of subsequent Western literature. As one writer puts it: "Without the Provençal and troubadour singers there would be precious little in our contemporary music worth the name. True, we could have had dirges and folk songs but the strange insistent call to something else, something which awaits us, something which as human beings we have to accomplish, would probably be missing from poetry and music alike." [10] (Pp. 318–320, 322.)

[8] New York: Macmillan, 1959, p. 26.
[9] Hitti, *History of the Arabs*, New York, 1951, p. 600.
[10] G. Butler, *The Leadership of the Strange Cult of Love*, Bristol, 1910, p. 17.

The Renaissance and Reformation

The Italian Renaissance and the Neoplatonic Revival

"The light of the Renaissance dawned gradually upon Europe," writes W. R. Inge. "Greek scholars had begun to visit the Latin countries some time before the fall of Constantinople [in 1453]; and there were many other reasons for the great emancipation of the human mind which spread from Italy all over the West. It was like an awakening from a deep sleep . . . the dropped threads are taken up again; civilization resumes its course with the recovered remains of the Classics in its hand." [1] Or, as the reincarnationist might audaciously suggest, the very souls who lived in Greece and Rome came back to carry on their work. G. F. Moore remarks in his Ingersoll lecture at Harvard: "It is not surprising . . . that with the revival of Platonism and Plotinianism at the renaissance, the theory of metempsychosis was revived in European philosophy." [2]

The Neoplatonic revival appeared first in the city of Florence and under the protection of the powerful house of Medici. Cosmo de Medici made the acquaintance of George Gemistus, a renowned Byzantine Platonic philosopher who attended the Council of Florence in 1439 as a deputy of the Greek Church. Gemistus, who lived for a time at Cosmo's court, gave him the idea of founding a Platonic academy. With this in view, Cosmo selected Marsilio Ficino, the son of his chief physician, for a thorough education in Greek language and philosophy. Ficino's natural aptitude was so great that he completed his first work on the Platonic Institutions

---

[1] *The Platonic Tradition in English Religious Thought.* London: Longmans, Green, 1926, pp. 21–22.
[2] *Op. cit.,* p. 56.

when only twenty-three years old. At thirty he began his translation of Plato, later making excellent translations of Plotinus, Iamblichus, Proclus, and Synesius. He also wrote a treatise on the Platonic doctrine of immortality.

When Lorenzo, Cosmo de Medici's grandson, was eight years old, Ficino became his tutor, imbuing him with a deep reverence for the Greeks. After Lorenzo (the "Magnificent") became the head of the house he brought his grandfather's plans to completion and going further, founded a university in Pisa, established public libraries for his people, and became a patron of Michelangelo, Botticelli, and Leonardo de Vinci.

Giovanni Pico, son of the Prince of Mirandola, joined forces with Lorenzo and Ficino and through their united efforts the revival of Neoplatonism made rapid headway. Although only a young man, Pico della Mirandola was deeply versed in the learning of the Chaldeans, Hebrews, and Arabians. He was a Hermetist as well as a Kabalist, but today he is chiefly known as the author of the humanist classic "An Oration on the Dignity of Man." Pico taught that "the soul passes out of one body and enters another." [3]

With the deaths of Pico, Lorenzo, and Ficino, the Platonic Academy went out of existence, but not without having made a major contribution to the advancement of art, science, and philosophy, and to the spread of Platonism in Germany, France, and England. The Platonic revival in each of these centers will receive separate treatment.

GEORGE GEMISTUS (1355–1450)
Byzantine Philosopher

[This Platonist, known also by the name of Gemistus Pletho, was an important precursor of the Italian renaissance, as we have just seen. "He is . . . chiefly memorable for having been the first person who introduced Plato to the Western world . . . Cardinal Bessarion became his disciple; he produced a great impression upon Cosmo de' Medici; and . . . effectually shook the exclusive domination which Aristotle had exercised over European thought for eight centuries." [1] Byzantium, or the eastern half of the Roman Empire, survived by a thousand years the fall of the western portion. It may be of more than passing significance that the Platonic ideas on

---

[3] This is one of Pico's *Conclusiones Kabalisticæ*, drawn by him from Zoharic works, and published by Archangelus de Burgo Nuovo in *Apologia pro Defensione Doctrinæ Cabalæ*, 1564. See *The Works of Thomas Vaughan*, ed. A. E. Waite, London: 1919, p. 6 fn.

---

[1] *Britannica*, 11th edition.

reincarnation were openly restored to the West through a Byzantine philosopher considering that it was the Byzantine Emperor Justinian who in the sixth century closed the door to a free dialogue on the subject. Pletho wrote, as quoted in Eva Martin's The Ring of Return.[2]]

As to ourselves, our soul, partaking of the divine nature, remains immortal and eternal in the precincts which are the limit of our world. Attached to a mortal envelope, it is sent by the gods now into one body, now into another, in view of the universal harmony, in order that the union of the mortal and immortal elements in human nature may contribute to the unity of the Whole. . . .

If, in man, the immortal nature is united for an instant to the mortal nature, only to abandon it for the rest of time, no permanent bond would be made between these two mortal and immortal elements, but a temporary union which, the mortal element once removed, would immediately dissolve, and dissolve with it the general harmony. It remains to be said that the union of these two natures exists partially, temporarily, and that whenever the body is destroyed each returns to its respective independence, and this process is renewed indefinitely throughout eternity.

The French Renaissance

Writing in the Spring, 1965 issue of The Philosopher—the journal of The Philosophical Society of England—Esmé Wynne-Tyson states: "The brief and glorious revival of Neoplatonic thought during the Renaissance [which] flourished in Italy under the Medicis . . . was carried from there to the French Court by an enthusiastic François I," who reigned from 1515 to 1547. In the volume The Century of the Renaissance in France by the French author Louis Batiffol,[1] he writes in chapter "The Court of Francis I":

Thanks to the invention of printing, fresh editions of Greek and Latin authors came into existence [in France] every day, and interest in the works of the ancients, which had hitherto been practically inaccessible, increased considerably. Publications such as Budé's Commentaires sur la Langue Grecque and Robert Estienne's Thesaurus Linguæ Latinæ facilitated acquaintance with the wisdom of antiquity, and a large number of people developed a taste for the careful study of Greek and Latin forms. Interested in everything connected with the exercise of the intellect, Francis I was greatly attracted by this movement.

[2] P. 107.

---

[1] New York: Putnam, 1916, pp. 104–105.

. . . The most famous scholars of his reign were gradually introduced into his circle. . . .

The most illustrious of these was Guillaume Budé, the omniscient Budé, who was jurist, theologian, mathematician, philologist, historian, critic, archæologist, and above all Hellenist. . . . [He was] one of the first scholars to apply himself to the study of antiquity. . . . There were also the Hellenist, Jacques Toussaint (*Tussanus*), Robert Estiennes' master; Robert Estienne himself . . . and above all Guillaume Postel, the Orientalist, one of the first to unravel the tangled skein of Oriental languages. . . . [He] was sent on a mission to the East to find manuscripts.

Jean Pierre Niceron in his noted *Memoires*[2] speaks of Postel as one of the most learned men of his age, a judgment confirmed by Postel's numerous works. He excelled particularly in languages, philosophy, cosmography, mathematics, and medicine. The king and his learned sister, the Queen of Navarre, regarded him as the marvel of the world. When in Constantinople, Postel embarked on Chaldean and Kabalistic studies under the tuition of a learned Jew, and while in the Levant is said to have been initiated by an Eastern Fraternity.

Postel's mystical ideas earned him endless abuse from the theologians. One of his contemporaries called him the "father of the deists." Accused of various heresies he nearly perished at the hands of the Inquisition. His *Clavis Absconditorum*, a key to things hidden and forgotten, was very celebrated. Postel speaks of reincarnation in his writings as well as various occult doctrines.

The English Renaissance

In *The Platonic Tradition in English Religious Thought*[1] W. R. Inge writes: "While the Italian Renaissance issued in a new school of art, in England there was born a new piety, a new poetry, and a new drama. . . . [English] Renaissance poetry is steeped in Platonic thoughts.[2] . . . The Renaissance proper . . . reached England in the time of Colet and Erasmus. The flame which they kindled . . . was lighted in Italy, where Grocyn and Linacre visited the famous Platonic Academy at Florence. These Oxford Platonists represented a new idea of humane learning in England; at Cambridge the study of Greek was promoted by the teaching of Erasmus in 1512 and 1513."

[2] *Mèmoires pour servir à l'Histoire des Hommes Illustres dans la République des Lettres.* Paris: 1729, Vol. VIII.

[1] Pp. 28, 36–37.
[2] See also John Smith Harrison, *Platonism in English Poetry of the Sixteenth and Seventeenth Centuries*. New York: Macmillan, 1903. (Eds.)

Further effects of the Italian Renaissance upon English thought will receive consideration in the section "The Cambridge Platonists."

The Rebirth of Platonism, Pythagoreanism, and Kabalism in Germany

In the fifteenth century a revival of Neoplatonism arose in Germany through the efforts of Nicolas de Cusa, a Catholic Cardinal of German birth, and a noted ecclesiastical and philosophical writer. Cusa directly opposed the anthropomorphic conception of God. His efforts to revive Neoplatonism were continued in Germany by Trithemius, John Reuchlin, and Cornelius Agrippa.

Trithemius, the Abbot of the Benedictine Monastery of Spanheim, was a Kabalist as well as a Platonist. His fame was perpetuted by his two distinguished pupils, Paracelsus and Agrippa. He originated the modern system of diplomatic cipher writing to convey teachings and messages that dared not be openly disclosed.

In the middle of this century appeared John Reuchlin, the celebrated humanist and teacher of whom Goethe wrote: "Reuchlin! who would himself with him compare, in his own time a sign so rare!" (*Zahm Zenien*, V.) While acting as Imperial Counsellor of Emperor Frederick III, Reuchlin found time to study Neoplatonism, several oriental languages, and to write books on the Kabala. When he denounced the burning of the Hebrew bibles, the Dominicans caused his expulsion for a time from Germany, and his own works were burned. But later when Erasmus, Martin Luther, and Melanchthon (the grandson of Reuchlin's sister, and for a long period under his care) came to him for instruction, Reuchlin set going a ferment of ideas which caused him to be called "the Father of the Reformation." [1] The *Britannica*[2] provides some significant details of his interest in Neoplatonism and Kabalism, and of his influence on German culture:

Reuchlin . . . in February 1482 left Stuttgart for Florence and Rome . . . [which] brought the German scholar into contact with several learned Italians. . . . Reuchlin's life at Stuttgart was often broken by important missions, and in 1490 he was again in Italy. Here he saw Pico to whose Cabbalistic doctrines he afterwards became heir. . . .

[Later in Heidelberg] Reuchlin's appointed function was to make translations from the Greek authors, in which his reading was already extremely wide . . . and formed an important element in his efforts to spread a knowledge of Greek. For, though Reuchlin had no public office as teacher, and even at Hei-

[1] Francis Barham, *The Life and Times of John Reuchlin, or Capnion, the Father of the German Reformation.* London: 1843.
[2] Ninth edition.

delberg was prevented from lecturing openly, he was during a great part of his life the real centre of all Greek teaching as well as of all Hebrew teaching in Germany. . . . His Greek studies had interested him in philosophy, and not least in those fantastical and mystical systems of later times with which the Cabbala has no small affinity. Following Pico, he seemed to find in the Cabbala a profound theosophy which might be of the greatest service for the defence of Christianity and the reconciliation of science with the mysteries of faith. . . . The most esoteric wisdom of the rabbis was in his eyes of the greatest value.

Reuchlin remarked in *De arte cabalistica* (1517): "Marsilio [Ficino] produced Plato for Italy. Lefèvre d'Estaples restored Aristotle to France. I shall complete the number and . . . show to the Germans, Pythagoras reborn through me." [3] Pythagoras, he believed, derived the heart of his philosophy from the wise men of the East. In an essay "An Explanation of the Pythagorean Doctrine," Reuchlin wrote: "It is commonly averred Pythagoras was of opinion, that the souls of men after death informed the bodies of beasts. We cannot imagine this of so knowing a person. This suspicion of this transanimation seems rather to have been raised by such, as were partly ignorant, partly envious, of the Pythagorean mysteries, as Timon, Xenophanes, Cratinus, Aristophon, Hermippus, and others, who have ascribed many things to Pythagoras which he never said nor wrote, and have perverted what he did say." [4]

Lewis Spitz writes that in Reuchlin's Kabalism he viewed man "as a unique creature, situated at the center of the great chain of being, able to descend or ascend until united with the One, as in Neplatonism [and that] the goal of both the Cabala and Pythagoras is to lead the souls of men back to the gods, that is, to raise them to perfect beatitude." [5]

Masonry, Alchemy, and the Hermetic Philosophers

In his small volume, *Mysteries of Antiquity*,[1] John Yarker, a high-ranking Mason, makes some significant linkages of the Freemasons, the Knights Templar, and the Rosicrucians, with such reincarnationist groups as the Gnostic Cathari and the Kabalists. (Reincarnation in modern Masonry has already been considered in Part Three.) Yarker writes:

There can be no doubt that the Operative Association of Freemasons and the Chivalric Order of Templars, both included searchers into Cabalism, Alchemy, and the recondite mysteries of nature and science. We have also arrived

---

[3] Lewis Spitz, *The Religious Renaissance of the German Humanists.* Harvard University Press, 1963, Chapter "Reuchlin—Pythagoras Reborn," p. 67.
[4] Thomas Stanley, *History of Philosophy.* London: 1687, p. 570.
[5] Spitz, p. 71.

---

[1] New York: 1878.

at the time when these were known as Rosicrucianism. . . . [In fact, our Masonic rites] were introduced by the Gnostics and Cabalists, and transferred to the Templars, Rosicrucians, and Freemasons. . . . There can be no doubt whatever that the Gnostic [Cathari] associations spread early into England [having emigrated from France]. The Abbé Pluqet, remarking on this says: ". . . They made their way into Germany and England, and everywhere gained many proselytes. The Manichees seduced numbers of people, and their sect was considered by the simple minded to be a society of Christians who made profession of an extraordinary perfection."

Another Gnostic branch, headed by Walter Lollard, and his twelve apostles, united with the followers of John Wycliffe [a leader of the English reformation]. Chaucer was one of their number, and obliged to quit England for a time; whilst in Italy he visited Petrarch[2] . . . ; throughout [Chaucer's] works we find the alchemical and otherwise veiled language and marked resemblance to our secret mysteries. . . .

It is well known that the Templar Order in England was dissolved on the proofs of Gnostic knowledge brought against them. . . . They doubtless acquired their knowledge [during the Crusades] in the East, where remnants of the Essenian and other secret schools [such as the Sufis] existed at the time. . . . In A.D. 1296 Edward I, of England, the son of Henry III, was admitted into the order by Raymond Lully—the great pioneer of the Rosicrucians . . . and the friend of John Cremer, Abbot of Westminster, and the celebrated monkish philosopher and alchemist, Roger Bacon.[3]

Sufism, one of the Islamic forms of Gnosticism, and which, as we have seen, teaches reincarnation, was "the Eastern parent of Freemasonry," according to Sir Richard Burton.[4] Robert Graves, in his introduction to Idries Shah's *The Sufis*, adds: "The Sufis are an ancient spiritual freemasonry. . . . Indeed, Freemasonry itself began as a Sufi society. It first reached England in the reign of King Aethelstan (924–939) and was introduced into Scotland disguised as a craft guild at the beginning of the fourteenth century, doubtless by the Knights Templar." (p. xix.) The word "Rosicrucian," meaning a follower of the path of the Rose Cross, Shah finds to be "a late mistranslation of the Sufi phrase 'Path of the Rose.' " (p. 245.)

Of the Rosicrucian alchemists "there were two orders," states the *Royal Masonic Cyclopædia*,[5] "those who laboured at the physical forge and crucible, and those who, by a theosophic process, sought to elevate the

---

[2] Petrarch (1304–1374) is considered the first great representative of Renaissance humanism. Revolting against late-medieval scholasticism, and replacing it with unbounded zeal for the study of classical antiquity, he regarded Plato as the greatest of all philosophers. See Paul O. Kristeller, *Eight Philosophers of the Italian Renaissance*. California: Stanford University Press, 1964, p. 9. (Eds.)
[3] Pp. 48–49, 51–52, 70.
[4] Francis Hitchman, *Richard F. Burton*. London: 1887, p. 286 fn.
[5] London: 1877, pp. 613–614.

mind into a knowledge of its constitution; thus perfecting a much higher series of investigations, and arriving at a mystical gold beyond all price." In other words, they sought to transmute the baser elements in human nature. Jung, convinced of this transcendental side to medieval alchemy, spent years investigating its psychological and symbolical aspects.[6] "I must confess," he wrote, "that it cost me quite a struggle to overcome the prejudice, which I shared with many others, against the seeming absurdity of alchemy. . . . But my patience has been richly rewarded. . . . True alchemy was never a business or a career, but a real *opus* that a man carried on in silent self-sacrificing labour." [7] Doubtless the peculiar jargon and the seemingly fantastic symbols of the alchemists were a necessity of the times. The dungeon, the rack, and the fagot employed against heretics were ample excuse for esotericism.

This process of self-transmutation was evidently regarded by some Rosicrucians as extending over more than one lifetime, for included in this work for their views on pre-existence and/or rebirth are a number of the noted members or friends of the Order, namely, Robert Fludd, Thomas Vaughan, Paracelsus, one of the Van Helmonts, Tommaso Campanella, and Jerome Cardan.

An evolutionary palingenesis was also taught—anticipating a spiritual form of Darwinism centuries before *The Origin of Species*. As Hargrove Jennings writes in his classic work *The Rosicrucians, Their Rites and Mysteries*,[8] the Rosicrucians believed that every form contains an "eager fire" or "jewel of light," the development of which brings about its evolution. "Thus all minerals, in this spark of life, have the rudimentary possibilities of plants and growing organisms . . . thus all plants and all vegetation might pass off into more distinguished highways, as it were, of independent, completer advance, allowing their original spark of light to expand and thrill with higher and more vivid force, and to urge forward with more abounding, informed purpose."

Robert Fludd and many another Rosicrucian were also Hermetists. (As previously indicated in the section "The Hermetic Works," the philosophy of reincarnation frequently appears in the Hermetic Fragments.) The allusions to Hermes Trismegistus in late medieval and Renaissance literature are extensive, and Ficino, Pico, Patricius and other learned Renaissance men regarded him as the source of the Orphic initiations and of the philosophy of Pythagoras and Plato. In fact, a strong movement was under

---

[6] C. G. Jung's *Collected Works*. New York: Pantheon, XII, *Psychology and Alchemy;* XIII, Alchemical Studies; XIV, *Mysterium Coniunctionis.*
[7] *The Integration of Personality.* New York: Farrar & Rinehart, 1939, pp. 28, 238.
[8] London: 5th revised edition, undated, p. 214.

way to supplant the Scholastics' model, Aristotle, with Trismegistus. An interesting work which yokes Hermetism to Neoplatonic, Rosicrucian, Kabalistic, and similar movements of this period is *Giordano Bruno and the Hermetic Tradition*, by Frances Yates.[9] The author shows how Renaissance Hermetism stimulated new attitudes toward the cosmos and affected the religious issues, leading toward toleration of nonorthodox viewpoints such as reincarnation. Bruno's open espousal of reincarnation philosophy, which contributed to his being martyred at the stake, will be considered a few pages hence.

PARACELSUS (1493–1541)
Swiss Physician and Alchemist

[The following excerpts from the writings of Paracelsus are taken from *The Life of Philippus Theophrastus Bombast of Hohenheim, known by the name of Paracelsus*, by Franz Hartmann, M.D.[1]]

Some children are born from heaven, and others are born from hell, because each human being has his inherent tendencies, and these tendencies belong to his spirit, and indicate the state in which he existed before he was born. Witches and sorcerers are not made at once; they are born with powers for evil.[2] The body is only an instrument; if you seek for man in his dead body, you are seeking for him in vain. . . . Life is something spiritual. Life is not only in that which moves, such as men and animals, but in all things; for what would be a corporeal form without a spirit? The form may be destroyed; but the spirit remains and is living, for it is the subjective life. . . .

The body which we receive from our parents . . . has no spiritual powers, for wisdom and virtue, faith, hope and charity, do not grow from the earth. These powers are not the products of man's physical organization, but the attributes of another invisible and glorified body, whose germs are laid within man. The physical body changes and dies, the glorified body is eternal. This eternal man is the real man, and is not generated by his earthly parents. He does not draw nutriment from the earth, but from the eternal invisible source from which he originated. . . . The temporal body is the house of the eternal, and we should therefore take care of it, because he who destroys the temporal body destroys the house of the eternal, and

[9] Chicago University Press, 1964.

[1] London: Kegan Paul, 2d revised edition, undated, pp. 278–279.
[2] They are born with the tendencies which they acquired in former lives upon the earth, or upon some other planet. (Franz Hartmann.)

although the eternal man is invisible, he exists nevertheless, and will become visible in time.

[The idea of an immortal "glorified body" is mentioned above. The Gnostics taught similarly.[3] The Hindus also speak of a highly refined body, the highest sheath of the soul, and the storehouse of the essence of experiences garnered from life to life. These are interesting theories to consider, for the basic argument of the materialist is that consciousness must dissolve with the destruction of the body, as there is then no body and brain to focus it. St. Paul stated that there is "a natural body, and there is a spiritual body . . . the first man is of the earth, earthy: the second man is the Lord from heaven." Immortality is derived only through the incorruptible body, he said (I Corinthians 15: 35–54). The ninth-century genius, John Scotus Erigena, who appeared in his age as "a meteor, none knew whence," [4] indicated in his celebrated work *The Division of Nature* that the soul and the spiritual body came into existence simultaneously "and the soul therefore precedes the [spiritual] body only in dignity, not in space or in time. . . . But where, then, is that spiritual and incorruptible body. . . ? It is hidden in the secret recesses of our nature, and it will reappear in the future, when this mortal shall put on immortality." [5] The soul will then, he says, "return into a former state which it lost by transgression." [6] According to some, the real meaning of the bodily resurrection of Jesus and of mankind still to come, may lie concealed in the foregoing ideas.]

GIORDANO BRUNO (1548–1600)
Italian Philosopher

[Born near Naples, of a distinguished Italian family, Bruno entered a Dominican monastery at 15. Dissatisfied with the dogmas of the Church, he found in the philosophy of Pythagoras, Plato, Hermes, and several of the Neoplatonists the teachings he was seeking. Later he made a deep study of the writings of Nicolas de Cusa and Raymond Lully. Accused of heresy, he fled the monastery at 24, from which time his wandering life began. He lectured and taught in Germany, Switzerland, The Prague, as well as in France and England. Under the protection of the King of France he taught

---

[3] G. R. S. Mead, *The Hymn of the Robe of Glory*. London: 1908.
[4] Reginald L. Poole, *Illustrations of the History of Medieval Thought and Learning*. London: SPCK, 1920, p. 48.
[5] Henry Bett, *Johannes Scotus Erigena* (New York: Russell & Russell, 1964), p. 56.
[6] *That Unknown Country*, an anthology on punishment after death (Springfield, Mass.: C. A. Nichols, 1891), p. 47.

philosophy at the University of Paris, and then went to London where he became a warm friend of Queen Elizabeth. At Oxford he delivered lectures on the Copernican theory, and on immortality and reincarnation, and consequently aroused the animosity of the Oxford professors who asked him to leave. Finally in Venice, Bruno was seized by the Inquisition. After seven years imprisonment and torture, and still refusing to recant, he was burnt at the stake on February 17, 1600. Among those particularly influenced by Bruno's philosophy were Spinoza, Descartes, and Leibniz.

The most popular of Bruno's many works, and the one that was singled out by the Roman tribunal at his trial, was *The Expulsion of the Triumphant Beast*, published in 1584. It was a daring indictment of the corruption of the social and religious institutions of the day. In one part he describes the condition of a soul who had misused its opportunities on earth, saying that such a soul would be "relegated back to another body, and should not expect to be entrusted with the government and administration of a better dwelling if it had conducted itself badly in the conduct of a previous one." But, he added, there are certain individuals whose "soul-flame" has burned more brightly with each succeeding incarnation, leading them by gradual stages to perfection. "These speak and act not as mere instruments of the divine, but rather as self-creative artists and heroes. The former *have* the divine spirit; the latter *are* divine spirits."

In his *De Rerum Principiis*, and in *De Monade Numero*, Bruno was the first European to teach the circulation of the blood, later demonstrated by Harvey. Dr. Félix Martí-Ibáñez, Director of the Department of the History of Medicine, New York Medical College, discloses this fact in his large volume *Centaur, Essays on the History of Medical Ideas*.[1] Interestingly enough, he shows that Bruno's ideas on the circulation of the blood were simply an application of his cosmic views, summarized by the doctor in these words: "Every movement that returns to its point of origin must adopt the form of a circle. Only circular movement is continuous and consistent. Every object of nature is, then, a circle, whose function and activity derive from its center point, which is the soul. From the soul the active principle tends, according to Bruno, to go to the periphery, whence it flows back to the center. Harvey's discovery, therefore, is bound to a philosophy of circles, and the circular motion of the blood is a microcosmic example of a macrocosmic pattern, it being the cycle that conducts the process of return to its point of departure." In other words, this is the ancient doctrine of the periodic emanation and return of worlds, atoms, and men, applied to physiology.

[1] New York: MD Publications, 1958, p. 143.

In addition to reincarnation, Bruno taught, as just mentioned, that other heresy of his day, the Copernican theory. This new-old Pythagorean concept of the perpetual motion of the planets around the sun was soon to give rise to an intense yearning to impart movement to everything. The Baroque period, as Dr. Martí-Ibáñez points out, "was essentially an explosion of movement." (p. 142.) Art and music became dynamic. "Spiral columns soared into space, replacing the old classical columns, and the stone of cathedrals and palaces was wrenched from its mystic Gothic placidity and turned into veritable whirlpools." In such an atmosphere it is perhaps not strange that the theory of reincarnation, with its perpetually revolving cycles, should have found a few ardent champions.

The first excerpt is from Bruno's *Ash Wednesday Conversation,* an address delivered at the London home of Sir Fulke Grevie. The final selection will be Bruno's last testament—his reported words before the tribunal of the Inquisition.]

Nature is a living unity of living units, in each of which the power of the whole is present.[2] . . . We ourselves, and the things we call our own, come and vanish and return again. . . . Within every man there is a soul-flame, kindled at the sun of thought, which lends us wings whereby we may approach the sun of knowledge. . . . The soul of man moves and governs the body, is superior to the body and cannot be constrained by it. . . . It is the Real Spirit in which, from which and through which are formed the different bodies, which have to pass through different kinds of existences, names and destinies. . . . Every act performed brings its appropriate reward or punishment in another life. In proportion as the soul has conducted itself in a body, it determines for itself its transition into another body.

La Cena de la Ceneri

In order not to burden too much the transmigrating souls, [Fate] interposes the drinking from the Lethean river . . . so that through oblivion everyone may be . . . eager to preserve himself in his present state. Therefore, youths do not recall their state of infancy; infants do not long for the state in their mothers' wombs; and none of these longs for the state in that life which he lived before he found himself in such a nature. The pig does not want to die for fear of not being a pig; the horse fears most to lose his equine nature. Jove . . . greatly fears not being Jove. But Fate's mercy and

[2] Bruno appears to have been the first European to employ the term "Monad," which Leibniz later used in formulating the key idea of his philosophy. Leibniz held with Bruno that each monadic center—whether of an atom or a man—is a mirror and replica in small of the entire Cosmos. (See under "Leibniz.")

grace will not change his state without having saturated him in the waters of that river. . . .

You see then, dear sister, how treacherous time subdues us, how we are all subject to mutation. And that which most afflicts us . . . is that we have neither certainty nor any hope of at all reassuming that same being in which we once found ourselves. We depart, and do not return the same; and since we have no recollection of what we were before we were in this being, so we cannot have a sample of that which we shall be afterward. . . . Only Truth, with Absolute Virtue, is immutable and immortal. And if she sometimes falls and is submerged, she, necessarily, in her time rises again, the same.

The Expulsion of the Triumphant Beast[3]

[When Bruno was turned over to the Father Inquisitor in Venice in May of 1592, his denouncer, Zuane Mocenigo, accused him of teaching various heretical ideas, among these were: "souls created by the operation of nature pass from one animal to another"; when the world is destroyed by deluge, souls are again reborn.[4] On these points Bruno replied at his trial:]

I have held and hold souls to be immortal. . . . Speaking as a Catholic, they do not pass from body to body, but go to Paradise, Purgatory or Hell. But I have reasoned deeply, and, speaking as a philosopher, since the soul is not found without body and yet is not body, it may be in one body or in another, and pass from body to body. This, if it be not [proved] true, seems at least likely, according to the opinion of Pythagoras. . . .[5]

In the circle, which comprehends in itself the beginning and the end, we have the figure of true being; and circular motion is the only enduring form of motion. From this Spirit, which is called the Life of the Universe, proceed the life and soul of everything which has soul and life,—which life, however, I understand to be immortal, as well in bodies as in their souls, all being immortal, there being no other death than division and congregation; which doctrine seems to be expressed in Ecclesiastes, where it is said nothing is new under the sun.[6]

From Bruno's Profession of Faith before
the Inquisition[7]

[3] Trans. Arthur D. Imerti. Rutgers University Press, 1963, First Dialogue, First Part, pp. 94–95, 102.
[4] I. Frith, *Life of Giordano Bruno*, Boston, 1887, p. 262 fn.
[5] William Boulting, *Giordano Bruno, His Life, Thought and Martyrdom*. London: Kegan Paul, 1914, pp. 163–164.
[6] Frith, *Life of Giordano Bruno*, pp. 278–279.
[7] These selections can be found in their original in *Vita di Giordano Bruno, con documenti editi e inediti*, Vincinzo Spampanato. Messina, Casa Editrice Principato, 1921, "Documenti veneti," XI, 711; XII, 720.

EDMUND SPENSER (1552–1599)
British Poet

[Spenser's *Faery Queene*, particularly "The Garden of Adonis" canto—
from which the lines below are taken—shows a pronounced Neoplatonic
influence. (See article "Spenser's Garden of Adonis" by Josephine Waters
Bennett.[1]) The influence of Ficino, Porphyry, and possibly Giordano
Bruno is considered in the Notes covering Books 3, 6, and 7 of *The Faery
Queene* in the nine-volume variorum edition of Spenser's works edited by
Edwin Greenlaw, et al.[2]]

[*The Garden of Adonis*] *is the first seminary*
Of all things that are born to live and die,
According to their kinds. . . .
Double gates it had which opened wide,
By which both in and out men must pass:
Th'one fair and fresh, the other old and dried.
Old Genius the porter of them was. . . .

He letteth in, he letteth out to wend
All that to come into the world desire:
A thousand thousand naked babes attend
About him day and night, which do require
That he with fleshly weeds would them attire:
Such . . . *he clothes with sinful mire,*
And sendeth forth to live in mortal state,
Till they again return back by the hinder gate.

After that they again returned been,
They in that Garden planted be again,
And grow afresh, as [if] they had never seen
Fleshly corruption, nor mortal pain.
Some thousand years so do they there remain,
And then of him are clad with other hue,[3]
Or sent into the changeful world again,
Till thither they return where first they grew;
So, like a wheel, around they run from old to new.

> The Faery Queene
> (Book III, Canto VI, Stanzas 30–33)

1 Modern Language Association Publications, Menasha, Wisconsin. March, 1932,
XLVII, 46–80.
2 Baltimore, Johns Hopkins Press, 1932–1938.
3 Form or appearance.

♦ * ●

Seventeenth Century

WILLIAM SHAKESPEARE (1564–1616)
British Dramatist

[In the first selection, Malvolio in *Twelfth Night* shares the prevalent misconception that Pythagoras taught that human beings can be reborn as
animals. In the next extract, Shakespeare's Gratiano reversing the picture,
suggests the possibility that souls of wild animals can become embodied in
evil men.]

CLOWN   What is the opinion of Pythagoras concerning wild fowl?
MALVOLIO   That the soul of our grandam might haply inhabit a bird.
CLOWN   What thinkest thou of his opinion?
MALVOLIO   I think nobly of the soul, and no way approve of his opinion.
CLOWN   Fare thee well. Remain thou still in darkness: thou shalt hold the
　　opinion of Pythagoras ere I will allow of thy wits; and fear to kill a
　　woodcock, lest thou dispossess the soul of thy grandam. Fare thee well.

Twelfth Night (IV. *ii*)

GRATIANO   O, be thou damn'd, inexecrable dog! . . .
　　Thou almost makest me waver in my faith
　　To hold opinion with Pythagoras,
　　That souls of animals infuse themselves
　　Into the trunks of men; thy currish spirit
　　Govern'd a wolf, who hang'd for human slaughter.
　　Even from the gallows did his fell soul fleet,
　　And, whilst thou lay'st in thy unhallow'd dam,
　　Infused itself in thee; for thy desires
　　Are wolvish, bloody, starved and ravenous.

The Merchant of Venice (IV. *i*)

[In this Sonnet we have the one clear reference in Shakespeare to the reincarnation of human souls in human bodies:]

If there be nothing new, but that which is
Hath been before, how are our brains beguiled,
Which labouring for invention, bear amiss
The second burthen [bearing] of a former child!
O, that record could with a backward look,
Even of five hundred courses of the sun,
Show me your image in some antique book,
Since mind at first in character was done!
That I might see what the old world could say
To this composèd wonder of your frame;
Whether we are mended, or whether better they,
Or whether revolution be the same.
*   O, sure I am, the wits of former days*
*   To subjects worse have been given admiring praise.*

Sonnet 59

TOMMASO CAMPANELLA (1568–1639)
Italian Poet and Philosopher

[This celebrated Renaissance philosopher and Dominican monk was imprisoned for twenty-seven years, undergoing much torture and misery, though his spirit remained unbroken. Many of his poems and philosophical works were written during this period. In desperate mood he penned these lines:]

I fear that by my death the human race
Would gain no vantage. Thus I do not die.
So wide is this vast cage of misery
That flight and change lead to no happier place.
Shifting our pains, we risk a sorrier case:
All worlds, like ours, are sunk in agony:
Go where we will, we feel; and this my cry
I may forget like many an old disgrace.
Who knows what doom is mine? The Omnipotent
Keeps silence; nay, I know not whether strife
Or peace was with me in some earlier life.
Philip in a worse prison hath me pent
These three days past.

"A Sonnet on Caucasus" [1]

[1] Trans. John Addington Symonds, *The Sonnets of M. A. Buonarroti and T. Campanella.* London: 1878, p. 177.

JOHN DONNE (1573–1631)
British Poet

[Dr. Donne's "The Progress of the Soul" is a satirical poem directed chiefly against the folly of believing in transmigration of human beings into animals. However, the following lines, from stanzas I, VI, and VII, are in another vein:]

I sing the progress of a deathless soul,
Whom Fate, which God made, but doth not control,
Placed in most shapes. . . .
For though through many straits and lands I roam,
I launch at paradise, and I sail towards home;
The course I there began, shall here be stay'd,
Sails hoisted there, struck here, and anchors laid
In Thames, which were in Tigris, and Euphrates weigh'd.
For the great soul which here amongst us now
Doth dwell, and moves that hand, and tongue, and brow. . . .
This soul, to whom Luther and Mahomet were
Prisons of flesh; this soul which oft did tear
And mend the wracks of th' Empire, and late Rome,
And lived when every great change did come,
Had first in paradise, a low, but fatal room.

"The Progress of the Soul"

JOHN WEBSTER (1580?–1625)
British Dramatist

[In *The Duchess of Malfi*, Webster is said to have "approached the tragic power and poetic genius of Shakespeare." (*Webster's Biographical Dictionary*.) In these lines therefrom one is reminded of verses from Spenser's *Faery Queene* previously quoted:]

I know death hath ten thousand several doors
For men, to take their Exits; and 'tis found
They go on such strange geometrical hinges,
You may open them both ways.

SIR THOMAS BROWNE (1605–1682)
British Physician and Author

[In Moore's famous work *Religio Medici* he suggests the pre-existence of the soul, but his belief in metempsychosis extends only to the rebirth of ideas and types of men.]

We are men, and we know not how: there is something in us that can be without us, and will be after us; though it is strange that it hath no history what it was before us, nor cannot tell how it entered in us. . . . Whilst I study to find how I am a Microcosm, or little World, I find myself something more than the great. There is surely a piece of Divinity in us, something that was before the Elements, and owes no homage unto the Sun. . . .

One General Council is not able to extirpate one single Heresy: it may be cancelled for the present, but revolution of time, and the like aspects from Heaven will restore it, when it will flourish till it be condemned again. For as though there were a Metempsychosis, and the soul of one man passed into another, Opinions do find, after certain Revolutions, men and minds like those that first begat them. To see ourselves again, we need not look for Plato's year: every man is not only himself: there have been many Diogenes, and as many Timons, though but few of that name: men are lived over again; the world is now as it was in Ages past; there was none then, but there hath been some one since that parallels him, and is, as it were, his revived self.

Religio Medici[1]

JOHN MILTON (1608–1674)
British Poet

[Milton imbibed from his college friend, Henry More, an early fondness for Plato. In the extracts that follow, the Platonic influence seems evident. Milton also "made use of Hermes Trismegistus and the works of the Cabalists," writes Professor Denis Saurat in *Literature and Occult Tradition*.[1]]

The soul grows clotted by contagion,
Imbodies and embrutes till she quite lose
The divine property of her first being.
> Comus, A Mask
> (Scene: "The Two Brothers")

[1] *Harvard Classics.* New York: P. F. Collier, 1909, III, 257, 289, 326.

[1] New York: Dial Press, 1930, p. 44.

Wert thou that just Maid who once before
Forsook the hated earth, O tell me sooth,
And cam'st again to visit us once more?
Or wert thou that sweet smiling Youth? . . .
Or any other of that heavenly brood
Let down in cloudy throne to do the world some good?
Or wert thou of the golden-wingèd host,
Who, having clad thyself in human weed,
To earth from thy prefixèd seat didst post,
And after short abode fly back with speed
As if to show what creatures heaven doth breed;
Thereby to set the hearts of men on fire,
To scorn the sordid world, and unto Heaven aspire?
"On the Death of a Fair Infant"

The Cambridge Platonists

In the seventeenth century, Cambridge University became the center of a movement which attracted considerable attention. Its leaders were known as the Cambridge Platonists, the most prominent of whom were Henry More, Ralph Cudworth, and John Smith. However, the movement was not confined to Cambridge. Two of its leading supporters, John Norris and Joseph Glanvill, were from Oxford.

Of Dr. More, who was a close friend of Addison and Milton, Hobbes said that if his own philosophy were not true he knew none that he should sooner adopt than Henry More's of Cambridge. Samuel Johnson esteemed him as "one of our greatest divines and philosophers and no mean poet." More's philosophical works, Coleridge declared, "contain more enlarged and elevated views of the Christian dispensation than I have met with in any other single volume; for More had both philosophical and poetic genius supported by immense erudition." [1] Dean Inge relates that in 1630 More took his degree at Christ's College and "began the study of 'the Platonic writers, Marsilius Ficinus, Plotinus himself, Mercurius Trismegistus, and the mystical divines. . . .' Here he found his own spiritual kin, and with them he lived to the end." [2]

The Cambridge Platonists, wise in the science of their day and schooled in precise Cartesian thinking, nevertheless rejected the materialism toward which Descartes had directed the awakening Western intellectuality. They rendered the moral inspiration of the Renaissance into an English idiom for future generations. The Neoplatonic revival of the Italian

[1] Walker's *Reincarnation*, p. 179.
[2] W. R. Inge, *The Platonic Tradition in English Religious Thought*, p. 55.

Renaissance was a major inspiration, the great Florentine Platonist Ficino being a frequently cited authority. Continuing the task begun by Philo Judæus, the English Platonists endeavored to reconcile the Platonic doctrines with the Hebrew Bible. In fact, Plato was considered to be Moses speaking Attic Greek! More's work on the Kabala appeared in 1653, entitled "A conjectural essay of interpreting the mind of Moses according to a threefold Cabbala," and John Milton became deeply learned in this mystical Jewish lore—which, as has already been shown, embraces the reincarnation perspective.

Cudworth's encyclopedic book, *The True Intellectual System of the Universe*, appeared in London in 1678. It has been called "a storehouse of learning on the ancient opinions of the nature, origin, pre-existence, transmigration, and future of the soul." Although he dismissed the Platonic doctrines of pre-existence and reincarnation as "offensive absurdities," he nevertheless focused attention on these ideas, and a number of his fellow Platonists gave them serious attention. Glanvill, who was the Chaplain to King Charles II, is quoted on reincarnation in the section "Christianity." Selections from More's writings follow shortly.

The relationship of the Cambridge group to the Platonic movement in the West is reviewed below by W. R. Inge in his Hulsean Lectures at Cambridge in 1925–1926, published as *The Platonic Tradition in English Religious Thought.*[3]

Burnet's judgment about [the Cambridge Platonists] is too familiar to be quoted at length. It was his deliberate opinion that the corruptions of the English clergy, their avarice, self-indulgence, and neglect of duty, were so notorious, that "if a new set of men had not appeared of another stamp, the Church had quite lost her esteem over the nation." . . . "I can come into no company of late," says a contemporary, "but I find the chief discourse to be about a certain new sect of men called Latitude-men." . . . Edward Fowler, afterwards Bishop of Gloucester, had also "heard them represented as a generation of people that have revived the abominable principles of the old Gnostics." . . . No one can read the books of these men without feeling that there was a real outpouring of the Spirit at Cambridge at this time, which in the future may engage more sympathetic attention than it has done yet.

HENRY MORE (1614–1687)
British Philosopher

[In the essay and poem that follows More touches on rebirth while mainly considering pre-existence, and cites a large number of reincarnationists to support his views.]

[3] Pp. 45–46, 65.

If it be good for the souls of men to be at all, the sooner they are, the better. . . . If they can enjoy themselves before they come into these terrestrial bodies . . . they must be before they come into these bodies; that is, they must be in a capacity of enjoying themselves without [bodies] for long periods of time, before they appeared here in this age of the world. . . .

Wherefore the pre-existence of souls is a necessary result of the wisdom and goodness of God. . . . Again, the face of Providence in the world seems very much to suit with this opinion, there being not any so natural and easy account to be given of those things that seem the most harsh in the affairs of men, as from this hypothesis: that their souls did once subsist in some other state . . . and of their own natures, they undergo several calamities and asperities of fortune, and sad drudgeries of fate, as a punishment inflicted, or a disease contracted from the several obliquities of their *apostasy*. Which key is . . . able to unlock that recondite mystery of some particular men's almost fatal averseness from all religion and virtue, their stupidity and dullness and even invincible slowness to these things from their very childhood, and their incorrigible propension to all manner of vice. . . . Which sad scene of things must needs exceedingly cloud and obscure the ways of Divine Providence, and make them utterly unintelligible; unless some light be let in from the present hypothesis. . . .

And as this hypothesis is rational in itself, so has it also gained the suffrage of all philosophers of all ages, of any note, that have held the soul of man incorporeal and immortal. . . . Let us cast our eye, therefore, into what corner of the world we will, that has been famous for wisdom and literature, and the wisest of those nations you shall find the asserters of this opinion. In Egypt, that ancient nurse of all hidden sciences, that this opinion was in vogue amongst the wisest men there, the fragments of Trismegistus do sufficiently witness . . . of which opinion, not only the Gymnosophists, and other wise men of Egypt, were, but also the Brahmans of India, and the Magi of Babylon and Persia. . . . To these you may add the abstruse philosophy of the Jews, which they call their Cabbala, of which the soul's pre-existence makes a considerable part, as all the learned of the Jews do confess. . . .

[You] may add Zoroaster, Pythagoras, Epicharmus, Cebes, Euripides, Plato, Euclid, Philo, Virgil, Marcus Cicero, Plotinus, Iamblichus, Proclus, Boethius, Psellus, and several others, which it would be too long to recite. And if it were fit to add [Church] fathers to philosophers, we might enter into the same list Synesius and Origen; the latter of whom was surely the greatest light and bulwark that ancient Christianity had. . . . But I have not yet ended my catalogue; that admirable physician Johannes Fernelius is also of this persuasion, and . . . discovers those two grand-masters of medicine, Hippocrates and Galen, to be so, too. Cardan, also, that famous philosopher of his age, expressly concludes that the rational soul is both a distinct being from the soul of the world, and that it does pre-exist before it comes into the body; and lastly, Pomponatius, no friend to the soul's immortality, yet cannot but confess that the safest way to hold it is also therewith to acknowledge her pre-existence.

The Immortality of the Soul [1]

I would sing the pre-existency
Of Human souls, and live once o'er again
By recollection and quick memory
All that is passed since first we all began.
But all too shallow be my wits to scan
So deep a point and mind too dull to clear
So dark a matter.

[*The poet later addresses the "Sacred Soul of*
Plotinus dear:"]

Tell what we mortals are. Tell what of old we were.
A spark or ray of Divinity
Clouded in earthly fogs, and clad in clay,
A precious drop sunk from eternity
Spilt on the ground, or rather slunk away. . . .
Show fitly how the pre-existing soul
Enacts and enters bodies here below
And then entire unhurt can leave this moul(d).
A Platonic Song of the Soul [2]

FRANCISCUS MERCURIUS VAN HELMONT (1614–1699)
Belgian Naturalist and Philosopher

Van Helmont, in his *De Revolutione Animarum*, adduced in two hundred problems all the arguments which may be urged in favor of the return of souls into human bodies according to Kabalistic ideas. The book as published in London, 1684, bears the title, *Two Hundred Queries Moderately Propounded Concerning the Doctrine of the Revolution of Human Souls.* This work, together with Baron Knorr von Rosenroth's book mentioned

[1] *A Collection of Several Philosophical Writings of Dr. Henry More*, 4th rev. ed. London: 1712, Book II, Chap. 12, pp. 114–116.
[2] Henry More, *Philosophical Poems.* Cambridge: 1647, pp. 225, 256, 261.

earlier, have the distinction of being the first volumes in Western, or for that matter, Eastern literature specifically devoted to reincarnation.

THOMAS VAUGHAN (1622?–1665)
British Hermetist, Neoplatonist, Kabalist, and Alchemist

[Thomas Vaughan, the twin brother of the poet, Henry Vaughan, was one of the mystical philosophers Sir Isaac Newton devotedly read. The Britannica[1] informs us that "Sir Isaac spent much time in the study of the works of the alchemists," also that he "diligently studied the works of Jacob Boehme." (XIX, 592.) From Vaughan's Anthroposophia Theomagica—or a Discourse on the Nature of Man and His State after Death—the following has been taken:[2]]

I look on this life as the progress of an essence royal: the soul but quits her court to see the country. . . . Thus her descent speaks her original. God in love with His own beauty frames a glass, to view it by reflection. But the frailty of the matter excluding eternity, the composure was subject to dissolution. Ignorance gave this release the name of death, but properly it is the soul's birth and a charter that makes for her liberty. She hath several ways to break up house, but her best is without a disease. This is her mystical walk, an exit only to return. . . . The magicians tell me that the soul passes out of one mode and enters another. . . .

The soul of man, while she is in the body, is like a candle shut up in a dark lanthorn, or a fire that is almost stifled for want of air. Spirits—say the Platonics—when they are "in their own country" are like the inhabitants of green fields who live perpetually amongst flowers, in a spicy, odorous air; but here below, "in the circle of generation," they mourn because of darkness and solitude, like people locked up in a pest-house. "Here do they fear, desire and grieve," etc. This makes the soul subject to so many passions, to such a Proteus of humors. Now she flourishes, now she withers—now a smile, now a tear; and when she hath played out her stock, then comes a repetition of the same fancies, till at last she cries out with Seneca: "How long this self-same round?" . . .

Who seeketh to be more than a man, or to know the harmony of the world and be born again? [3]

Anthroposophia Theomagica

---

[1] Eleventh edition.
[2] *The Works of Thomas Vaughan*, ed., A. E. Waite. London: 1919, pp. 5–6, 46–47, 50.
[3] In this sentence, Vaughan of course speaks of spiritual rebirth.

JOHN DRYDEN (1631–1700)
British Poet

If thy pre-existing soul
Was form'd at first with myriads more,
It did through all the mighty poets roll
Who Greek or Latin laurels wore,
And was that Sappho last, which once it was before.
If so, then cease thy flight, O heaven-born mind!
Thou hast no dross to purge from thy rich ore:
Nor can thy soul a fairer mansion find,
Than was the beauteous frame she left behind:
Return to fill or mend the choir of thy celestial kind.
   "Ode to the Memory of Mrs. Anne Killigrew"

BENEDICT SPINOZA (1632–1677)
Dutch Philosopher

It is impossible for us to remember that we had existence prior to the body, since the body can have no vestige of it, and eternity cannot be defined in terms of time or have any relation to time. But, nevertheless, we have in our experience a perception that we are eternal. For the mind is sensible no less of what it understands than of what it remembers. . . . Although, therefore, we do not remember that we existed before the body, yet we perceive that our mind is eternal, in so far as it involves the body's essence under the category of eternity, and that this its existence cannot be defined by time or interpreted by duration.

   Ethics (Book V, Proposition 23)

LEIBNIZ (1646–1716)
German Philosopher and Mathematician

[Macneile Dixon writes of Leibniz—"the greatest intellectual genius since Aristotle"—that he "appears as a bright prophetic star, forerunner and foreteller of new ways of thought. . . . Nearly three centuries ago, the scientific acumen and prescience of Leibniz enabled him to foresee, and even in a measure anticipate, many conclusions arrived at by the most recent science." Matter is but another name for energy, he said. Empty space is a fiction; space and time are inseparable. He arrived by his own acute and original route at the modern theory of "the unconscious." "In the view of this most suggestive and remarkable thinker," continues Dixon, "just as a nation is composed of persons, so the universe may best be understood as consisting of an infinite variety of living and active beings, monads, as he called them. . . . 'The world,' said Leibniz, 'is not a machine. Everything in it is force, life, thought, desire.' The monads reflect the universe, each from its own angle, each in its own degree. . . . This great community extends both upwards and downwards from man through the whole creation. The world, in brief . . . is a living society." [1]

From the context of the statements that follow, Leibniz does not appear to limit the term "body" to the physical instrument, but includes the inner bodies of men and animals, and believing that these invisible constituents never completely die, he prefers the term "metamorphosis," to "metempsychosis."]

There is nothing waste, nothing sterile, nothing dead in the universe; no chaos, no confusions, save in appearance. . . . We must not imagine . . . that each soul has a mass or portion of matter appropriated or attached to itself for ever. . . . For all bodies are in a perpetual flux like rivers, and parts are passing in and out of them continually. Thus the soul only changes its body bit by bit and by degrees, so that it is never despoiled of all its organs all together . . . neither are there any entirely *separate souls, nor superhuman spirits* without bodies.

Monadology[2]

As animals are usually not born completely in conception or *generation,* so neither do they perish completely in what we call *death;* for it is reasonable that what does not begin naturally should not come to an end in the order of nature either. Thus, casting off their masks or their rags, they merely return to a more subtle scene, on which, however, they can be as sensible and as well ordered as on the greater one. . . . Thus not only souls but animals also are ingenerable and imperishable; they are only developed, enveloped, reclad, stripped, transformed; souls never leave the whole of their body, and do not pass from one body to another which is entirely new to them. Thus there is no *metempsychosis,* but there is *metamorphosis.*

Principles of Nature[3]

[James Ward in his Gifford Lectures, *The Realm of Ends,*[4] summarizes Leibniz's views on pre-existence and reincarnation:]

[1] *The Human Situation,* pp. 315–316.
[2] Trans. Mary Morris, *Leibniz: Philosophical Writings.* London: J. M. Dent, 1934, p. 16.
[3] *Ibid.,* p. 25.
[4] Cambridge University Press, 1911, pp. 204–205, 212–213.

According to the pluralistic, as according to the Leibnizian view, all the individuals there are have existed from the first and will continue to exist indefinitely. Birth and death, then, cannot really be what they seem to be. . . . [Leibniz believes] that all souls have pre-existed "always in a sort of organized body," which at the time of generation undergoes a certain transformation and augmentation. . . . Death, as the more or less complete dissolution of the organism, means that the soul in consequence, so far as it is thus deprived of its *locus standi*, is, to use Leibniz's phrase, in the position of a deserter from the general order. Temporarily it is in a like position during sleep; and death for Leibniz was but a longer and profounder sleep: in neither case did he believe that the continuity of the individual's life was completely broken. . . .

Is there some principle of "conservation of value" tending to prevent rational, self-conscious spirits from lapsing back into merely animal souls? This question Leibniz answered with a decided affirmative. . . .[5]

JOSEPH ADDISON (1672–1719)
British Essayist, Poet, and Statesman

Eternity—thou pleasing, dreadful thought!
Through what variety of untried being,
Through what new scenes and changes must we pass!
The wide, th' unbounded prospect lies before me;
But shadows, clouds, and darkness, rest upon it.
. . . . I shall never die.
The soul, secure in her existence, smiles
At the drawn dagger, and defies its point.
The stars shall fade away, the sun himself
Grow dim with age, and Nature sink in years,
But thou shall flourish in immortal youth,
Unhurt amidst the war of elements,
The wreck of matter, and the crush of worlds.

Cato (Act V, Scene 1)

[5] Lettre à Arnauld, *Philosophische Schriften*, Gerhardt's ed., II, 99 f.

♦ * ●

Eighteenth Century

EMANUEL SWEDENBORG (1688–1772)
Swedish Scientist, Philosopher, Theologian

[In these extracts from the essay "Swedenborg; or, the Mystic,"[1] Ralph
Waldo Emerson touches upon Swedenborg's view of reincarnation, but
first suggests how this doctrine might explain the seership of the famous
mystics of history, including the Swedish seer.]

The Arabians say, that Abul Khain, the mystic, and Abu Ali Seena, the
philosopher, conferred together; and, on parting, the philosopher said, "All
that he sees, I know;" and the mystic said, "All that he knows, I see." If
one should ask the reason of this intuition, the solution would lead us into
that property which Plato denoted as Reminiscence, and which is implied
by the Brahmins in the tenet of Transmigration. The soul having been
often born, or, as the Hindoos say, "travelling the path of existence through
thousands of births," having beheld the things which are here, those which
are in heaven and those which are beneath, there is nothing of which she
has not gained the knowledge: no wonder that she is able to recollect, in
regard to any one thing, what formerly she knew. . . .

That metempsychosis which is familiar in the old mythology of the
Greeks, collected in Ovid and in the Indian Transmigration, and is there
objective, or really takes place in bodies by alien will,—in Swedenborg's
mind has a more philosophic character. It is *subjective*, or depends entirely
upon the thought of the person.[2] All things in the universe arrange them-

---

[1] *Emerson's Complete Works*, Boston, Houghton Mifflin, 1886, IV, pp. 93–4, 120–21,
139.
[2] Swedenborg believed that animal-like men became animals in the after death world,
while the virtuous were transformed into pure spirits. He did not teach of reincarnation
on this earth. (Eds.)

selves to each person anew, according to his ruling love. . . . Everyone makes his own house and state. . . .

I think of [Swedenborg] as of some transmigrating votary of Indian legend, who says "Though I be dog, or jackal, or pismire, in the last rudiments of nature, under what integument or ferocity, I cleave to right, as the sure ladder that leads up to man and to God."

VOLTAIRE (1694–1778)
French Philosopher and Author

Pherecydes was the first among the Greeks who believed that souls existed from all eternity; and not the first, as has been supposed, who said that the soul survived the body. Ulysses, long before Pherecydes, had seen the souls of heroes in the infernal regions; but that souls were as old as the world was a system which had sprung up in the East, and was brought into the West by Pherecydes. I do not believe that there is among us a single system which is not to be found among the ancients. The materials of all our modern edifices are taken from the wreck of antiquity.

Voltaire's Philosophical Dictionary
(Section X, under "Soul")

The doctrine of metempsychosis is, above all, neither absurd nor useless. . . . It is not more surprising to be born twice than once; everything in nature is resurrection.[1]

SOAME JENYNS (1704–1787)
British Writer and Member of Parliament

The ancient doctrine of Transmigration seems the most rational and most consistent with [God's] wisdom and goodness; as by it all the unequal dispensations of things so necessary in one life, may be set right in another, and all creatures serve the highest and lowest, the most eligible and most burdensome offices of life by an equitable kind of rotation; by which means their rewards and punishments may not only be well proportioned to their behavior, but also subservient towards carrying on the Business of the Universe, and thus at the same time answer the purposes of both justice and utility.

Miscellaneous Pieces in Verse and Prose[1]

---

[1] Quoted in Emil Bock's *Wiederholte Erdenleben*, Stuttgart: 1952, p. 31: "La doctrine de la metempsychose surtout n'est ni absurde ni inutile? . . . Il n'est pas plus surprenant de naître deux fois qu'une. Tout est résurrection dans la nature."

---

[1] London, 1770, 3d ed., p. 288.

That mankind had existed in some state previous to the present was the opinion of the wisest sages of the most remote antiquity. . . . It is confirmed by reason, which teaches us that it is impossible that the conjunction of a male and female can create, or bring into being, an immortal soul: they may prepare a material habitation for it, but there must be an immaterial pre-existent inhabitant ready to take possession. Reason assures us that an immortal soul, which will exist eternally after the dissolution of the body, must have eternally existed before the formation of it.

"Disquisition on a Præexistent State"
Disquisitions on Several Subjects

BENJAMIN FRANKLIN (1706–1790)
American Statesman, Scientist, and Philosopher

[Benjamin Franklin's epitaph, written by himself at the age of twenty-two, is called by Carl Van Doren "the most famous of American epitaphs," [1] although it was never used on Franklin's tombstone. It appears, slightly modified, in almost a dozen versions, which is not surprising as he often made copies for friends and did not confine himself to the original wording. (See *The Papers of Benjamin Franklin*, ed. Leonard W. Labaree,[2] and article "B. Franklin's Epitaph" by L. H. Butterfield, in *New Colophon*.[3] The epitaph reads:]

The Body of B. Franklin,
Printer,
Like the Cover of an Old Book,
Its Contents Torn Out
And
Stripped of its Lettering and Gilding,
Lies Here
Food for Worms,
But the Work shall not be Lost,
For it Will as He Believed
Appear Once More
In a New and more Elegant Edition
Revised and Corrected
By the Author.

[Franklin thus explained his views:]
When I see nothing annihilated (in the works of God) and not a drop of water wasted, I cannot suspect the annihilation of souls, or believe that

1 *Benjamin Franklin.* New York: Viking, 1952, p. 123.
2 Yale University Press, I, 310.
3 III, 1950, pp. 9–30.

He will suffer the daily waste of millions of minds ready made that now exist, and put himself to the continual trouble of making new ones. Thus, finding myself to exist in the world, I believe I shall, in some shape or other, always exist; and, with all the inconveniences human life is liable to, I shall not object to a new edition of mine, hoping, however, that the *errata* of the last may be corrected.[4]

[In Emerson's *Journals*[5] he quotes Franklin, then eighty years old, as writing to a friend:]

I feel as if I was intruding among posterity when I ought to be abed and asleep. I look upon death to be as necessary to the constitution as sleep. We shall rise refreshed in the morning.

HENRY FIELDING (1707–1754)
British Novelist and Playwright

Fielding's novel, A *Journey from This World to the Next*, narrates the tale of one who has just died. En route to heaven numerous souls are met returning to earth life. In heaven he finds several historically famous characters, including Julian, the "Apostate," and is amazed to see the latter, thinking he surely would have been entitled to the bottomless pit. "He told me, that several lies had been raised on him in his former capacity, nor was he so bad a man as he had been represented. However, he had been denied admittance [to Elysium], and forced to undergo several subsequent pilgrimages on earth." A long list of these incarnations is given with details thereof. The story may be found in *The Works of Henry Fielding*, ed. James P. Browne.[1]

DAVID HUME (1711–1776)
Scottish Philosopher and Historian

Reasoning from the common course of nature, and without supposing any new interposition of the Supreme Cause, which ought always to be excluded from philosophy; what is incorruptible must also be ungenerable. The soul, therefore, if immortal, existed before our birth: And if the former existence noways concerns us, neither will the latter. . . . The Metempsychosis is, therefore, the only system of this kind, that philosophy can hearken to.

"The Immortality of the Soul" [1]

---

[4] Lady Caithness, *Old Truths in a New Light*. London: 1876, pp. 396–397.
[5] Boston: Houghton Mifflin, 1909, I, 320.

---

[1] London: 1871, IV.

---

[1] David Hume, *Essays, Moral, Political and Literary*. London: 1875, II, 400, 404.

FREDERICK THE GREAT (1712–1786)
King of Prussia

[Shortly before his death, Frederick said:]

Well, I feel that soon I shall have done with my earthly life. Now, since I am convinced that nothing existing in nature can be annihilated, so I know for a certainty that the more noble part of me will not cease to live. Though I may not be a king in my future life, so much the better: I shall nevertheless live an active life and, on top of it, earn less ingratitude.

King Frederick's Sayings and Thoughts
Compiler R. Rehlen

JOHANN GEORG SULZER (1720–1779)
Swiss Philosopher

If there are laws that unite the soul to a physical body, why should we doubt that under similar laws a second union of the soul with another body could take place?

Miscellaneous Philosophical Writings[1]

The German Transcendentalists

Professor Bertholet writes in *Transmigration of Souls*[1]: "During the classical period of German literature metempsychosis attracted such attention that that period may almost be styled the flourishing epoch of the doctrine."

The classical period had its distinct origin in the transcendental philosophy of Immanuel Kant, whose *Critique of Pure Reason*, published in 1781, opened a new era in metaphysical thought. Kant undertook to transfer attention from the objects that engaged the mind to the mind itself. He proposed a revolution in metaphysics comparable to the Copernican revolution in astronomy. As Copernicus, finding it impossible to explain the movements of the heavenly bodies on the supposition of their turning round the earth, posited the sun as the center, so Kant, perceiving the confusion that resulted from making man a satellite of the external world, resolved to place him in the central position. Carlyle speaks of August Schlegel's view that in its influence on the moral culture of Europe, Kant's philosophy was as important as the Reformation itself.[2]

[1] *Vermischte Philosophische Schriften*, II, 80 *et. seq.*

[1] New York: Harper and Row, 1909, p. 103.
[2] O. B. Frothingham, *Transcendentalism in New England*. New York: Putnam, 1876, p. 52.

Fichte became an enthusiastic interpreter of Kant's teachings, endeavoring to render them intelligible and attractive to minds of ordinary culture. Others whose brilliance added light and ardor to the Kantian revolution were: Lessing, Herder, Schleirmacher, Goethe, Schiller, Jean Paul Richter, the brothers August and Friedrich Schlegel, Hegel, and Schopenhauer—all of whom are quoted in the present work.

The transcendental movements in England and America were considerably influenced by these German thinkers, as pointed out by Frothingham.[3] Carlyle undertook the study of German and championed the cause of German philosophy and literature in the English reviews. He also made excellent translations, e.g., Goethe's *Wilhelm Meister*. Coleridge commenced the study of German when he was twenty-four, and at twenty-six visited Germany in company with Wordsworth, spending fourteen months there in hard study.

In America we find Frederic Hedge translating Herder's *Dialogues on Metempsychosis*, as well as other German works. In Emerson's papers, "Carlyle's Miscellanies," he presented Carlyle's articles on Kant, Fichte, Novalis, Goethe, and Richter.

The influence of oriental thought was pronounced among the German transcendentalists. August Schlegel published the first German translation of The Bhagavad-Gita, as well as other Sanskrit works, and paid tribute to the author of the Gita in these words:

By the Brahmins, reverence of masters is considered the most sacred of duties. Thee therefore, first, most holy prophet, interpreter of the Deity, by whatever name thou wast called among mortals, the author of this poem by whose oracles the mind is rapt with ineffable delight to doctrines lofty, eternal, and divine—thee first, I say, I hail, and shall always worship at thy feet.

Beethoven later came under the spell of the Orient. He was fond of copying mystical sentences from Eastern literature, and permanently framed on his desk this quotation: "I am that which is. I am all that was, that is, and that shall be." [4]

IMMANUEL KANT (1724–1804)
German Philosopher and Metaphysician

[Kant, in his teaching of an "unending progression," opposed static immortality in favor of progressive growth of the soul after death. In an early

---

[3] *Ibid.*, Chaps. 1–3.
[4] J. W. N. Sullivan, *Beethoven, His Spiritual Development*. New York: Knopf, 1927, pp. 212–213.

paper, "General History of Nature and Theory of the Heavens," he speculated that souls start imperfect from the sun, and travel by planet stages farther and farther away to a paradise in the coldest and remotest planet of our system. He wrote:]

In view of the endless duration of the immortal soul throughout the infinity of time, which even the grave itself does not interrupt . . . shall the soul remain forever attached to this one point of world-space, our earth? Will it never participate in a closer contemplation of the remaining wonders of creation? Who knows but that the intention is for it to become acquainted at close range, some day, with those far distant globes of the cosmic system and the excellence of their institutions, which from this distance already provoke our curiosity? Perhaps for just such a purpose some globes of the planetary system are in state of preparation as a new dwelling place for us to occupy after we have completed the period of time allotted for our sojourn here. Who knows but that the satellites coursing around Jupiter will some day shine on us?

General History of Nature[1]

Generation in the human race . . . depends on . . . many accidents . . . on the views and whims of government, nay, even on vice, so that it is difficult to believe in the eternal existence of a being whose life has first begun under circumstances so trivial, and so entirely dependent on our own choice. . . . It would seem as if we could hardly expect so wonderful an effect from causes so insignificant. But, in answer to these objections, we may adduce the transcendental hypothesis, that all life is properly intelligible, and not subject to the changes of time, and that it neither began in birth, nor will end in death. . . . If we could see ourselves and other objects *as they really are*, we should see ourselves in a world of spiritual natures, our community with which neither began at our birth nor will end with the death of the body.

Critique of Pure Reason (Part II: 1, iii)

[James Ward, who in his Gifford Lectures, *The Realm of Ends* (p. 404 fn), calls attention to the above passage, states that in Kant's lectures on metaphysics shortly before the publication of the *Critique* he taught the pre-existence of the soul. Ward cites Max Heinze's *Vorlesungen Kant's über Metaphysik*, 1894, p. 547 of the reprint from the Transactions of the Royal Society of Saxony.]

[1] *Allgemeine Naturgeschichte und Theorie des Himmels.* (Koenigsberg and Leipzig: 1755, pp. 198–199 (Part III, Appendix, "Conclusion").

G. E. LESSING (1729–1781)
German Dramatist and Critic

Is it after all so certain that my soul has only once inhabited the form of man? Is it after all so unreasonable to suppose that my soul, upon its journey to perfection, should have been forced to wear this fleshly veil more than once? Possibly this migration of the soul through several human bodies was based on a new system of thought. Possibly this new system was merely the oldest of all.

Observations Upon Campe's Philosophical Dialogues

[The following selection constitutes the famous conclusion of Lessing's *Education of the Human Race*, and has been called his "religious testament." This translation, as well as the extract just quoted, may be found in Bertholet's *Transmigration of Souls*.[1]]

Is this hypothesis [of metempsychosis] ridiculous merely because it is the oldest, because the human intellect adopted it without demur, before men's minds had been distracted and weakened by the sophistry of the schools? . . . On the contrary, the first and earliest opinion in matters of speculation is invariably the most probable, because it was immediately accepted by the sound understanding of mankind. . . . Why should I not return as often as I am capable of acquiring fresh knowledge and further power? Do I achieve so much in one sojourning as to make it not worth my while to return? Never! Or, is it that I forget my former life? Well for me that I forget. The recollection of my former state would enable me to turn my present condition to but poor account. And have I forgotten forever what I must forget for the time being? Or is it that I should lose so much time? Lose time! What need have I for haste? Is not the whole of eternity mine?

Education of the Human Race

JOHANN LAVATER (1741–1801)
Swiss Poet, Philosopher, and Mystic

[Writes Bertholet in *The Tranmigration of Souls*, pp. 110–111:]

As Lessing tells us, his theory of metempsychosis was based upon the ideas of Charles Bonnet, a physicist of Geneva, who wrote a treatise in French in 1769 upon philosophical palingenesis (rebirth), giving many so-

[1] London and New York: Harper and Row, 1909, pp. 105–108.

called proofs to show how from the original matter of the brain all created beings were transformed from corporeal to ethereal natures. Bonnet's ideas seem to have fallen upon fruitful soil elsewhere. In 1770 Lavater translated his treatise into German with annotations, and his social environment also shows how the belief in soul-transmigration haunted the minds of that age. . . . The diary of a woman of Zurich, who may be quoted as an eye-witness of that interesting period, . . . says: "The friends of Lavater at Copenhagen believe in a transmigration of the soul. They believe that several of Jesus' apostles live again on earth, without any recollection of their former lives as apostles."

GEORGE CHRISTOPH LICHTENBERG (1742–1799)
German Physicist and Mathematician

Lichtenberg relates in "Remarks of the Author about Himself," that at the age of eight he was guided to the idea of metempsychosis by an unusual boy of his acquaintance.[1] In *Selbstcharacteristik* ("Self-Study") he writes: "I cannot get rid of the thought that I died before I was born. . . . I feel so many things that were I to write them down the world would regard me as a madman. Consequently, I prefer to hold my peace." [2]

J. G. VON HERDER (1744–1803)
German Philosopher

Do you not know great and rare men who cannot have become what they are at once, in a single human existence? Who must often have existed before in order to have attained that purity of feeling, that instinctive impulse for all that is true, beautiful and good—in short, that elevation and natural supremacy over all around them? . . .

Have you never observed that children will sometimes, of a sudden, give utterance to ideas which makes us wonder how they got possession of them, which presuppose a long series of other ideas and secret self-communings, which break forth like a full stream out of the earth, an infallible sign that the stream was not produced in a moment from a few rain-drops, but had long been flowing concealed beneath the ground? . . .

Have you never had remembrances of a former state, which you could find no place for in this life? . . . Have you not seen persons, been in places, of which you were ready to swear that you had seen those persons, or

[1] *Vermischte Schriften* ("Miscellaneous Writings"), I, 9.
[2] *Ibid.*, II, 16–17.

had been in those places before? . . . And such are we; we who, from a hundred causes, have sunk so deep and are so wedded to matter, that but few reminiscences of so pure a character remain to us. The nobler class of men who, separated from wine and meat, lived in perfect simplicity, temperate and according to the order of Nature, carried it further, no doubt, than others, as we learn from the example of Pythagoras, of Iarchas, of Apollonius, and others, who remembered distinctly what and how many times they had been in the world before.

If we are blind, or can see but two steps beyond our noses, ought we therefore to deny that others may see a hundred or a thousand degrees farther, even to the bottom of time, into the deep, cool well of the foreworld, and there discern everything plain and bright and clear? . . .

I am not ashamed of my half-brothers, the brutes; on the contrary as far as they are concerned, I am a great advocate of metempsychosis. I believe, for a certainty, that they will ascend to a higher grade of being, and am unable to comprehend how anyone can object to this hypothesis which seems to have the analogy of the whole creation in its favour.

> *Dialogues on Metempsychosis*[1]
> *Trans. Frederic H. Hedge*

SIR WILLIAM JONES (1746–1794)
British Orientalist and Jurist

[Sir William Jones was "one of the great scholars of England. He was famous in jurisprudence and in oriental languages. . . . Founded the Asiatic Society of Bengal at Calcutta, through which, as well as through his publications, he had a great influence on literature, Oriental study, and philology in Western Europe." (*Columbia Encyclopedia.*[1]). Radhakrishnan in *The Brahma Sutra*[2] quotes from J. A. Arberry's *Asiatic Jones*[3] this excerpt from a letter of Sir William Jones to Earl Spencer, dated September 4, 1787, as illustrative of a westerner who looked with favor on the doctrine of rebirth:]

I am no Hindu; but I hold the doctrine of the Hindus concerning a future state to be incomparably more rational, more pious, and more likely to deter men from vice, than the horrid opinions inculcated by Christians on punishments without end.

---

[1] Frederic H. Hedge, *Prose Writers of Germany*. Philadelphia: 1852, pp. 248, 250–251, 257.

---

[1] Second edition, 1950.
[2] New York: Harper and Row, 1960, p. 206.
[3] 1946, p. 37.

JOHANN EHLERT BODE (1747–1826)
German Astronomer

Like his contemporary, Immanuel Kant, this celebrated astronomer (after whom Bode's Law was named) speculated upon the soul's progress among the various heavenly bodies. The French science writer, Louis Figuier, in his book *The Tomorrow of Death*,[1] reports that "Bode has written that we start from the coldest planet of our solar system (Uranus), and advance progressively from planet to planet, ever drawing near the Sun. In the Sun will live, in the opinion of this astronomer, the most perfect beings. . . ."

[1] Boston: 1888, p. 310.

Nineteenth Century

J. W. VON GOETHE (1749–1832)
German Poet

[Professor Denis Saurat writes that "Goethe interested himself in occult-ism all his life; and was one of the first to become acquainted with the literature of India." [1]

In his essay entitled "Goethe's Faust," George Santayana explains briefly Goethe's view of reincarnation: "A deep mind has deep roots in nature,—it will bloom many times over. But what a deep mind carries over into its next incarnation—perhaps in some remote sphere—is not its con-ventional merits and demerits, its load of remorse, or its sordid memories. These are washed away in its new baptism. What remains is only what was deep in that deep mind, so deep that new situations may again imply and admit it." [2] Goethe states in a letter to his close friend Charlotte von Stein: "How well it is that men should die, if only to erase their impressions and return clean washed.[3] A poem addressed to Frau von Stein appears below, followed by a letter concerning her written by Goethe in 1776 to Christoph Wieland—the German Voltaire.]

Tell me, what is Destiny preparing?
Tell me why we two have drawn so near?
Aeons since, you were my sister, sharing
Kin with me, or else my wife most dear.
Everything I am, my every feature,
You divined, my every nerve could thrill,

[1] *Literature and Occult Tradition.* New York: Dial Press, 1930, p. 44.
[2] George Santayana, *Three Philosophical Poets.* Harvard University, 1910.
[3] Bertholet, *op. cit.*, p. 104.

Read me at a glance—no other creature
Knows me as you know, nor ever will.
        "To Charlotte von Stein" [4]

I cannot explain the significance to me of this woman or her influence over me, except by the theory of metempsychosis.[5] Yes, we were once man and wife. Now our knowledge of ourselves is veiled, and lies in the spirit world. I can find no name for us—the past, the future, the All!
        Letter to Christoph Wieland [6]

The soul of man is like to water;
From Heaven it cometh
To Heaven it riseth
And then returneth to earth,
Forever alternating.
        "Song of the Spirits over the Waters" [7]

. . . .   Two souls contend
In me and both souls strive for masterdom,
Which from the other shall the scepter rend.
The first soul is a lover, clasping close
To this world tentacles of corporal flame,
The other seeks to rise with mighty throes
To those ancestral meadows whence it came.
        Faust (Act I, Scene 2)

As long as you are not aware of the continual law of Die and Be Again, you are merely a vague guest on a dark earth.
        "Selige Sehnsucht" [8]

[At Wieland's funeral, January 25, 1813, Johannes Falk asked Goethe what Wieland was now doing. In the course of his lengthy reply, Goethe stated:]

[4] Emil Ludwig, *Goethe.* New York: Putnam, 1928, p. 141.
[5] Frau von Stein apparently shared Goethe's views on rebirth, for in a memorial discourse delivered at Zwickau (Saxony) in 1892 by a Professor Keller on the occasion of the 150th anniversary of her birth, the professor stated: "Frau von Stein considered life as a school into which the human spirit enters, coming from its heavenly home. Laden therein with weakness, sin and doubts, after having overcome this difficult ordeal, grown in knowledge, and been purified, it enters again through the gates of death, its spiritual home, and continues thus in different forms of existence, which are always renewing themselves." (London: *Lucifer*, January, 1894, p. 428.)
[6] Bertholet, *op. cit.*, p. 104.
[7] *The Works of J. W. von Goethe*, ed. Nathan Haskell Dole. New York: 1902, vol. "Poetical Works," p. 192.
[8] One of Goethe's later poems. *West-Oestlicher Divan*, Book I.

I am certain that I have been here as I am now a thousand times before, and I hope to return a thousand times. . . . Respecting ourselves, however, it almost seems that our previous sojourns were too commonplace to deserve a second thought in the eyes of nature. . . . I cannot deny that there may be higher natures than our own among the Monads [Souls]. A World-Monad may produce out of the womb of its memories that which will prove prophetic but is actually a dim remembrance of something long expired. Similarly, human genius in a lightning flash of recollection can discover the laws involved in producing the universe, because it was present when those laws were established. . . .

As to the Monad to whom we are indebted for Wieland's appearance on earth, I cannot see what would prevent it from entering into the highest relations with the universe. . . . It would not astonish me if thousands of years hence I should meet him as a World-Monad—a star of the first magnitude. . . . When one reflects upon the eternity of the universe, one can conceive of no other destiny than that the Monads should eventually participate in the bliss of the Gods as joyfully cooperating forces. The work of creation will be entrusted to them. . . . Man is the dialogue between nature and God. On other planets this dialogue will doubtless be of a higher and profounder character. What is lacking is Self-Knowledge. After that the rest will follow.

Conversation with Johannes Falk [9]

WILLIAM BLAKE (1757–1827)
British Poet, Artist, and Mystic

In my brain are studies and chambers filled with books and pictures of old, which I wrote and painted in ages of eternity before my mortal life; and these works are the delight and study of archangels. . . . You, O dear Flaxman, are a sublime archangel, my friend and companion from eternity. I look back into the regions of reminiscence, and behold our ancient days before this earth appeared and its vegetative mortality to my mortal vegetated eyes. I see our houses of eternity which can never be separated, though our mortal vehicles should stand at the remotest corners of heaven from each other.

Letter to John Flaxman, the Sculptor [1]

Tell me where dwell the thoughts forgotten till thou call them forth?
Tell me where dwell the joys of old? and where the ancient loves,

[9] *Memoirs of Johannes Falk.* Leipzig: 1832. Reprinted in *Goethe-Bibliothek*, Berlin: 1911.

[1] William Scoones' *English Letters.* 1880, p. 361.

And when they will renew again, and the night of oblivion past,
That I might traverse times and spaces far remote, and bring
Comforts into a present sorrow and a night of pain?
"Visions of the Daughters of Albion"

. . . . [Man] stores his thoughts
As in a store house in his memory. He regulates the forms
Of all beneath and all above . . . he rises to the Sun,
And to the Planets of the Night, and to the stars that gild
The Zodiacs, and the stars that sullen stand to north and south;
He touches the remotest pole, and in the center weeps
That Man should Labour and sorrow, and learn and forget, and return
To the dark valley whence he came, and begin his labour anew.
In pain he sighs, in pain he labours in his universe. . . .
And in the cries of birth and in the groans of death his voice
Is heard throughout the Universe; wherever a grass grows,
Or a leaf buds, The Eternal Man is seen, is heard, is felt,
And all his sorrows, till he reassumes his ancient bliss.
"Vala, or The Four Zoas" (Night the Eighth)

THOMAS TAYLOR (1758–1835)
British Classicial Scholar

[This friend of William Blake stands out as the giant Platonic scholar of all times. Surnamed "The Platonist," he published more than sixty books covering the writings of Plato, Aristotle, and the Neoplatonists, most of these being translated into English for the first time. Professor Alexander Wilder writes of him: "It must be conceded that he was endowed with a superior qualification—that of an intuitive perception of the interior meaning of the subjects which he considered. Others may have known more Greek, but he knew more Plato." Emerson called him "that eminent benefactor of scholars and philosophers." [1] Quoting from Taylor's introduction to his translation of *The Works of Plato*:[2]]

Let not the reader . . . be surprised at the solitariness of the paths through which I shall attempt to conduct him, or at the novelty of the objects which will present themselves in the journey: for perhaps he may fortunately recollect that he has travelled the same road before, that the scenes were once familiar to him, and that the country through which he is passing is his native land. . . .

As the human soul, according to Plato, ranks among the number of

[1] *The Dial*, April, 1844.
[2] London: 1804, I, iv, lxii–lxiii.

those souls that *sometimes* follow the mundane divinities [and sometimes do not] hence it possesses a power of descending infinitely into generation, or the sublunary region, and of ascending from generation to real being. . . . It remains, therefore, that every soul must perform periods, both of ascensions from generation, and of descensions into generation; and that this will never fail, through an infinite time. From all this it follows that the soul, while an inhabitant of earth, is in a fallen condition, an apostate from deity, an exile from the orb of light.

Introduction to "The Works of Plato"

FRIEDRICH SCHILLER (1759–1805)
German Poet and Dramatist

Were our Beings once together twin'd?
Was it therefore that our bosoms pin'd?
Were we in the light of suns now dead,
In the days of rapture long since fled,
Into One united?
Aye, we were so!—thou wert link'd with me
In Æone that has ceas'd to be;
On the mournful page of vanish'd time.
"The Mystery of Reminiscence" 1

[Schiller at the age of twenty-one, upon completion of his studies at the Karlsshule in Stuttgart, wrote a thesis entitled "Concerning the Connection between the Animal and the Spiritual Nature of Man." In Section 27, treating of death, he stated:]

Matter decomposes into its final elements, which now wander through the kingdoms of nature in other forms and conditions. . . . The soul continues to exercise its power of thought and views the universe from other aspects. Of course, one can say, that it has not in the least exhausted this sphere as yet. . . . Can one be sure that this earth is forever lost? Do we not lay aside many a book we do not understand, to take it up again years later when we will understand it better?

J. G. FICHTE (1762–1814)
German Philosopher and Metaphysician

These two systems, the purely spiritual and the sensuous—which last may consist of an immeasurable series of particular lives—exist in me from the

1 Another translation: *The Works of Friedrich Schiller*, ed. Nathan Haskell Dole (New York: Bigelow, Brown, 1902), volume *Poems*, pp. 9–10.

moment in which my active reason is developed, and pursue their parallel course. . . . The former alone gives to the latter meaning, and purpose, and value. I am immortal, imperishable, eternal, so soon as I form the resolution to obey the law of Reason. . . . After an existence of myriad lives [the supersensuous world] cannot be more present than at this moment. Other conditions of my sensuous existence are to come; but these are no more the true life than the present condition. . . . Even because [Nature] puts me to death she must quicken me anew. It can only be my higher life, unfolding itself in her, and that which mortals call death is the visible appearing of a second vivification. . . .

Man is not a product of the world of sense; and the end of his existence can never be attained in that world. His destination lies beyond time and space and all that pertains to sense.

The Destination of Man [1]
Trans. Frederic H. Hedge

JEAN PAUL RICHTER (1763–1825)
German Author

[From Jean Paul's *Selina: On the Immortality of the Soul*, called his swan song:[2]]

The least valid objection to the theory of soul-circulation is that we forget these journeyings. Even during this life and without experiencing a "change of clothes," multifarious conditions vanish from our memories. How then should we expect to remember the different bodies and the still more varied conditions experienced in previous lives? Why not allow a way of thinking to enjoy full light that a Plato, a Pythagoras, and whole nations and eras have not disdained? . . . Let the soul return as often as it wishes. Certainly the earth is rich enough to bestow ever new gifts, new centuries, new countries, new minds, new discoveries and hopes.

Selina

Always employ a language some years in advance of the child (men of genius in their books speak to us from the vantage-ground of centuries) . . . Let the teacher, especially he who is too much in the habit of attributing all learning to teaching, consider that the child already carries half his world, that of mind—the objects, for instance, of moral and metaphysical contemplation—ready formed within him; and hence language, being pro-

---

[1] F. H. Hedge, *Prose Writers of Germany*. Philadelphia: 1852, pp. 398, 401, 404.

[1] *Jean Paul's Werke*. Berlin and Stuttgart: Paul Nerrlich, undated, I. lxvii.

vided only with physical images, cannot give, but merely illumine, his mental conceptions.

Levana; or the Doctrine of Education[2]

NAPOLEON BONAPARTE (1769–1821)
Emperor of France (Napoleon I)

Here was a man born in the humblest possible condition of life, rising until he dominated empires and sent kings from their thrones at a single word, a man who, in those strange, abnormal conditions into which he sometimes passed, would cry out to his Marshals: "I am Charlemagne. Do you know who I am? I am Charlemagne." Emil Ludwig quotes him as stating: "Tell the Pope that I am keeping my eyes open; tell him that I am Charlemagne, the Sword of the Church, his Emperor, and as such I expect to be treated.[1]

Prince Talleyrand in his *Memoirs*[2] writes thus of a stormy meeting on June 18, 1811 between Bonaparte and several dignitaries of the Church:

The phrase which follows, and which he repeated every three or four minutes . . . revealed the depth of his thought. "Messieurs," he exclaimed to them, "you wish to treat me as if I were Louis le Débonnaire. Do not confound the son with the father. You see in me Charlemagne. . . . I am Charlemagne, I . . . yes, I am Charlemagne."

G. W. F. HEGEL (1770–1831)
German Philosopher

Change while it imports dissolution, involves at the same time the rise of a *new* life—that while death is the issue of life, life is also the issue of death. This is a grand conception; one which the Oriental thinkers attained, and which is perhaps the highest in their metaphysics. In the idea of *Metempsychosis* we find it evolved in its relation to individual existence; but a myth more generally known, is that of the *Phoenix* as a type of the Life of *Nature*; eternally preparing for itself its funeral pile, and consuming itself upon it; but so that from its ashes is produced the new, renovated, fresh life. . . . Spirit—consuming the envelope of its existence—does not merely pass into another envelope, nor rise rejuvenescent from the ashes of its previous form; it comes forth exalted, glorified, a purer spirit. It certainly makes war upon itself—consumes its own existence; but in this very destruction it works up that existence into a new form, and each successive

[2] Boston: 1863, p. 348.

[1] Emil Ludwig, *Napoleon*. New York: Boni & Liveright, 1926, p. 245.
[2] Paris and Boston: Napoleon Society, 1895, II, 77.

phase becomes in its turn a material, working on which it exalts itself to a new grade. . . .

Nothing in the past is lost for it, for the Idea is ever present; Spirit is immortal; with it there is no past, no future, but an essential now. This necessarily implies that the present form of Spirit comprehends within it all earlier steps. . . . The life of the ever present Spirit is a circle of progressive embodiments, which looked at in one aspect still exist beside each other, and only as looked at from another point of view appear as past. The grades which Spirit seems to have left behind it, it still possesses in the depths of its present.

The Philosophy of History (Introduction)
Trans. J. Sibree

WILLIAM WORDSWORTH (1770–1850)
Poet Laureate of England (1843–1850)

[An article in the weekly London periodical *The Spectator*[1] states: "There did not seem, until recently, to be any definite reference to the belief [of reincarnation] in Wordsworth's poems, for the well-known lines, 'Our birth is but a sleep and a forgetting,' are a statement of the soul's pre-existence, rather than of its repeated returns to earth. But the newly discovered poem in [his sister] Dorothy Wordsworth's handwriting (the MS. of which is to be sold at Sotheby's on December 15th) provides remarkable evidence of the poet's interest in this age-old doctrine. The lines are addressed to an infant, and begin as follows:"]

Oh, sweet new-comer to the changeful earth,
If, as some darkling seers have boldly guessed,
Thou hadst a being and a human birth,
And wert erewhile by human parents blessed,
Long, long before thy present mother pressed
Thee, helpless stranger, to her fostering breast.

[In view of the foregoing, Wordsworth's famous "Ode to Immortality,"—extracts from which will follow—may be invested with new significance. Walter Pater wrote in *Appreciations, Wordsworth:*[2] "He had pondered deeply . . . on those strange reminiscences and forebodings which seem to make our lives stretch before and behind us. . . . Following the soul backwards and forwards, on these endless ways, his sense of man's dim, poten-

[1] December 10, 1927, p. 1041.
[2] London: 1904, pp. 53–54.

tial powers became a pledge to him, indeed, of a future life, but carried him back also to that mysterious notion of an earlier state of existence—the fancy of the Platonists—the old heresy of Origen."]

Our birth is but a sleep and a forgetting;
The Soul that rises with us, our life's Star,
Hath had elsewhere its setting,
And cometh from afar.
Not in entire forgetfulness
And not in utter nakedness,
But trailing clouds of glory do we come
From God who is our home.
Heaven lies about us in our infancy!

Shades of the prison-house begin to close
Upon the growing Boy;
But He beholds the light, and whence it flows
He sees it in his joy.
The Youth, who daily farther from the east
Must travel, still is Nature's Priest,
And by the vision splendid
Is on his way attended;
At length the Man perceives it die away,
And fade into the light of common day.

Earth fills her lap with pleasures of her own. . . .
The homely Nurse doth all she can
To make her Foster-child, her Inmate Man,
Forget the glories he hath known,
And that imperial palace whence he came . . .
Though nothing can bring back the hour
Of splendour in the grass, of glory in the flower . . .
Yet in my heart of hearts I feel your might. . . .

> "Intimations of Immortality from
> Recollections of Early Childhood"

SAMUEL T. COLERIDGE (1772–1834)
British Poet and Critic

[A 25-page article entitled "Coleridge—Metempsychosis . . ." by Irene H. Chayes, appearing in the *Journal of English Literary History*[1] published by Johns Hopkins University, traces Coleridge's interest in reincarnation to

[1] December, 1958.

the works of two authors he was studying when the poem below was written in September, 1796, namely, the writings of Chevalier Ramsay and Thomas Taylor, both of whom are quoted in the present volume:]

Oft o'er my brain does that strange fancy roll
Which makes the present (while the flash doth last)
Seem a mere semblance of some unknown past,
Mixed with such feelings as perplex the soul
Self-questioned in her sleep; and some have said
We lived, ere yet this robe of flesh we wore.
O my sweet baby! when I reach my door,
If heavy looks should tell me thou art dead,
(As sometimes, through excess of hope, I fear)
I think that I should struggle to believe
Thou wert a spirit, to this nether sphere
Sentenc'd for some more venial crime to grieve;
Dids't scream, then spring to meet Heaven's quick reprieve
While we wept idly o'er thy little bier!

"On a Homeward Journey upon
Hearing of the Birth of a Son"

FRIEDRICH VON SCHLEGEL (1772–1829)
German Philosopher

Philosophy has primarily to refute two basic errors: firstly, that the human soul can dissolve into nothingness, and secondly, that man, without any effort of his own, is already fully endowed with immortality. . . . Man as he is now is entirely too imperfect, too material, to claim that higher kind of immortality. He will have to enter into other earthly, yet far more refined and transfigured forms and developments before he can directly partake of the eternal glory of the divine world of light. . . .

The idea of metempsychosis, embraced by mysticism, is remarkable in itself for its antiquity. . . . It does not permit the soul to pass to full freedom before it has incarnated in many bodies. Here we view metempsychosis in its most general meaning as continuance of spirit, alternately using organic forms, and not in the sense of . . . an aggravating punishment ever accelerating.

Cologne Lectures (1804–1806)[1]

Inasmuch as the true Indian teaching of metempsychosis, as we now know it correctly from the sources, is too serious and solemn to find much

[1] *Kölner Vorlesungen*, ed. von Windischmann. Bonn: 1837, pp. 202–203, 205–206.

credence and applause in our time, the attempt has been made recently to carry it entirely into the realm of romanticism and to paint the future life in glowing colors as a sort of astronomical excursion from one star to another. . . . Would it not be more advisable, and more appropriate to human intellect, if man would first turn his gaze upon himself and his present dwelling place, the earth, instead of at once disappearing into the starry skies? May not he find that which he seeks so often in the distance far closer at hand?

The Philosophy of Life[2]

CHARLES FOURIER (1772–1837)
French Social Scientist and Reformer

[Fourier is generally regarded as the founder of Socialism. A famous example of a Fourieristic experiment, Brook Farm in the United States, captured the interest of the American Transcendentalists. Emerson, however, found a number of drawbacks in Fourier's ideas, but nevertheless wrote in his article, "Fourierism and the Socialists": "The increasing zeal and numbers of the disciples of Fourier, in America and in Europe, entitle them to an attention which their theory and practical projects will justify and reward. . . . In a day of small, sour, and fierce schemes, one is admonished and cheered by a project of such friendly aims, and of such bold and generous proportion; there is an intellectual courage and strength in it, which is superior and commanding." [1]

Fourier was a reincarnationist, as his various books including his well-known *Theory of Universal Unity* reveal. In introducing *The Passions of the Human Soul*,[2] the translator, the Reverend John Reynell Morell, states that Fourier believed in an "alternating passage from the visible into the invisible world, and *vice versa*, [which] commenced with the existence of humanity on this globe, and will continue to the end of time; that is, until the decline of this planet Earth, and the final transmigration of humanity *en masse* unto another planet." In the book itself Fourier states:[3]]

I do not reckon the numerous revivals or incarnations of our souls on the globe as the future life. . . . In fact, at the epochs when it is freed from the human body, it revives instantly in the great soul of the globe, whereof it is part and parcel, and disdains the present life, as at the mo-

---

[2] *Philosophie des Lebens.* Vienna Lectures, 1827, Lecture VI, p. 193. *The Philosophy of Life*, trans. A. J. W. Morrison. London: 1847, p. 139. The translation above is a new one.

[1] *The Dial*, July, 1842.
[2] London: 1851.
[3] I, 220–221.

ment of waking we despise or cherish a dream, according as it has been happy or unhappy. Now the civilizee and barbarian state is an ugly dream to 99/100 of souls. . . . After a period passed in the great soul, they go to sleep and are born again upon the globe in a new body. . . . Some exceptional individuals . . . remember their past existences.

The Passions of the Human Soul

ROBERT SOUTHEY (1774–1843)
Poet Laureate of England (1813–1843)

I have a strong and lively faith in a state of continued consciousness from this stage of existence, and that we shall recover the consciousness of some lower stages through which we may previously have passed seems to me not impossible. . . . The system of progressive existence seems, of all others, the most benevolent; and all that we do understand is so wise and so good, and all we do or do not, so perfectly and overwhelmingly wonderful, that the most benevolent system is the most probable.

Letters[1]

JOHN LEYDEN (1775–1811)
Scottish Poet and Orientalist

Ah, sure, as Hindoo legends tell,
When music's tones the bosom swell
The scenes of former life return,
Ere sunk beneath the morning star,
We left our parent climes afar,
Immured in mortal forms to mourn.
      "Ode to Scottish Music"

SIR HUMPHRY DAVY (1778–1829)
British Chemist

We sometimes, in sleep, lose the beginning and end of a dream, and recollect the middle of it, and one dream has no [seeming] connection with another, and yet we are conscious of an infinite variety of dreams, and there is a strong analogy for believing in an infinity of past existences, which must have had connection . . . With its present organization, the intellect of man is naturally limited and imperfect; but this depends upon its material machinery; and in a higher organized form, it may be imagined to possess infinitely higher powers. . . . It does not, however, appear improbable to me, that some of the more refined machinery of thought may adhere, even

[1] E. D. Walker, *Reincarnation*, p. 94.

in another state, to the sentient principle; for though the organs of gross sensation, the nerves and brain, are destroyed by death, yet something of the more ethereal nature . . . may be less destructible. And I sometimes imagine, that many of those powers which have been called instinctive belong to the more refined clothing of the spirit; conscience, indeed, seems to have some undefined source, and may bear relations to a former state of being.

Consolations in Travel (Dialogue IV)

THOMAS MOORE (1779–1852)
Irish Poet

Though new the frame
Thy soul inhabits now, I've tracked its flame
For many an age, in every chance and change
Of that existence, through whose varied range—
As through a torch-race, where, from hand to hand,
The flying youths transmit their shining brand—
From frame to frame the unextinguished soul
Rapidly passes, till it reach the goal!

Lalla Rookh[1]

PIERRE JEAN DE BÉRANGER (1780–1857)
French Lyric Poet

In Philosophic mood, last night, as idly I was lying,
That souls may transmigrate methought there could be no denying:
So, just to know to what I owe propensities so strong,
I drew my soul into a chat—our gossip lasted long.
"A votive offering," she observed, "well might I claim from thee;
For thou in being hadst remained a cipher but for me:
Yet not a virgin soul was I when first in thee enshrined."
Ah! I suspected, little soul, thus much that I should find!

"La Métempsycose" [1]

ARTHUR SCHOPENHAUER (1788–1860)
German Philosopher

[A philosophy of optimism is apparent in the selections here presented, yet, as is well known, Schopenhauer's theorizing frequently led him to utmost despair. This seems to have arisen because an impassable gulf was believed to exist between the conscious personality and what Schopenhauer called

[1] "The Veiled Prophet of Khorassan," Stanza 7.

[1] See complete poem in Walker's *Reincarnation*, pp. 173–74.

the Will, and von Hartmann was later to call the Unconscious. As the personal consciousness was thought to dissolve completely at death without transferring its memories or experiences to the Will or the Unconscious, its life was purely illusory, meaningless to itself, and its struggles and sufferings were forever unrewarded. The root of the difficulty may possibly be traced to Schopenhauer's rather limited view of Hindu and Buddhist metaphysics. This is readily understandable, for the translated versions of Eastern scriptures available in his day were more than inadequate. The Upanishads, for example, so highly prized by this great philosopher, could be read only in Anquetil Duperron's Latin translation (1801) of the Persian version made at the instance of the sixteenth-century Mogul Emperor Akbar. Gustave Geley, a noted French medical doctor, makes an interesting analysis of what he calls the missing element in the philosophy of Schopenhauer and von Hartmann, and asks:

Why should consciousness be exclusively bound to the temporary semblances which make up the universe? Why should not all that falls within its domain be registered, assimilated, and preserved by the eternal essence of being? What! The divine principle, the will or the unconscious, is to be allowed all potentialities except one, and that the most important of all—the power to acquire and retain the knowledge of itself?[1] How much more logical it is to presume that this real and eternal will which is objectified in transitory and factitious personalities, will keep integrally the remembrances acquired during these objectifications.[2]

The following selections suggest, however, that Schopenhauer often took a more fluidic and hopeful position than the foregoing comments would indicate:]

The individuality disappears at death, but we lose nothing thereby for it is only the manifestation of quite a different Being—a Being ignorant of time, and, consequently, knowing neither life nor death. . . . When we die, we throw off our individuality like a worn-out garment, and rejoice because we are about to receive a new and better one. . . .

Were an Asiatic to ask me for a definition of Europe, I should be forced to answer him: It is that part of the world which is haunted by the incredible delusion that man was created out of nothing, and that his present birth is his first entrance into life.

Parerga and Paralipomena[3]

---

[1] Through experiments in age regression, psychologists have now demonstrated that at least within the span of this life the subconscious mind preserves the record of even the most fleeting experience. (Eds.)
[2] *From The Unconscious to The Conscious.* New York: Harper and Row, 1920, p. 198.
[3] Vol. II, Chaps. 10 and 15.

We find the doctrine of metempsychosis, springing from the earliest and noblest ages of the human race, always spread abroad in the earth as the belief of the great majority of mankind. . . .

In the succession of births . . . the persons who now stand in close connection or contact with us will also be born along with us at the next birth, and will have the same or analogous relations and sentiments towards us as now, whether these are of a friendly or a hostile description. . . .

What sleep is for the individual, death is for the will. . . . It would not endure to continue the same actions and sufferings throughout an eternity without true gain, if memory and individuality remained to it. It flings them off, and this is lethe; and through this sleep of death it reappears refreshed and fitted out with another intellect, as a new being—"a new day tempts to new shores." . . .

These constant new births, then, constitute the succession of the life-dreams of a will which in itself is indestructible. . . . Every new-born being indeed comes fresh and blithe into the new existence, and enjoys it as a free gift: but there is, and can be, nothing freely given. Its fresh existence is paid for by the old age and death of a worn-out existence which has perished, but which contained the indestructible seed out of which this new existence has arisen: they are one being. To show the bridge between the two would certainly be the solution of a great riddle.

The World as Will and Idea[4]

FRIEDRICH RÜCKERT (1788–1866)
German Poet and Orientalist

First, Nature builds the body,
A house with doors of sense,
Wherein a strange child, the Spirit is born.
Tools he finds and uses at his pleasure.
Leaving the house, it crumbles,
But the architect always builds anew
And beckons the heavenly guest again to earthly accommodation.
"Wisdom of the Brahmins"

JOHAN LUDVIG HEIBERG (1791–1860)
Danish Author

[Heiberg states that his long poem "The Newly Married" is based on the events that transpired during his own honeymoon. The poem depicts, in part, a newly-wed couple seeking shelter in the home of a poor widow and

4 Trans. R. B. Haldane and J. Kemp. London: Kegal Paul, 1906, III, 299–300, 302.

her adopted son Fredrik, who as an orphaned child found her in a strange way. The little fellow filled an empty place in her heart, her own son being dead. Fredrik, now grown, falls so passionately in love with the young bride that he secretly schemes to kill the husband on a hunting trip. The mother has a fearful premonition and speaks to Fredrik thus:]

"I have never told you, my son . . . maybe the heart gets rest, when I speak to you of my fate; maybe it becomes easier, when we are two to carry the secret tortures. That son, which was given me in my marriage, oh—you don't know how he died!—he was decapitated and his blood covered the scaffold. Rejected by a young and beautiful maiden, who was deaf and blind to his love, he killed a more lucky lover . . . while hunting."

"That morning, when he was to suffer his horrible doom . . . my son sank to my breast and exclaimed: 'Give me a word, a powerful word, which will comfort me on my last walk alive!' And I said—Fredrik, you frighten me! . . . You stare at me as white as a corpse."

"Oh mother! stop!—You said: 'When before your saviour you stand say: My God and my Brother! Forgive me for your martyr-wounds; for my anger and for my mother!' "

[Mother:] "How do you know that?" [Fredrik:] "It was I! I am your real son, and now he lives the life anew." [Mother:] "Fredrik, has insanity overtaken your mind?" [Fredrik:] "No, mother, don't be afraid! But up to now, I walked as one blind, through all these long years. My consciousness awoke in this hour. Now I see my entire self, now I see the basis of my life and at the same time I hope and I tremble. Ah, I feel again my horrible fear, when my head I laid on the block. But still my thought held the comforting words you spoke.

"When the ax fell my consciousness left me. I woke up in strange places; and in my wanderings my eye rested on a man in white garments. I know not . . . maybe he was my Saviour, but ah! I did not know him, so my prayer to him I did not say, though his eyes were so mild looking . . . his hair was shining light. He said: 'Turn around! Your place is not here. On earth you suffered death for your crime; here is no punishment, no penalty. So go back, down to earth to live over again your days.'

"Then I turned back on fearful foot; wandering ever so long. . . . I needed rest and slept a sleep so deep I knew nothing of what happened. But, when I woke up as a child I sensed I was another. Oh, mother, look at me; I need you to console me now. Not another time, that I can promise for certain, shall your son make sad your heart.—She does not answer! . . . What a deep sigh she draws—She is dead!"

"The Newly Married"

PERCY BYSSHE SHELLEY (1792–1822)
British Poet

[In Dowden's *Life of Shelley*,[1] the following anecdote of the poet is reported as told by his friend Hogg:]

One morning we had been reading Plato together so diligently that the usual hour of exercise passed away unperceived. We sallied forth hastily to take the air for half an hour before dinner. In the middle of Magdalen Bridge we met a woman with a child in her arms. Shelley was more attentive at that instant to our conduct in a life that was past, or to come, than to a decorous regulation . . . of his behavior. . . . With abrupt dexterity he caught hold of the child. The mother . . . held it fast by its long train.

"Will your baby tell us anything about pre-existence, madam?" he asked in a piercing voice and with a wistful look. The mother made no answer, but perceiving that Shelley's object was not murderous, but altogether harmless, she . . . relaxed her hold. "Will your baby tell us anything about pre-existence, madam?" he repeated, with unabated earnestness. "He cannot speak, sir," said the mother seriously.

"Worse and worse," cried Shelley with an air of deep disappointment. . . . "But surely the babe can speak if he will. . . . He may fancy perhaps that he cannot, but it is only a silly whim. He cannot have forgotten entirely the use of speech in so short a time. The thing is absolutely impossible." . . .

Shelley sighed deeply as we walked on. "How provokingly close are those newborn babes! but it is not the less certain, notwithstanding the cunning attempts to conceal the truth, that all knowledge is reminiscence. The doctrine is far more ancient than the times of Plato, and as old as the venerable allegory that the Muses are the daughters of Memory; not one of the nine was ever said to be the child of Invention."

[In his brief essay "On a Future State," Shelley asks: "Have we existed before birth? It is difficult to conceive the possibility of this." Could there exist "a principle or substance which escapes the observation of the chemist and anatomist" and pre-exists our birth?]

It certainly may be; though it is sufficently unphilosophical to allege the possibility of an opinion as a proof of its truth. Does it see, hear, feel, before its combination with those organs on which sensation depends?

[1] London: 1886, I, 81.

Does it reason, imagine, apprehend . . . ? If there are no reasons to suppose that we have existed before that period at which our existence apparently commences, then there are no grounds for [the] supposition that we
shall continue to exist after our existence has apparently ceased. So far as
thought and life is concerned, the same will take place with regard to us,
individually considered, after death, as had [taken] place before our birth.

"On a Future State" [2]

Worlds on worlds are rolling ever
From creation to decay,
Like the bubbles on a river,
Sparkling, bursting, borne away.
But they are still immortal
Who, through birth's orient portal
And death's dark chasm hurrying to and fro,
Clothe their unceasing flight
In the brief dust and light
Gathered around their chariots as they go;
New shapes they still may weave,
New gods, new laws receive:
Bright or dim are they as the robes they last
On Death's bare ribs had cast.

"Hellas" (Lines 196–210)

[In the poem below, Shelley casts Ariel, from Shakespeare's *Tempest*, in
the role of a transcendent Self in man—a Self which is "crucified" when
neglected. In the scene here portrayed, Ariel is offering the lovely Miranda
the gift of a guitar:]

Ariel to Miranda: . . . Take
This slave of music for the sake
Of him, who is the slave of thee. . . .
Poor Ariel sends this silent token
Of more than ever can be spoken;
Your guardian spirit, Ariel, who
From life to life must still pursue
Your happiness;—for thus alone
Can Ariel ever find his own. . . .
When you die, the silent moon,
In her interlunar swoon,
Is not sadder in her cell
Than deserted Ariel;

[2] *The Complete Works of Percy Bysshe Shelley*. New York: Scribner, 1929, VI, 208.

When you live again on earth,
Like an unseen star of birth
Ariel guides you o'er the sea
Of life from your nativity.
Many changes have been run
Since Ferdinand and you begun
Your course of love, and Ariel still
Has tracked your steps, and served your will;
Now, in humbler, happier lot,
This is all remembered not;
And now, Alas! the poor sprite is
Imprisoned, for some fault of his
In a body like a grave.

"With a Guitar, to Jane"

THOMAS CARLYLE (1795–1881)
Scottish Essayist and Historian

[In the myth "The Twilight of the Gods"] the Gods and Jötuns, the divine Powers and the chaotic brute ones, after long contest and partial victory by the former, meet at last in universal world-embracing wrestle and duel; World-serpent against Thor, strength against strength; mutually extinctive; and ruin, "twilight," sinking into darkness, swallows the created Universe. The old Universe with its God is sunk; but it is not final death: there is to be a new Heaven and a new Earth. . . .

Curious; this law of mutation, which also is a law written in man's inmost thought, had been deciphered by these old earnest Thinkers in their rude style; and how, though all dies, and even gods die, yet all death is but a phœnix fire-death, and new-birth into the Greater and the Better! It is the fundamental Law of Being for a creature made of Time, living in this Place of Hope. All earnest men have seen into it; may still see into it.

Heroes and Hero-Worship (Lecture 1)

Whatsoever sensibly exists, whatsoever represents Spirit to Spirit, is properly a Clothing, a suit of Raiment, put on for a season, and to be laid off. . . . Nay, if you consider it, what is Man himself, and his whole terrestrial Life, but an Emblem; a Clothing or visible Garment for that divine life of his, cast hither, like a light-particle down from Heaven? . . . Are we not Spirits, that are shaped into a body, into an Appearance; and that fade away again into air and Invisibility? . . . Ghosts! There are nigh a thousand million of them walking the earth openly at noontide; some half hundred have vanished from it, some half hundred have arisen in it, ere thy watch tick one. . . . Death and birth are the vesper and matin bells that summon mankind to sleep and to rise refreshed for new advancement.

Sartor Resartus[1]

HEINRICH HEINE (1797–1856)
German Lyric Poet and Critic

[The selections below are from Heine's *Norderney*, published as Book II in his *Travel-Pictures*,[1] translated by Francis Storr. Elsewhere Heine speaks of a vision experienced in Venice: "I could not eat, still less could I drink. Hot tears fell into my glass, and in that glass I saw my beloved home, the blue waters of the sacred Ganges; the Himalayas, with their eternal snows. . . ." [2]]

I know that I am laying myself open to ridicule, but the truth must be told: I am tormented not a little by the disproportion between body and soul . . . and I often ponder on the doctrine of metempsychosis. Who can understand the divine irony which delights in accentuating the manifold contradictions between body and soul? Who can tell what tailor now inherits the soul of a Plato, what dominie is heir to Caesar's spirit? . . . Perchance the soul of Yenghis Khan now animates a reviewer who, without knowing it, daily slashes the souls of his faithful Bashirs and Kalmucks in the pages of a critical journal. . . . But who is able to look down on the ways of mortals from the heights of omniscience of the past? As I walk by night on the seashore, and listen to the song of the waves, all sorts of visions and memories flood my brain. I seem as though I had once looked down from above on the same shifting scene, and, dizzy with terror, had fallen to the earth. I seem as though, with telescopic eyes, I had seen the stars moving through the heavens large as life . . . then, as from millennial depths, there surge up . . . thoughts of primeval wisdom, but all so misty that I know not what they mean.

Norderney

H.: Regarding my actions in this world, I care little about the existence of heaven or hell; self-respect does not allow me to guide my acts with an eye to heavenly reward or fear of hellish punishment. I pursue the good because it is beautiful and attracts me, and shun the bad because it is ugly and repulsive. All our actions should originate from the spring of unselfish love, whether there be continuation after death or not.

---

[1] Book I, Chap. 11; Book III, Chaps. 7 and 8.

[1] London: George Bell, 1907, pp. 94–95.

[2] *Ibid.*, Book III, p. 120. Heine's *Ideen oder das Buch Le Grand*, or "Book of Ideas."

M.: Then, you do not believe in immortality?

H.: I, doubt it? I, whose heart is rooted in the most distant milleniums of the past . . . I, should not believe in immortality?

Die Bader von Lucca (Chap. 17)

PIERRE LEROUX (1797–1871)
French Philosopher, Journalist, and Statesman

Leroux was co-founder with George Sand of *Revue Indépendante*. A number of French writers of this period viewed with sympathy the doctrine of many lives. Among those to be shortly quoted are De Balzac, George Sand, Victor Hugo and Flaubert. In an article in the *Fortnightly Review*, Leroux's views on reincarnation are given as found in his well known work *De l'Humanite:*

Pierre Leroux shows that, according to Plato and Descartes, the being who lives before you, and that you imagine to have been born yesterday only to die tomorrow, is an eternal being who has already lived . . . It is the principle of Reminiscence of Plato and of Innate Ideas of Descartes. What then matters it that the various beings coming again into life should have no *formal* recollection of their previous existence? Each of their existences is a link in the chain; but they do not repeat one another, they are not the useless reproduction of a single manifestation. . . . In sleep our ideas, our sensations, our sentiments of the evening before, seem to become incarnate in us, become ourselves by a phenomenon analogous to that of the digestion and assimilation of our bodily food. It is thus that sleep regenerates us, and that we emerge from it the stronger, with a certain oblivion. In death, which is a mightier oblivion, it seems that our life becomes digested and elaborated. Then comes the awakening, or new birth. . . . We are in our potentiality the exact sequel of what we were; still the same being but grown larger.[1]

A. BRONSON ALCOTT (1799–1888)
American Educator and Transcendentalist

[The first selections are from *The Record of a School* by Elizabeth P. Peabody, a book that contains her eye-witness reports of classes conducted by Alcott while she was his assistant at the Temple School in Boston. In the preface to the third edition (1874), Miss Peabody wrote:

The great interest inspired by Louisa May Alcott's *Little Men* has led to the inquiry if ever there was or could be a school like Plumfield; and she has proposed the republication of the *Record of a School*, which was published thirty-eight years ago, and which suggested some of the scenes described in *Lit-*

[1] Vol. 17, 1872, p. 330.

tle Men. . . . What I witnessed in his schoolroom threw for me a new light into the profoundest mysteries that have been consecrated by the Christian symbols; and the study of childhood made there I would not exchange for any thing else I have experienced in life.

That her feeling was shared by the children at their own level is abundantly evident throughout these remarkable journals. One day, for example, Alcott asked the children whether a conversation on ideas, such as they had just finished, was more interesting than one on steam engines. Many said it was. A little boy exclaimed, "I never knew I had a mind till I came to this school"; and a great many more burst out with the same idea. To quote now from the journals,[1] to be followed by direct quotations from Alcott's own writings:]

January 15 [1835] . . . What is the meaning of the word *recollect?* . . . Are you now collecting or re-collecting the impressions of childhood? Some thought they had begun to re-collect, as well as to collect. Shall I tell you an idea some people have of recollecting, reminiscence, remembrance? Yes, said several of them. Mr. Alcott continued (pointing to the bust of Plato), That man believed that all our feelings and thoughts were the remembrances of another state of existence, before we came into the world in our present bodies. And he (pointing to the cast of Jesus Christ) used to say of himself that he came forth from God; that he had lived before. In the Gospel of St. John there are many passages in which he refers to his pre-existent state. . . .

January 30 . . . What do you mean by *birthday?* . . . Birthday is the day on which the spirit is put into the body, said [one] boy. Did you get that idea in this school? said Mr. Alcott. I never thought of such subjects before I came to this school, said he. . . . One of the boys added, that he had always had an indistinct idea that the soul lived before the body, that there was a transmigration of souls. . . .

February 4 . . . Some expressed the idea that the soul shaped and made the body; others that the body was made, and the soul put into it. Which is right? said one boy. That is more than I can tell, but I incline to the first opinion. You are all nearly right, however; you have the important ideas; birth is not the beginning of the spirit; life is the remembrance, or a waking up of spirit. All the life of knowledge is the waking up of what is already within. [The class had been discussing Wordsworth's "Ode to Immortality."]

The Record of a School

[1] Pp. 104, 132–133, 147–148.

To conceive a child's acquirements as originating in nature, dating from his birth into his body, seems an atheism that only a shallow metaphysical theology could entertain in a time of such marvelous natural knowledge as ours. "I shall never persuade myself," said Synesius, "to believe my soul to be of like age with my body." And yet we are wont to date our birth, as that of the babes we christen, from the body's advent . . . as if time and space could chronicle the periods of the immortal mind.

Concord Days[2]

Life is a current of spiritual forces. In perpetual tides, the stream traverses its vessels to vary its pulsations and perspective of things. . . . Vast systems of sympathies, antedating and extending beyond our mundane experiences, absorb us within their sphere, relating us to other worlds of life and light. . . . Memory sometimes dispels the oblivious slumber, and recovers for the mind recollections of its descent and destiny. Some relics of the ancient consciousness survive, recalling our previous history and experiences.

Tablets[3]

[Alcott's favorite daughter and companion, Louisa May Alcott, once wrote to a friend:]

I think immortality is the passing of a soul through many lives or experiences, and such as are truly lived, used, and learned, help on to the next, each growing richer, happier and higher, carrying with it only the real memories of what has gone before. . . . I seem to remember former states and feel that in them I have learned some of the lessons that have never since been mine here and in my next step I hope to leave behind many of the trials I have struggled to bear here and begin to find lightened as I go on. This accounts for the genius and great virtue some show here. They have done well in many phases of this great school and bring into our class the virtue or the gifts that make them great or good. We don't remember the lesser things. They slip away as childish trifles, and we carry on only the real experiences.[4]

[2] Boston: Roberts Bros., 1872, p. 83.
[3] Boston: Roberts Bros., 1879, pp. 201–3.
[4] *Sunrise*. Pasadena, California, August, 1959, p. 333.

HONORÉ DE BALZAC (1799–1850)
French Novelist

All human beings go through a previous life in the sphere of Instinct, where they are brought to see the worthlessness of earthly treasures, to amass which they gave themselves such untold pains! Who can tell how many times the human being lives in the sphere of Instinct before he is prepared to enter the sphere of Abstractions, where thought expends itself on erring science, where mind wearies at last of human language? For, when Matter is exhausted, Spirit enters. Who knows how many fleshly forms the heir of heaven occupies before he can be brought to understand the value of that silence and solitude whose starry plains are but the vestibule of Spiritual Worlds? He feels his way amid the void, makes trial of nothingness, and then at last his eyes revert upon the Path. Then follow other existences—all to be lived to reach the place where Light effulgent shines. Death is the post-house of the journey.

A lifetime may be needed merely to gain the virtues which annul the errors of man's preceding life. . . . The virtues we acquire, which develop slowly within us, are the invisible links that bind each one of our existences to the others—existences which the spirit alone remembers, for Matter has no memory for spiritual things. Thought alone holds the tradition of the bygone life. The endless legacy of the past to the present is the secret source of human genius. . . .

The final life, the fruition of all other lives, to which the powers of the soul have tended, and whose merits open the Sacred Portals to perfected man, is the life of Prayer. . . . Silence and meditation are the means of following [that] Way. . . . It is thus that the separation takes place between Matter, which so long has wrapped its darkness round you, and Spirit, which was in you from the beginning . . . now brings noon-day to your soul.

Seraphita (Chap. 6)
Trans K. P. Wormeley

VICTOR HUGO (1802–1885)
French Author

Each time we die we gain more of life. Souls pass from one sphere to another without loss of personality, become more and more bright. . . . I am a soul. I know well that what I shall render up to the grave is not myself. . . . Earth, thou art not my abyss! . . . The whole creation is a perpetual ascension, from brute to man, from man to God. To divest ourselves more and more of matter, to be clothed more and more with spirit, such is the law.

Victor Hugo's Intellectual Autobiography[1]

[In the research annals of reincarnation literature there are a number of reports of children dying at an early age supposedly being reborn within a few years to the same parents.[2] Hugo's poem, "The Return," from his volume *Contemplations*, is on this theme. Reincarnationists hold that such a rapid return is natural because the quickly departing soul had no time to garner experience requiring a long heavenly state of assimilation.]

Mothers who mourn—your cries are not unheard,
Divine Love notes the fall of even one small bird;
And oft returns the fledgling to its mother's nest,
The link 'tween cradle and grave is thus expressed.
[*A woman had a beloved son, who succumbed to a fatal*
illness at the age of three. The mother was inconsolable.]
And still her grief would not abate.
At last she bore another child, and great
Was the father's joy; and loud his cry: "A Son!"
That day, to thus rejoice—he was the only one.
Dejected and wan the mother lay; her soul was numb . . .
Then suddenly she cried with anguish wild,
Her thoughts less on the new than on the absent child . . . .
"My angel in his grave, and I not at his side!" . . .
Speaking through the babe now held in her embrace
She hears again the well-known voice adored:
" 'Tis I,—but do not tell!" He gazes at her face.

"The Return"

[The translation that follows is from *The Philosophy of Life*, by A. M. Baten.[3] Another translation appeared in *Victor Hugo and His Time*, by Alfred Barbou,[4] and was introduced with these words: "According to Arsène Houssaye, [Hugo] has given a general exposition of his religious creed in something like the following terms":]

[1] Trans. Lorenzo O'Rourke. New York: Funk & Wagnalls, 1907, pp. 260, 269.
[2] Ian Stevenson, "The Evidence for Survival from Claimed Memories of Former Incarnations," *Journal of American Society for Psychical Research*, April, 1960, pp. 70–71. Leslie D. Weatherhead, *The Christian Agnostic*. London: Hodder and Stoughton, 1965, p. 216.
[3] Hammond, Indiana: 1930, p. 163.
[4] New York: Harper and Row, 1882, p. 254.

I feel in myself the future life. I am like a forest once cut down; the new shoots are stronger and livelier than ever. . . . You say the soul is nothing but the resultant of the bodily powers. Why, then, is my soul more luminous when my bodily powers begin to fail? . . . The nearer I approach the end the plainer I hear around me the immortal symphonies of the worlds which invite me. It is marvelous, yet simple. It is a fairy tale, and it is history.

For half a century I have been writing my thoughts in prose and in verse, history, philosophy, drama, romance, tradition, satire, ode and song; I have tried all. But I feel I have not said the thousandth part of what is in me. When I go down to the grave I can say like many others "I have finished my day's work," but I cannot say, "I have finished my life." My day's work will begin again the next morning. The tomb is not a blind alley; it is a thoroughfare. It closes on the twilight, it opens on the dawn.

GEORGE SAND (1803–1876)
French Author

"Consuelo," he said to her . . . "I am going to leave you for a time, and then I shall return to earth by means of a new birth. I shall return accursed and despairing if you abandon me now, in my last hour. . . . We are brethren; ere we become lovers, death must once more separate us. But we must be united by the marriage-vow, that I may be reborn calm and strong, and free, like other men, from the memory of past lives which has been my torment and my punishment for so many centuries. Consent to this vow. It will not bind you to me in this life, which I am about to leave, but it will reunite us in eternity. It will be as a seal to help us to recognise one another when the shades of death have effaced the clearness of our memories."

Consuelo[1]
Trans. Eva Martin

Cast into this life, as it were, into an alembic, where, after a previous existence which we have forgotten, we are condemned to be remade, renewed, tempered by suffering, by strife, by passion, by doubt, by disease, by death. All these evils we endure for our good, for our purification, and, so to speak, to make us perfect. From age to age, from race to race, we accomplish a tardy progress, tardy but certain, an advance of which, in spite of all the skeptics say, the proofs are manifest. If all the imperfections of our being and all the woes of our estate drive at discouraging and terrifying us,

[1] *The Ring of Return*, compiled by Eva Martin. London: Philip Allan, 1927, pp. 147–149.

on the other hand, all the more noble faculties, which have been bestowed on us that we might seek after perfection, do make for our salvation, and deliver us from fear, misery and even death. Yes, a divine instinct that always grows in light and strength helps us to comprehend that nothing in the whole world wholly dies and that we only vanish from the things that lie about us in our earthly life, to reappear among conditions more favorable to our eternal growth in good.[2]

SIR EDWARD BULWER-LYTTON (1803–1873)
British Novelist

[The works of Bulwer-Lytton contributed to the wave of interest in mystical and occult literature that flowed over the West in the latter half of the nineteenth century. If one can gauge Lord Lytton's popularity from the fact that the 1890 edition of *The Britannica* devoted five closely printed columns to his life, his novels must have been widely read. Occasional references to reincarnation are found therein. In *Godolphin* he wrote: "Why cheat ourselves with words so vague as life and death! What is the difference? At most, the entrance in and the departure from one scene in our wide career. How many scenes are left to us! We do but hasten our journey, not close it." [1] In *Zanoni*, his chief mystical work, he remarked: "A short time,—like a day in thy incalculable life,—and the form thou dotest on is dust! Others . . . go hand in hand, each with each, unto the tomb; hand in hand they ascend from the worm to new cycles of existence." [2]

The selections below are from *A Strange Story*. The underlying theme is that a man's lower self may lose its indwelling soul. The reincarnationist who believes in the awful possibility of such a wasted incarnation is likely to be unimpressed by the oft-repeated argument that the prospect of many lives encourages procrastination. Dr. Fenwick, the teller of the tale, has been deeply disturbed by the behavior of an evil acquaintance named Margrave. The doctor had been inclined to doubt the existence of soul, having come under the influence of the then growing school of materialism. Through the agency of a magical potion, he "enters" the brain and inner consciousness of Margrave as it existed at the time of a serious moral crisis three years previously. The selections are from volume 10 of the thirty-volume edition of Lytton's works.[3]]

2 *Lucifer*. London, April, 1889, p. 93.

---

1 Book II, Chap. 25.
2 Book V, Chap. ix.
3 New York: P. F. Collier, 1901, 185–190, 271.

If Sir Philip Derval could be believed, Margrave was possessed of powers, derived from fragmentary recollections of a knowledge acquired in a former state of being, which would render his remorseless intelligence infinitely dire. . . .

The brain now opened on my sight, with all its labyrinth of cells. I seemed to have the clue to every winding in the maze. I saw therein a moral world, charred and ruined, as, in some fable I have read, the world of the moon is described to be; yet withal it was a brain of magnificent formation. . . . I observed three separate emanations of light; the one a pale red hue, the second of pale azure, the third a silvery spark. The red light . . . undulated from the brain along the arteries, the veins, the nerves. And I murmured to myself, "Is this the principle of animal life?" The azure light equally permeated the frame, crossing and uniting with the red, but in a separate and distinct ray . . . And again I murmured to myself, "Is this the principle of intellectual being, directing or influencing that of animal life; with it, yet not of it?"

But the silvery spark! What was that? Its centre seemed the brain. But I could fix it to no single organ. Nay, wherever I looked through the system, it reflected itself as a star reflects itself upon water . . . so independent of all which agitated and vexed the frame, that I became strangely aware that if the heart stopped in its action, and the red light died out, if the brain were paralyzed, that energetic mind smitten into idiocy . . . still that silver spark would shine the same, indestructible by aught that shattered its tabernacle. . . . "Can that starry spark speak the presence of the soul?" . . . And gazing yet more intently on the spark, I became vaguely aware that it was not the soul, but the halo around the soul, as the star we see in heaven is not the star itself, but its circle of rays. . . .

In the heart of the light, [the soul] reflected back on my own soul its ineffable trouble, humiliation, and sorrow; for those ghastly wrecks of power placed at its sovereign command it was responsible: and, appalled by its own sublime fate of duration, was about to carry into eternity the account of its mission in time. . . . I saw that the mind was storming the soul, in some terrible rebellious war—all of thought, of passion, of desire. . . . I could not comprehend the war, nor guess what it was that the mind demanded the soul to yield. Only the distinction between the two was made intelligible by their antagonism. And I saw that the soul, sorely tempted, looked afar for escape from the subjects it had ever so ill-controlled, and who sought to reduce to their vassal the power which had lost authority as their king. . . . And suddenly the starry spark rose from the ruins and the tumult around it—rose into space and vanished. And where my soul had recognized the presence of soul, there was a void. . . .

As my eyes, in the Vision, followed the azure light, undulating as before . . . I perceived that [its] essence . . . had undergone a change: it had lost that faculty of continuous and concentrated power by which man improves on the works of the past, and weaves schemes to be developed in the future of remote generations; it had lost all sympathy in the past, because it had lost all conception of a future beyond the grave; it had lost conscience, it had lost remorse. . . . The azure light was even more vivid in certain organs useful to the conservation of existence . . . secretiveness, destructiveness, and the ready perception of things immediate to the wants of the day [but] the mind wanted the *something*, without which men never could found cities, frame laws, bind together, beautify, exalt the elements of this world. . . . The ant, and the bee, and the beaver congregate and construct; but they do not improve. Man improves because the future impels onward that which is not found in the ant, the bee, and the beaver— that which was gone from the being before me. I shrank appalled into myself. . . . "Have I ever then doubted that soul is distinct from mind?"

A Strange Story

The American Transcendentalists

The August, 1959 issue of the magazine *Sunrise* contained a symposium entitled "The Transcendentalists on Reincarnation," and included a number of the selections used in this portion of the present work. The symposium was prefaced by these informative remarks:

In 1836 a group of younger Unitarians who dared to believe in the inherent worth of man, the divinity of all Nature and the continuity of the soul's life after death, openly revolted against the "corpse-cold Unitarianism" of their Harvard associates and, spearheaded by Emerson, Hedge and Ripley, formed the Transcendental Club of America. Whereas these ideas so long ago taught in India, Persia and Greece and more currently by Kant and Goethe, Wordsworth, Coleridge and Carlyle, were not at all new, they had for centuries in Europe remained the property of the intellectual élite. Now, germinating in the soil of the New World, they blossomed with extraordinary vigor, taking the form of a practical crusade against every form of tyranny—of soul as well as of body.

In a letter dated October 1, 1840, George Ripley wrote to Unitarian friends: "There is a class of persons who desire a reform in the prevailing philosophy of the day. These are called Transcendentalists, because they believe in an order of truths which transcends the sphere of the external senses. Their leading idea is the supremacy of mind over matter. Hence they maintain that the truth of religion does not depend on tradition, nor historical facts, but has an unerring witness in the soul. There is a light, they believe, which enlighteneth every man that cometh into the world; there is a faculty in all—the most degraded, the most ignorant, the most obscure—to perceive spiritual truth when distinctly presented; and the ultimate appeal on all moral questions is not to a jury of scholars, a hierarchy of divines, or the prescriptions of a creed, but to the common sense of the human race." [1]

The marked influence of the German Transcendentalists upon the American movement has already been considered. The contribution of ancient Greece was abundantly manifest. The Platonic philosophers, incidentally, were not studied in translations but in the original Greek. The English Transcendentalists also played a prominent part. Coleridge, Carlyle, and Wordsworth were everywhere read and talked about.

An immeasurably influential contribution came from the Orient. Scarce copies of the first English translations of The Bhagavad-Gita, Upanishads, Vedas, and Puranas somehow found their way into the hands of Emerson, Thoreau and the others. Thoreau translated from the French a Sanskrit story entitled The Transmigration of Seven Brahmins, and had it published.

In 1824, the Unitarians in America took a lively interest in the Hindu leader Ram Mohun Roy, who had "adopted Unitarianism." A British-Indian Unitarian Association was formed here, and the Reverend Charles H. A. Dall was sent to Calcutta, where he effected an alliance with the Brahmo-Samaj. George Willis Cooke in his volume Unitarianism in America[2] states that "the two potent influences shaping the ancient Puritanism of Salem into Unitarianism were foreign commerce and contact with the Oriental religions."

Arthur Christy's The Orient in American Transcendentalism[3] devotes 367 pages to exploring this merging of Eastern and Western cultures, and in doing so concentrates particularly upon the part played by Emerson, Thoreau, and Bronson Alcott. In prefacing the book, Christy quotes Romain Rolland's Prophets of the New India:[4] "It would be a matter of deep interest to know exactly how far the American spirit had been impregnated, directly or indirectly, by the infiltration of Hindu thought during the xixth century; for there can be no doubt that it has contributed to the strange moral and religious mentality of the modern United States. . . . I do not know whether any historian will be found to occupy himself seriously with

[1] O. Frothingham, George Ripley. Boston: 1882, pp. 84–85.
[2] Boston: 1902, p. 72.
[3] Columbia University Press, 1932.
[4] Book II, Chap. iv.

the question. It is nevertheless a psychological problem of the first order, intimately connected with the history of our civilisation." Christy envisioned his own book "as an attempt to write the first chapter of the general study Romain Rolland suggests."

With the blending in America of four streams of transcendental philosophy—the Greek, German, English, and Oriental—each bearing the impress of the reincarnation perspective, it is but natural to find fairly frequent references to rebirth in the writings of the New England group. From the quotations that appear in this section it will be observed how refreshingly original was the viewpoint of these men. In addition to Thoreau, Emerson and his scholarly brother Charles, the Transcendentalists to be included are: Frederic Hedge, James Freeman Clarke, Cyrus Bartol, and William Potter, each of the last-named four, being Unitarian clergymen. Selections from Bronson Alcott's writings have already been presented.

RALPH WALDO EMERSON (1803–1882)
American Philosopher and Essayist

It is the secret of the world that all things subsist and do not die, but only retire a little from sight and afterwards return again. . . . Nothing is dead; men feign themselves dead, and endure mock funerals and mournful obituaries, and there they stand looking out of the window, sound and well, in some new strange disguise. Jesus is not dead; he is very well alive: nor John, nor Paul, nor Mahomet, nor Aristotle; at times we believe we have seen them all, and could easily tell the names under which they go.

"Nominalist and Realist" [1]

Where do we find ourselves? In a series of which we do not know the extremes, and believe that it has none. We wake and find ourselves on a stair; there are other stairs below us which we seem to have ascended; there are stairs above us, many a one, which go upward and out of sight. But the Genius which according to the old belief stands at the door by which we enter, and gives us the lethe to drink, that we may tell no tales, mixed the cup too strongly, and we cannot shake off the lethargy now at noonday. Sleep lingers all our lifetime about our eyes.

"Experience" [2]

Perchance not he but Nature ailed,
The world and not the infant failed.

[1] *The Selected Writings of Ralph Waldo Emerson*, ed. Brooks Atkinson. New York: Modern Library, 1950, p. 445.
[2] *Ibid.*, p. 342.

It was not ripe yet to sustain
A genius of so fine a strain. . . .
They could not feed him, and he died,
And wandered backward as in scorn
To wait an aeon to be born. . . .
"Threnody" 3

We must infer our destiny from the preparation. We are driven by instinct to hive innumerable experiences which are of no visible value, and we may revolve through many lives before we shall assimilate or exhaust them. Now there is nothing in nature capricious, or whimsical, or accidental, or unsupported. Nature never moves by jumps, but always in steady and supported advances. . . . If there is the desire to live, and in larger sphere, with more knowledge and power, it is because life and knowledge and power are good for us, and we are the natural depositaries of these gifts. The love of life is out of all proportion to the value set on a single day, and seems to indicate . . . a conviction of immense resources and possibilities proper to us, on which we have never drawn. . . .

[Quoting from the Katha Upanishad:] "The soul is not born; it does not die; it was not produced from any one. Nor was any produced from it. Unborn, eternal, it is not slain, though the body is slain; subtler than what is subtle, greater than what is great. . . . Thinking the soul as unbodily among bodies, firm among fleeting things, the wise man casts off all grief. The soul cannot be gained by knowledge, not by understanding, not by manifold science. It can be obtained by the soul by which it is desired. It reveals its own truths."

"Immortality" 4

Man is that noble endogenous plant which grows, like the palm, from within outward. . . . The best discovery the discoverer makes for himself. It has something unreal for his companion until he too has substantiated it. It seems as if the Deity dressed each soul which he sends into nature in certain virtues and powers not communicable to other men, and sending it to perform one more turn through the circle of beings, wrote "Not transferable," and "Good for this trip only," on these garments of the soul. . . . Each is uneasy until he has produced his private ray unto the concave sphere and beheld his talent also in its last nobility and exaltation.

"Uses of Great Men" 5

3 *Ibid.*, p. 779.
4 *Letters and Social Aims.* Boston: Houghton, Mifflin, 1887, pp. 319–320, 333. (Vol. VIII of Emerson's Complete Works.)
5 *Representative Men.* Boston: Houghton, Mifflin, 1886, pp. 12, 32, 35. (Vol. IV of Emerson's Complete Works.)

[The entries below are from Emerson's journals. The first, written when Emerson was twenty-seven, appears to be the first inkling of his sympathy toward the philosophy of reincarnation.]

[1830] The soul is an emanation of the Divinity, a part of the soul of the world, a ray from the source of light. It comes from without into the human body, as into a temporary abode, it goes out of it anew; it wanders in ethereal regions, it returns to visit it . . . it passes into other habitations, for the soul is immortal.

[1841] Should not man be sacred to man? What are these thoughts we utter but the reason of our incarnation? To utter these thoughts we took flesh, missionaries of the everlasting Word which will be spoken. . . . These hands, this body, this history of Waldo Emerson are profane and wearisome but . . . above his life, above all creatures, I flow down forever, a sea of benefit into races of individuals. Nor can the stream ever roll backward, or the sin or death of a man taint the immutable energy which distributes itself into men, as the sun into rays, or the sea into drops.

[1843] Life itself is an interim and a transition; this, O Indur, is my one and twenty thousandth form, and already I feel old Life sprouting underneath in the twenty thousand and first, and I know well that he builds no new world but by tearing down the old for materials.

[1848] Yes, the Zoroastrian, the Indian, the Persian scriptures are majestic and more to our daily purpose than this year's almanac or this day's newspaper. . . . I owed—my friend and I owed—a magnificent day to the Bhagavat Geeta.—It was the first of books; it was as if an empire spake to us, nothing small or unworthy, but large, serene, consistent, the voice of an old intelligence which in another age and climate had pondered and thus disposed of the same questions which exercise us.

Journals of Ralph Waldo Emerson[6]

[Christy writes (p. 23): "No one oriental volume that ever came to Concord was more influential than the *Bhagavadgita*. This is evident from the manner and frequency in which the Concordians spoke of it. Sanborn states[7] that for years Emerson was one of the very few Americans who owned a copy, and that his was even more widely used than that in the Harvard College Library."]

[6] Cambridge, Mass.: Houghton, Mifflin, II, 341 (1901); V, 533 (1911); VI, 419–420 (1912); VII, 510–511 (1912).
[7] *The Nation*, May 10, 1910, p. 481.

FREDERIC H. HEDGE (1805–1890)
American Transcendentalist and Unitarian Minister

[Hedge translated Herder's "Dialogues on Metempsychosis." See under "Herder."]

We reach back with our recollection and find no beginning of existence. Who of us knows anything except by report of the first two years of earthly life? . . . We began to exist for others before we began to exist for ourselves. Our experience is not co-existensive with our being, our memory does not comprehend it. We bear not the root, but the root us.

What is that root? We call it soul. Our soul, we call it; properly speaking, it is not ours, but we are its. It is not a part of us, but we are a part of it. It is not one article in an inventory of articles which together make up our individuality, but the root of that individuality. It is larger than we are, and older than we are,—that is, than our conscious self. The conscious self . . . is not aboriginal, but a product,—as it were, the blossoming of an individuality. . . . And the soul which does so blossom exists before that blossom unfolds. . . . The supposition of pre-existence . . . seems best to match the supposed continued existence of the soul hereafter. . . . The eternal destination which faith ascribes to the soul presupposes an eternal origin. . . . This was the theory of the most learned and acute of the Christian Fathers, (Origen) . . .

A new body and organism I hold to be an essential part of the soul's destination.

Ways of the Spirit, and Other Essays (Chap. 14)

GIUSEPPE MAZZINI (1805–1872)
Italian Liberator

[*The Columbia Encyclopedia*[1] states of Mazzini: "His youth was spent in literary and philosophical studies. He early joined the Carbonari, was imprisoned (1830–1), and went into exile. In Marseilles he founded the secret society Giovine Italia (Young Italy), which led a vigorous campaign for Italian unity. . . . His influence on Italian liberals was tremendous. . . . Mazzini's work was inspired by his great moral strength. His program was not only political, but deeply social, aiming at human redemption on a religious and moral basis, at liberty, and at justice. His literary style is re-

[1] Second edition.

markably fine. He wrote on politics, social science, philosophy, and literature." Quoting from Bolton King's *The Life of Mazzini*:[2]]

[Mazzini] speaks of memory as the consciousness of the soul's progress up from earlier existences; love would be a mockery, if it did not last
beyond the grave; the unity of the race implies a link between the living
and the dead; science teaches there is no death but only transformation. He
held passionately to his faith in immortality. . . . The individual soul, he
thought, progresses through a series of reincarnations, each leading it to a
more perfect development, and the rapidity of its advance depends on its
own purification. And as the individual has his progress through a series of
existences, so collective man progresses ever through the human generations.

[On behalf of himself and the Movement he represented, Mazzini addressed a letter to the 1869–1870 Ecumenical Council in Rome. The letter
was subsequently printed in the London *Fortnightly Review*. The following excerpts are to be found in *Modern Essays* by F. W. H. Myers:[3]]

The arch of the Christian heaven is too narrow to embrace the earth.
Beyond that heaven, across the fields of the infinite, we discover a vaster
sky, illumined by the dawn of a new dogma; and on the rising of its sun
your own heaven will disappear. We are but the precursors of that
dogma. . . .

You believe—thus depriving yourselves of every basis of intellectual
certainty and criterion of truth—in *miracles*; in the supernatural; in the
possible violation of the laws regulating the universe. We believe in the
Unknown, in the Mysterious—to be one day solved—which now encom-
passes us on every side; in the secrets of an *intuition* inaccessible to analysis;
in the truth of our strange presentiment of an Ideal, which is the primitive
fatherland of the soul . . . but we believe all these things the preordained
consequence of laws hitherto withheld from our knowledge.

You believe in a heaven extrinsic to the universe. . . . We believe in
One Heaven in which we live, and move, and love; which embraces—as an
ocean embraces the islands that stud its surface—the whole indefinite series
of existences through which we pass. We believe in the *continuity* of life; in
a connecting link uniting all the various periods through which it is transformed and developed; in the eternity of all noble affections; in the progres-

---

[2] New York: Dutton, 1911, Chap. 13.
[3] London: Macmillan, 1883, pp. 66–67.

sive sanctification of every germ of good gathered by the pilgrim soul in its journey upon earth and otherwhere.

Letter to Ecumenical Council

ELIZABETH BARRETT BROWNING (1806–1861)
British Poet

. . . . *Let who says*
"The soul's a clean white paper," rather say
A palimpsest, a prophet's holograph,
Defiled, erased, and covered by a monk's—
The apocalypse, by a Longus! poring on
Which obscene text, we may discern perhaps
Some fair, fine trace of what was written once,
Some upstroke of an alpha and omega.

"Aurora Leigh"

JEAN REYNAUD (1806–1863)
French Philosopher

Compared to eternal knowledge, our memory is emptiness. Not only is it helpless regarding the periods that preceded our birth, but often during our present life it plays us false. . . . How glorious the light that would be cast on the present order of things by a knowledge of our former existences! . . . Who dares affirm that in the depths of our being our soul will not some day be able to shed light on these successive journeyings? . . . Let us try to conceive of the infinite treasures of a memory enriched by the recollections of a long series of incarnations—each different, yet all linked together. . . . From life to life man is ever approaching closer and closer to his celestial ideal.

Philosophie Religieuse Terre et Ciel [1]

HENRY WADSWORTH LONGFELLOW (1807–1882)
American Poet

[Listed in Christy's *The Orient in American Transcendentalism* are fifty-seven books constituting "The Oriental Library of Henry Wadsworth Longfellow." Among them are the 1785 and 1867 editions of Sir Charles Wilkins' translation of The Bhagavad-Gita. Longfellow was also interested in Hermetic philosophy. His last poem was a lyrical ode in honor of Hermes Trismegistus, and was quoted in Part Two.]

[1] Paris, 1854, pp. 305–8.

Thus the seer,
With vision clear,
Sees forms appear and disappear,
In the perpetual round of strange,
Mysterious change
From birth to death, from death to birth;
From earth to heaven, from heaven to earth;
Till glimpses more sublime,
Of things, unseen before,
Unto his wondering eyes reveal
The Universe, as an immeasurable wheel
Turning forevermore
In the rapid and rushing river of Time.
                    "Rain in Summer"

JOHN GREENLEAF WHITTIER (1807–1892)
American Poet

[Whittier's interest in oriental religion and philosophy is summarized in two articles by Arthur Christy appearing in *The Aryan Path*.[1] The stanza that follows from Whittier's poem "The Preacher" is a paraphrase of several verses from Chapter 2 of The Bhagavad-Gita—the chapter which treats of the periodic return of the soul.]

In the Indian fable Arjoon hears
The scorn of a god rebuke his fears:
"Spare thy pity!" Krishna saith;
"Not in thy sword is the power of death!
All is illusion,—loss but seems;
Pleasure and pain are only dreams;
Who deems he slayeth doth not kill;
Who counts as slain is living still.
                    "The Preacher"

The river hemmed with leaving trees
Wound through its meadows green,
A low blue line of mountains showed
The open pines between. . . .

No clue of memory led me on,
But well the ways I knew;
A feeling of familiar things
With every footstep grew. . . .

[1] Bombay: June, 1933; May, 1934.

A presence, strange at once and known,
Walked with me as my guide;
The skirts of some forgotten life
Trailed noiseless at my side.

Was it a dim-remembered dream?
Or glimpse through aeons old?
The secret which the mountains kept
The river never told.
                    "A Mystery"

We shape ourselves the joy or fear
Of which the coming life is made
And fill our Future's atmosphere
With sunshine or with shade.

The tissue of the Life to be
We weave with colors all our own,
And in the field of Destiny
We reap as we have sown. . . .

We live our life again:
Or warmly touched or coldly dim
The pictures of the Past remain,—
Man's works shall follow him!
                    "Raphael"

CHARLES C. EMERSON (1808–1836)
Brother of Ralph Waldo Emerson

The reason why Homer is to me like a dewy morning is because I too lived while Troy was, and sailed in the hollow ships of the Grecians to sack the devoted town. The rosy-fingered dawn as it crimsoned the tops of Ida, the broad seashore dotted with tents, the Trojan hosts in their painted armor, and the rushing chariots of Diomede and Idomeneus,—all these I too saw: my ghost animated the frame of some nameless Argive. . . . We forget that we have been drugged with the sleepy bowl of the Present. But when a lively chord in the soul is struck, when the windows for a moment are unbarred, the long and varied past is recovered. We recognize it all. We are no more brief, ignoble creatures; we seize our immortality, and bind together the related parts of our secular being.

"Notes from the Journal of a Scholar"
(The Dial, I, 14)

EDGAR ALLAN POE (1809–1849)
American Author

We walk about, amid the destinies of our world-existence, encompassed by dim but ever present Memories of a Destiny more vast—very distant in the bygone time, and infinitely awful. . . . We live out a Youth peculiarly haunted by such dreams; yet never mistaking them for dreams. As Memories we know them. *During our Youth the distinction is too clear to deceive us even for a moment.* . . . Existence—self-existence—existence from all Time and to all Eternity—seems, up to the epoch of Manhood, a normal and unquestionable condition:—*seems, because it is.*

Essay "Eureka" [1]

It is mere idleness to say that I had not lived before—that the soul has no previous existence. . . . You deny it?—let us not argue the matter. Convinced myself, I seek not to convince. There is, however, a remembrance of aerial forms—of spiritual and meaning eyes—of sounds, musical yet sad; a remembrance which will not be excluded; a memory like a shadow—vague, variable, indefinite, unsteady; and like a shadow, too, in the impossibility of my getting rid of it while the sunlight of my reason shall exist.

"Berenice" [2]

OLIVER WENDELL HOLMES (1809–1894)
American Author

[Holmes here describes the beautiful spiral sea shells of the Pearly Nautilus. The spiral is composed of a series of ever-larger "rooms." Retreat into last year's "residence" is prevented by the sea creature walling up the doorway.]

Year after year beheld the silent toil
That spread his lustrous coil;
Still, as the spiral grew,
He left the past year's dwelling for the new,
Stole with soft step its shining archway through,
Built up its idle door,
Stretched in his last-found home, and knew
  the old no more. . . .

[1] *The Works of the late Edgar Allan Poe*, New York, 1859, II, pp. 117, 212.
[2] *Ibid.*, I, 43.

Build thee more stately mansions, O my soul!
As the swift seasons roll!
Leave thy low-vaulted past!
Let each new temple, nobler than the last,
Shut thee from heaven with a dome more vast,
Till thou at length art free,
Leaving thine outgrown shell by life's unresting sea!
                         "The Chambered Nautilus"

ALFRED LORD TENNYSON (1809–1892)
Poet Laureate of England (1850–1892)

[The first of Tennyson's early sonnets:]

As when with downcast eyes we muse and brood,
And ebb into a former life, or seem
To lapse far back in a confusèd dream
To states of mystical similitude,
If one but speaks or hems or stirs his chair
Ever the wonder waxeth more and more,
So that we say, "All this hath been before,
All this hath been, I know not when or where:"
So, friend, when first I looked upon your face,
Our thoughts gave answer each to each, so true—
Opposed mirrors each reflecting each—
Although I knew not in what time or place,
Methought that I had often met with you,
And either lived in either's heart and speech.
                         Early Sonnets No. 1

[On the birth of a son:]

Out of the deep, my child, out of the deep,
Where all that was to be, in all that was,
Whirl'd for a million aeons thro' the vast
Waste dawn of multitudinous-eddying light—
Out of the deep, my child, out of the deep,
Thro' all this changing world of changeless law,
And every phase of ever-heightening life,
And nine long months of antenatal gloom . . .
Thou comest . . . A babe in lineament and limb
Perfect, and prophet of the perfect man . . .
Live thou! and of the grain and husk, the grape
And ivy-berry, choose; and still depart
From death to death thro' life and life, and find

Nearer and ever nearer Him, who wrought
Not matter, nor the finite-infinite,
But this main-miracle, that thou art thou,
With power on thine own act and on the world.

De Profundis

This truth within thy mind rehearse,
That in a boundless universe
Is boundless better, boundless worse. . . .

Yet how should I for certain hold,
Because my memory is so cold,
That I first was in human mould? . . .

It may be that no life is found,
Which only to one engine bound
Falls off, but cycles always round.

As old mythologies relate,
Some draught of Lethe might await
The slipping thro' from state to state. . . .

But, if I lapsed from nobler place,
Some legend of a fallen race
Alone might hint of my disgrace. . . .

Or, if thro' lower lives I came—
Tho' all experience past became
Consolidate in mind and frame—

I might forget my weaker lot;
For is not our first year forgot?
The haunts of memory echo not.

The Two Voices

JAMES FREEMAN CLARKE (1810–1888)
American Transcendentalist and Unitarian Minister

[In Volume II of Clarke's *Ten Great Religions*[1], he devotes chapter 6 to "The Soul and Its Transmigrations in All Religions." He writes:]

That man has come up to his present state of development by passing through lower forms is the popular doctrine of science today. What is

[1] Boston: Houghton, Mifflin, 1887, Vol. II, Preface, p. ix; 190.

called evolution teaches that we have reached our present state by a very long and gradual ascent from the lowest animal organizations. It is true that the Darwinian theory takes no notice of the evolution of the soul, but only of the body. But it appears to me that a combination of the two views would remove many difficulties which still attach to the theory of natural selection and the survival of the fittest. . . . The modern doctrine of evolution of bodily organisms is not complete, unless we unite with it the idea of a corresponding evolution of the spiritual monad, from which every organic form derives its unity. Evolution has a satisfactory meaning only when we admit that the soul is developed and educated by passing through many bodies. . . . If we are to believe in evolution, let us have the assistance of the soul itself in this development of new species.

Ten Great Religions

[Darwin did take note of the possibility of immortality and by inference some form of reincarnation when he wrote: "Believing as I do that man in the distant future will be a far more perfect creature than he now is, it is an intolerable thought that he and all other sentient beings are doomed to complete annihilation after such long continued progress. To those who fully admit the immortality of the human soul, the destruction of our world will not appear so dreadful." (*The Life and Letters of Charles Darwin*, ed. Francis Darwin.[2]]

FRANCIS BOWEN (1811–1890)
American Philosopher, Harvard University

We can easily imagine and believe that every person now living is a representation of some one who lived perhaps centuries ago under another name, in another country. . . . He has entered upon a new stage of probation, and in it he has now to learn what the character which he there formed naturally leads to when tried upon a new and perhaps broader theatre. . . .

I know not how it may seem to others, but to me there is something inexpressibly consolatory and inspiring in the thought that the great and good of other days have not finally accomplished their earthly career, have not left us desolate, but that they are still with us. . . . We are unwilling to believe that their beneficent activity was limited to one short life on earth, at the close of which there opened to them an eternity without change, without further trial or action, and seemingly having no other purpose than unlimited enjoyment. . . .

[2] New York: Appleton, 1887, I, 282.

Why should it be thought incredible that the same soul should inhabit in succession an indefinite number of mortal bodies . . . ? Even during this one life our bodies are perpetually changing, though by a process of decay and restoration which is so gradual that it escapes our notice. Every human being thus dwells successively in many bodies, even during one short life.

"Christian Metempsychosis"
(Princeton Review, May 1881)

[*The New York Times* for September 29, 1954, reports that Dr. Paul C. Aebersold, director of the isotopes division of the United States Atomic Energy Commission, stated in the Annual Report of the Smithsonian Institute: "Tracer studies show that the atomic turnover in our bodies is quite rapid and complete. . . . In a year approximately 98 percent of the atoms in us now will be replaced by other atoms we take in our air, food, and drink." In fifty-three weeks, then, the turnover will be complete. Thus a man of seventy-five has had at least seventy new brains and bodies, and this naturally raises significant questions for physiology and psychology: Where are the memories of a lifetime stored? How is the sense of individual identity preserved throughout these numerous "re-embodiments"?]

ROBERT BROWNING (1812–1889)
British Poet

I shall never, in the years remaining,
Paint you pictures, no, nor carve you statues,
This of verse alone, one life allows me . . .
Other heights in other lives, God willing.
"One Word More"

Delayed it may be for more lives yet
Through worlds I shall traverse, not a few:
Much is to learn and much to forget
Ere the time be come for taking you.
"Evelyn Hope"

There's a fancy some lean to and others hate—
That, when this life is ended, begins
New work for the soul in another state,
Where it strives and gets weary, loses and wins:
Where the strong and the weak, this world's congeries,
Repeat in large what they practised in small,

Through life after life in unlimited series;
Only the scale's to be changed, that's all.

"Old Pictures in Florence"

At times I almost dream
I too have spent a life the sages' way,
And tread once more familiar paths. Perchance
I perished in an arrogant self-reliance
Ages ago; and in that act, a prayer
For one more chance went up so earnest, so
Instinct with better light led in by death,
That life was blotted out—not so completely
But scattered wrecks enough of it remain,
Dim memories, as now, when seems once more
The goal in sight again. . . .

There is an inmost centre in us all,
Where truth abides in fulness; and around,
Wall upon wall, the gross flesh hems it in,
This perfect, clear perception—which is truth.
A baffling and perverting carnal mesh
Binds it, and makes all error, and "to know"
Rather consists in opening out a way
Whence the imprisoned splendour may escape,
Than in effecting entry for a light
Supposed to be without.

"Paracelsus" (Part I)

RICHARD WAGNER (1813–1883)
German Composer

[At twenty-five, when Wagner made his initial investigation of Buddhism, he was living with his brother-in-law, Hermann Brockhaus, who inspired these studies. Brockhaus was a Sanskrit scholar, later to become Professor of Oriental Languages at Leipzig University. Wagner completed his first opera, *Rienzi*, soon thereafter, and in the original version, the dying Roman hero is made to sing: "You think to destroy me? So long as Rome's seven hills remain, you shall see Rienzi return again."

Later, upon taking up Buddhism again, Wagner had a strong compulsion to compose a reincarnation opera, *Die Sieger* (The Victors). In a very interesting article "Buddhism and Wagner," Granville Pyne, a Wagnerian specialist and Chairman of the Wagner Society (England), writes:

[Wagner records in his autobiography:[1]] ". . . Bournouff's *Introduction a l'Histoire du Bouddhisme* interested me most among my books [during the winter of 1855–56], and I found material for a dramatic poem, which has stayed in my mind ever since, though only vaguely sketched." This was *The Victors* (*Die Sieger*). . . . Wagner found great underlying beauty in this material, and saw the possibility of dealing with reincarnation through the special techniques of music-drama, in which the music could describe the past while the words spoke of the present. He thought that this greatly influenced his subsequent development. *The Victors* continued to haunt his imagination for twenty years, but it never came to fruition. The emotional and metaphysical impulse aroused in Wagner by *The Victors* was discharged in *Tristan and Isolde*, and the rest of his thought on the subject found a natural outlet in his last work, *Parsifal.* . . . One thing is certain: Buddhism laid a hand on the volcanic genius and tempestuous personality of Richard Wagner, whereby his works are different from what they otherwise would have been.[2]

From other sources the following extracts from Wagner's writings have been gathered together, the first two of which concern *Die Sieger:*]

[Sketch for *Die Sieger*, Zurich, May 16, 1856:] The Buddha on his last journey. Ananda [his favorite disciple] given water from the well by Prakriti, the Tchandala maiden. Her tumult of love for Ananda; his consternation. . . . Prakriti goes to Buddha . . . to plead for union with Ananda. He asks if she is willing to fulfill the stipulations of such union? . . . She sinks horrified and sobbing to the ground, when she hears at length that she must share Ananda's vow of chastity. . . . [Buddha] tells of Prakriti's previous incarnation; she then was the daughter of a haughty Brahmin. The Tchandala King, remembering a former existence as Brahmin, had craved the Brahmin's daughter for his son, who had conceived a violent passion for her; in pride and arrogance the daughter had refused return of love, and mocked at the unfortunate. This she had now to expiate, reborn as Tchandala to feel the torments of a hopeless love; yet to renounce withal, and be led to full redemption by acceptance into Buddha's flock . . . Ananda welcomes her as sister. Buddha's last teachings. All are converted by him. He departs to the place of his redemption.

Richard Wagner's Prose Works[3]

To the mental eye of Buddha the past life of any being he meets is like an open book. . . . The simple story [of *Die Sieger*] assumed significance by having the previous life of the leading characters merge into the present existence by means of an accompanying musical reminiscence. Hav-

[1] Richard Wagner: *My Life*. Constable. Reissued 1963, p. 638.
[2] *The Aryan Path*, September, 1966.
[3] Trans. William Ashton Ellis. London: Kegan Paul, 1899, VIII, 385–386.

ing immediately realized how to present clearly this double life through simultaneously sounding music, I applied myself to the execution of the poem with particular devotion.

Collected Writings[4]

From all time the minds that have attained . . . to a clear perception, have turned to the minds of the multitude still in bondage . . . and, having compassion on them, have sought a means of communication with them. Foremost among these enlightened spirits have been the founders of religions. . . . Certainly the Indian Prince Buddha spoke the language which most nearly gives expression to that lofty enlightenment. . . . If we are to speak of this highest perception in terms understood by the people it can only be done under the form of pure and primitive Buddhist teaching. Especially important is the doctrine of the transmigration of souls as the basis of a truly human life.

Letter to August Roeckel (1855)[5]

I cannot take my life, for the Will to accomplish the Object of Art would draw me back into life again until I realized that Object, and so I would only be re-entering this circle of tears and misery.

Letter to Hans Bülow (Sept. 27, 1858)[6]

[In a letter to Mathilde Wesendonck—who inspired the composing of *Tristan and Isolde*—Wagner wrote: "In contrast to reincarnation and karma all other views appear petty and narrow." [7] In another letter, written from Paris in August, 1860, he confided to her:]

A prose translation of the four pieces, *Hollander, Tannhäuser, Lohengrin,* and *Tristan,* is soon to be issued. . . . I have just gone through these translations and in so doing I was obliged to recall clearly to mind all the details of my poems. Yesterday *Lohengrin* touched me very much, and I cannot but hold it to be the most tragic poem of all, since only an immensely wide outlook upon life can provide a reconciliation between Lohengrin and Elsa. Only the profoundly conceived idea of Reincarnation could give me any consolation, since that belief shows how all at last can reach complete redemption. . . . According to the beautiful Buddhist belief, the spotless purity of Lohengrin finds a simple explanation in the fact

[4] Kapp ed., VI, 278.
[5] *Richard Wagner's Letters to August Roeckel,* trans. Eleanor C. Sellar. London: 1897, pp. 137–138. *Richard Wagner an August Röckel,* Leipzig: 1912, p. 60.
[6] *Richard Wagner Briefe an Hans von Bülow.* Jena: 1916, p. 107.
[7] Georg Neidhart, *Werden Wir Wieden Geboren.* Munich, undated, p. 59.

that he is the continuation of Parsifal, who had to fight for his purity. Even so Elsa in her rebirth would reach to the height of Lohengrin. . . . Thus all the terrible tragedy of life is seen to be nothing but the sense of Separateness in Time and Space.

Letter to Mathilde Wesendonck[8]

[In *Parsifal*, Wagner's last opera, the Knight Gurnemanz sings these words in Act I respecting Kundry, the leading woman character, who is supposed to have lived during the time of Christ, mocked him on the cross, and for centuries was condemned to a tormented existence:]

Here she lives today—perhaps anew to suffer penance for debts incurred in former life, for which forgiveness still is due.

Parsifal

[The excerpt below is from the closing lines of the Götterdämmerung. Wagner specifically directed that they be unsung because "the musician cannot help seeing for himself that the verses have to be omitted in the live production inasmuch as their meaing is emphatically expressed in the orchestral music itself." [9] Contrary to Wagner's apparent intention, the stanza is omitted in current librettos. When the composer has Brünhilde, in these last moments of the immolation scene, say that she will return no more to earthly incarnation, he is adhering to the original Scandinavian and Germanic myth we have briefly considered in Part Four.]

The home of desire I leave behind
Illusions forever avoid.
The open door of return and being
I close forever.
Yearning for regions of peace,
The holy land of choice,
Released from the path of return,
So wanders the Wise one forth.
    The Gotterdämmerung

SOREN KIERKEGAARD (1813–1855)
Danish Religious Philosopher

[The following is a note from the year 1842 found in Kierkegaard's "Nachlass" (literary remains):]

---

[8] *Richard Wagner an Mathilde Wesendonk Lagebuchblätter und Briefe 1853–1871.* Leipzig: 1922, p. 285. (Letter 106a.)
[9] Richard Wagner, *Gesammelte Schriften und Dichtungen* (Collected Writings and Poetry), Leipzig: 1872, edited by himself, VI, 362–363.

"Write," said that voice, and the prophet answered: "For whom?" The voice said: "For the dead, for those you have loved in antiquity." "Will they read me?"—"Yes, for they will come back as posterity."

CYRUS AUGUSTUS BARTOL (1813–1900)
American Transcendentalist and Unitarian Minister

In some sense, I was born and must die. In some sense, my dwelling holds me; your babe is in the crib, and your sires in the tomb. But there is an *I*, by which all these contents and consignments are disallowed. Before Abraham was, I am [John 8:58]; *I have power to lay down my life and power to take it up again.* I am conscious of Eternal Generation, that I am what never lay in the cradle and no coffin can hold, but sits behind smiling at what was brought forth and expires.

The Rising Faith[1]

HENRY DAVID THOREAU (1817–1862)
American Transcendentalist and Author

July 8, 1843, to Emerson: And Hawthorne, too, I remember as one with whom I sauntered in old heroic times along the banks of the Scamander amid the ruins of chariots and heroes.

April 3, 1850 to Harrison Blake: I lived in Judea eighteen hundred years ago, but I never knew that there was such a one as Christ among my contemporaries.

February 27, 1853, to Harrison Blake: As the stars looked to me when I was a shepherd in Assyria, they look to me now a New-Englander.

Letters[2]

November 12, 1841: Methinks the hawk that soars so loftily and circles so steadily and apparently without effort, has earned this power by faithfully creeping on the ground as a reptile in a former state of existence.

1845–47: Why should we be startled of death? Life is a constant putting off of the mortal coil—coat, cuticle, flesh and bones, all old clothes.

May 6, 1851: [Quoting from The Harivansa, which forms part of the great Hindu epic The Mahabharata:] "A being returns to life in consequence of the affection which he has borne for terrestrial things: he finds himself emancipated when he has felt only indifference for them."

[1] Boston: Roberts Bros., 1874, p. 241.
[2] *The Writings of Henry David Thoreau.* Cambridge, Mass.: Houghton, Mifflin, 1894, XI, 110, 215, 253.

June 26, 1851: Visited a menagerie this afternoon. . . . What constitutes the difference between a wild beast and a tame one? How much more human the one than the other! Growling, scratching, roaring, with whatever beauty and gracefulness, still untamable, this royal Bengal tiger or this leopard. They have the character and the importance of another order of men. The majestic lions, the king of beasts,—he must retain his title. . . . It is unavoidable, the idea of transmigration; not merely a fancy of the poets, but an instinct of the race.

July 16, 1851: As far back as I can remember I have unconsciously referred to the experiences of a previous state of existence.

Journals[3]

I am conscious of the presence and criticism of a part of me, which, as it were, is not a part of me, but spectator, sharing no experience, but taking note of it and that is no more I than it is you. When the play, it may be the tragedy, of life is over, the spectator goes his way. It was a kind of fiction, a work of the imagination only, so far as he was concerned. (Chapter 5.)

In the morning [at Walden Pond] I bathe my intellect in the stupendous and cosmogonal philosophy of the Bhagvat Geeta, since whose composition years of the gods have elapsed, and in comparison with which our modern world and its literature seem puny and trivial; and I doubt if that philosophy is not to be referred to a previous state of existence, so remote is its sublimity from our conceptions. I lay down the book and go to my well for water, and lo! there I meet the servant of the Brahmin, priest of Brahma and Vishnu and Indra, who still sits in his temple on the Ganges reading the Vedas, or dwells at the root of a tree with his crust and water jug. I meet his servant come to draw water for his master, and our buckets as it were grate together in the same well. The pure Walden water is mingled with the sacred water of the Ganges. (Chapter 16.)

Walden

WALT WHITMAN (1819–1892)
American Poet

[In the leading article in the *Saturday Review* for October 31, 1959, entitled "Walt Whitman's Buried Masterpiece," Malcolm Cowley wrote:

Whitman believed . . . that there is a distinction between one's mere personality and the deeper Self [and that] by means of metempsychosis and

---

[3] *The Writings of Henry David Thoreau.* Houghton, Mifflin, 1892, VII, 255; *The Journal of Henry D. Thoreau.* Houghton, Mifflin, 1949, I, 419; II, 190–191, 271, 306.

karma we are all involved in a process of spiritual evolution that might be compared to natural evolution. Even the latter process, however, was not regarded by Whitman as strictly natural or material. He believed that animals have a rudimentary sort of soul ("They bring me tokens of myself"), and he hinted or surmised, without directly saying, that rocks, trees, and planets possess an identity, or "eidolon," that persists as they rise to higher states of being. The double process of evolution, natural and spiritual, can be traced for ages into the past, and he believed that it will continue for ages beyond ages. . . . All men are divine and will eventually be gods. . . . The universe was an eternal becoming for Whitman, a process not a structure, and it had to be judged from the standpoint of eternity.

Whitman's "Song of Myself," from which the selections below are taken, constitutes the bulk of the first edition of *Leaves of Grass* (1855), and has been included in all subsequent editions. Emerson called it "the most extraordinary piece of wit and wisdom that America has yet contributed." (Letter to Whitman, July 21, 1855.[1])

The parallels between *Leaves of Grass* and oriental teachings have been carefully presented in *Whitman in the Light of Vedantic Mysticism* by V. K. Chari.[2] However, as stated by Cowley five years previously in the article just quoted:

What is extraordinary about this Eastern element is that Whitman, when he was writing the poems of the first edition, seems to have known little or nothing about Indian philosophy. It is more than doubtful that he had even read the "Bhagavad-Gita," one of the few Indian works then available to Americans in translation. He does not refer to it in his notebooks of the early 1850s, where he mentions most of the books he was poring over. A year after the first edition was published, Thoreau went to see him in Brooklyn and told him that "Leaves of Grass" was "wonderfully like the Orientals." Had Whitman read them, he asked. The poet answered. "No: tell me about them." He seems to have taken advantage of Thoreau's reading list, since words from the Sanskrit (notably *Maya* and *Sudra*) appear in some of the poems written after 1858. They do not appear in "Song of Myself," in spite of the recognizably Indian ideas expressed in the poem.]

I wish I could translate the hints about the dead young men and women,
And the hints about old men and mothers, and the offspring taken
soon out of their laps.
What do you think has become of the young and old men?
And what do you think has become of the women and children?
They are alive and well somewhere,
The smallest sprout shows there is really no death. . . .

[1] *Walt Whitman's Leaves of Grass*, the First (1855) Edition, ed. Malcolm Cowley. New York: Viking, 1959, p. ix.
[2] University of Nebraska Press, 1964.

I know I am deathless,
I know this orbit of mine cannot be swept by a carpenter's compass. . . .
And whether I come to my own today or in ten thousand or ten
  million years,
I can cheerfully take it now, or with equal cheerfulness I can wait . . .
I laugh at what you call dissolution,
And I know the amplitude of time. . . .
To be in any form, what is that?
(Round and round we go, all of us, and ever come back thither). . . .
Believing I shall come again upon the earth after five thousand
  years . . . .

The clock indicates the moment—but what does eternity indicate?
We have thus far exhausted trillions of winters and summers,
There are trillions ahead, and trillions ahead of them.
Births have brought us richness and variety,
And other births will bring us richness and variety. . . .
I am an acme of things accomplish'd, and I an encloser of things
  to be. . . .
Rise after rise bow the phantoms behind me,
Afar down I see the huge first Nothing, I know I was even there. . . .
Immense have been the preparations for me,
Faithful and friendly the arms that have help'd me.
Cycles ferried my cradle, rowing and rowing like cheerful boatmen. . . .

I tramp a perpetual journey, (come listen all!). . . .
Not I, not any one else can travel that road for you,
You must travel it for yourself.
It is not far, it is within reach. . . .
And as to you Life I reckon you are the leavings of many deaths,
(No doubt I have died myself ten thousand times before.) . . .
This day before dawn I ascended a hill and look'd at the crowded
  heaven,
And I said to my spirit, When we become the enfolders of those
  orbs, and the pleasure and knowledge of everything in them,
  shall we be fill'd and satisfied then?
And my spirit said, No, we but level that lift to pass and continue
  beyond.
You are also asking me questions and I hear you,
I answer that I cannot answer, you must find out for yourself.

                                              "Song of Myself"
                                              Leaves of Grass[3]

[This poem is from later editions of Leaves of Grass:]

[3] Book 3, Parts 6, 20, 27, 43–44, 46, 49.

Facing west from California's shores,
Inquiring, tireless, seeking what is yet unfound,
I, a child, very old, over waves, towards the house
*   of maternity, the land of migrations, look afar,*
Look off the shores of my Western sea, the circle
*   almost circled;*
For starting westward from Hindustan, from the vales
*   of Kashmere,*
From Asia, from the north, from the God, the sage, and
*   the hero,*
From the south, from the flowery peninsulas and the
*   spice islands,*
Long having wander'd since, round the earth having wander'd,
Now I face home again, very pleas'd and joyous,
(But where is what I started for so long ago?
And why is it yet unfound?)

                    Facing West from California's Shores

HERMAN MELVILLE (1819–1891)
American Novelist

[In 1851 appeared Melville's epic-drama *Moby Dick*. Unfavorably received, the career of a promising author was permanently eclipsed. In 1921 a noted English critic announced that he had been induced to read this forgotten book, and that "having done so, I hereby declare that since letters began there never was such a book, and that the mind of man is not constructed so as to produce such another; that I put its author with Rabelais, Swift, Shakespeare." [1] Whether we may agree with this view or not, within a decade Melville was regarded as one of the great writers of all time.

Commenting on the story, D. H. Lawrence wrote: "It is the Gethsemane of Ahab, before the last fight; the Gethsemane of the human soul seeking the last self-conquest, the last attainment of extended consciousness—infinite consciousness."[2] J. B. Priestley viewed it this way: The whale, Moby Dick, "is entirely evil only in the mind of Captain Ahab . . . the mind in its complete self-dependence, in its ruthless opposition to the whale as a force of Nature. . . . The whale is neither good nor evil. It is the mighty Other or Opposite, what we leave when we split totality and claim half as our own before demanding the whole again . . . and the

---

[1] Max Eastman, "The Man Who Wrote Moby Dick," *Reader's Digest*, March, 1965, p. 192.
[2] D. H. Lawrence, *Studies in Classic American Literature*. New York: Viking, 1961, pp. 158–159.

more we separate ourselves from it, challenge it, hunt it and hope to destroy it, the more powerful, menacing, and finally destructive it becomes." [3] Quoting from the book:]

In the sperm fishery, this is perhaps one of the most remarkable incidents in all the business of whaling: One day the planks stream with freshets of blood and oil; on the sacred quarter-deck enormous masses of the whale's head are profanely piled. . . . But a day or two after, you look about you . . . you would all but swear you trod some silent merchant vessel, with a most scrupulously neat commander. . . . Many is the time, when, after the severest uninterrupted labours . . . continuing straight through for ninety-six hours, [and after which all hands] have finally bestirred themselves to cleanse the ship, and make a spotless dairy room of it . . . the poor fellows . . . are startled by the cry of "There she blows!" and away they fly to fight another whale, and go through the whole weary thing again.

"Oh! my friends, but this is man-killing! Yet this is life. For hardly have we mortals by long toilings extracted from this world's vast bulk its small but valuable sperm; and then, with weary patience, cleansed ourselves from its defilements, and learned to live here in clean tabernacles of the soul; hardly is this done, when—There she blows!—the ghost is spouted up, and away we sail to fight some other world, and go through young life's old routine again. Oh! the metempsychosis! Oh! Pythagoras, that in bright Greece, two thousand years ago, did die, so good, so wise, so mild; I sailed with thee along the Peruvian coast last voyage—and, foolish as I am, taught thee, a green simple boy, how to splice a rope! . . .

The mingled, mingling threads of life are woven by warp and woof: calms crossed by storms, a storm for every calm. . . . [We pass] through infancy's unconscious spell, boyhood's thoughtless faith, adolescence, doubt (the common doom), then scepticism, then disbelief, resting at last in manhood's pondering repose of If. But once gone through, we trace the round again: and are infants, boys, and men, and Ifs eternally. Where lies the final harbour, whence we unmoor no more? In what rapt ether sails the world of which the weariest will never weary? . . .

[Captain Ahab, a New England Quaker, addresses three white flames that lightning caused to appear on the ship's masts and which were silently burning like gigantic wax tapers before an altar:] Oh! thou clear spirit of clear fire, whom on these seas I as Persian once did worship, till in the

[3] J. B. Priestley, *Literature and Western Man*. New York: Harper and Row, 1960, p. 238.

sacramental act so burned by thee, that to this hour I bear the scar; I now know thee, thou clear spirit, and I know that thy right worship is defiance. . . . No fearless fool now fronts thee. I own thy speechless, placeless power; but to the last gasp of my earthquake life will dispute its unconditional, unintegral mastery in me. In the midst of the personified impersonal, a personality stands here. Though but a point at best; whencesoe'er I came; wheresoe'er I go, yet while I earthly live, the queenly personality lives in me, and feels her royal rights. . . . Now I do glory, in my genealogy. . . .

[As the point of no return approaches, a more contrite Ahab thinks these thoughts:] Forty—forty—forty years of continual whaling! forty years of privation, and peril . . . has Ahab forsaken the peaceful land, for forty years to make war on the horrors of the deep! . . . But do I look very old, so very, very old? I feel deadly faint, bowed, and humped, as though I were Adam, staggering beneath the piled centuries since Paradise. . . . What is it, what nameless, inscrutable, unearthly thing is it; what hidden lord and master, and cruel, remorseless emperor commands me; that against all natural lovings and longings, I so keep pushing, and crowding, and jamming myself on all the time; recklessly making me ready to do what in my own proper, natural heart, I durst not so much as dare? . . . Ye see an old man cut down to the stump; leaning on a shivered lance; propped up on a lonely foot. 'Tis Ahab—his body's part; but Ahab's soul's a centipede, that moves upon a hundred legs. . . . Ahab is for ever Ahab, man. This whole act's immutably decreed. 'Twas rehearsed by thee and me a billion years before this ocean rolled.

Moby Dick 4

JAMES RUSSELL LOWELL (1819–1891)
American Poet, Essayist, and Diplomat

Sometimes a breath floats by me,
An odor from Dreamland sent,
That makes the ghost seem nigh me
Of a splendor that came and went,
Of a life lived somewhere, I know not
In what diviner sphere. . . .
A something too vague, could I name it,
For others to know,
As if I had lived it or dreamed it,
As if I had acted or schemed it
Long ago!

"In the Twilight"

4 Chapters 98, 114, 119, 132, and 134.

CHARLES KINGSLEY (1819–1875)
British Novelist and Clergyman

[From Kingsley's fairy story The Water Babies, Chapters 2 and 3:]

When you came into this world, and became a land baby, you remembered nothing. . . . Then have you lived before? My dear child, who can tell? One can only tell that, by remembering something which happened where we lived before. . . . There was a wise man once, a very wise man, and a very good man, who wrote a poem about the feeling which some children have about having lived before; and this is what he said: [Wordsworth's "Ode to Immortality" is quoted.] There, you can know no more than that. But if I were you, I would believe that. For then the great fairy Science, who is likely to be queen of all the fairies for many a year to come, can only do you good, and never do you harm. And instead of fancying, with some people, that your body makes your soul, as if a steam engine could make its own coke; or, with some people, that your soul has nothing to do with your body, but is only stuck into it like a pin into a pincushion, to fall out with the first shake—you will believe the one true doctrine of this wonderful fairy tale, which is that your soul makes your body, just as a snail makes his shell. . . .

[Quatrefages said:] "Who would not exclaim that a miracle had come to pass, if he saw a reptile come out of the egg dropped by the hen in his poultry yard, and the reptile give birth at once to an indefinite number of fishes and birds? Yet the history of the jellyfish is quite as wonderful as that would be." . . . If the changes of the lower animals are so wonderful, and so difficult to discover . . . may not man, the crown and flower of all things, undergo some change as much more wonderful than all the rest . . . ? Does not each of us, in coming into this world, go through a transformation just as wonderful as that of a sea egg or a butterfly? And do not reason and analogy, as well as Scripture, tell us that that transformation is not the last?

The Water Babies

[In his novel Hypatia (Chapter 8), Kingsley places these words in the mouth of his heroine, the Neoplatonic philosopher who in the fifth century taught at the famous Museum in Alexandria:]

Truth! Where is truth but in the soul itself? Facts, objects, are but phantoms matter-woven—ghosts of this earthly night . . . Yet, even as our nightly dreams stir in us the suspicion of mysterious and immaterial presences, unfettered by the bonds of time and space, so do these waking dreams which we call sight and sound. They are divine messengers, whom Zeus, pitying his children, even when he pent them in this prison-house of flesh, appointed to arouse in them dim recollections of that real world of souls whence they came. . . .

It is but a little time—a few days longer in this prison-house of our degradation, and each thing shall return to its own fountain; the blood-drop to the abysmal heart, and the water to the river, and the river to the shining sea; and the dewdrop which fell from heaven shall rise to heaven again, shaking off the dust-grains which weighted it down . . . , upward and upward ever through stars and suns, through gods, and through the parents of the gods, purer and purer through successive lives, till it enters The Nothing, which is The All, and finds its home at last.

Hypatia

LOUIS FIGUIER (1819–1894)
French Naturalist and Science Writer

The English philosopher, Locke, immortalized himself by the discovery that the human understanding has ideas called "innate"; that is, ideas that we bring with us into life. This fact is certain in itself. In our day, a Scotch philosopher, Dugald Stewart, has more precisely stated the discovery of Locke, in showing that the only and true innate idea, that which exists universally in the human mind from birth, is the idea or principle of causality,—a principle which makes us say and think that there is no effect without a cause, which is the beginning of reason. . . .

Innate ideas and the principle of causality are very easily explained. . . . Our souls, having already existed . . . have preserved traces of the impressions they received during such existences. They have lost, it is true, the memory of actions done during their first incarnations; but the abstract principle of causality . . . must endure in the soul at its second [and later] incarnation[s] . . . Natural apititudes, special faculties and vocations, are traces of impressions received long before, of knowledge already acquired, and which, betraying itself from the cradle, can be accounted for only on the hypothesis of a former life. . . . The soul of man remains always the same, notwithstanding its numerous peregrinations.

The Tomorrow of Death [1]
Trans. S. R. Crocker

[1] Boston: Robert Bros., 1888, pp. 251–252, 281, 287.

GUSTAVE FLAUBERT (1821–1880)
French Novelist

[From a letter of Flaubert written in 1866 to George Sand, and published in *The George Sand—Gustave Flaubert Letters:*[1]]

I don't experience, as you do, this feeling of a life which is beginning, the stupefaction of a newly commenced existence. It seems to me, on the contrary, that I have always lived! And I possess memories which go back to the Pharaohs. I see myself very clearly at different ages of history, practising different professions and in many sorts of fortune. My present personality is the result of my lost personalities. . . . Many things would be explained if we could know our real genealogy. . . . Thus heredity is a just principle which has been badly applied.

Lettres à George Sand

FEODOR DOSTOEVSKY (1821–1881)
Russian Novelist

"This legend is about Paradise. There was, they say, here on earth a thinker and philosopher. He rejected everything, 'laws, conscience, faith,' and above all, the future life. He died; he expected to go straight to darkness and death and he found a future life before him. He was astounded and indignant. 'This is against my principles!' he said. And he was punished for that . . . he was sentenced to walk a quadrillion kilometres in the dark . . . and when he has finished the quadrillion, the gates of heaven would be opened to him and he'll be forgiven. . . . Well, this man who was condemned to the quadrillion kilometres, stood still, looked round and lay down across the road. 'I won't go, I refuse on principle!' . . . He lay there almost a thousand years and then he got up and went on."

"What an ass!" cried Ivan, laughing nervously. . . . "Does it make any difference whether he lies there for ever or walks the quadrillion kilometres? It would take a billion years to walk it?"

"Much more than that. . . . But he got there long ago and that's where the story begins."

"What, he got there? But how did he get the billion years to do it?"

"Why, you keep thinking of our present earth! But our present earth may have been repeated a billion times. Why, it's become extinct, been frozen; cracked, broken to bits, disintegrated into its elements, again 'the water above the firmament,' then again a comet, again a sun, again from the sun it becomes earth—and the same sequence may have been repeated endlessly and exactly the same to every detail."

The Brothers Karamazov[1]

MATTHEW ARNOLD (1822–1888)
British Poet and Critic

And then we shall unwillingly return
Back to this meadow of calamity,
This uncongenial place, this human life;
And in our individual human state
Go through the sad probation all again,
To see if we will poise our life at last,
To see if we will now at last be true
To our own only true, deep-buried selves,
Being one with which we are one with the whole world;
Or whether we will once more fall away
Into some bondage of the flesh or mind,
Some slough of sense, or some fantastic maze
Forged by the imperious lonely thinking-power.

Empedocles on Etna (Act II)

SÁNDOR PETÖFI (1823–1849)
Hungarian National Poet and Revolutionary

[In America, and probably other places, there are a number of Petöfi societies in honor of this lyric poet, who apparently lost his life in the Hungarian revolution of 1848–49.]

The Soul is immortal—this I believe
But not into another world it goes
Instead here on earth remains
On earth to live and to wander.
Among other things, I remember
In Rome I was Cassius,
In Helvetia, William Tell,
In Paris, Desmoulins Kamill
Here, too, perhaps, I will become something.

"The Soul Is Immortal" [1]

---

[1] Trans. Constance Garnett. Part IV, Book XI, Chap. 9.

---

[1] Potöfi Sándor Összes Költeményei (Complete Verses), ed. Albert Kardos. Debrecen: 1916, p. 448.

ERNEST RENAN (1823–1892)
French Historian, Philologist, Critic

[From Renan's address at the tomb of Ivan Turgenev, delivered October 1, 1883, and to be found in Turgenev's *Oeuvres Dernieres*:[1]]

We cannot let the remains which are about to be returned to his country return without a farewell to the spirit of the genius, who it was our privilege for many years to know and to love. . . . I will but speak to you of his soul such as it was revealed to me in the beautiful retreat which gave us the opportunity of an illustrious friendship. . . . He was born essentially impersonal. His conscience was . . . the conscience of a people. Before his birth, he had lived thousands of years and infinite succession of dreams concentrated in the depths of his soul. . . .

The silent genius of the collective masses is the source of all great things. But the mass is without voice. It knows but to suffer and to stammer. It needs an interpreter, a prophet to speak for it. . . . The great man is that prophet when he is at the same time a genius and a man of heart. That is why the great man is the least free of men. He can neither do nor say what he wishes. A God speaks in him—ten centuries of sorrows and hopes obsess and command him. . . . Like the universe itself, [Turgenev] recommenced a thousand times the unfinished work.

"At the Tomb of Turgenev"

* NOTE *
From this point onward, selections from the writings of scientists, psychologists, and philosophers will be found in Part Six. The remainder of Part Five, while treating chiefly of reincarnation in Western literature, also includes the views of men of action, and pioneers in various fields of occidental life. As to Western literature, the numerous novels and plays that have used the reincarnation theme mainly as a backdrop for romance, though probably not without significance, have been omitted. For additional material see Reincarnation, an East-West Anthology, Part Two.

CONRAD FERDINAND MEYER (1825–1898)
Swiss Poet and Historical Novelist

In the last few years I have gone through more than I am ever willing to confess. Truly what sustained me was a thought on reincarnation. I told

[1] Paris: 1885, pp. 298, 302.

myself: evidently you did something terrible in a former existence. Said the voice of fate: just for that the fellow shall go to earth and become a Meyer. Now both have to suffer through honestly, before a change for the better may be attained.[1]

Letter to Friedrich von Wiss, August 7, 1889

COUNT LEO TOLSTOY (1828–1910)
Russian Novelist and Philosopher

"How quiet you young people are!"

"Yes, we're talking philosophy," said Natasha. . . . "Do you know, I think . . . that one goes on remembering, and remembering; one remembers till one recalls what happened before one was in this world."

"That's metempsychosis," said Sonya, who had been good at lessons. . . . "The Egyptians used to believe that our souls had been in animals, and would go into animals again."

"No, do you know, I don't believe that we were once in animals," said Natasha . . . "but I know for certain that we were once angels somewhere beyond, and we have been here, and that's why we remember everything." . . .

"If we had been angels, why should we have fallen lower?" said Nikolay. "No, that can't be!"

"Not lower . . . who told you we were lower? . . . This is how I know I have existed before," Natasha replied, with conviction: "The soul is immortal, you know, . . . so, if I am to live for ever, I have lived before too, I have lived for all eternity.

"Yes, but it's hard for us to conceive of eternity," said Dimmler, who had joined the young people, with a mildly condescending smile, but now talked as quietly and seriously as they did.

"Why is it hard to conceive of eternity?" said Natasha. "There will be today, and there will be tomorrow, and there will be forever, and yesterday has been, and the day before."

War and Peace (Part VII, Chap. 10)
Trans. Constance Garnett

[In 1904 Tolstoy completed an arrangement in four volumes of the thoughts of great men under the title *The Circle of Reading*, grouped to provide reading matter for each day of the year. Frequently he headed a page with a contribution of his own, as was the case for March 12:]

[1] *Briefe*, I, 95.

The deeds of the preceding life give the direction to the present life. This is what the Hindus call Karma.

Krug Tchtenia

How interesting it would be to write the story of the experiences in this life of a man who killed himself in his previous life; how he now stumbles against the very demands which had offered themselves before, until he arrives at the realization that he must fulfil those demands. Remembering the lesson, this man will be wiser than others.

Diary Entry, February 13, 1896 [1]

You are asking me about the Buddhist idea of "Karma." . . . Now our whole life, from birth unto death, with all its dreams, is it not in its turn also a dream, which we take as the real life, the reality of which we do not doubt only because we do not know of the other more real life? . . . The dreams of our present life are the environment in which we work out the impressions, thoughts, feelings of a former life. . . . As we live through thousands of dreams in our present life, so is our present life only one of many thousands of such lives which we enter from the other, more real life . . . and then return after death. Our life is but one of the dreams of that more real life, and so it is endlessly, until the very last one, the very real life,—the life of God. . . . I wish you would understand me; I am not playing, not inventing this: I believe in it, I see it without doubt.

Letter [2]

HENRIK IBSEN (1828–1906)
Norwegian Dramatist and Poet

[As already mentioned, the Roman Emperor Julian believed himself to be a reincarnation of Alexander the Great. The following lines from Ibsen's tragedy on Julian point up this idea:]

MAXIMUS   Must I remind you how fortune has borne you, as on mighty pinions, through an agitated and perilous life? Who are you, sire? Are you Alexander born again, not, as before in immaturity, but perfectly equipped for the fulfillment of the task?

JULIAN   Maximus!

MAXIMUS   There is One who ever reappears, at certain intervals, in the course of human history. He is like a rider taming a wild horse in

---

[1] *Diary of Leo Nickolaevich Tolstoy*, ed. V. G. Chertkov. Moscow: 1906, I, 17.
[2] Moscow: magazine *The Voice of Universal Love*, 1908, No. 40.

the arena. Again and yet again it throws him. A moment, and he is in the saddle again, each time more secure and more expert; but off he has had to go, in all his varying incarnations, until this day. Off he had to go as the god-created man in Eden's grove; off he had to go as the founder of the world-empire; off he must go as the prince of the empire of God. Who knows how often he has wandered among us when none have recognized him? . . .

JULIAN (looking far away)   Oh, unfathomable riddle—!

The Emperor Julian[1]

DANTE GABRIEL ROSSETTI (1828–1882)
British Painter and Poet

I have been here before,
But when or how I cannot tell;
I know the grass beyond the door,
The sweet keen smell,
The sighing sound, the lights around the shore.

You have been mine before,—
How long ago I may not know:
But just when at that swallow's soar
Your neck turned so,
Some veil did fall,—I knew it all of yore.

"Sudden Light"

[Rossetti has also written a reincarnation story entitled "St. Agnes of Intercession." [1]]

EMILY DICKINSON (1830–1886)
American Poet

Afraid? Of whom am I afraid?
Not death; for who is he?
The porter of my father's lodge
As much abasheth me.

Of life? 'Twere odd I fear a thing
That comprehendeth me
In one or more existences
At Deity's decree.

[1] Act IV, Scene I. *Collected Works of Henrik Ibsen,* ed. William Archer. New York: Scribner, 1911, p. 393.

[1] *Collected Works,* I, 399.

Of resurrection? Is the east
Afraid to trust the morn?
Collected Poems[1]

WILLIAM J. POTTER (1830–1893)
American Transcendentalist and Unitarian Minister

It is possible, perhaps probable, that the soul will always have some form of body and some material limitation . . . now taking this form, now that— yet always ascending in form as giving larger freedom of nature . . . as the scale of being ascends. But over and above all change, independent of all limitations of time and matter, beyond the reach of the accidental and fluctuating relations of individual existence, there enters into human nature another factor by which it lays hold of a substance that is Infinite and Everlasting, and draws its being therefrom. There is somewhat of the absolute and eternal in every human soul . . . something that transcends time and space and organic form, and makes eternity for the soul to be the continuous unfolding of a perpetual and indestructible principle of life rather than the infinite multiplication of days and years.

"The Doctrine of Pre-Existence and the Fourth Gospel"
The Radical, April 1868

ROBERT G. INGERSOLL (1833–1899)
American Agnostic and Iconoclast

We cannot say that death is not a good. We do not know whether the grave is the end of this life, or the door of another, or whether the night here is not somewhere else a dawn. . . . Another life is nought, unless we know and love again the ones who love us here. . . . The dead do not suffer. If they live again, their lives will surely be as good as ours. . . . We [the Agnostics], too, have our religion, and it is this: Help for the living— hope for the dead.

"At a Child's Grave" 1

GEORGE DU MAURIER (1834–1896)
French-Born British Artist and Novelist

O reader, if you be but sound in mind and body, it most seriously behooves you . . . to go forth and multiply exceedingly . . . to select the very best

---

1 *The Poems of Emily Dickinson.* Boston: Little, Brown, 1930, p. 167.

1 A. M. Baten, *The Philosophy of Life.* Hammond, Indiana: 1930, pp. 114–115.

of your kind in the opposite sex for this most precious, excellent, and blessed purpose; that all your future reincarnations (and hers), however brief, may be many. . . . If anything can keep us well within the thorny path that leads to happiness and virtue, it is the certainty that those who come after us will remember having been ourselves, if only in a dream.

Peter Ibbetson (Part Fifth)

MARK TWAIN (1835–1910)
American Author and Humorist

[In an article "About Play-Acting," [1] Mark Twain urged the more frequent performance of serious tragedy on the American and British stage, and enthusiastically recommended the German production "The Master of Palmyra."]

I have just been witnessing a remarkable play, here at the Burg Theatre in Vienna. I do not know of any play that much resembles it. In fact, it is such a departure from the common laws of the drama that the name "play" doesn't seem to fit it quite snugly. However, whatever else it may be, it is in any case a great and stately metaphysical poem, and deeply fascinating. . . . This piece is "The Master of Palmyra." . . . It is by Wilbrandt, and is his masterpiece and the work which is to make his name permanent in German literature. It has never been played anywhere except in Berlin and in the great Burg Theatre in Vienna. Yet whenever it is put on the stage it packs the house, and the free list is suspended. I know people who have seen it ten times; they know the most of it by heart. . . .

There is a dash of metempsychosis in it—and it is the strength of the piece. . . . The scene of it is Palmyra in Roman times. It covers a wide stretch of time . . . and in the course of it the chief actress is reincarnated several times. . . . In the first act she is Zoë. . . . In this character she is wholly spiritual, a religious enthusiast, a devotee who covets martyrdom— and gets it. After many years she appears in the second act as *Phœbe*, a graceful and beautiful young light-o'-love from Rome, whose soul is all for the shows and luxuries and delights of this life. . . . In the third act, after an interval of many years, she reappears as *Persida*, mother of a daughter in the fresh bloom of youth. She is now a sort of combination of her two earlier selves: in religious loyalty and subjection she is Zoë; in triviality of character and shallowness of judgment . . . she is *Phœbe*. After a lapse of years she appears in the fourth act as *Nymphas*, a beautiful boy, in whose

---

[1] *Mark Twain's Works.* New York: Harper and Row, 1906, XXIII, pp. 202–205, *The Man That Corrupted Hadleyburg and Other Stories and Essays.*

character the previous incarnations are engagingly mixed. And after another stretch of years all these heredities are joined in the *Zenobia* of the fifth act—a person of gravity, dignity, sweetness, with a heart filled with compassion for all who suffer, and a hand prompt to put into practical form the heart's benignant impulses.

You will easily concede that the actress who proposes to discriminate nicely these five characters, and play them to the satisfaction of a cultivated and exacting audience, has her work cut out for her. Mme. Hohenfels has made these parts her peculiar property. . . . You perceive, now, where the chief part of the absorbing fascination of this piece lies; it is in watching this extraordinary artist melt these five characters into each other—grow, shade by shade, out of one and into another through a stretch of four hours and five minutes. . . . The aging men and the aging scenery together convey a profound illusion of that long lapse of time: they make you live it yourself! You leave the theatre with the weight of a century upon you.

"About Play-Acting"

The First time I was in Egypt a Simplified Spelling epidemic had broken out and the atmosphere was electrical with feeling engendered by the subject. This was four or five thousand years ago—I do not remember just how many thousand it was, for my memory for minor details has suffered some decay in the lapse of years. I am speaking of a former state of existence of mine, perhaps my earliest reincarnation; indeed I think it was the earliest. I had been an angel previously, and I am expecting to be one again—but at the time I speak of I was different.

"Simplified Spelling" [2]

[Mark Twain's true story "My Platonic Sweetheart" tells of an unusual dream that recurred in manifold forms over a period of forty years. Therein he meets a girl of fifteen for whom he has a deep, reverent, chaste love. Frequently in the dreams she, as well as he, has a new name, and her appearance and facial characteristics also change. The place of the vision varies: it might be India, or England, or America. In "Hawaii" he saw her die a terrible death, and the pain, the grief, and the misery of it transcended many sufferings he had known in waking life. Of his next meeting her in Greece he writes:]

What now follows occurred while I was asleep. . . . I was in Athens —a city which I had not then seen, but I recognized the Parthenon from the pictures, although it had a fresh look and was in perfect repair. I passed

[2] Included in Mark Twain's posthumously published *Letters from the Earth*, ed. B. Devoto. New York: Harper and Row, 1962, p. 159.

by it and climbed a grassy hill toward a palatial sort of mansion which was built of red terra cotta and had a spacious portico, whose roof was supported by a rank of fluted columns with Corinthian capitals. . . . I passed into the house and entered the first room. It was very large and light, its walls were of polished and richly tinted and veined onyx, and its floor was a pictured pattern in soft colors laid in tiles. I noted the details of the furniture and the ornaments . . . and they took sharp hold and remained in my memory; they are not really dim yet, and this was more than thirty years ago.

There was a person present—Agnes. I was not surprised to see her, but only glad. She was in the simple Greek costume, and her hair and eyes were different as to color from those she had had when she died in the Hawaiian Islands half an hour before. . . . I remembered her death. . . . I was grateful to have her back, but there was no realizable sense that she had ever been gone, and so it did not occur to me to speak about it, and she made no reference to it herself. It may be that she had often died before, and knew that there was nothing lasting about it, and consequently nothing important enough in it to make conversation out of. . . .

While Agnes and I sat talking in that grand Athens house, several stately Greeks entered from another part of it, disputing warmly about something or other, and passed us by with courteous recognition; and among them was Socrates. I recognized him by his nose. . . .

In my waking hours, when the inferior artist in me is in command, I cannot draw even the simplest picture. . . . In our dreams—I know it!— we do make the journeys we seem to make; we do see the things we seem to see; the people, the horses, the cats . . . are real, not chimeras; they are living spirits, not shadows; and they are immortal and indestructible. . . . My Dreamland sweetheart . . . to me . . . is a real person, not a fiction. . . . Everything in a dream is more deep and strong and sharp and real than is ever its pale imitation in the unreal life which is ours when we go about awake and clothed with our artificial selves in this vague and dull-tinted artificial world. When we die we shall slough off this cheap intellect, perhaps, and go abroad into Dreamland clothed in our real selves, and aggrandized and enriched by the command over the mysterious mental magician who is here not our slave, but only our guest.

"My Platonic Sweetheart" [3]

[3] The Mysterious Stranger and Other Stories. New York: Harper and Row, 1950, pp. 300–304.

SAMUEL BUTLER (1835–1902)
British Author and Satirist

We commonly know that we are going to die, though we do not know that we are going to be born. But are we sure this is so? We may have had the most gloomy forebodings on this head and forgotten all about them. . . .

I must have it that neither are the good rewarded nor the bad punished in a future [after death] state, but every one must start anew quite irrespective of anything they have done here and must try his luck again and go on trying it again and again *ad infinitum*. Some of our lives, then, will be lucky and some unlucky and it will resolve itself into one long eternal life during which we shall change so much that we shall not remember our antecedents very far back (any more than we remember having been embryos) nor foresee our future very much, and during which we shall have our ups and downs *ad infinitum*—effecting a transformation scene at once as soon as circumstances become unbearable.

The Note-Books of Samuel Butler[1]

We have been three lights to one another and now we are two,
For you go far and alone into the darkness;
But the light in you was stronger and clearer than ours . . .
Out, out into the night you go,
So guide you and guard you Heaven and fare you well! . . .

Yet for the great bitterness of this grief
We three, you and he and I,
May pass into the hearts of like true comrades hereafter,
In whom we may weep anew and yet comfort them,
As they too pass out, out, out into the night,
So guide them and guard them Heaven and fare them well! . . .
　　　"In Memoriam, February 14, 1895, To H. R. F." [2]

Not on sad Stygian shore, nor in clear sheen
Of far Elysian plain, shall we meet those
Among the dead whose pupils we have been. . . .
We shall not argue saying " 'Twas thus" or "Thus,"
Our argument's whole drift we shall forget;
Who's right, who's wrong, 'twill be all one to us;
We shall not even know that we have met.

[1] Ed. Henry Festing Jones. New York: Dutton, 1917, pp. 16, 362.
[2] *Ibid.*, p. 394.

Yet meet we shall, and part, and meet again,
Where dead men meet, on lips of living men.
                    "The Life After Death" [3]

ALGERNON CHARLES SWINBURNE (1837–1909)
British Poet

[Swinburne wrote to Seymour Kirkup, an artist friend of William Blake: "I was much struck by the passage in your last letter to me, where you speak of the Theory of Transmigration. Whether or not it be affirmed or denied by spirits [Kirkup was interested in Spiritualism] I know that it has always appeared to me a very probable article of faith." August 11, 1865, *The Swinburne Letters*.[1]]

I am that which began;
Out of me the years roll;
Out of me God and man;
I am equal and whole:
God changes, and man, and the form of them bodily;
I am the soul.
Before ever land was.
Before ever the sea,
Or soft hair of the grass,
Or fair limbs of the tree,
Or the flesh-coloured fruit of my branches,
I was, and thy soul was in me.
                    "Hertha"

QUEEN ELISABETH OF AUSTRIA (1837–1898)
German-Born Empress of Austria, Wife of Franz Joseph

[Constantin Christomanos, the Queen's Greek tutor, who often accompanied her on her long walks, wrote in his *Vienna Diary*:[1]]

Speaking of the difference between culture and civilization, she says: "Civilization is reading, culture is the thoughts. . . . Everyone has culture within himself as heritage of all his pre-existences, absorbs it with every breath and in this lies the great unity." . . . Of Dante and other great ones, she says: "They are souls, who, from ages past have come anew to

[3] *Ibid.*, p. 397.

[1] Yale University Press, 1959, I, 128.

[1] *Tagebuchblätter Wien*, 1899, pp. 81, 97, 227.

earth to continue their work and to anticipate the development of others still to come. . . . Our innermost being is more valuable than all titles and honors. These are colored rags with which we try to cover our nudities. Whatever is of value in us we bring from our previous lives that were spiritual."

JOHN MUIR (1838–1914)
American Naturalist

Trees towering in the sky, braving storms of centuries, flowers turning faces to the light for a single day or hour, having enjoyed their share of life's feast—all alike pass on and away under the law of death and love. Yet all are our brothers and they enjoy life as we do, share heaven's blessings with us, die and are buried in hallowed ground, come with us out of eternity and return into eternity. "Our little lives are rounded with a sleep." . . . Death is a kind nurse saying, "Come, children, to bed and get up in the morning"—a gracious Mother calling her children home.

John of the Mountains
The Unpublished Journal of John Muir[1]

EDWARD CARPENTER (1844–1929)
British Author

[After leaving Cambridge, Edward Carpenter entered the Anglican ministry for five years. On a visit to the United States in 1877 he met Emerson, Whitman, Lowell, Bryant, and Oliver Wendell Holmes, and a few years later devoted himself to writing. "After Long Ages," and "When a Thousand Years have Passed," are some of his reincarnation poems.]

Every man feels doubtless that his little mortal life is very inadequate, and that to express and give utterance to all that is in him would need many lives, many bodies. . . . The important thing . . . is to see that undoubtedly various orders of consciousness do exist, *actually embedded within us*; and that the words I and Thou do not merely cover our bodily forms and the outlines of our minds as we habitually represent them to ourselves, but cover also immense tracts of intelligence and activity lying behind these and only on occasions coming into consciousness. . . . To command these tracts in such a way as to be able to enter in and make use of them at will, and to bring them into permanent relation with the conscious ego, will I think be the method of advance, and the means by which all

[1] Boston: Houghton Mifflin, 1938, pp. 438–440.

these questions of the perduration and reincarnation of the ego, and its real relation with other egos, will at length be solved.

The Art of Creation (Chap. 11)

WILLIAM ERNEST HENLEY (1849–1903)
British Poet, Editor, and Playwright

Or ever the knightly years were gone
With the old world to the grave,
I was a King in Babylon
And you were a Christian Slave.
I saw, I took, I cast you by,
I bent and broke your pride. . . .
And a myriad suns have set and shone
Since then upon the grave
Decreed by the King in Babylon
To her that had been his Slave.
The pride I trampled is now my scathe,
For it tramples me again.
The old resentment lasts like death,
For you love, yet you refrain.
I break my heart on your hard unfaith,
And I break my heart in vain.

"*To W.A.*"

AUGUST STRINDBERG (1849–1912)
Swedish Dramatist and Novelist

The teacher said: "Life is hard to live, and the destinies of men appear very different. . . . It is therefore difficult to know how one should behave in life, what one should believe, what views one should adopt, or to which party one should adhere. This destiny is not the inevitable blind fate of the ancients, but the commission which each one has received, the task he must perform. The Theosophists call it Karma, and believe it is connected with a past which we only dimly remember. . . ."

The pupil asked: "If it is so, why is not one informed of one's Karma from the beginning?"

The teacher answered: "That is pure pity for us. No man could endure life, if he knew what lay before him. Moreover, man must have a certain measure of freedom; without that, he would be only a puppet. Also the wise think that the voyage of discovery we make to discover our destiny is instructive for us. . . ."

Darwinism made it seem probable that men derived their origin from animals. Then came the Theosophists with the opinion that our souls are in process of transmigration from one human body to another. Thence comes this excessive feeling of discomfort, this longing for deliverance, this sensation of constraint, the pain of existence, the sighing of the creature. Those who do not feel this uneasiness, but flourish here, are probably at home here. Their inexplicable sympathy for animals and their disbelief in the immortality of the soul points to a connection with the lower forms of existence of which they are conscious, and which we cannot deny.

Zones of the Spirit 1

LAFCADIO HEARN (1850–1904)
Author and Journalist

[Born on a Greek island of Greek mother and English father, Lafcadio Hearn lived for over twenty years in the United States as journalist and writer. In later years he became in all ways a Japanese, and admirably served the function of interpreter of the East to the West.]

Proof that a reconsideration of the problem of the Ego is everywhere forcing itself upon Occidental minds, may be found not only in the thoughtful prose of the time, but even in its poetry and romance. . . . Creative art, working under larger inspiration, is telling . . . what marvellous deepening of emotional power, may be gained in literature with the recognition of the idea of pre-existence. Even in fiction we learn that we have been living in a hemisphere only, that we have been thinking but half-thoughts, that we need a new faith to join past with future over the great parallel of the present, and so to round out our emotional world into a perfect sphere.

Kokoro: Hints and Echoes of Japanese Inner Life (Chap. 12)

I seemed to understand as never before, how the mystery that is called the Soul of me must have quickened in every form of past existence, and must as certainly continue to behold the sun, for other millions of summers, through eyes of other countless shapes of future being. . . . For thousands of years the East has been teaching that what we think or do in this life really decides—through some inevitable formation of atom-tendencies or polarities—the future place of our substance, and the future state of our sentiency. . . . Acts and thoughts, according to Buddhist doctrines, are creative. . . . What we think or do is never for the moment

1 New York: Putnam, 1913, pp. 50, 145.

only, but for measureless time; it signifies some force directed to the shaping of worlds—to the making of future bliss or pain. . . . And when all the stars of the visible Night shall have burnt themselves out, those atoms will doubtless again take part in the orbing of Mind—and will tremble again in thoughts, emotions, memories—in all the joys and pains of lives still to be lived in worlds still to be evolved. . . . The very delusion of delusions is the idea of death as loss.

Kotto[1]

The child is incomparably superior to the average man in seeing the character of things. . . . If I were to ask twenty little children—say, five or six years old—to look at the same tree . . . and to tell me what they think of it, I am sure that many of them would say wonderful things. They would come much nearer to the truth than the average university student, and this just because of their absolute innocence. To the child's imagination everything is alive—stones, trees, plants, even household objects. For him everything has a soul. . . . Nor is this the only reason for the superiority of the child's powers of observation. His instinctive knowledge, the knowledge inherited from millions of past lives, is still fresh, not dulled by the weight of the myriad impressions of education, and personal experience.

Talks to Writers (Chap. 2, Part II)

Great music is a psychical storm, agitating to unimaginable depth the mystery of the past within us. Or we might say that it is a prodigious incantation—every different instrument and voice making separate appeal to different billions of prenatal memories. There are tones that call up all ghosts of youth and joy and tenderness; there are tones that evoke all phantom pain of perished passion; there are tones that resurrect all dead sensation of majesty and might and glory—all expired exultations, all forgotten magnanimities. Well may the influence of music seem inexplicable to the man who idly dreams that his life began less than a hundred years ago! But the mystery lightens for whomsoever learns that the substance of Self is older than the sun. . . . To every ripple of melody, to every billow of harmony, there answers within him, out of the Sea of Death and Birth, some eddying immeasurable of ancient pleasure and pain.

In Ghostly Japan[2]

Hopeless . . . any attempt to tell the real pain of seeing my former births. I can say only that no combination of suffering possible to *individual*

[1] London and New York: Macmillan, 1902, pp. 175–176, 182–184.
[2] Boston: Little, Brown, 1899, pp. 239–240.

being could be likened to such pain—the pain of countless lives interwoven. It seemed as if every nerve of me had been prolonged into some monstrous web of sentiency spun back through a million years. . . . For, as I looked backward, I became double, quadruple, octuple . . . I became hundreds and thousands—and feared with the terror of thousands—and despaired with the anguish of thousands . . . yet knew the pleasure of none. . . .

Then in the moment when sentiency itself seemed bursting into dissolution, one divine touch ended the frightful vision, and brought again to me the simple consciousness of the single present. Oh! how unspeakably delicious that sudden shrinking back out of the multiplicity into unity!—that immense, immeasurable collapse of Self into the blind oblivious numbness of individuality!

"To others also," said the voice of the divine one who had thus saved me—"to others in the like state it has been permitted to see something of their pre-existence. But no one of them ever could endure to look far. Power to see all former births belongs only to those eternally released from the bonds of Self. Such exist outside of illusion—outside of form and name; and pain cannot come nigh them. But to you, remaining in illusion, not even the Buddha could give power to look back more than a little way."

"Within the Circle"
Gleanings in Buddha-Fields

◆ ✳ ●

Twentieth Century

CHARLES KELSEY GAINES (1854–1944)

American Educator

[Dr. Gaines' once widely read novel, Gorgo; a Romance of Old Athens,[1] was acclaimed by some reviewers as one of the best historical novels ever written. His stories therein of Socrates teaching a child are priceless. Gaines was Professor of Greek Philosophy at St. Lawrence University. Quoting from the prologue to Gorgo:]

I stopped short; I flung down the book. "It is a lie," I cried bitterly, "a cruel, hateful lie," I almost shouted,—and the whole class stared at me in amazement. A strange outburst was that for the dingy, drowsy Greek-room of the little New England college. I was as much surprised as any; I stood confounded at myself. For then it was that I remembered. The passage which I was translating seemed innocent enough—to all the rest. We were reading at sight—the professor's particular hobby; and he was exploiting upon us the Twelfth Oration of Lysias. . . .

And although he has been the author of all these and still other disasters and disgraces, both old and new, both small and great, some dare to profess themselves his friends; although it was not for the people that Theramenes died, but because of his own villainy—

Then I choked and stopped. Tears swam in my eyes, and a hot flush scalded my cheeks. . . . "It is a lie," I burst forth. "A cruel, hateful lie. . . . I will not read it—I will not read another line.". . . For the past had opened like a darkness lightning-cleft; all in one moment I felt the injus-

[1] Boston: Lothrop, 1903.

tices of ages, the shame of an aeon of scorn—and they asked me to read against myself the lying record. . . . After that they nicknamed me Theramenes: I was nicknamed after myself, and none suspected. . . .

Forget! I have far too much to remind me. What is this seething democracy in which we live but Athens renewed? In a thousand ways I am reminded—but I forbear. Yet—do you imagine that I alone among living men have walked those ancient streets? Not so: but the rest do not remember.

Gorgo

GEORGE BERNARD SHAW (1856–1950)
Irish Playwright, Novelist, and Critic

JOAN   And now tell me: shall I rise from the dead, and come back to you a living woman? . . . What! Must I burn again? Are none of you ready to receive me? . . . O God that madest this beautiful earth, when will it be ready to receive Thy saints? How long, O lord, how long?

Saint Joan (Epilogue)

PART I *The Garden of Eden*

THE SERPENT   The serpent never dies. Some day you shall see me come out of this beautiful skin; a new snake with a new and lovelier skin. That is birth. . . . I made the word "dead" to describe my old skin that I cast when I am renewed. I call that renewal being born.

EVE   Born is a beautiful word.

THE SERPENT   Why not be born again and again as I am, new and beautiful every time? . . .

PART II *The Twentieth Century*

SAVVY   I believe the old people are the new people, reincarnated, Frank. I suspect I am Eve. I am very fond of apples, and they always disagree with me.

CONRAD   You are Eve in a sense. The Eternal Life persists, only it wears out Its bodies and minds and gets new ones, like new clothes. You are only a new hat and frock on Eve.

FRANKLYN   Yes. Bodies and minds ever better fitted to carry out Its eternal pursuit.

LUBIN (with quiet scepticism)   What pursuit, may one ask, Mr. Barnabas?

FRANKLYN   The pursuit of omnipotence and omniscience. Greater power and greater knowledge: these are what we are all pursuing even at the risk of our lives and the sacrifice of our pleasures. Evolution is that pursuit and nothing else. It is the path to godhead. A man differs from a microbe only in being further on the path.

Back to Methuselah

AXEL MUNTHE (1857–1949)
Swedish Physician, Psychiatrist, and Writer

[Munthe's memoirs, *The Story of San Michele*, have been translated into twenty-three languages, the editions in English alone accounting for almost a million copies. Written at the suggestion of Henry James, the book treats, in part, of the reconstruction by Dr. Munthe of the chapel built on the Isle of Capri by the Roman Emperor Tiberius (42 B.C.-A.D. 37), who retired to Capri during the last eleven years of his life.

Although neither Munthe nor the illiterate peasants who helped him had any knowledge of architectural techniques—the answer to problems often appearing in sleep—the wondrous beauty of the completed work was the envy of kings and queens, who were its frequent visitants. When one reads of the unusual psychic adventures that involved Dr. Munthe from boyhood onward in the project, it is not surprising that friends speculated that he must be Tiberius returned. The English sculptor and author, Clare Sheridan, wrote in her autobiography *The Naked Truth:*[1] "I called him Tiberio; the name seemed to belong to him. He had the qualities and faults of Tiberius; his tyranny and kindliness. . . . He might have been, and I believed he was, a reincarnation of the Imperator, drawn back to the scene of his past and doomed in this life to pay back an overburdened Karma." Quoting now from *The Story of San Michele:*[2]]

[A "goblin" is asking Munthe about Time:] "Do you always carry it about with you in that gold box [Munthe's watch]?"

"Yes, it never rests, it never sleeps, it never ceases to repeat the same word in my ears. . . . It tells me every second, every minute, every hour of the day and of the night that I am getting older, and that I am going to die. Tell me, little man, before you go, are you afraid of Death?"

"Afraid of what?"

"Afraid of the day when the beating of your heart will cease, the cogs and wheels of the whole machinery fall to pieces, your thoughts stand still, your life flicker out like the light of that dim tallow candle on the table."

"Who has put all that nonsense in your head? Don't listen to the voice

[1] New York: Harper and Row, 1928, p. 62.
[2] Chaps. 7 and 31.

inside the gold box with its silly past, present and future, don't you understand that it all means the same thing! Don't you understand that somebody is making fun of you inside that gold box! . . . Don't believe a word of what it tells you, it is nothing but lies! You will always remain a child, you will never grow old, you will never die. You just lie down and get to sleep for a while! The sun will soon rise again over the fir-tops, the new day will soon look in through the window, you will soon see much clearer than you ever saw by the light of that tallow candle."

[Pacciale, an old Italian fisherman of Capri] had become my friend, the honour was mine, he was a far better man than I. . . . During the long days and nights we were together alone on the sea he taught me many things I had not read in my books or heard from the lips of other men. . . . His thoughts were few and so much the better for him. But his sayings were full of poetry and the archaic simplicity of his similes were pure Greek. Many of his very words were Greek; he remembered them from the time he had sailed down that very coast as one of the crew in Ulysses' ship.

The Story of San Michele

H. FIELDING HALL (1859–1917)
British Author

[Fielding Hall was a British officer stationed in Burma. In his several books he wrote most perceptively of the Burmese people.]

Was it an Oriental who wrote "The earth is the living garment of God"? . . . That is a universal thought that comes to every one who lives near nature. So with the life before this life, what is there Eastern in that? All the world naturally knows it, that we did not begin at birth. . . . Men have always known it till it was crushed in them. They know it even still, the truth does not die. It will rise again, must rise and burst the tombstones placed on it to keep it down.

The Inward Light (Chap. 22)

Love does not die with the body . . . it lives for ever and ever, through incarnation after incarnation. . . . Love is stronger than death. Not any dogmas of any religion, not any philosophy, nothing in this world, nothing in the next, shall prevent him who loves from the certainty of rejoining some time the soul he loves.

The Soul of a People (Chap. 22)

GUSTAV MAHLER (1860–1911)
German Composer

[Mahler's biographer, Richard Specht, relates of his visit to the composer in Hamburg, in 1895:]

In the course of the conversation Mahler said very emphatically: "We all return; it is this certainty that gives meaning to life and it does not make the slightest difference whether or not in a later incarnation we remember the former life. What counts is not the individual and his comfort, but the great aspiration to the perfect and the pure which goes on in each incarnation." [1]

ERNEST THOMPSON SETON (1860–1946)
American Nature Writer, and
Founder of Boy Scouts of America

[Julia Seton writes in the foreword to *The Gospel of the Red Man*,[1] a small volume by Ernest Thompson Seton and his wife:]

In March, 1905, we were in Los Angeles on a lecture tour. The morning after the lecture, we were met at the Van Nuys Hotel by some Eastern friends who, addressing the Chief,[2] said: "We have a message for you. There is a strange woman in the Hills who wishes to see you." Accordingly, we took the tram to the end of the track, then set out on foot to climb what, I think, are now called the Beverly Hills. On the green slope higher up was a small white cottage; in front of this, a woman dressed like a farmer's wife. . . .

She was introduced to us as a Mahatma from India, although born in Iowa. She had left her home as a small child, had spent many years studying under the Great Masters, and was now back on a mission to America. She was a strange-looking person. We could not tell whether she was thirty or a hundred and thirty years old. . . . Her eyes had the faraway veiled look of a mystic. Her talk was commonplace as she served coffee and cakes. We wondered why she had sent the summons. Finally, after an hour, we rose to leave.

[1] Richard Specht, *Gustav Mahler*. Berlin: Schuster & Loeffler, 1913, p. 39.

[1] Seton's books are available at Seton Village, Sante Fe, New Mexico.
[2] "Ernest Thompson Seton was known the world over as "The Chief," a title bestowed originally when he headed the Boy Scouts of America" [from the inception of that organization in 1910 until 1916]. (Julia Seton.)

Then, suddenly, she turned on the Chief with a total change of look and demeanor. Her eyes blazed as she said, in tones of authority: "Don't you know who you are?" We were all shocked into silence as she continued: "You are a Red Indian Chief, reincarnated to give the message of the Redman to the White race, so much in need of it. Why don't your get busy? Why don't you set about your job?"

The Chief was moved like one conscience-stricken. He talked not at all on the road back, and the incident was not mentioned for long after. But I know that the strange woman had focussed his thoughts on the mission he had been vaguely working on for some years. He has never since ceased to concentrate on what she had termed "his job."

The Gospel of the Red Man

RUDOLF STEINER (1861–1925)
Austrian Educator and Philosopher: Founder of Anthroposophical Society

Question: Is it possible to understand, according to the law of reincarnation and karma, how a highly developed human soul can be reborn in a helpless, undeveloped child? To many a person the thought that we have to begin over and over again at the childhood stage is unbearable and illogical.

Answer: . . . Just as the pianist must wait until the piano builder has made a piano on which he can express his musical ideas, so does the soul have to wait with its faculties acquired in the previous life until the forces of the physical world have built up the bodily organs to the point where they can express these faculties. . . . Were [the soul] simply to enter the world in his former state he would be a stranger in it. The period of childhood is gone through in order to bring about harmony between the old and the new conditions. How would one of the cleverest ancient Romans appear in our present world, were he simply born into our world with his acquired powers? A power can only be employed when it is in harmony with the surrounding world. . . . The thought that we have to be born as a child is, therefore, neither illogical nor unbearable. On the contrary, it would be unbearable were we born as a fully developed man into a world in which we are a stranger.

Reincarnation and Karma; How Karma Works[1]

A vast transformation will take place in life when the ideas of reincarnation and karma are no longer theories held by a few people. . . . It can truly be said that there are numbers of people today who believe in reincarnation and karma; but they act as if there were no such realities, as though

[1] New York: Anthroposophic Press, 1962, pp. 50–51.

life were actually confined to the one period between birth and death. Nor can it be otherwise, for habits change less quickly than ideas. Only when we introduce into our lives right and concrete ideas of reincarnation and karma . . . shall we find how life can be fertilized by them. . . .

What does [reincarnation] mean for the whole of man's consciousness, for his whole life of feeling and thinking? . . . The people belonging to earlier epochs of Western civilization and the great majority of those living at the present time . . . still cling to the belief . . . that man's spiritual life after death is entirely separate from earthly existence. . . . Knowledge of reincarnation and karma changes this idea entirely. What is contained in the soul of a man who has passed through the Gate of Death has significance not only for a sphere beyond the earth, but the future of the earth itself depends upon what his life has been between birth and death. . . . The whole future configuration of the planet, as well as the social life of men in the future, depends upon how men have lived in their earlier incarnations. . . . A man who has assimilated these ideas knows: According to what I was in life, I shall have an effect upon everything that takes place in the future, upon the whole civilization of the future! . . . The feeling of responsibility will be intensified to a degree that was formerly impossible, and other moral insights will necessarily follow.

Reincarnation and Karma, Their Significance in Modern Culture[2]

MAURICE MAETERLINCK (1862–1949)
Belgian Poet, Dramatist, Essayist

Let us return to reincarnation . . . for there never was a more beautiful, a juster, a purer, a more moral, fruitful and consoling, nor to a certain point, a more probable creed than theirs [the Theosophists]. It alone, with its doctrine of successive expiations and purifications, accounts for all the physical and intellectual inequalities, all the social iniquities, all the hideous injustices of fate. But the quality of a creed is no evidence of its truth. Even though it is the religion of six hundred millions of mankind, the nearest to the mysterious origins, the only one that is not odious and the least absurd of all, it will have to do what the others have not done, to bring unimpeachable testimony; and what it has given us hitherto is but the first shadow of a proof begun.

Our Eternity[1]

We parted, and not a word was spoken, but at one and the same moment had we understood our inexpressible thought. We know now that

[2] London: Anthroposophical Pub. Co., 1960, pp. 85–87.

[1] Trans. Alexander Teixeira de Mattos. New York: Dodd, Mead, 1913, pp. 169–170.

another love had sprung to life, a love that demands not the words, the little attentions and smiles of ordinary love. We have never met again. Perhaps centuries will elapse before we ever do meet again.

'Much is to learn, much to forget,
Through worlds I shall traverse not a few'

before we shall again find ourselves *in the same movement of the soul* as on that evening: but we can well afford to wait. . . .

Perhaps [human beings] do not yet know what the word "to love" means. . . . It is a thing that lies a thousand fathoms deeper, where our softest, swiftest, strongest words cannot reach it. At moments we might believe it to be a recollection, furtive but excessively keen, of the great primitive unity. . . . The souls of all our brethren are ever hovering about us, craving for a caress, and only waiting for the signal. But how many beings there are who all their life long have not dared make such a signal! It is the disaster of our entire existence that we live thus away from our soul, and stand in such dread of its slightest movement. Did we but allow it to smile frankly in its silence and its radiance, we should be already living an eternal life.

The Treasure of the Humble[2]

SIR CHARLES ELIOT (1862–1931)
British Diplomat and Scholar

[In his volumes *Hinduism and Buddhism, an Historical Sketch*,[1] Sir Charles remarks that reincarnation is preferable to the common view of specially created souls. He adds that "there is a psychological and temperamental objection to the doctrine, which goes to the root of the matter" of why so many in the West reject the idea:[2]]

Love of life and the desire to find a field of activity are so strong in most Europeans that it might be supposed that a theory offering an endless vista of new activities and new chances would be acceptable. . . . [However, many Westerners feel that] another life with similar struggles and fleeting successes, similar sorrows and disappointments, is not satisfying and is almost shocking. We do not like it, and not to like any particular view about the destinies of the soul is generally, but most illogically considered a reason for rejecting it.

Hinduism and Buddhism

[2] Trans. Alfred Sutro and A. B. Walkley. New York: Dodd, Mead, pp. 160, 162–164.

---

[1] London: Edward Arnold, 1921.
[2] I, lviii.

WINCENTY LUTOSLAWSKI (1863-?)
Polish Educator

[The extract below is from Professor Lutoslawski's *Pre-Existence and Rein-carnation*.[1] He is quoted elsewhere in this work. At Harvard in 1899, William James wrote the preface to Lutoslawski's work *The World of Souls*, a book which also discusses reincarnation. James wrote: "The author of the book to which I write this Preface has shown by that weighty English work, *The Logic of Plato*, that he is an accomplished philosopher in the technical and scholarly sense of that much-abused term. . . . [He] honours philosophy; he even adores it, along its platonising traditions; but he finds little use for its sceptical scruples and inhibitions. He is a genuine transcendentalist, in the Emersonian sense."]

In the nineteenth century the number of those who professed belief in palingenesis increased very considerably all over the world, but in no other country is the unanimity in this respect so complete as in Poland. All the greatest poets of Poland, such as Mickiewicz, Slowacki, Krasinski, Norwid, Wyspianski, mention their past lives as a matter of course, and the greatest masterpiece of Polish literature, the *Spirit-King* of Slowacki, is a mystic autobiography in which the poet narrates his past incarnations. Besides the poets also the famous philosopher Cieszkowski and the mystic Towianski admit palingenesis.

Pre-Existence and Reincarnation

DAVID LLOYD GEORGE (1863-1945)
British Prime Minister (1916-1922)

[In a diary entry for September 3, 1919, Lord Riddell recorded these words of his friend, Lloyd-George:]

When I was a boy, the thought of Heaven used to frighten me more than the thought of Hell. I pictured Heaven as a place where there would be perpetual Sundays with perpetual services, from which there would be no escape, as the Almighty, assisted by cohorts of angels, would always be on the look-out for those who did not attend. It was a horrible nightmare. The conventional Heaven with its angels perpetually singing, etc., nearly drove me mad in my youth and made me an atheist for ten years. My opinion is that we shall be reincarnated . . . and that hereafter we shall suffer or benefit in accordance with what we have done in this world. For example, the

[1] London: Allen & Unwin, 1928, p. 24.

employer who sweats his workpeople will be condemned to be sweated himself . . .

Lord Riddell's Intimate Diary of
the Peace Conference and After[1]

HENRY FORD (1863–1947)
American Businessman

[The following appeared in the Hearst papers for April 27 and 28, 1938, being a copyrighted account of an interview with Henry Ford:]

When I was a young man I, like so many others, was bewildered. I found myself asking the question. . . . "What are we here for?" I found no answer. Without some answer to that question life is empty, useless. Then one day a friend handed me a book.[1] . . . That little book gave me the answer I was seeking. It changed my whole life. From emptiness and uselessness, it changed my outlook upon life to purpose and meaning. I believe that we are here now and will come back again. . . . Of this I am sure . . . that we are here for a purpose. And that we go on. Mind and memory—they are the eternals.

[Another interview with Ford is reported by George Sylvester Viereck:[2]]

I adopted the theory of Reincarnation when I was twenty-six. . . . Religion offered nothing to the point. . . . Even work could not give me complete satisfaction. Work is futile if we cannot utilize the experience we collect in one life in the next. When I discovered Reincarnation it was as if I had found a universal plan. I realized that there was a chance to work out my ideas. Time was no longer limited. I was no longer a slave to the hands of the clock. . . . Genius is experience. Some seem to think that it is a gift or talent, but it is the fruit of long experience in many lives. Some are older souls than others, and so they know more. . . .

The discovery of Reincarnation put my mind at ease. . . . If you preserve a record of this conversation, write it so that it puts men's minds at ease. I would like to communicate to others the calmness that the long view of life gives to us.

---

[1] London: Victor Gollancz, 1933, pp. 122–123.

[1] *A Short View of Great Questions,* by Orlando J. Smith. It marshalls the philosophical arguments for reincarnation. (Eds.)
[2] *San Francisco Examiner,* August 28, 1928.

RUDYARD KIPLING (1865–1936)
British Author

[In *The Diary and Sundry Observations of Thomas Alva Edison*[1] one finds this entry: "Rudyard Kipling, in one of his best stories, had a London bank clerk get a glimpse of a former reincarnation when he was a Greek galley slave. . . ." This is Kipling's "The Finest Story in the World" and is contained in his volume *Many Inventions*.[2] The hero envisions writing a book containing the memories of his past lives and lifting the veils of future ones, but after falling in love with a lady the memory of the past gradually faded, and so the "finest story in the world" was never written.]

Strangers drawn from the ends of the earth, jewelled and plumed were we.
I was the Lord of the Inca race, and she was the Queen of the Sea.
Under the stars beyond our stars where the reinless meteors glow
Hotly we stormed Valhalla, a million years ago.
            "The Sack of the Gods" (Naulahka)[1]

When earth's last picture is painted, and the tubes are twisted and dried,
When the oldest colors are faded, and the youngest critic has died;
We shall rest, and faith, we shall need it—lie down for an aeon or two,
Till the Master of all Good Workmen shall put us to work anew.
            "When Earth's Last Picture is Painted" [2]

JEAN SIBELIUS (1865–1957)
Finnish Composer

[A friend of the Sibelius' family reports to the editors that Sibelius spoke openly with intimate friends of his conviction in reincarnation, and also of what appeared to him to be remembrances of previous lives. The former music critic, and later drama critic, for the *New York Times*, Howard Taubman, stated in a feature article in honor of Sibelius on the occasion of his ninetieth birthday:[1]]

The interrelationship between life and art is one of Sibelius' chief concerns. . . . Sibelius' identification with the fields, the woods, the sea and

---

[1] New York: Philosophical Library, 1948, p. 215.
[2] Boston: Houghton, Mifflin, 1891.

---

[1] *The Writings in Prose and Verse of Rudyard Kipling*, New York, Scribner's, 1898–1910, X, 263.
[2] *Collected Verse of Rudyard Kipling*, New York, Doubleday, Page, 1907, p. 131.

---

[1] *The New York Times*, December 4, 1955.

the sky is so profound that it has always permeated his music. . . . As a boy, Sibelius wandered in the wilderness of his native province of Häme. Birds always fascinated him. "Millions of years ago, in my previous incarnations," he once told Jalas [his son-in-law], "I must have been related to swans or wild geese, because I can still feel that affinity."

THE IRISH LITERARY RENAISSANCE

John Eglinton, in his biography of George Russell, A Memoir of Æ,[1] observed:

> Probably there has never been in any country a period of literary activity which has not been preceded or accompanied by some stimulation of the religious interest. Anyone in search of this in Ireland at this time may find it if he looks for it. . . . He will find it, unless he disdains to look in that direction, in the ferment caused in the minds of a group of young men by the early activities of the Theosophical Movement in Dublin. The proof is, not only that there was no other religious movement in Ireland at this time, but that Yeats and Russell, who were to be the principal leaders of the Literary Revival, were closely associated with this one.

Ernest Boyd's large volume, *Ireland's Literary Renaissance*[2] contains a chapter "The Dublin Mystics," with subtitle "The Theosophical Movement." He writes:

> The Theosophical Movement provided a literary, artistic and intellectual centre from which radiated influences whose effect was felt even by those who did not belong to it. Further, it formed a rallying-ground for all the keenest of the older and younger intellects, from John O'Leary and George Sigerson, to W. B. Yeats and A.E. It brought into contact the most diverse personalities, and definitely widened the scope of the new literature, emphasizing its marked advance on all previous national movements. . . . It was an intellectual melting-pot from which the true and solid elements of nationality emerged strengthened, while the dross was lost.

Boyd mentions the prominent part played in the awakening by Yeats, Charles Johnston, George Russell, Charles Weekes, and other writers associated with the Dublin Theosophical Society, later reorganized by Russell as the Hermetic Society, and which subsequently attracted many of the younger Irish poets. Æ actively conducted the Society until his departure for London in 1933, two years before his death. Concerning the work of

[1] London: Macmillan, 1937, p. 1.
[2] New York: Knopf, 1922.

this group he wrote: "It waxed and waned and waxed again, and I felt inwardly satisfied that they all more or less passed through a bath of Theosophical ideas. . . . My own writing is trivial, and its only merit is that it was written in a spiritual atmosphere generated by a study of H. P. Blavatsky and the sacred books . . . the Bhagavad-Gita, Upanishads, Patanjali, and one or two other scriptures." [3] The Dublin Theosophical Society was founded in 1886 by Charles Johnston, a boyhood friend of Yeats, and Æ joined in 1887 at Yeats' instigation. From 1892 to 1897 they published a monthly magazine called *The Irish Theosophist.*

William Q. Judge, the Irish-born American Theosophist and close colleague of Mme. Blavatsky, was in intimate contact with the Dublin Theosophists and their special hero.[4] Æ wrote of him in 1932: "Judge was the most impressive man I ever met, not by any air of dignity but simply from what he was." (*A Memoir of Æ*, p. 13.) James Joyce in *Ulysses* also speaks of the group's regard for "Judge, the noblest Roman of them all." [5]

An excerpt from a poem of Yeats appears next, to be followed shortly by selections from Æ's writings, and later James Stephens and James Joyce will receive treatment.

WILLIAM BUTLER YEATS (1865–1939)
Irish Poet and Playwright

[The reviewer of *The Collected Poems of W. B. Yeats*, in *Newsweek*,[1] suggests that Yeats' perception of rebirth did not come in intuitive flashes, but was the result of study and reflection. The reviewer adds: "Toward the end of his life, Yeats began to find personal strength and a fiery poetic imagery in the realm of the transcendental. . . . His interest in religion was especially confusing to many readers because of the unorthodox, occult terms in which he expressed it. As a youth, he was fascinated by the Russian theosophist Madame Blavatsky, and he went on to explore other avenues of Eastern mysticism." In 1923 he was awarded the Nobel Prize for Literature.

One of Yeats' last poems, "Under Ben Bulben," is dated September 4, 1938, three months before he died. It concludes with his inscribed epitaph and gives directions for his burial. The second stanza of the poem reads:]

Many times man lives and dies
Between his two eternities,

[3] P. G. Bowen, "*Æ and Theosophy*," *Aryan Path*. Bombay, Dec., 1935, pp. 722–726.
[4] *Ibid.*, p. 724.
[5] New York: Modern Library, 1961, p. 185.

[1] April 9, 1956.

That of race and that of soul,
And ancient Ireland knew it all.
Whether man die in his bed
Or the rifle knocks him dead,
A brief parting from those dear
Is the worst man has to fear.
Though grave-diggers' toil is long,
Sharp their spades, their muscles strong,
They but thrust their buried men
Back in the human mind again.
"Under Ben Bulben"

WASSILY KANDINSKY (1866–1944)
Russian Abstract Expressionist Artist

"Abstract art of one kind or another has changed the face of the modern world," writes Hilton Kramer, art news editor of *The New York Times*, in an article "Kandinsky, No Great Master But a Great Influence." [1] "It is a bit of a shock to realize that the abstract movement is over half a century old," he adds. "How much more of a shock, then, to find ourselves observing the centenary of one of its principal founders, possibly THE founder—Wassily Kandinsky . . . who first provided abstract art with a comprehensive theory . . ." Tracing Kandinsky's development, Kramer discusses the crucial period when the artist studied Theosophy, enabling him "to make his revolutionary leap into abstraction." "Kandinsky needed a theoretical framework, an ideology, for carrying painting beyond the realm of representation. . . . With a mind like [his]—at once intellectual and mystical, seeking 'laws' and principles before committing itself to practice—the idea must always precede its realization."

The article continues: Kandinsky's "commitment to theosophy guaranteed—to him, at least—that abstract art would attain a higher spiritual meaning. . . . His concept of the spiritual counted for a great deal, for Kandinsky was a theosophist for whom painting was a medium of the highest spiritual purpose. Kandinsky was not alone in this respect. One of the other great initiators of abstraction, the Dutch geometrical painter Piet Mondrian, was also deeply immersed in theosophy at the time. [This was also true of Malenkov and to some degree of Paul Klee. (Eds.)] The exact relation of these theosophical concerns to the origin of abstract art remains one of the most beguiling and unexplored mysteries in the history of the modern movement."

The subject has been exhaustively explored by Laxmi Sihare of the

[1] *The New York Times Magazine*, Dec. 18, 1966, pp. 28 *et seq.*

Institute of Fine Arts of New York University. We understand that his investigations are to be published under the title *Oriental Influences on Kandinsky and Mondrian*, to be followed probably by a similar volume on Klee and Malinkov. Dr. Sihare focusses largely on the writings of H. P. Blavatsky as the chief source of inspiration of the pioneers of modern art. (See Part Three of the present work for reincarnation views of theosophists.)

H. G. WELLS (1866–1946)
British Historian and Novelist

"I have had a dream, a whole lifetime, two thousand years ago! . . . I have lived through a whole life in that old world. . . ." (Chap. 1.)

"That tale," said the guest-master, stoutly, "was no dream. It was a memory floating up out of the deep darkness of forgotten things into a kindred brain." . . .

"Sometimes before this in my dreams I have had a feeling that I lived again forgotten lives. Have none of you felt that?" . . .

"Maybe life from its very beginning has been spinning threads and webs of memories. Not a thing in the past, it may be, that has not left its memories about us. Some day we may learn to gather in that forgotten gossamer, we may learn to weave its strands together again, until the whole past is restored to us and life becomes one. . . ."

"It was a life," said Sarnac, "and it was a dream, a dream within this life; and this life too is a dream. Dreams within dreams, dreams containing dreams, until we come at last, maybe, to the Dreamer of all dreams, the Being who is all beings. (Chap. 8.)

The Dream

ROMAIN ROLLAND (1866–1944)
French Author

When staff in hand in later years I scoured the roads of thought, I found nothing that was strange in any country. All the aspects of mind that I found or felt were in their origin the same as mine. Outside experience merely brought me the realization of my own mind, the states of which I had noted but to which I had no key. Neither Shakespeare nor Beethoven nor Tolstoy nor Rome, the master that nurtured me, ever revealed anything to me except the "Open Sesame" of my subterranean city, my Herculaneum, sleeping under its lava. And I am convinced that it sleeps in the depths of many of those around us. But they are ignorant of its existence just as I was. . . .

I have just rediscovered the key of the lost staircase. . . . The staircase in the wall, spiral like the coils of a serpent, winds from the subterranean depths of the Ego to the high terraces crowned by the stars. But nothing that I saw there was unknown country. I had seen it all before and I knew it well—but I did not know where I had seen it before. More than once I had recited from memory, though imperfectly, the lesson of thought learned at some former time (but from whom? One of my very ancient selves. . . .)

Prophets of the New India[1]

GEORGE W. RUSSELL (1867–1935)
Irish Author, Painter, Editor

[The British scientist, Raynor Johnson, writes of George Russell in his book *The Light and the Gate:*[1]

If it is greatness to become the embodiment of spirituality to many others, Æ may be counted probably the greatest Irishman of his day. . . . All who met him felt that he was "different"—in some way apart from them, as though he had strayed into this world from an older and wiser one with which he was more familiar. . . . Dr. Monk Gibbon said, "He saw things in their eternal procession." [2]

He had an intense sympathy with man in his outcast state. . . . He [wrote]: "I remember the deep peace which came to me when I had the intuition that Christ, Prometheus, are in every heart, that we all took upon ourselves the burden of the world like the Christ, and were foreseers as Prometheus was, of the agony of the labour he undertook, until the chaos is subdued and wrought in some likeness to the image in the divine imagination." [3] Much of his poetry speaks of Man at this age-long task—the outcast from the "Ancestral Self"—the "fallen majesty"—making his slow way back again.

Quoting from Æ's best known work, *The Candle of Vision:*]

To those who cry out against romance I would say, You yourself are romance. You are the lost prince herding obscurely among the swine. The romance of your spirit is the most marvellous of stories. Your wanderings have been greater than those of Ulysses. . . .

[1] New York: Charles Boni, 1930, pp. xxiii-xxiv.

---

[1] London: Hodder & Stoughton, 1964, pp. 15, 40.
[2] *The Living Torch*. London: Macmillan & Co. Ltd., p. 67.
[3] *Song and Its Fountains*, p. 90.

From long pondering I have come to believe in the eternity of the spirit and that it is an inhabitant of many spheres, for I know not how otherwise I can interpret to myself the myriad images that as memories or imaginations cling to it, following it into the body as birds follow the leader in the migratory flock. . . . Looking back upon that other life through the vistas of memory I see breaking in upon the images of this world forms of I know not what antiquity. I walk out of strange cities steeped in the jewel glow and gloom of evening, or sail in galleys over the silvery waves of the antique ocean. I reside in tents, or in palace chambers, go abroad in chariots, meditate in cyclopean buildings, am worshipper of the Earth gods upon the mountains, lie tranced in Egyptian crypts, or brush with naked body through the long sunlit grasses of the prairies. Endlessly the procession of varying forms goes back into remote yesterdays of the world. . . . Are they not . . . memories of the spirit incarnated many times?

And if so, again I ask myself is it only on earth there has been this long ancestry of self? For there is another self in me which seemed to know not the world but revealed itself to the listening bodily life in cosmic myths, in remote legends of the Children of Darkness and the Children of Light, and of the revolt against heaven. And another self seemed to bring with it vision or memory of elemental beings, the shining creatures of water and wood, or who break out in opalescent color from the rocks or hold their court beneath the ponderous hills. And there was another self which was akin to the gloomy world of the shades, but recoiled shuddering from them. And there was yet another self which sought out after wisdom, and all these other selves and their wisdom and memories were but tributary to it. . . .

It is only when I turn to the literature of vision and intuition, to the sacred books and to half sacred tradition, to the poets and seers, that I find a grandiose conception of nature in which every spiritual experience is provided for. . . . What little I know finds its place in the universe of their vision. Whether they are Syrian, Greek, Egyptian or Hindu, the writers of the sacred books seem to me as men who had all gazed upon the same august vision and reported of the same divinity.

"The Memory of the Spirit"
The Candle of Vision

[Claude Bragdon writes in his book *Merely Players*:[4]]

One story . . . gives a hint of the possible derivation of [Russell's] pseudonym, Æ.[5] He said that when he was a boy he was just like other

---

[4] New York: Knopf, 1929, pp. 173–175.
[5] "Æ" was the result of a printer's difficulty with "Æon," with which Russell had signed an aticle. (Eds.)

boys . . . except that he seemed to have a more vivid imagination, for he was always telling himself wonderful stories of gods and demi-gods, and miraculous happenings in some Valhalla, and to these characters he assigned names. He had no other idea but that he invented these stories and these names.

But one day while waiting at the desk of the village library for the librarian to bring him a story book, he happened to glance at the open page of a book that was lying there, and his eye encountered the word "Aeon." He declared that his surprise and excitement were so great that he left the library empty-handed and walked about the streets for two hours before he could muster up sufficient calmness and courage to ask the librarian what book it was, and if he might look at it. For the name Aeon was one which he had given to the hero of one of his own stories, a name which he regarded as peculiarly his own . . . and it was upsetting to discover that such was plainly not the case.

The book proved to be a treatise on Gnostic religion and cosmogony and in it, to his utter amazement, he found recorded, in a mass of legendary lore, those very stories which he thought he had invented—even the names of the characters were the same. This forced him to the conclusion that either his imaginings were recovered memories of things learned or experienced in some antecedent life, or that in some inexplicable manner he had tapped, so to speak, the memory of nature.

[Æ discussed these possible past-life recalls with the biologist, Sir Julian Huxley. Their conversation is reported in Part Six.]

MARY JOHNSTON (1870–1936)
American Novelist

As Curtin rode he thought that he faintly remembered all the forests of the world. . . . "Is it because I have been—and surely I have been in all the forests of the world?" . . . A sense of hut and cave, so often, so long, in so many lands, that there was a feel of eternity about it. Rain and the cave and the fire, and the inner man still busied with his destiny! There was something that awed in the perception that ran from one to another, that held them in a swift, shimmering band. "How old—how old! How long have we done this?" The rhythm of the storm, the rhythm of the room, the rhythm of the fire, passed into a vast, still sense of ordered movement. "Of old, and now, and tomorrow—everywhere and all time—until we return above time and place, and division is healed."

Sweet Rocket [1]

[1] New York: Harper, 1920, pp. 98, 176. See also pp. 51–52.

SOMERSET MAUGHAM (1874–1965)
British Novelist and Playwright

[Maugham speaks of reincarnation in his novel, *The Razor's Edge*, his leading character discussing the subject in relation to visions experienced of possible previous lives. In his autobiography, *The Summing Up*,[1] published six years earlier, we learn that Maugham found only one explanation of the problem of evil "that appealed equally to my sensibility and to my imagination. This is the doctrine of the transmigration of souls." Yet he could not accept it. "There is no explanation for evil." (P. 285.) He wrote:[2]]

It would be less difficult to bear the evils of one's own life if one could think that they were but the necessary outcome of one's errors in a previous existence, and the effort to do better would be less difficult too when there was the hope that in another existence a greater happiness would reward one. But if one feels one's own woes in a more forcible way than those of others (I cannot feel your toothache, as the philosophers say) it is the woes of others that arouse one's indignation. It is possible to achieve resignation in regard to one's own, but only philosophers obsessed with the perfection of the Absolute can look upon those of others, which seem so often unmerited, with an equal mind. If Karma were true one could look upon them with pity, but with fortitude. Revulsion would be out of place and life would be robbed of the meaninglessness of pain which is pessimism's unanswered argument. I can only regret that I find the doctrine . . . impossible to believe.

The Summing Up

SIR WINSTON CHURCHILL (1874–1965)
British Statesman and Historian

[A few days after Sir Winston's death, the noted foreign correspondent, C. L. Sulzburger, devoted his column in *The New York Times* for February 1, 1965, to some thoughts on the occasion:]

Despite his immense gusto for life, in a rather jovial cozy way Churchill never minded contemplating the mystery of death. . . . [One] time he was asked if he believed in an afterlife. After a moment's hesitation he said no, that he thought there was only "some kind of velvety cool blackness,"

[1] New York: Doubleday, 1938.
[2] P. 264.

adding then: "Of course, I admit I may be wrong. It is conceivable that I might well be reborn as a Chinese coolie. In such a case I should lodge a protest."

ROBERT FROST (1875-1963)
American Poet

I'd like to get away from earth awhile
And then come back to it and begin over.
May no fate wilfully misunderstand me
And half grant what I wish and snatch me away
Not to return. Earth's the right place for love:
I don't know where it's likely to go better.
"Birches"

Sarcastic Science she would like to know,
In her complacent ministry of fear,
How we propose to get away from here
When she has made things so we have to go
Or be wiped out. Will she be asked to show
Us how by rocket we may hope to steer
To some star off there say a half light-year
Through temperature of absolute zero?
Why wait for Science to supply the how
When any amateur can tell it now?
The way to go away should be the same
As fifty million years ago we came—
If anyone remembers how that was
I have a theory, but it hardly does.
"Why Wait for Science"

RAINER MARIA RILKE (1875-1926)
German Lyric Poet and Writer

W. H. Auden calls Rilke almost the first poet since the seventeenth century to find a fresh solution for the poet's eternal problem of expressing abstract ideas in concrete form. The Princess Marie of Thurn and Taxis writes in her *Recollections of R. M. Rilke* that "deep down he considered Russia his soul-home, convinced that in a former incarnation he lived in Moscow." [1] In his "Sonnets to Orpheus," Rilke yearningly asks: "But when, in which of all our lives do we finally become open and receptive?"

[1] *Erinnerungen an Rainer Maria Rilke*, p. 83.

Elsewhere, speaking of death and return to earth life, he wrote: "Perhaps one only seeks a homecoming and welcome, pursues it, till the circle rounds, back to that home, feeling with a strange certainty, dreamlike and sad, that he had lost it once before." (*Briefe und Tagebücher* 1899–1902, p. 8.)

GENERAL HOMER LEA (1876–1912)
American Soldier and Author

Few today recall General Homer Lea, the American cripple who with Dr. Sun Yat Sen overthrew the Manchu Dynasty of China, setting in motion the wheels of a new Asiatic era. As a small boy he had a dream which left an unforgettable impression. In it appeared strange men and strange sounds. At ten, the dream reappeared. This time he knew the men to be Chinese soldiers. The dream came for the third time at sixteen; and this time he knew the sounds for Chinese war trumpets. It returned a fourth time, years later, just before his departure for China.

After leaving college he turned his entire attention to military strategy. In some way he gained ascendency over the Chinese youth of San Francisco and Los Angeles, organized them, cut off their queues—the mark of servitude to the Manchu Dynasty—and began shipping them to China. Shortly afterward he followed. Then began the first unsuccessful rebellion. Lea came back with a price on his head, in all Oriental usage a disgraced man, yet Kang Yu Wei, ex-Premier of China, and Liang Ki Chew, an Imperial Prince, attached themselves to him like servitors. His military record caused him at various times to be consulted by Lord Roberts, Commander-in-chief of the British Army, and Kaiser Wilhelm. The latter had a special carriage built to enable Lea to see army maneuvers.

Lea came to know Dr. Sun Yat Sen and together they plotted and carried out the uprising which made a Republic—in name—of China. He died soon after, having played jackstraws with the destinies of more human beings than Napoleon probably ever realized were in the world. Like Napoleon, he considered himself a "man of destiny"; and like Napoleon, speculated upon his own peculiarities as derived from other lives of the past. A Buddhist monk, "reading" his palm, grew pale and pronounced the hand that of a king—or so they say.[1]

[1] Harry Carr, a noted columnist and personal acquaintance of Lea, made known some of the foregoing in an article in the *Los Angeles Times*, Nov. 15, 1931.

JACK LONDON (1876–1916)
American Novelist

[In James Jones's *From Here to Eternity*, Jack London's novels are extolled, particularly those that explain reincarnation.[1] One of these, *The Star Rover*—published in London as *The Jacket*—sounds the note of rebirth on almost every page. The story concerns a prisoner in San Quentin who learns to outwit the maddening boredom of solitary confinement and the torture of the strait jacket through a special technique of separating the mind from the body. Thus "liberated" he begins to relive portions of previous incarnations. The novel is actually based on the recorded experience of Ed Morrell, a prisoner of San Quentin, whose autobiography was published as *The Twenty-Fifth Man*. London's interest in reincarnation may derive from a contact with Theosophy. In *Martin Eden*[2] he has his hero—after an encounter with a theosophist—reading Madame Blavatsky's *Secret Doctrine*. *Martin Eden* was published in 1908. Quoting now from *The Star Rover*:]

All my life I have had an awareness of other times, and places. I have been aware of other persons in me. . . . I, whose lips had never lisped the word "king," remembered that I had once been the son of a king. More—I remembered that once I had been a slave and a son of a slave, and worn an iron collar round my neck. (Chap 1.)

I, like any man, am a growth. I did not begin when I was born, nor when I was conceived. I have been growing, developing, through incalculable myriads of millenniums. All these experiences of all these lives, have gone to the making of the soul-stuff or the spirit-stuff that is I. . . . I am all of my past, as every protagonist of the Mendelian law must agree. All my previous selves have their voices, echoes, promptings in me. . . . I am man born of woman. My days are few, but the stuff of me is indestructible. I have been woman born of woman. I have been a woman and borne my children. And I shall be born again. Oh, incalculable times again shall I be born; and yet the stupid dolts about me think that by stretching my neck with a rope they will make me cease. (Chap. 18.)

The Star Rover

[1] See Index under Jones.
[2] New York: Macmillan, 1957, pp. 50–51, 98.

EDGAR CAYCE (1877–1945)
American Healer and Clairvoyant

[A great deal of interest in reincarnation has been evoked through the reputed healings of Edgar Cayce, who it is claimed had the power, while entranced, of reading the past lives of people and detecting karmic causes leading to present troubles. Cayce, a devout Christian, was very disturbed to find himself relating the supposed previous incarnations of patients, and it was only after much study and searching of the scriptures that he eventually reconciled himself to the concept of rebirth. Two books on his life work are: *Many Mansions* by Dr. Gina Cerminara[1] and *There Is a River* by Thomas Sugrue.[2] To those avidly desirous of knowing who they were in a former life, Cayce said: "Just to find out that you lived, died, and were buried under a cherry tree in grandmother's garden does not make you one whit better as a neighbor, citizen, father, or mother. But to know that you spoke unkindly in the past and suffered for it, and in the present may correct it by being kind—THAT is worth while!" (G. Cerminara, *The World Within.*[3]) To a man who had written several times for help, Cayce said:]

Yes, we have the body here; this we have had before. As we find, there have been physical improvements in the body, yet there is much, much to be desired. As already indicated, this is a karmic condition and there must be measures taken by the entity to change its attitude toward things, conditions, and its fellow man. So long as mechanical things were applied for physical correction, improvements were seen. But when the entity becomes so self-satisfied, so self-centered, as to refuse spiritual things, and does not change its attitude; so long as there is hate, malice, injustice, jealousy; so long as there is anything within at variance with patience, long suffering, brotherly love, kindness, gentleness, there cannot be a healing of the condition of this body. What does the entity want to be healed *for*? That it may gratify its own physical appetites? That it may add to its own selfishness? Then, if so, it had better remain as it is. . . . Will you accept, will you reject? It is up to you. We are through—unless you make amends." [4]

---

[1] New York: Wm. Sloane.
[2] New York: Henry Holt.
[3] New York: Wm. Sloane, pp. 200–201.
[4] *Many Mansions*, pp. 88–89.

HERMANN HESSE (1877–1962)
German-Swiss Author

[Hesse was ranked with Thomas Mann as the greatest contemporary German author. His novels have enjoyed great popularity on the continent and in South America. His *Siddhartha*, a favorite among college students in England and the United States, has been reprinted many times. It is the story of a soul's quest for the ultimate answer to the enigma of man's role on earth. As a youth, the young Indian Siddhartha meets the Buddha but cannot accept the teachings of even this "greatest of men." He must work out his own destiny and solve his own doubt through experience, just as the Buddha himself did. Brief selections are first offered from Hesse's major work *Das Glasperlenspiel*, published in English under the title *Magister Ludi*,[1] and for which he won the Nobel Prize for Literature in 1946. The *New York Times* review states: "Hesse plunges into the realm of universal humanity, with all the wide-ranging love of Saint Francis, the mysticism of Buddha, the psychological insight of Dostoevsky, the world-embracing striving of Goethe, and the Europeanism of Nietzsche."]

Numbed and paralyzed . . . he had had enough of it all. He desired no more wife or child, neither throne nor victory nor revenge, neither happiness nor cleverness, neither might nor virtue: he desired nothing but peace, nothing except an end, wanted nothing except to bring this eternally revolving wheel, this endless picture-show to a standstill and to extinguish it. . . . But what then? Then there would be a pause of unconsciousness, slumber or death, and immediately one would be awake once more, would be obliged to let in the stream of life into one's heart again, and the beautiful, terrifying flood of pictures—endless and inescapable—would ensue until the next consciousness, until the next death. . . . There was no extinction, no end! . . .

Ah! If only one could really know! . . . If only there were a doctrine —something in which one could believe! . . . One can interpret the whole of world history as development and progress, and yet, on the other hand, one can just as well see in it nothing but decline and insanity. Is there no truth then, is there no true and valid doctrine? . . . Yes, there is truth. . . . The Godhead is in *yourself*, not in theories and in books. Truth must be lived, not taught.

Magister Ludi

[1] New York: Frederick Ungar, 1957, pp. 76–77, 499–501.

Often [Siddhartha and the ferryman Vasudeva] sat together in the evening on the tree trunk by the river. They both listened silently to the water, which to them was not just water, but the voice of life, the voice of Being, of perpetual Becoming. . . . The water continually flowed and flowed and yet it was always there; it was always the same and yet every moment it was new. Who could understand, conceive this? . . . The river knows everything; one can learn everything from it. . . .

"Have you also learned [this] secret from the river; that there is no such thing as time? . . . The river is everywhere at the same time, at the source and at the mouth, at the waterfall, at the ferry, at the current, in the ocean and in the mountains, everywhere, and that the present only exists for it, not the shadow of the past, nor the shadow of the future?"

"That is it," said Siddhartha, "and when I learned that, I reviewed my life and it was also a river, and Siddhartha the boy, Siddhartha the mature man and Siddhartha the old man, were only separated by shadows, not through reality. Siddhartha's previous lives were also not in the past, and his death and his return to Brahma are not in the future. Nothing was, nothing will be, everything has reality and presence." Siddhartha spoke with delight. This discovery had made him very happy. Was then not all sorrow in time, all self-torment and fear in time? Were not all difficulties and evil in the world conquered as soon as one conquered time?

Siddhartha[2]

JOHN MASEFIELD (1878–   )
Poet Laureate of England (1930–   )

[The London *Daily Telegraph* (Supplement) for May 28, 1965, contains an article "The Pioneer Laureate"—a tribute to Masefield on his eighty-seventh birthday, written by his long-time friend J. H. B. Peel. Commenting on Masefield's affirmation that "he is a simple Christian," Peel states: "His creed is not so simple. As the poems reveal, he picks an eclectic path, even to the point of many reincarnated returns." (Masefield was a close friend of another reincarnationist, W. B. Yeats. A room they shared in London is now a museum.) Mr. Peel cites in particular Masefield's well-known reincarnation poem "A Creed," which is given below. This was an early poem. Later Masefield must have experienced doubts for a time, for in the 1923 edition of his *Collected Poems* the first lines of stanza one and two were changed to read: "I held that when a person dies . . ." "Such was my own belief and trust. . . ." In the 1935 and all subsequent editions, Mase-

2 New York: New Directions, 1951, pp. 104, 108–111.

field reverted to the original wording and in this form the poem is here reprinted:]

I hold that when a person dies
His soul returns again to earth;
Arrayed in some new flesh-disguise,
Another mother gives him birth.
With sturdier limbs and brighter brain
The old soul takes the road again.

Such is my own belief and trust;
This hand, this hand that holds the pen,
Has many a hundred times been dust
And turned, as dust, to dust again;
These eyes of mine have blinked and shone
In Thebes, in Troy, in Babylon. . . .

I know that in my lives to be
My sorry heart will ache and burn,
And worship, unavailingly
The woman whom I used to spurn,
And shake to see another have
The love I spurned, the love she gave.

And I shall know, in angry words,
In gibes, and mocks, and many a tear,
A carrion flock of homing-birds,
The gibes and scorns I uttered here.
The brave word that I failed to speak
Will brand me dastard on the cheek.

And as I wander on the roads
I shall be helped and healed and blessed;
Dear words shall cheer and be as goads
To urge to heights before unguessed.
My road shall be the road I made;
All that I gave shall be repaid.

So shall I fight, so shall I tread,
In this long war beneath the stars;
So shall a glory wreathe my head,
So shall I faint and show the scars,

Until this case, this clogging mould,
Be smithied all to kingly gold.
                    "A Creed"

LORD HUGH DOWDING (1882–)
British Air Chief Marshall

[Lord Dowding was chief of the Royal Air Force Fighter Command in the Battle of Britain, World War II. In *Lynchgate*[1] he wrote: "I am personally convinced beyond any shadow of a doubt that reincarnation is a fact." In a speech delivered in the House of Lords (July 18, 1957), on "Painful Experiments on Animals," Lord Dowding applied his reincarnationist philosophy to the subject:]

I firmly believe that painful experiments on animals are morally wrong, and that it is basically immoral to do evil in order that good may come—even if it were proved that mankind benefits from the suffering inflicted on animals. . . . I cannot leave this subject without some reference to its esoteric side—to the place of the animal kingdom in the scheme of things, to man's responsibility to animals, and to the results of man's failure to meet this responsibility.

As the human race evolves, it becomes ready for fresh revelation, and the defect in most of the world's religions is that they fail to realise this very important fact. The priests are inclined to say "everything that is necessary for salvation is contained in this Book. It is unnecessary and, indeed impious, to search elsewhere." It is I think, this aspect of our childhood's teaching which leads to the idea that animals have no continuing life after physical death. That phrase in the 49th Psalm, "The beasts that perish," has much to answer for, for it is a fact that the beasts do not perish any more than do men. All life is one, and all its manifestations with which we have contact are climbing the ladder of evolution. The animals are our younger brothers and sisters, also on the ladder but a few rungs lower down than we are. It is an important part of our responsibilities to help them in their ascent, and not to retard their development by cruel exploitation of their helplessness.

                    "Painful Experiments on Animals"

[1] London: Rider, 1945.

JAMES STEPHENS (1882–1950)
Irish Poet and Novelist

[In Hilary Pyle's biography *James Stephens*,[1] she calls his work "the important bridge between the first Irish writers of the Celtic Twilight period and the new, more sophisticated writers." (P. x.) Stephens was a protégé of George Russell. Chapter IV of Miss Pyle's book is entitled "The Influence of Blake and of Theosophy." In Stephen's *The Demi-Gods* he attempts an account of the theosophical ideal of evolution, and describes his view of reincarnation: "While generation succeeds generation a man has to fight the same fight. At the end he wins, and he never has to fight that battle again, and then he is ready for Paradise. . . ." Miss Pyle states (p. 42) : "As early as *Insurrections*, Stephens saw that in evolution lies our hope of deliverance. In *The Hill of Vision* he examined it in connection with the doctrine of reincarnation, picturing all live things coming to the Source of Life for refreshment before they set out again." Quoting from the latter work:[2]]

Deep Womb of Promise! Back to thee again
And forth, revivified, all living things
Do come and go,
Forever wax and wane into and from thy garden;
There the flower springs,
Therein does grow
The bud of hope, the miracle to come,
For whose dear advent we are striving, dumb
And joyless. . . .
Until our back and forth, our life and death
And life again, our going and return
Prepare the way: until our latest breath,
Deep-drawn and agonized, for him shall burn
A path: for him prepare
Laughter and love and singing everywhere,
A morning and a sunrise and a day!
                                        "A Prelude and a Song"

[1] New York: Barnes & Noble, 1965.
[2] Pp. 24–26.

JAMES JOYCE (1882–1941)
Irish Author

In the study, *James Joyce's Ulysses*, prepared in Paris with Joyce's constant help, Stuart Gilbert tells of Joyce's contact with Theosophy and the Irish Theosophists, and writes in the preface: "When we chanced to be discussing . . . Mme. Blavatsky's entertaining *Isis Unveiled*, [Joyce] asked me if I had read any of Sinnett's work. (A. P. Sinnett, a cultured and intelligent man, was a member of Mme. Blavatsky's circle in India, and her biographer.) Naturally I took the hint and procured his [volumes on Theosophy] *Esoteric Buddhism* and *Growth of the Soul*, well-written books from which Joyce certainly derived some of his material." [1]

In chapter 3, part 1, headed "MET-HIM-PIKE-HOSES," Gilbert writes:

In the first episode of Mr. Bloom's day ("Calypso") several themes are stated which will recur frequently throughout *Ulysses*, and it is characteristic of the Joycean method that one of the most important of these *leitmotifs* should be presented in a casual manner and a ludicrous context. Mrs. Bloom has been reading in bed *Ruby: The Pride of the Ring* . . . She asks her husband what that word in the book means—"met him pike hoses." He leaned downward and read near her polished thumbnail. "Metempsychosis?" . . . Mr. Bloom explains. "Some people believe that we go on living in another body after death, that we lived before. They call it reincarnation. That we all lived before on the earth thousands of years ago or on some other planet. They say we have forgotten it. Some say they remember their past lives." . . .

The passages [several more of which are quoted] indicate the persistence of the idea, or, rather, word "metempsychosis," in Mr. Bloom's memory. But it is not only as one of Mr. Bloom's possessions that the doctrine of reincarnation is mentioned in *Ulysses*. Allusions, direct or indirect, to it are frequent, and . . . [it] is, in fact, one of the directive themes of the work. . . . That these conceptions and their corollaries have an important place in the highly complex structure of *Ulysses* will become apparent when I come to deal with the Homeric correspondences and historical analogies. References to the eternal recurrence of personalities and things abound in *Ulysses* and many of the obscurer passages can be readily understood if this fact be borne in mind.

The American poet, Eugene Jolas, writes that in *Finnegans Wake* Joyce has "painted the rotations of the wheel of life." "He made a hero out of Time: incessant creation and return. He rebuilt the city across the ages in Finn's multiple metamorphoses." [2]

[1] New York: Vintage paperback (Knopf), 1952; England: Penguin, 1963.
[2] *We Moderns*, 1920–1940 anniversary catalog of The Gotham Book Mart, New York, N.Y., in which well-known authors commented on fellow authors of the day.

In James Atherton's *The Books of the Wake*[3] he states in the chapter "Other Sacred Books" used in *Finnegans Wake:* "There are many schools of Buddhism and the first attempt to unite them was made by an American, Colonel H. S. Olcott [President-Founder of The Theosophical Society], whose *Buddhist Catechism* was used by Joyce. . . . [Joyce] believed that rebirth was the recompense for death; not . . . the result of ignorance and unsatisfied desire, and the cause of sorrow. It is probably because of their insistence on rebirth that Joyce combines Vishnuism with Buddhism."

In a small volume on Joyce, Leon Edel concludes with this evaluation of his life and work:

All of Joyce, from the sermons on Hell in the *Portrait of the Artist* to the last words of *Finnegans Wake*, echoes of Life, Death and Resurrection; the cycles of history, which from the beginning measure the life of Man, were ever present in his mind; he found in them a kind of cosmic mockery. In that spirit perhaps Joyce's own words in which Stephen Dedalus [before embarking on his career] invokes guidance at the end of the *Portrait*, might have appropriately been pronounced over the bier in the Fluntern Chapel: "I GO TO ENCOUNTER FOR THE MILLIONTH TIME THE REALITY OF EXPERIENCE AND TO FORGE IN THE SMITHY OF MY SOUL THE UNCREATED CONSCIENCE OF MY RACE. OLD FATHER, OLD ARTIFICER, STAND ME NOW AND EVER IN GOOD STEAD." To Joyce even death must have been an encounter with "the reality of experience." Before he was born he had, as Renan said of Turgenev, lived for thousands of years and "infinite successions of reveries had amassed themselves in the depths of his heart." [4] (*The Last Journey.*[5])

KAHLIL GIBRAN (1883–1931)
Lebanese-born American Poet

Brief were my days among you, and briefer still the words I have spoken. But should my voice fade in your ears, and my love vanish in your memory, then I will come again, and with a richer heart and lips more yielding to the spirit will I speak. Yes, I shall return with the tide, and though death may hide me and the greater silence enfold me, yet again will I seek your understanding. . . . Know, therefore, that from the greater silence I shall return. . . . Forget not that I shall come back to you. . . . A little while, a moment of rest upon the wind, and another woman shall bear me.

The Prophet [1]

[3] New York: Viking, 1960.
[4] See index under "Renan." (Eds.)
[5] New York: Gotham Book Mart, 1947, p. 42.

[1] Reprinted from *The Prophet* by Kahlil Gibran (pp. 83–84, 94–95), with permission of the publisher, Alfred A. Knopf, Inc. Copyright 1923 by Kahlil Gibran; renewal copyright 1951 by Administrators C.T.A. of Kahlil Gibran Estate and Mary G. Gibran.

[Barbara Young wrote in her biography of Gibran, *This Man from Leba-non*:[2]]

One evening when we were doing *Sand and Foam*, I piled cushions on the floor and sat upon them instead of occupying my usual chair. Then I had a strange feeling of familiarity about the gesture, and I said, "I feel as if I've sat like this beside you many times—but I really haven't." [Gibran] waited a moment—as he often did before replying. . . . Then he said, "We have done this a thousand years ago, and shall do it a thousand years hence."

And during the writing of *Jesus, The Son of Man*, the drama of some incident, now and again, was so overwhelming that I felt, and said, "It is so real. It seems as if I had been there." And his answer came, almost like a cry, "You were there! And so was I!" Thus Gibran expressed over and over again, his utter belief in what he called "the continuity of life." The Theosophist . . . and divers other trends of thought and belief, call it reincarnation. He never used the word. It was his profound certainty that the life that is the human spirit has lived and shall live timelessly, that the bonds of love, devotion, and friendship shall bring together these endlessly reborn beings, and that animosity, evil communications, and hatred have the same effect of reassembling groups of entities from one cycle to another. Indifference acts as a separating influence. Those souls who neither love nor hate, but remain entirely self-contained as regards one another, meet but once in the pattern of the ages.

This Man from Lebanon

D. H. LAWRENCE (1885–1930)
British Novelist

Although Lawrence does not often speak directly of future lives in his writings, we learn from William York Tindall's *D. H. Lawrence and Susan His Cow*,[1] he was more than casually interested in Theosophy. Professor Tindall traces Lawrence's debt to the Hindu Upanishads through Madame Blavatsky and Theosophy in general, and more particularly to a Theosophist, James M. Pryse, a one-time resident of Dubin, who lived in the same household with Yeats, Æ, and Charles Johnston. Quoting from chapter "Susan Unveiled":

In a letter to a friend who was evidently in spiritual distress, Lawrence recommended Mme. Blavatsky's *Isis Unveiled* . . . he especially recommended

[2] New York: Knopf, 1945, pp. 93–94.

[1] New York: Columbia University Press, 1939.

her *Secret Doctrine*.[2] . . . Mrs. Lawrence informed me that her husband read and delighted in all of Mme. Blavatsky's works. . . . Symbolic clues to the past were never more knowingly followed by the most orthodox Theosophist. The Foreword to [Lawrence's] *Fantasia of the Unconscious*, 1922 . . . might have been written by Mme. Blavatsky herself. [Lawrence wrote therein:] "I honestly think that the great pagan world of which Egypt and Greece were the last living terms . . . had a vast and perhaps perfect science of its own, a science in terms of life. . . . I believe that this great science . . . was universal, established all over the then-existing globe. I believe it was esoteric, invested in a large priesthood. Just as mathematics and mechanics and physics are defined and expounded in the same way in the universities of China or Bolivia or London or Moscow today, so, it seems to me, in the great world previous to ours a great science and cosmology were taught esoterically in all countries of the globe, Asia, Polynesia, America, Atlantis and Europe." . . . This is simple theosophy.

Tindall adds that "although Lawrence seems elsewhere to have taken little interest in metempsychosis, *The Plumed Serpent* contains several references to the cyclical development of races and to reincarnation under the law of Karma."

EDNA FERBER (1887–   )
American Novelist

In her autobiography, *A Peculiar Treasure*,[1] Edna Ferber recalls that as a child the sound of circus wagon wheels evoked vague and terrible sensations of "something that went back, back, perhaps to Egyptian days and the heavy wheels of chariots." Prompted by great expectations, she later visited Egypt, only to experience intense dislike for most of the country. "I can only venture to say, at the risk of being hooted, that somewhere in Egypt a couple of thousand years ago I probably had a very tough time of it."

The chance remark of a friend about the floating theatres on the Mississippi, set Miss Ferber on the trail of a new novel, *Show Boat*. She had hardly suspected that such a romantic aspect of America existed: the wandering, drifting life of the show boat players, the drama of the river towns, the mystery and terror of the Mississippi itself. "At the very thought of the Mississippi there welled up in me from some hidden treasure-trove in my memory or imagination a torrent of visualized pictures, people, incidents. I don't to this day know where that river knowledge came from. Perhaps, centuries and centuries ago, I was a little Jewish slave girl on the Nile." When *Show Boat* was set to music, Jerome Kern apparently caught something of this imagery in his powerful song, "Old Man River."

[2] *The Letters of D. H. Lawrence*, ed. Aldous Huxley, p. 476.

[1] New York: Doubleday, 1960, pp. 50, 283, 360.

EUGENE O'NEILL (1888–1953)
American Playwright

[The selections here are from O'Neill's *The Great God Brown*.[1] An unusual feature of this psychological drama is the wearing of masks by the characters when their ordinary selves talk, but when the inner man speaks, the masks are removed.]

ACT I

DION   (wearily bitter). I'll take the job. One must do something to pass away the time, while one is waiting—for one's next incarnation. . . .

ACT II

DION   (sadly). You've given me strength to die.

CYBEL   You may be important, but your life's not. There's millions of it born every second. . . . And it's not sacred—only the you inside is. The rest is earth.

DION   "Into thy hands, O Lord," . . . (Suddenly with a look of horror). Nothing! To feel one's life blown out like the flame of a cheap match . . . ! (He claps on his mask and laughs harshly). To fall asleep and know you'll never, never be called to get on the job of existence again! "Swift be thine approaching flight! Come soon—soon!" . . .

DION   . . . What haunted, haunting ghosts we are! We dimly remember so much it will take us so many million years to forget! . . .

ACT IV

BROWN   [is dying]. And when I wake up . . . ?

CYBEL   The sun will be rising again. . . . Always spring comes again bearing life! Always again! Always, always forever again!—Spring again!—life again!—summer and fall and death and peace again! But always, always, love and conception and birth and pain again—spring bearing the intolerable chalice of life again!—bearing the glorious, blazing crown of life again! . . .

[From the closing lines of the play:] So long ago! And yet I'm still the same Margaret. It's only our lives that grow old. We are where centuries only count as seconds and after a thousand lives our eyes begin to open.

The Great God Brown

[1] New York: Modern Library, 1959, pp. 333, 337, 343, 374, 377.)

HERVEY ALLEN (1889–1949)
American Novelist

The accounts of the good and evil of a lifetime cannot be balanced by explanations, and the books closed. The balance is carried forward into other lives; into actions and reactions until equilibrium results. Only time can liquidate [it] in full.

Anthony Adverse (Chap. 62)

In North America, especially in the newer settlements, Masonry in sundry and various ways filled vital and long-felt wants. . . . To many a simple frontier youth, in particular, the experience of initiation was frequently overwhelming. . . . For, instead, of arriving in some rude loft . . . the new initiates would now seem to have been translated into the finished cavernlike abode of some powerful magician or spiritual personage, a being superior to and aloof from the wild self-planted nature without. . . . Only a missing password had been needed—and they had at last gained entrance to his very house.

"At last"—because this place and the spirit that dwelt there must after all have always been quite close by. . . . In the recesses of their lonely minds they had sought this dwelling through forests of dream-afflicted nightmare. Somehow, somewhere it had been lost. Now they had suddenly come upon it—again! . . . "Why, this was not a garret! No, this was that old place!" They would be astonished. But that was not what would astonish them most. It was this: Each would suddenly feel that he had been alive for ages. He would instantly "remember" that he had often and often seen this familiar place before.

Bedford Village (Chap. 12)

ROBERT STROUD (1890–1963)
"The Birdman of Alcatraz"

[Robert Stroud, probably the most celebrated prisoner of recent times, died at the age of seventy-three after fifty-four years of imprisonment, forty-two years of which were spent in complete isolation—the longest period of solitary confinement experienced by anyone in United States history. Despite unbelievable hardships and the opposition of prison officials, this man, who had only a third-grade education, learned mathematics, astronomy, languages, music, painting, law, gained world-wide recognition as a foremost authority on bird diseases, and devoted many years to planning prison reforms. Stroud's biography, told by Thomas Gaddis in *Birdman of Alcatraz*,[1] was later dramatized in the motion picture of that name, Burt Lancaster playing the leading role. Concerning Stroud's early days in Leavenworth prison, Gaddis relates:[2]]

His hatred of punishment grew with his reading and his pent-up ego swelled with the view of worlds he could not reach. He became grave and inwardly ardent. He studied and worked deeper into astronomy, seeing, in his mind's eye, the sky and its heavenly bodies swimming in limitless space. . . . But now he discovered something truly illimitable, beyond astronomy, in the spacious metaphysics of the Orient. He stumbled upon theosophy. One of his letters to his mother revealed that, even as a boy, he had held the persistent notion that he had lived before. . . . Enthralled by his reading, Stroud embraced the brotherhood of Karma, thought-transference and reincarnation. . . . "I soon saw the two phases of theosophy," he wrote his mother, "the theory and practice of occultism, and the holding of life with respect to the theory of brotherhood, *karma*. . . . The second was of the highest value attainable. I started to live by the second phase."

HENRY MILLER (1 8 9 1 –   )
American Author

[Henry Miller's interest in Eastern religion is mentioned in W. G. Rogers' biography of Frances Stelhoff, *Wise Men Fish Here*.[1] The extract below is from an interview with Miller in London, 1961, published in "The Art of Fiction" series of *The Paris Review*:[2]]

I no longer want to write about my personal experiences. I wrote all these autobiographical books not because I think myself such an important person but—this will make you laugh—because I thought when I began that I was telling the story of the most tragic suffering any man had endured. As I got on with it I realized that I was only an amateur at suffering. Certainly I had my full share of it, but I no longer think it was so terrible. That's why I called the trilogy *The Rosy Crucifixion*. I discovered that this suffering was good for me, that it opened the way to a joyous life, through acceptance of the suffering. When a man is crucified, when he dies to himself, the heart opens up like a flower. Of course you don't die, nobody dies,

[1] New York: Signet paperback.
[2] Pp. 28–29.

---

[1] New York: Harcourt, Brace, 1965, p. 217.
[2] Summer-Fall, 1962.

death doesn't exist, you only reach a new level of vision, a new realm of consciousness, a new unknown world. Just as you don't know where you came from, so you don't know where you're going. But that there is something there, before and after, I firmly believe.

PEARL S. BUCK (1892–   )

American Author

[In *The Living Reed*, a historical novel about Korea, Pearl Buck writes of Liang, a baby born to Yul-han and his wife Induk:[1]]

At first Yul-han thought of the child only as his son, a part of himself, a third with Induk. As time passed, however, a most strange prescience took hold of [Yul-han's] mind and spirit. . . . He perceived that the child possessed an old soul. It was not to be put in words, this meaning of an old soul. Yul-han, observing the child, saw in his behaviour a reasonableness, a patience, a comprehension, that was totally unchildlike. He did not scream when his food was delayed, as other infants do. Instead, his eyes calm and contemplative, he seemed to understand and was able to wait. These eyes, quietly alive, moved from Yul-han's face to Induk's when they talked, as though he knew what his parents said. . . . He gazed at them with such intelligence, such awareness, that it was as if he spoke their names, not as his parents, but as persons whom he recognized. . . . Yul-han, watching, felt a certain awe, a hesitancy in calling him "my son," as though the claim were presumption. "If I were a Buddhist," he told Induk one day, "I would say that this child is an incarnation of some former great soul."

[Liang meets his uncle Yul-chun, for the first time. Yul-chun was a Korean hero known to the people as "The Living Reed."] The child was barely awake but being amiable and benign by nature, he roused himself and smiled at his uncle at first without much concern. Suddenly, however, an inexplicable change took place. The smile left his face, he leaned forward in his mother's arms and gazed most earnestly into his uncle's eyes. He gave a cry of joy, he reached out his arms . . . while Yul-han and Induk stood transfixed in amazement. [Recalling the event years later, the uncle remarks to Liang:] "You sprang into my arms . . . you knew me from some other life."

The Living Reed

1 New York: John Day, 1963, pp. 305–306, 322–323, 473.

J. B. PRIESTLEY (1894–)
British Novelist, Critic, and Playwright

[Priestley's play, *I Have Been Here Before*[1] is briefly summarized by André Maurois in his article "Tragic Decline of the Humane Ideal":[2] "The subject of this play was the Eternal Return, the idea that the same events occur over and over again, that men find themselves, after millions of years, in situations which they have previously encountered, and that, each time, they make the same mistakes which cause the same tragedies. But the author of the play . . . admits that certain men, at the moment when they find themselves on the threshold of their drama, remember confusedly their previous misfortunes and find in this memory the strength to thwart destiny by a free action which breaks the fatal chain." Quoting now from Act III:]

ORMUND If I'd any sense I'd use [my revolver to kill myself]. No more questions that can't be answered, twisting like knives in your guts. Sleep, a good sleep, the only good sleep.

DR. GÖRTLER I am afraid you will be disappointed. It will be a sleep full of dreams—like this. And the questions will still be there. You cannot blow them to bits with a pistol.

ORMUND . . . I suppose you believe that if I take the jump into the dark, I'll find myself back again on the old treadmill. Well, I don't believe it. I can find peace.

DR. GÖRTLER You can't. Peace is not somewhere just waiting for you. . . . You have to create it. . . . Life is not easy. It provides no short cuts, no effortless escapes. . . . Life is penetrated through and through by our feeling, imagination and will. In the end the whole universe must respond to every real effort we make. We each live a fairy tale created by ourselves.

ORMUND What—by going around the same damned dreary circle of existence as you believe?

DR. GÖRTLER We do not go round a circle. That is an illusion just as the circling of the planets and stars is an illusion. We move along a spiral track. It is not quite the same journey from the cradle to the grave each time. Sometimes the differences are small. Sometimes they are very important. We must set out each time on the same road but along that road we have a choice of adventures.

I Have Been Here Before

[1] London: Wm. Heineman, 1937.
[2] *The New York Times*, June 19, 1938.

ALDOUS HUXLEY (1894–1963)
British-American Author

The eschatologists of the Orient affirm that there are certain posthumous conditions in which meritorious souls are capable of advancing from a heaven of happy personal survival to genuine immortality in union with the timeless, eternal Godhead. And, of course, there is also the possibility (indeed, for most individuals, the necessity) of returning to some form of embodied life, in which the advance towards complete beatification, or deliverance through enlightenment, can be continued. . . .

Orthodox Christian doctrine does not admit the possibility, either in the posthumous state or in some other embodiment, of any further growth towards the ultimate perfection of a total union with the Godhead. But in the Hindu and Buddhist versions of the Perennial Philosophy the divine mercy is matched by the divine patience: both are infinite. For oriental theologians there is no eternal damnation; there are only purgatories and then an indefinite series of second chances to go forward towards not only man's, but the whole creation's final end—total reunion with the Ground of all being. . . .

In the Vedanta cosmology there is . . . something in the nature of a soul that reincarnates in a gross or subtle body, or manifests itself in some incorporeal state. This soul is not the personality of the defunct, but rather the particularized I—consciousness out of which a personality arises. [This conception] is logically self-consistent and can be made to "save the appearances"—in other words, to fit the odd and obscure facts of psychical research.

The Perennial Philosophy (Chap. 14)

LOUIS BROMFIELD (1896–1956)
American Author

There have been moments in my experience when I have been sharply aware of the "strange intimations" of which Dr. Alexis Carrel writes—intimations which have scarcely been touched upon in the realms of science—"strange intimations" of worlds which I had known before, of places which in the spirit I had touched and heard and smelled.

France was one of the places I had always known. From the time I was old enough to read, France had a reality for me, the one place in all the world I felt a fierce compulsion to see. Its history fascinated me, its pictures, its landscapes, its books, its theatres. It was, during all my childhood and early youth, the very apotheosis of all that was romantic and beautiful. And finally when, the morning before we were allowed ashore, the gray landscape of Brittany appeared on the horizon, there was nothing strange about it. I had seen those shores before, when I do not know. And afterward during all the years I lived there, during the war when I served with the French army and in the strange, melodramatic truce between wars, it was always the same. Nothing ever surprised or astonished me; no landscape, no forest, no chateau, no Paris street, no provincial town ever seemed strange. I had seen it all before. It was always a country and its people a people whom I knew well and intimately.

Pleasant Valley (autobiography)[1]

NEVIL SHUTE (1899–1960)
British Author

[Nevil Shute's novel *In the Wet* returns to the reincarnation theme of an earlier book, *An Old Captivity*:]

"You'll be all right," I said quietly. "God is very merciful, and he won't judge you too hard."

"You don't know nothing," the old man muttered weakly. "I could tell you things. . . . I ain't done so good. I know it. I'll start lower down next time. But I'll be right. Everyone gets another shot, however low you go, and I'll be right. . . . I ain't afraid of dying . . . that's nothing. It's just going off to sleep and sliding off into the next time . . . I reckon that I'd rather be there than here."

In the Wet (Chap. 2)

LORAN HURNSCOT
British Author

[In the journal, *A Prison, a Paradise*,[1] the author, using the above pseudonym, writes:]

My first genuine memory is about the Fall. There is darkness before and after it, but the memory itself is clear. A baby in a pram, in a late autumn garden, waking suddenly from sleep, at thirteen or fourteen months old. The fingerless infant-gloves tied rather too tightly round the wrists; the strap of the pram an uncomfortable restraint. And then the over-

[1] New York: Harper and Row, 1945, pp. 3–4.

[1] New York: Viking, 1959, pp. 161, 263–264, 275.

whelming, terrible discovery: "I'm in a body." I began to wail, to scream, to weep distractedly. In a few moments there were three women standing round the pram, comforting, speculating. "Something must have frightened her—but what?" "Could it have been an insect-sting? No, it's getting too late in the year for that." I sobbed in the helpless prison of before-one-can-talk, understanding telepathically, as it were, the gist of what they said. "It isn't that, it isn't that, it's not the sort of thing you think at all—it's that I've found out I'm locked up in a body, and its dreadful." . . .

Now and then I become passionately pre-occupied by the idea of reincarnation. Is there evidence? [Several stories are told of acquaintances who seem to remember the past.] . . . Had a rather irritable telephone conversation with my parsonical friend. I said that Buddhism was more christian than Christianity: that in the end it promised salvation to all—it did not look on the multitudes as chaff to be burned eternally. He said that there had to be a certain urgency: that with endless lives in prospect, one would always put off making the effort until the next. I said that to hinge eternal salvation on one single, confused and handicapped lifetime seemed to me a diabolical idea. He didn't agree; he said that everyone had their chance in this life, and if they wouldn't take it, "well, you've had it." If this is orthodoxy, then may God save me from it.

A Prison, a Paradise

THOMAS WOLFE (1900–1938)
American Novelist

[Thomas Wolfe's Look Homeward, Angel, an autobiographical novel, bids fair to becoming an American classic. Chapter 1 opens with the reincarnation theme which is unfolded later when Eugene Gant reminisces as a babe in the crib, and then as a boy during pre-school days:]

Each of us is all the sums he has not counted; subtract us into nakedness and night again, and you shall see begin in Crete four thousand years ago the love that ended yesterday in Texas. . . . Each moment is the fruit of forty thousand years. (Chapter 1.)

Lying darkly in his crib, washed, powdered, and fed, he thought quietly of many things before he dropped off to sleep. . . . He saw his life down the solemn vista of a forest aisle, and he knew he would always be the sad one: caged in that little round skull, imprisoned in that beating and most secret heart, his life must always walk down lonely passages. . . . He had been sent from one mystery into another: somewhere within or without his consciousness he heard a great bell ringing faintly, as if it sounded undersea, and as he listened, the ghost of memory walked through his mind, and for a moment he felt that he had almost recovered what he had lost. (Chapter 4.)

Secure and conscious now in the guarded and sufficient strength of home, he lay with well-lined belly before the roasting vitality of the fire, poring insatiably over great volumes in the bookcase. The books he delighted in most were . . . called *Ridpath's History of the World*. Their numberless pages were illustrated with hundreds of drawings, engravings, wood-cuts: he followed the progression of the centuries pictorially before he could read. . . . The past unrolled to him in separate and enormous visions; he built unending legends upon the pictures of the kings of Egypt, charioted swiftly by soaring horses, and something infinitely old and recollective seemed to awaken in him as he looked upon fabulous monsters, the twined beards and huge beast-bodies of Assyrian kings, the walls of Babylon. (Chapter 6.)

[In the closing paragraphs of the volume, Eugene Gant, as a young man, is shown venturing forth into the world:] He stood naked and alone in darkness . . . he stood upon the ramparts of his soul, before the lost land of himself. . . . Lost in the thickets of myself, I will hunt you down until you cease to haunt my eyes with hunger. I heard your foot-falls in the desert, I saw your shadow in old buried cities, I heard your laughter running down a million streets, but I did not find you there. And no leaf hangs for me in the forest; I shall lift no stone upon the hills; I shall find no door in any city. But in the city of myself, upon the continent of my soul, I shall find the forgotten language, the lost world, a door where I may enter. . . .

Look Homeward, Angel [1]

CHARLES A. LINDBERGH (1 9 0 2 –   )
American Aviator

Lindbergh's *The Spirit of St. Louis*[2] is far more than a tale of courage and adventure concerning his historic flight across the Atlantic. It reveals the strange dissociation of states of consciousness that went on within himself as the thirty-four-hour flight proceeded and he waged a superhuman battle to keep awake. (He had not slept during the night and day preceding.) First, a separation was observed to take place between mind and body—aspects of himself usually regarded as indivisible. Overwhelmed with drowsi-

[1] New York: Scribner, 1952, pp. 1, 36–37, 63, 662.
[2] New York: Scribner, 1953, pp. 352–353, 361–362, 375, 378, 387, 389–391.

ness the senses and organs sought sleep though obviously it meant their certain death, but the mind entity standing "apart" held firm. In turn the mind became unable to preserve wakefulness, only to give way to a transcendent power that Lindbergh hardly suspected was within him. Finally, in mid-ocean, the conscious mind fell fast asleep, and this third element, this new "extraordinary mind" which at first he feared to trust, now directed the flight. Here, in brief, is what he says occurred:

The fuselage behind became crowded with ghostly human presences, transparent, riding weightless with him in the plane. No surprise is experienced at their arrival, and without turning his head he sees them all, for his skull has become "one great eye, seeing everywhere at once." They seem able to disappear or show themselves at will, to pass through the walls of the plane as though no walls existed. Sometimes voices from afar off resound in the plane, familiar voices, advising him on his flight, encouraging him, conveying messages unattainable in normal life.

What connection exists between these "spirits" and himself? It is more like a reunion of friends after years of separation, "as though I've known all of them before in some past incarnation." Perhaps they are the products of the experience of ages, dwellers of a realm closed to the men of our world. He feels himself in a transitional state between earthly life and a vaster region beyond, as if caught in the magnetic field between two planets and propelled by forces he cannot control "representing powers incomparably stronger than I've ever known." Only when his conscious direction of the plane's course seems imperative does he find himself momentarily wakened, to be soon followed by these long, strange interludes of "sleep" with eyes wide open.

Values are changing within his consciousness. For twenty-five years it has been imprisoned in walls of bone, and he had not recognized the endlessness of life, the immortal existence that lies outside. Is he already "dead" and about to join these "phantoms"? Death ceases to be the final end he thought it was. Simultaneously, he lives in the past, the present, and the future. Around him are "old associations, bygone friendships, voices from ancestrally distant times." Yes, he is flying in a plane over the Atlantic, but he is also living in ages long past.

SALVADOR DALI (1904–   )
Spanish Painter

[In Lord Beaverbrook's book, *Courage: The Story of Sir James Dunn,* an incident is related concerning a chance meeting between Dali and Sir James. During the course of conversation Dali is reported to have exclaimed: "I am a believer in reincarnation and I am sure you are descended from the Great Caesar." The following extract, from an article "Dali Greets the World" by Ben Martin, appeared in the *New York Herald Tribune*'s magazine *Today's Living* for January 24, 1960, being an account of an interview with the famous artist:]

[Dali stated:] "If you will study the entire series of cards [he had painted] you will find one theme runs through almost all—the butterfly. The butterfly is not present only because it is in itself a thing of beauty. It is present because to one of the greatest Spanish mystics, St. Theresa of Avila, the butterfly was the symbol of the soul. The ugly, ungainly caterpillar, our body, enters a form of the grave, the cocoon. Out of this death emerges the butterfly—beautiful, free, no longer earthbound. To me, as to St. Theresa, the butterfly is the soul of man." . . .

"*All* Spaniards are mystics," he replied [to the query "Are you a mystic?"] "All Spaniards are both Don Quixote, who is pure spirit, and Sancho Panza, who is pure materialism. That is why 'Don Quixote' is the most Spanish of all books. As for me, I am not only a mystic; I am also the reincarnation of one of the greatest of all Spanish mystics, St. John of the Cross. I can remember vividly my life as St. John, of experiencing divine union, of undergoing the dark night of the soul of which he writes with so much feeling. I can remember the monastery and I can remember many of St. John's fellow monks."

RUMER GODDEN (1907–   )
British Author

[Rumer Godden's *The River*, as those who read the book or saw and loved Jean Renoir's memorable film will recall, is the story of Harriet, a young girl growing up in India, where Miss Godden herself lived as a child. A work of great delicacy and sensitivity, it portrays the wonder and innocence of childhood against the background of nature and oriental life. These brief glimpses into the book are from the Viking Press edition:[1]]

Harriet . . . went back to the house, and on her way she passed Victoria with her doll. "I play so beautifully with my baby," she said to Harriet as Harriet passed. "She was born again yesterday."

"You are always having her born," said Harriet scornfully.

"Why not?" asked Victoria. "You can be born again and again, can't you?"

[1] New York: 1946, pp. 41, 49–50.

It was puzzling. Every time Harriet examined somebody's silly remark, it seemed not to be so silly. . . .

Sometimes, in the night, Harriet thought about death. She thought about Father and Mother dying, or Nan, who was really very old; then she would hastily wake Bea to comfort her. When Ram Prasad's wife died, she was carried on a string bed to the river and put on a pyre and burned. Afterwards her ashes were thrown on the water. . . . Harriet . . . had not seen the body, only those ashes, and they did not seem to have anything to do with a person who had lived and walked and talked and eaten food and played with her baby and laughed. . . .

She asked Father what Buddhists did when they died; he took down a book and read to her about a drop sliding into the crystal sea. . . . She asked Mother, and Mother pointed out that Harriet knew already that Jesus rose from the dead; some people, she added, believe that you come back over and over again, to live another life each time, "A better life," said Mother.

"Goodness, how good you must be in the end," said Harriet.

That was the idea, Mother thought, and if you were not good, she went on to say, you came back as something lower. . . . Bogey, who did not like to be labelled good or bad, was bored with the idea. "I should rather have done with it," said Bogey.

All these thoughts seemed like cracks in the wholeness of Harriet's unconsciousness. It had cracked before, of course, but now she was growing rapaciously.

The River

NANCY WILSON ROSS (1907–   )
American Author

[From *The Return of Lady Brace*,[1] a widely read novel:]

[A Buddhist monk is speaking:] This law of Karma—it is really very much misunderstood, not only in the East where it is believed, but in the West where it is rejected. . . . In the West, people dislike the idea of inheriting their personal destiny from past existences. This seems to them so fatalistic, so fixed, that therefore they view Karma as a negative concept, and finally they reject it as dangerous altogether. . . . Karma, as we see it, is not a negative concept [but] a positive one. We see it not as blind destiny, but as opportunity. We believe it involves the use of that particular human trait the West values so highly—namely the *will*. . . . Two thou-

[1] New York: Random House, 1957, pp. 227–228.

sand five hundred years ago our great Teacher was concerned with helping man to get control of his own life, that is, his individual Karma, at the only point where such a thing is possible—namely, in the present moment. This was because the Teacher saw what is so true, and so very hard to grasp, that there is, indeed, only the Now!

The Return of Lady Brace

J. D. SALINGER (1919–   )
American Author

[Salinger's short story, "Teddy," [1] concerns a phenomenal ten-year-old who matter-of-factly recalls a previous incarnation in India. Brought before several panels of skeptical professors, they are soon confounded by his knowledge and clairvoyant powers. Teddy's casual attitude toward death—even his own foreseen tragic death within the hour—seems evident from these brief selections:]

Nicholson: "As I understand it . . . you hold pretty firmly to the Vedantic theory of reincarnation."

"It isn't a theory, it's as much a part—"

"All right," Nicholson said quickly. He smiled, and gently raised the flats of his hands, in a sort of ironic benediction. "We won't argue that point, for the moment. Let me finish. . . . From what I gather, you've acquired certain information through meditation, that's given you some conviction that in your last incarnation you were a holy man in India, but more or less fell from Grace—"

"I wasn't a holy man," Teddy said. "I was just a person making very nice spiritual advancement. . . . I met a lady, and I sort of stopped meditating. . . . I would have had to take another body and come back to earth again anyway—I mean I wasn't so spiritually advanced that I could have died, if I hadn't met that lady, and then gone straight to Brahma and never again have to come back to earth. But I wouldn't have had to get incarnated in an *American* body if I hadn't met that lady. I mean it's very hard to meditate and live a spiritual life in America. People think you're a freak if you try to. . . ."

"Is it true, or isn't it, that you informed the whole Leidekker examining bunch . . . when and where and how they would eventually die? . . ."

"I didn't tell them when they were actually going to die. That's a very

[1] J. D. Salinger, *Nine Stories*. New York: Signet paperback, 1954.

false rumor," Teddy said. "I *could* have, but I knew that in their hearts they really didn't want to know. I mean I knew that even though they teach Religion and Philosophy and all, they're still pretty afraid to die." Teddy sat, or reclined, in silence for a minute. "It's so silly," he said. "All you do is get the heck out of your body when you die. My gosh, everybody's done it thousands and thousands of times. Just because they don't remember it doesn't mean they haven't done it. It's so silly." . . .

Nicholson said: "Ever think you might like to do something in research when you grow up? Medical research, or something of that kind? It seems to me, with your mind, you might eventually—" . . .

"That wouldn't interest me very much. Doctors stay too right on the surface. They're always talking about cells and things. . . . as if they didn't really belong to the person that has them. . . . I grew my own body. Nobody else did it for me. So if I grew it, I must have known *how* to grow it. Unconsciously, at least. I may have lost the *conscious* knowledge of how to grow it sometime in the last few hundred thousand years, but the knowledge is still *there*, because—obviously—I've used it. . . . It would take quite a lot of meditation and emptying out to get the whole thing back—I mean the conscious knowledge—but you could do it if you wanted to. If you opened up wide enough."

"Teddy"

[In his stories about the Glass family, published as *Franny and Zooey*,[2] Salinger continues to discuss religion, particularly Eastern religions, and again speaks of reincarnation. See pp. 196–97.]

JAMES JONES (1921–   )
American Novelist

"Some day they will rank Joe Hill right up alongside old John the Baptist. He must have done something great, back a long time ago before he was ever Joe Hill, to have earned a chance at a ticket like that one." When Prewitt asked what he meant, he said, "In one of his previous lives." . . .

Jack Malloy believed in reincarnation, because to his logical mind, it was the only logical explanation. And it was for this same reason that he worshipped the memory of Joseph Hillstrom so. "He was a saint. He had to be one, to have been given the life he was allowed to have."

[Prewitt] remembered one day for no good reason how Jack Malloy had always talked about Jack London all the time, and how he had wor-

[2] Boston, Little Brown, 1955.

shipped him almost as much as Joe Hill. . . . So he started to [read London's books] in earnest. Of them all, he liked *Before Adam* and *The Star Rover* the best because for the first time they gave him a clear picture of what Malloy had meant by reincarnation of souls. He thought he could see now, how there could just as easily be an evolution of souls in different bodies, just like there had been an evolution of bodies in different souls from . . . prehistoric times. . . . It seemed to be logical. . . .

From Here to Eternity[1]

PETER USTINOV (1921–)
British Actor, Director, Playwright

A newly born child is striking by its expression of immense old age and omniscience, whereas the face of a man engaged in dying peacefully is remarkable for its serenity and the smiling tolerance of the human activities he still dimly sees. There is a mystic link between the margins of life, a cool majesty in which some secret is shared, a secret far removed from the high summer of love, sex, ambition and fretful jockeying for position. I am in what is known as the flower of middle age, and over the noise of traffic and ticker tapes, of canned music and of prattle, I am endlessly jealous of this secret.

Life (April 19, 1963)

[1] New York: Scribner, 1951, pp. 647–648, 723.

PART VI

Modern Scientists, Psychologists
and Philosophers on Reincarnation

Scientific truth is characterized by its exactness and the certainty of its predictions. But these admirable qualities are contrived by science at the cost of remaining on a plane of secondary problems, leaving intact the ultimate and decisive questions. . . . If the physicist detains, at the point where his method ends, the hand with which he delineates the facts, the human being behind each physicist prolongs the line thus begun and carries it on to its termination, as an eye beholding an arch in ruins will of itself complete the missing curve. . . .

The past century, resorting to all but force, tried to restrict the human mind within the limits set to exactness. Its violent effort to turn its back on last problems is called agnosticism. . . . How can we live turning a deaf ear to the last dramatic questions? Where does the world come from and whither is it going? Which is the supreme power of the cosmos, what the essential meaning of life? We cannot breathe confined to a realm of secondary and intermediate themes. We need a comprehensive perspective, foreground and background, not a maimed scenery, a horizon stripped of infinite distances. . . . We are given no escape from last questions. In one fashion or another they are in us, whether we like it or not.

JOSÉ ORTEGA Y GASSET
Toward a Philosophy of History

It would be curious if we should find science and philosophy taking up again the old theory of metempsychosis, remodeling it to suit our present modes of religious and scientific thought, and launching it again on the wide ocean of human belief. But stranger things have happened in the history of human opinion.

JAMES FREEMAN CLARKE

THOMAS H. HUXLEY (1825–1895)
British Biologist and Darwinist

In the doctrine of transmigration, whatever its origin, Brahmanical and Buddhist speculation found, ready to hand, the means of constructing a plausible vindication of the ways of the Cosmos to man. . . . Yet this plea of justification is not less plausible than others; and none but very hasty thinkers will reject it on the ground of inherent absurdity. Like the doctrine of evolution itself, that of transmigration has its roots in the world of reality; and it may claim such support as the great argument from analogy is capable of supplying.

Evolution and Ethics and Other Essays[1]

   I understand the main tenet of Materialism to be that there is nothing in the universe but matter and force. . . . *Kraft und Stoff*—force and matter—are paraded as the Alpha and Omega of existence. . . . Whosoever does not hold it is condemned by the more zealous of the persuasion to the Inferno appointed for fools or hypocrites. But all this I heartily disbelieve. . . . There is a third thing in the universe, to wit, consciousness, which . . . I can not see to be matter or force, or any conceivable modification of either. . . .

   The student of nature, who starts from the axiom of the universality of the law of causation, can not refuse to admit an eternal existence; if he admits the conservation of energy, he can not deny the possibility of an eternal energy; if he admits the existence of immaterial phenomena in the form of consciousness, he must admit the possibility, at any rate, of an *eternal series of such phenomena.* (Italics added.) . . .

[1] New York: Appleton, 1894, pp. 60–61.

Looking at the matter from the most rigidly scientific point of view, the assumption that, amidst the myriads of worlds scattered through endless space, there can be no intelligence, as much greater than man's as his is greater than a blackbeetle's; no being endowed with powers of influencing the course of nature as much greater than his, as his is greater than a snail's, seems to me not merely baseless, but impertinent. Without stepping beyond the analogy of that which is known, it is easy to people the cosmos with entities, in ascending scale until we reach something practically indistinguishable from omnipotence, omniprescence, and omniscience.

Essays Upon Some Controverted Questions[2]

SIR EDWARD B. TYLOR (1832–1917)
British Anthropologist

[From Tylor's well-known work *Primitive Culture:*[1]]

Metempsychosis never became one of the great doctrines of Christendom, though not unknown in mediæval scholasticism, and though maintained by an eccentric theologian here and there into our own times. It would be strange were it not so. It is in the very nature of the development of religion that speculations of the earlier culture should dwindle to survivals, yet be again and again revived. Doctrines transmigrate, if souls do not; and metempsychosis, wandering along the course of ages, came at last to animate the souls of Fourier and Soame Jenyns.

We have traced the theory of metempsychosis in stage after stage of the world's civilization, scattered among the native races of America and Africa, established in the Asiatic nations . . . rising and falling in classic and mediæval Europe, and lingering at last in the modern world as an intellectual crotchet, of little account but to the ethnographer who notes it down as an item of evidence for his continuity of culture. . . .

Far different has been the history of the other doctrine, that of the independent existence of the personal soul after the death of the body, in a Future Life [or heaven]. Passing onward through change after change in the condition of the human race . . . this great belief may be traced from its crude and primitive manifestations among savage races to its establishment in the heart of modern religion, where the faith in a future existence forms at once an inducement to goodness, a sustaining hope through suffering and across the fear of death, and an answer to the perplexed problem of the allotment of happiness and misery in this present world, by the expectation of another world to set this right.

Primitive Culture

[2] New York: Appleton, 1892, pp. 27, 171, 178.

[1] Second edition, 1873, II, Chap. 2.

CARL DU PREL (1839–1899)
German Philosopher

In Darwinism, well understood, there lies the germ of Palingenesis; to the materialist, of course, it will seem not only paradoxical, but (as usual) "impossible"; though Voltaire (I think it is) somewhere observes: "Not to be twice-born, but once, is wonderful." . . . The hypothesis of a transcendental consciousness, which many followers of Darwin might repudiate, is . . . completely compatible with Darwinism. . . . According to Darwin, habits are transmitted to the germ-cells, and so to all later generations, species, and kinds; according to the transcendental psychologists, habits pass as predispositions to the transcendental Subject, and so determine its later phenomenal forms. . . . These two views are not opposed to each other. Those who think the metaphysical Darwinism, tending to Palingenesis, a crude explanation of individuality, should consider that the alternative explanations offered by materialism and pantheism are by no means less crude. . . .

Our transcendental Subject not only introduces us into life and determines our particular individuality, but also leads us through life; but it cares only for our transcendental good. . . . Man is his own heir, the Subject inherits from the person, and what I have acquired morally and intellectually remains with me. The law of the Conservation of Energy . . . avails also for the psychical world. So should we again arrive at the oldest of philosophical conceptions of man, the migration of souls; but this old theory would be revived in a new and incomparably higher form, which could only be described as Palingenesis.

The Philosophy of Mysticism[1]

WILLIAM JAMES (1842–1910)
American Psychologist and Philosopher

[Professor James's essay *Human Immortality*, an Ingersoll Lecture delivered at Harvard in 1893, shows how the assumption that physiological psychology has taken away the basis for belief in immortality is without scientific justification. It rests on the view that the brain functions only in a productive capacity in relation to thought. The brain, however, could as easily transmit ideas that have an origin elsewhere. He further explains that "when finally a brain stops acting altogether, or decays, that special stream of consciousness which it subserved will vanish entirely from this natural

[1] Trans. C. C. Massey. London: 1889, II, 230–232.

world. But the sphere of being that supplied the consciousness would still be intact; and in that more real world with which, even whilst here, it was continuous, the consciousness might, in ways unknown to us, continue still." [1] In his preface to the second edition, James enlarges upon his views and speaks of reincarnation:]

So many critics have made one and the same objection to the doorway to immortality which my lecture claims to be left open by the "transmission theory" of cerebral action, that I feel tempted, as the book is again going to press, to add a word of explanation. If our finite personality here below, the objectors say, be due to the transmission through the brain of portions of a pre-existing larger consciousness, all that can remain after the brain expires is the larger consciousness itself as such. . . . But this, the critics continue, is the pantheistic idea of immortality, survival, namely, in the soul of the world; not the Christian idea of immortality, which means survival in strictly personal form. . . .

The plain truth is that one may conceive the mental world behind the veil in as individualistic a form as one pleases, without any detriment to the general scheme by which the brain is represented as a transmissive organ. If the extreme individualistic view were taken, one's finite mundane consciousness would be an extract from one's larger, truer personality, the latter having even now some sort of reality behind the scenes. And in transmitting it . . . one's brain would also leave effects upon the part remaining behind the veil; for when a thing is torn, both fragments feel the operation.

And just as (to use a very coarse figure) the stubs remain in a checkbook whenever a check is used, to register the transaction, so these impressions on the transcendent self might constitute so many vouchers of the finite experiences of which the brain had been the mediator; and ultimately they might form that collection within the larger self of memories of our earthly passage. . . .

It is true that all this would seem to have affinities rather with pre-existence and with possible reincarnations than with the Christian notion of immortality. But my concern in the lecture was not to discuss immortality in general. It was confined to showing it to be not incompatible with the brain-function theory of our present mundane consciousness. I hold that it is so compatible, and compatible moreover in fully individualized form. The reader would be in accord with everything that the text of my lecture intended to say, were he to assert that every memory and affection of his present life is to be preserved, and that he shall never in sæcula sæculorum

[1] The Will to Believe, and Human Immortality. New York: Dover, 1956, pp. 17–18.

cease to be able to say to himself: "I am the same personal being who in old times upon the earth had those experiences."

Human Immortality[2]

I am ignorant of Buddhism and speak under correction, and merely in order the better to describe my general point of view; but as I apprehend the Buddhistic doctrine of Karma, I agree in principle with that. All supernaturalists admit that facts are under the judgment of higher law. . . . I state the matter thus bluntly, because the current of thought in academic circles runs against me, and I feel like a man who must set his back against an open door quickly if he does not wish to see it closed and locked. In spite of its being so shocking to the reigning intellectual tastes, I believe that a candid consideration of piecemeal supernaturalism and a complete discussion of all its metaphsyical bearings will show it to be the hypothesis by which the largest number of legitimate requirements are met. That of course would be a program for other books than this; what I now say sufficiently indicates to the philosophic reader the place where I belong. (Postscript.)

The Varieties of Religious Experience
Gifford Lectures, 1901–02

JAMES WARD (1843–1925)
British Philosopher and Psychologist

[James Ward was Professor of Mental Philosophy at Cambridge from 1897 to 1925. In addition to his philosophical and psychological pursuits he was interested in science and received doctorates in that field from both Cambridge and Oxford. The following is from Chapter 18, "Theories of a Future Life," in *The Realm of Ends*, Dr. Ward's Gifford Lectures for 1907–1910:[1]]

I make bold to deny, that the theory of pre-existence [and reincarnation] "creates new difficulties." It involves "a ramifying network" of assumptions unquestionably; but if it "is certainly not capable of positive disproof," the objector is bound to show that the result of the whole is worthless. Till then, summarily to reject it involves the still more extravagant assumption that we have exhausted all possibilities and that what may be only our lack of knowledge of its empirical conditions is tantamount to a proof of its impossibility. As Kant, whose words I have adopted, has said, this arrogance of negation does not eliminate in the least the practical value

[2] *Ibid.*, pp. v–ix.

[1] Cambridge University Press, 1911, pp. 402–405.

of such hypotheses. The appeal to ignorance no doubt cuts both ways: it does not allow us to treat hypotheses as knowledge, but on the other hand it does not destroy their working utility if, consistently with what we do know, they enable us even tentatively to reach a completer and more satisfactory Weltanschauung.

As regards this particular hypothesis of pre-existence and a plurality of lives, its complexity is no advantage certainly; but even so the disadvantage is reduced in proportion as the separate assumptions are analogous with actual experience and consilient with each other. After all it should give the scornful objector pause, to think how many of the vital processes, about which we have definite knowledge, involve an elaborate adjustment of multifarious details that would be utterly incredible but for its familiarity. Is it then unreasonable to expect still more marvelous conjunctions in the wider dimensions of the world beyond the grave? And is it not also possible—just because of such wider dimensions—that what to us seems complicated or impossible is really as simple as say movement into a third dimension, which yet a being confined to two might fail to understand? . . .

The objection to transmigration or metempsychosis [on the grounds of personal discontinuity between lives] has been met by assuming that the personal discontinuity is only temporary, and that the successive lives of a given subject may be eventually connected through continuous but latent memories that are revived after death or when all the soul's Wanderjahre are over. So, for example, Professor Campbell Fraser thinks. Cf. his Theism, Vol. II, p. 249. And still more definitely Renouvier, Le Personnalisme, 1903, p. 220. A similar view was held by Max Drossbach, J. Reynaud and many others. . . .

Between one active life and another there may well be . . . an intermediate state of mental rumination, and reflection, as many theologians have assumed. This state, it has been said, "is not a domain of deeds and works, for the external conditions for these are wanting . . . it is the domain of inwardness, of silent consideration and pondering, a domain of recollection (Erinnerung) in the full sense of the word." (Martensen, Die Christliche Dogmatik.[2]) Such a self-purgatory of all souls seems a worthier idea than the one-sided expiatory purgatory of the Romish Church, which has so little moral efficacy that it may be curtailed by extraneous ceremonial. We can perhaps suppose that this process [of rumination] may be a preparation for a new life [on earth], provided . . . the change in character is notwithstanding still somehow retained. . . .

But even so, if this series [of rebirths] is to have any real continuity or meaning, if it is to be not merely a series but a progression, then at every

[2] 1856, §275.

return to life, either Providence must detemine, or the naturient soul must itself select, its appropriate reincarnation. Otherwise, if disembodied souls are to be blown about by the winds of circumstance like other seeds, we should only have a repetition of that outrageous fortune which the doctrine of transmigration was supposed to redress. . . .

This difficulty in turn has been met by the further and bolder assumption, that disembodied souls do in fact steer their own way back to a suitable rebirth. An atom liberated from its molecular bonds is described as manifesting an unwonted activity, technically known as "the nascent state"; but still it does not recombine indifferently with the first free atom that it encounters, but only with one for which it has an "affinity." And "there seems to be nothing more strange or paradoxical in the suggestion that each person enters into connection with the body that it is most fitted to be connected with him." [3] . . . A liberated spirit ought to be credited with vastly more *savoir vivre* than a liberated atom. Further it must be allowed that this suggestion is quite in keeping with the conservation of values, which men like Lotze and Höffding regard as axiomatic—at any rate experience often verifies, and never certainly belies it. Finally it minimises the objection to personal continuity that is often based on the facts of heredity.

The Realm of Ends
Gifford Lectures, 1907–10

FRIEDRICH NIETZCHE (1844–1900)
German Philosopher and Poet

[In Nietzsche's celebrated work *Thus Spake Zarathustra*, he expounds the philosophy of the Superman, and for many decades this was equated with fanatical German nationalism. It is now known that this image was fabricated and propagandized by his sister, an avid apostle of the Super-Race Cult, while to Nietzsche these ideas were extremely repugnant. In his autobiography *Ecce Homo*, he writes: "My life-task is to prepare for humanity a moment of supreme self-consciousness, a Great Noontide when it will gaze both backwards and forwards, when it will emerge from the tyranny of accident and the priesthood, and for the first time pose the question of the Why and Wherefore of humanity as a whole." [1]

Regarding *Thus Spake Zarathustra*, Nietzsche states in *Ecce Homo:* "The fundamental idea of my work—namely, the Eternal Recurrence of all things—this highest of all possible formulæ for a Yea-saying philosophy, first occurred to me in August 1881. I made a note of the thought on a

[3] McTaggart, *Some Dogmas of Religion*, 1906, p. 126.

[1] *The Philosophy of Nietzsche* (a collection of his writings), New York: Modern Library, 1954, p. 887.

sheet of paper, with the postscript: 6,000 feet beyond men and time! That day I happened to be wandering through the woods alongside of the lake of Silvaplana, and I halted beside a huge pyramidal and towering rock. . . . It was then that the thought struck me." [2] In his "Explanatory Notes to 'Thus Spake Zarathustra' " Nietzsche further affirms: "The doctrine of the Eternal Recurrence is the turning point of history. . . . The moment in which I begot recurrence is immortal, for the sake of that moment alone I will endure recurrence. . . . We must desire to perish in order to arise afresh,—from one day to the other. Wander through a hundred souls,—let that be thy life and thy fate! And then finally: desire to go through the whole process once more!" [3] Quoting now from *Thus Spake Zarathustra:*]

Everything goeth, everything returneth; eternally rolleth the wheel of existence. Everything dieth, everything blossometh forth again; eternally runneth on the year of existence. . . .

A long twilight limped on before me, a fatally weary, fatally intoxicated sadness, which spake with yawning mouth.

"Eternally he returneth, the man of whom thou art weary, the small man"—so yawned my sadness. . . . "Ah, man returneth eternally! The small man returneth eternally!"

Naked had I once seen both of them, the greatest man and the smallest man: all too like one another—all too human, even the greatest man!

All too small, even the greatest man!—that was my disgust at man! And the eternal return also of the smallest man!—that was my disgust at all existence! . . . (Part 57.)

[After painfully struggling with these ideas, Zarathustra comes forth with a more jubilant conception in the section "The Seven Seals." Each of the seven short stanzas concludes with these lines:]

Oh, how could I not be ardent for Eternity and for the marriage-ring of rings—the ring of the return?

Never yet have I found the woman by whom I should like to have children, unless it be this woman whom I love: for I love thee, O Eternity!

For I love thee, O Eternity!

Thus Spake Zarathustra[4]
Trans. Thomas Common

[2] *Ibid.,* p. xxiv; another translation, p. 892.
[3] *The Complete Works of Friedrich Nietzsche,* ed. Oscar Levy. New York: Russell & Russell, 1964, XVI, Notes 41, 60, 62.
[4] *The Philosophy of Nietzsche,* pp. 245–248, 256–260.

[Anthony Ludovici, the translator of Nietzsche's notes "Eternal Recurrence" [5] states in his preface: "The notes concerning the Eternal Recurrence are said by Mrs. Foerster-Nietzsche to have been the first that Nietzsche ever wrote on the subject of his great doctrine. This being so, they must have been composed toward the autumn of the year 1881. I have already pointed out elsewhere . . . how much importance Nietzsche himself ascribed to this doctrine, and how, until the end, he regarded it as the inspiration which had led to his chief work, *Thus Spake Zarathustra*."

The selections below are from "Eternal Recurrence." [6] In the attempt to remove the faintest shadow of a Personal Creator from his scheme, Nietzsche went to the length of denying plan and purpose in the periodic repetition of worlds and beings: "Let us guard against believing that the universe . . . aims at becoming more beautiful, more perfect, more complicated! All that is anthropomorphism. . . . We must guard against ascribing any aspiration or any goal to this circular process," [7] and yet he adds: "Likewise we must not . . . regard it as either monotonous or foolish."]

The political mania at which I smile just as merrily as my contemporaries smile at the religious mania of former times is above all Materialism, a belief in the world, and in the repudiation of a "Beyond," of a "backworld." . . . My doctrine is: Live so that thou mayest desire to live again,—that is thy duty,—for in any case thou wilt live again! . . . The question which thou wilt have to answer before every deed that thou doest: "is this such a deed as I am prepared to perform an incalculable number of times?" is the best ballast. . . .

In every one of these cycles of human life there will be one hour where for the first time one man, and then many, will perceive the mighty thought of the eternal recurrence of all things:—and for mankind this is always the hour of Noon. . . . From the moment when this thought begins to prevail all colours will change their hue and a new history will begin. . . .

"But if everything is necessary, what control have I over my actions?" . . . The mightiest of all thoughts absorbs a good deal of energy which formerly stood at the disposal of other aspirations, and in this way it exercises a modifying influence; it creates new laws of motion in energy, though no new energy. But it is precisely in this respect that there lies some possibility of determining new emotions and new desires in men. . . .

[5] *Complete Works*, XVI, 237–256.
[6] Pp. 251–252, 254–256.
[7] Pp. 247–248.

Let us stamp the impress of eternity upon our lives! This thought contains more than all the religions which taught us to contemn this life as a thing ephemeral, which bade us squint upwards to another and indefinite existence.—We must not strive after distant and unknown states of bliss and blessings and acts of grace, but must live so that we would fain live again and live for ever so, to all eternity!—Our duty is present with us every instant. . . . We must implant the love of life, the love of every man's own life in every conceivable way! . . . This life is thy eternal life! . . .

This doctrine is lenient towards those who do not believe in it. It speaks of no hells and it contains no threats. He who does not believe in it has but a fleeting life in his consciousness. . . .

Let us guard against teaching such a doctrine as if it were a suddenly discovered religion! It must percolate through slowly, and whole generations must build on it and become fruitful through it,—in order that it may grow into a large tree which will shelter all posterity.

"Eternal Recurrence"

THOMAS EDISON (1847–1931)
American Inventor

[Edison was one of the early members of the Theosophical Society.[1] During his last illness reporters inquired if he believed in survival after death. He answered: "The only survival I can conceive is to start a new earth cycle again" (*St. Louis Star-Times*). On his eightieth birthday he was asked: "Do you believe man has a soul?" His reply was: "No one understands that man is not a unit of life. He is as dead as granite. The unit of life is composed of swarms of billions of highly charged entities which live in the cells. I believe that when a man dies, this swarm deserts the body and goes out into space, but keeps on and enters another cycle of life and is immortal."[2] In *The Diary and Sundry Observations of Thomas Alva Edison*,[3] Edison expanded these views, stating:]

I cannot believe for a moment that life in the first instance originated on this insignificant little ball which we call the earth . . . The particles which combined to evolve living creatures on this planet of ours probably came from some other body elsewhere in the universe. . . . The more we learn the more we realize that there is life in things which we used to regard as inanimate, as lifeless. . . .

[1] Art. "The Cycle Moveth," *Lucifer*. London, March, 1890, p. 8.
[2] R. F. Goudey, *Reincarnation a Universal Truth*. Los Angeles: Aloha Press, 1928, pp. 120–121.
[3] New York: Philosophical Library, 1948, pp. 235–236.

I don't believe for a moment that one life makes another life. Take our own bodies. I believe they are composed of myriads and myriads of infinitesimally small individuals, each in itself a unit of life, and that these units work in squads—or swarms, as I prefer to call them—and that these infinitesimally small units live forever. When we "die" these swarms of units, like a swarm of bees, so to speak, betake themselves elsewhere, and go on functioning in some other form or environment.

Diary and Sundry Observations

BERNARD BOSANQUET (1848–1923)
British Philosopher and Writer

[From Bosanquet's Gifford Lectures, 1912, published as *Value and Destiny of the Individual*:[1]]

[Metempsychosis has been] of enormous influence in the history of philosophy and religion. . . . It is, I am convinced, the form which Plato preferred to give to his working conceptions of human survival, and, in shapes largely borrowed and spiritualized from Oriental tradition, it is exceedingly popular today. Dr. McTaggart's advocacy of it on strict philosophical grounds is familiar to students. . . . In the doctrine of metempsychosis . . . the bare subject or ego, the naked form of personality, the soul-thing is supposed to persist; but no content of the personality goes with it. We are offered chains of personalities linked together by impersonal transitions. We need only point out in passing the difficulty, which Aristotle put his finger on, in the conception of an identical soul animating wholly different bodies in succession. . . .

Advocates of [metempsychosis] point to the fact that character and the principles of knowledge can persist in the soul through intervals of oblivion and unconsciousness, wholly apart from specific memories of the incidents of their acquisition. Why, it is asked, should they not persist from life to life, as they persist from day to day, and from youth to age, unimpaired by intervals of unconsciousness and by the loss of particular memories? Such a conception affords, to minds of any elevation, a motive for self-improvement which for them is all the stronger that it is wholly divorced from ideas of a personal self-satisfaction in a future world. . . .

[As to the theory of creationism] I may draw attention here to a difficulty which Mr. Bradley mentions, nearly following Plato, *Rep.* 611 A. "A constant supply of new souls, none of which ever perished, would obviously land us in an insoluble difficulty" (the universe being held incapable of

[1] London: Macmillan, 1913, pp. 267–268.

increase) (*Appearance*, ed. 2, 502). It would follow that some souls must perish, or be used over again as in metempsychosis.

Value and Destiny of the Individual
Gifford Lectures, 1912

LUTHER BURBANK (1849–1926)
American Horticulturist

[From *Our Beloved Infidel*, the biography of Luther Burbank, by Frederick Clampett:[1]]

In no phase of his religious belief is Luther Burbank less understood and more inaccurately reported than that pertaining to the subject of personal immortality. . . . In the long procession of distinguished scientists and scholars . . . who traveled the well-worn path to the door of Luther Burbank's cottage were many Hindu leaders and disciples of the Vedanta philosophy of India. So close was the bond between their philosophy of life and that of Burbank that a hospitable welcome always awaited them. . . . It may safely be affirmed that the inspiring motive of his desire to master the Vedantic theory of reincarnation had no connection with a yearning after personal immortality . . . [Rather] he was deeply interested in the claim that reincarnation was based on evolution, and in the sequel to that claim that reincarnation was founded on the law of cause and effect. . . . [thus] his own hesitation in affirming a belief in the pre-existence of soul . . . was the logical outcome of a life trained to slow methods in the field of science. If his life-work had placed restraint upon his judgment in things mortal, how much more in things immortal! . . . Often had he seen life portrayed, he professed to me, as did Walt Whitman in his *Leaves of Grass*, when he said:

As to you, Life, I reckon you are the leavings of many deaths;
No doubt I have died, myself ten thousand times before.

Our Beloved Infidel

SIGMUND FREUD (1856–1939)
Austrian Psychiatrist and Psychoanalyst

To anyone who listened to us [in the West] we were prepared to maintain that death was the necessary outcome of life. . . . In reality, however, we . . . showed an unmistakable tendency to put death on one side, to eliminate it from life. . . . The complement to this cultural and conventional

[1] New York: Macmillan, 1926, pp. 107, 117–119.

attitude towards death is provided by our complete collapse when death has struck down someone whom we love. . . . But this attitude . . . towards death has a powerful effect on our lives. Life is impoverished . . . when the highest stake in the game of living, life itself, may not be risked. . . . We dare not contemplate a great many undertakings which are dangerous . . . . It is an inevitable result of all this that we should seek in the world of fiction, in literature and in the theatre compensation for what has been lost in life. . . . In the realm of fiction we find the plurality of lives which we need. We die with the hero . . . yet we survive him and are ready to die again just as safely with another hero. . . .

When primeval man saw someone who belonged to him die . . . then, in his pain, he was forced to learn that one can die, too, and his whole being revolted against the admission. . . . So he devised a compromise: he conceded the fact of his own death . . . but denied it the significance of annihilation. . . . His persisting memory of the dead became the basis for assuming other forms of existence and gave him the conception of a life continuing after apparent death.

These subsequent existences were at first no more than appendages to the existence which death had brought to a close—shadowy, empty of content, and valued at little. . . . It was only later that religions succeeded in representing this after-life as the more desirable, the truly valid one. . . . After this it was no more than consistent to extend life backwards into the past, to form the notion of earlier existences, of the transmigration of souls and of reincarnation, all with the purpose of depriving death of its meaning as the termination of life.

"Thoughts for the Times on War and Death" [1]

[As we have seen in Part Four and elsewhere in the present work,[2] anthropologists and other researchers tend to find pre-existence and rebirth to be the *first* conception of immortality embraced by ancient man, not simply an afterthought as the great psychiatrist would have us believe. To primeval man the mystery of birth was evidently as important as the mystery of death, and had first to be solved before the latter could be understood.]

The Cambridge Reincarnationists

By a happy coincidence of proximity of birth dates, the three individuals next to be considered are G. Lowes Dickinson, John McTaggart (both of Cambridge University), and W. Macneile Dixon, whose Gifford Lectures

---

[1] *The Standard Edition of the Complete Psychological Works of Sigmund Freud.* London: Hogarth Press, 1957, XIV, 289–295.
[2] See Index under "Antiquity of Reincarnation Belief."

have been extensively quoted in the Introduction. Their efforts to revive reincarnation philosophy in Western thought are reminiscent of the work of the seventeenth-century Cambridge Platonists already considered. Perhaps it is not by chance, then, that in the present section Cambridge seems particularly well represented, for in addition to McTaggart and Dickinson, are to be found James Ward, Francis Cornford, C. D. Broad, Alban Widgery, and A. C. Ewing.

G. LOWES DICKINSON (1862–1932)
British Humanist and Philosopher

[From Dickinson's Ingersoll Lecture on Immortality, delivered at Harvard University in 1909, under the title "Is Immortality Desirable?":]

The scientific denial of immortality is based upon the admitted fact of the connection between mind and brain, when it is assumed that death of the brain must involve death of that, whatever it be, which has been called soul. This may indeed be true, but it is not necessarily or obviously true; it does not follow logically from the fact of the connection. . . . The soul, as Plato thought, may be capable of existing without the body, though it be imprisoned in it as in a tomb. It looks out, we might suppose, through the window of the senses; and its vision is obscured or distorted by every imperfection of the glass. "If a man is shut up in a house," Dr. McTaggart has remarked, "the transparency of the windows is an essential condition of his seeing the sky. But," he wittily adds, "it would not be prudent to infer that if he walked out of the house he could not see the sky, because there was no longer any glass through which he might see it." . . . That the soul therefore dies with the brain is an inference, and quite possibly a mistaken one. If to some minds it seems inevitable, that may be as much due to a defect of their imagination as to a superiority of their judgment. . . .

It may be held that life, as we know it, is so desirable that though it would not be a good thing to prolong it indefinitely, it would be a good thing to repeat it over and over again. That we may treat this notion fairly, I will ask you to suppose that in none of these repetitions is there any memory of the previous cycles; for every one, I expect, would agree that the repetition of a life, every episode of which is remembered to have occurred before is a prospect of appalling tediousness. Supposing, however, that memory were extinguished at each death, we have a position that may be worth examining. It is, as many of you will remember, the position of that remarkable man of genius, Nietzsche; and, if only for that reason, deserves a moment's consideration . . . [He said:] "Oh! How could I fail to be eager for eternity, and for the marriage ring of rings, the ring of recurrence? . . . For I love thee, O eternity!" [1]

Do we, too, love this eternity? The answer seems plain. So far as a man judges any life, his own or another's, to be valuable, here and now, in and for itself, apart from any consideration of immortality, he will reasonably desire that it should be repeated as often as possible, rather than occur once and never again; for the positive value he finds in it will be reproduced in each repetition. On the other hand, so far as he finds any life in itself not to be valuable, or that its value depends upon some other kind of immortality, the prospect held out by Nietzsche will leave him cold or fill him with dismay. . . . But at this point it may really be more modest to say "I," to tell you simply how I feel, and to ask you whether you feel the same.

I find, then, that, to me, in my present experience, the thing that at bottom matters most is the sense I have of something in me making for more life and better. All my pain is at last a feeling of the frustration of this; all my happiness a feeling of its satisfaction. I do not know what that is; I am not prepared to give a coherent account of it; I ought not, very likely, to call it "it," and to imply the category of substance. I will abandon, if necessary, under criticism, any particular terms in which I may try to describe it; I will abandon anything except Itself. For it is real. It governs all my experience, and determines all my judgments of value. If pleasure hampers it, I do not desire pleasure; if pain furthers it, I do desire pain. And what I feel in myself, I infer in others. If I may be allowed to use that ambiguous and question-begging word "soul," then I agree with the poet Browning that "little else is worth study save the development of soul." This is to me the bottom fact of experience. And no one can go any further with me in my argument who does not find in my words an indication, however imperfect, of something which he knows, in his own life, to be real.

What, then, is it that this which I call the "soul" seeks? It seeks what is good; but it does not know what is the ultimate Good. As a seventeenth-century writer has well put it: "We love we know not what, and therefore everything allures us. As iron at a distance is drawn by the loadstone, there being some invisible communication between them, so is there in us a world of Love to somewhat, though we know not what in the world that should be. There are invisible ways of conveyance by which some great thing doth touch our souls, and by which we tend to it. Do you not feel yourself drawn by the expectation and desire of some great thing?" [2]

This "great thing" it is our business to find out by experience. We do

---

[1] *Thus Spake Zarathustra*, translated by A. Tille.
[2] Thomas Traherne, *Centuries of Meditation*, p. 3.

find many good things, but there are always other and better beyond. That is why it is hazardous to fix one's ideal, and say finally, "This or that would be heaven." For we may find, as the voyagers did in Browning's "Paracelsus," that the real heaven lies always beyond; beyond each Good we may attain here; but also, which is my present point, beyond death. The whole strength of the case for immortality, as a thing to be desired, lies in the fact that no one in this life attains his ideal. The soul, even of the best and most fortunate of us, does not achieve the Good of which she feels herself to be capable and in which alone she can rest. The potentiality is not fully realized. I do not infer from this that life has no value if the Beyond is cut off. . . . But what I do maintain is that life here would have indefinitely more value if we knew that beyond death we should pursue, and ultimately to a successful issue, the elusive ideal of which we are always in quest.

"Is Immortality Desirable?" [3]

JOHN MCTAGGART ELLIS MCTAGGART
(1866–1925)
British Philosopher

[By the time he was twenty-five, McTaggart had gained the reputation of being the most distinguished dialectician and metaphysician since Hegel. In 1897 he became Lecturer in the Moral Sciences at Trinity College, Cambridge. C. D. Broad, who after McTaggart's death succeeded him at Cambridge, declared that his system was the work of genius which places its author "in the front rank of the great historical philosophers," and one that "may quite fairly be compared with the *Enneads* of Plotinus, the *Ethics* of Spinoza, and the *Encyclopædia* of Hegel." [1]

The selections below are from Part II of McTaggart's small volume *Human Immortality and Pre-existence*,[2] which originally formed part of his larger work *Some Dogmas of Religion* (1906).]

If we succeed in proving immortality, it will be by means of considerations which would also prove pre-existence. I do not see how existence in future time could be shown to be necessary in the case of any being whose existence in past time is admitted not to be necessary. If the universe got on without me a hundred years ago, what reason could be given for denying that it might get on without me a hundred years hence? . . .

---

[3] G. Lowes Dickinson, *Religion and Immortality.* Cambridge, Mass.: Houghton, Mifflin, 1911.

[1] *Proceedings of the British Academy*, 1927.
[2] London: Edward Arnold, 1915.

Even the best men are not, when they die, in such a state of intellectual and moral perfection as would fit them to enter heaven immediately. . . . This is generally recognized, and one of two alternatives is commonly adopted to meet it. The first is that some tremendous improvement—an improvement out of all proportion to any which can ever be observed in life—takes place at the moment of death. . . . The other and more probable alternative is that the process of gradual improvement can go on in each of us after the death of our present bodies. . . .

Now it might be said that our chief ground for hoping for a progressive improvement after death would be destroyed if memory periodically ceased [when we are reborn]. Death, it might be argued, would not only remove us from the field of our activity, but would deprive us of all memory of what we had done, and therefore whatever was gained in one life would be lost at death. We could no more hope for a permanent improvement than a man on the treadmill can hope to end higher than he started. . . .

We must ask, therefore, what elements of value are carried on by memory from the present to the future. And then we must consider whether they can be carried on *without* memory.

I think I shall be in agreement with most people when I say that memory is chiefly of value in our lives in three ways. In the first place, it may make us wiser. The events which we have seen, and the conclusions at which we have arrived, may be preserved in memory, and so add to our present knowledge. In the second place, it may make us more virtuous. The memory of a temptation, whether it has been resisted or successful, may under various circumstances help us in resisting present temptation. In the third place, it may tell us that people with whom we are now related are the people whom we have loved in the past, and this may enter as an element into our present love of them. . . . If the past could help the present in a like manner *without* the aid of memory, the absence of memory need not destroy the chance of an improvement spreading over many lives.

Let us consider wisdom first. Can we be wiser by reason of something which we have forgotten? Unquestionably we can. Wisdom is not merely, or chiefly, amassed facts, or even recorded judgments. It depends primarily on a mind qualified to deal with facts, and to form judgments. Now the acquisition of knowledge and experience, if wisely conducted, may strengthen the mind. Of that we have sufficient evidence in this life. And so a man who dies after acquiring knowledge—and all men acquire some— might enter his new life, deprived indeed of his knowledge, but not deprived of the increased strength and delicacy of mind which he had gained in acquiring the knowledge. And, if so, he will be wiser in the second life because of what has happened in the first. Of course he loses something in losing the actual knowledge. . . . And is not even this loss really a gain? For the mere accumulation of knowledge, if memory never ceased, would soon become overwhelming, and worse than useless. . . .

With virtue the point is perhaps clearer. For the memory of moral experiences is of no value to virtue except in so far as it helps to form the moral character, and, if this is done, the loss of the memory would be no loss to virtue. Now we cannot doubt that a character may remain determined by an event which has been forgotten. I have forgotten the greater number of the good and evil acts which I have done in my present life. And yet each must have left a trace on my character. And so a man may carry over into his next life the dispositions and tendencies which he has gained by the moral contests of this life. . . .

There remains love. The problem here is more important, if, as I believe, it is in love, and in nothing else, that we find not only the supreme value of life, but also the supreme reality of life, and, indeed, of the universe. . . . Much has been forgotten in any friendship which has lasted for several years within the limits of a single life—many confidences, many services, many hours of happiness and sorrow. But they have not passed away without leaving their mark on the present. They contribute, though they are forgotten, to the present love which is not forgotten. In the same way, if the whole memory of the love of a life is swept away at death, its value is not lost if the same love is stronger in a new life because of what passed before. . . .

The chance of a love recurring in any future life, must depend primarily on the conditions which determine where and how the lovers are born in the future life. For if memory does not survive death, it will be impossible for love to occur in any life in which people do not meet. If the conditions which determine the circumstances of our birth, and through them our juxtapositions throughout life, were themselves determined by chance, or by some merely mechanical external necessity, the probability of meeting our friends in another life would be too small to be regarded. . . . If immortality is to give us an assurance or a hope of progressive improvement, it can only be if we have reason to believe that the interests of spirit are so predominant a force in the universe that they will find, in the long run, satisfaction in the universe. And, in this case, the constitution of the universe would be such that, whether with or without memory, love would have its way. . . .[3]

[3] In a letter, dated August, 1804, to a Miss Bird in New Zealand, McTaggart wrote: "I can't help thinking it probable that people who meet once will meet often on the way up. That they should meet at all seems to show that they must be connected with the same part of the pattern of things, and if so they would probably often be

The most effective way of proving that the doctrine of preexistence is bound up with the doctrine of immortality would be to prove directly that the nature of man was such that it involved a life both before and after the present life. But . . . such a demonstration, if it is possible at all, as I believe it to be, would be far beyond the scope of this book, since it would involve a determination of some of the most fundametal characteristics of reality. . . . In the nine years which have passed since I first wrote these pages, I have become more firmly convinced that the nature of reality can be shown to be such as to justify a belief both in immortality and in preexistence. I hope at some future time to publish my grounds for this conviction, as part of a treatise on the general question of the fundamental nature of reality.

Human Immortality and Pre-Existence

[Dr. McTaggart fulfilled this hope in his two-volume work *The Nature of Existence*.[4] Dr. Broad writes: "If subtle analysis, rigid reasoning and constructive fertility, applied with tireless patience to the hardest and deepest problems of metaphysics, and expressed in language which always enlightens the intellect and sometimes touches the emotions, be a title to philosophical immortality, then McTaggart has fully earned his place among the immortals by *The Nature of Existence*."[5] As one reads the selections that follow,[6] it becomes apparent how far removed the author was from the plane of wishful thinking.]

Let us turn from the effect of the loss of memory to the more general question of the effect of a plurality of lives. If there is such a plurality extending over a long future, our prospects after leaving our present bodies have possibilities of evil much greater than those generally admitted by theories of immortality which reject . . . the possibility of an endless hell. Such theories hold, in some cases, that we shall pass immediately at death to a state of complete and endless beatitude. . . .

We have, however, no right, on the view which we have taken, to share this optimism as to the immediate temporal future. The temporal future will consist of a greater number of successive lives. It is true that, in the long run, the later will be better than the earlier. But the rate of im-

---

working together. Very fanciful, no doubt, but more probable than thinking that it goes by chance, like sand grains in a heap, which is what one thinks in these scientific days, unless one thinks for oneself." (*J. McT. E. McTaggart* by G. Lowes Dickinson, Cambridge, 1931, p. 37.) (Eds.)
[4] Cambridge University Press, 1921, 1927.
[5] G. Lowes Dickinson, *J. McT. E. McTaggart*, p. 128.
[6] II, 396–397, 479.

provement may be very slow—so slow that it might be imperceptible for centuries—and it may be broken by periods of oscillation in which a man was actually in a worse condition than he had been previously. With regard to knowledge, to virtue, and to love, we have no ground for supposing that improvement will not be very slow, and that it will not be broken by intervals of deterioration. And with regard to happiness, there is no form of suffering which history records to have happened in the past, which may not lie in the path of any one of us in the future. . . . The universe has evil in it—that is beyond doubt. . . . All that we can say is that this evil, however great it may be, is only passing. . . . The very greatness of the evil which we endure gives us some slight anticipation of the greatness of the good which outweighs it infinitely. . . .

The prospect of many such lives as ours has [also] a bright as well as a dark aspect. . . . Such life as ours now, in which sin jostles with virtue, and doubt with confidence, and hatred with love, cannot satisfy us, but it can teach us a great deal—far more than can be learned between a single birth and a single death. Not only because the time is so short, but because there are so many things which are incompatible within a single life. No man can learn fully in one life the lessons of unbroken health and of bodily sickness, of riches and of poverty, of study and action, of comradeship and of isolation, of defiance and of obedience, of virtue and of vice. And yet they are all so good to learn. Is it not worth much to be able to hope that what we have missed in one life may come to us in another?

And though the way is long, it can be no more wearisome than a single life. For with death we leave behind us memory and old age, and fatigue. We may die old but we shall be born young. And death acquires a deeper and more gracious significance when we regard it as part of the continually recurring rhythm of progress—as inevitable, as natural, and as benevolent as sleep.

The Nature of Existence

W. MACNEILE DIXON (1866–1946)
British Philosopher and Educator

[The paragraphs below complete the reincarnation selections from Dixon's Gifford Lectures presented in the Introduction, and expand the just-expressed views of Dr. McTaggart as to the purpose of rebirths.]

It is Plato's doctrine, and none more defensible, that the soul before it entered the realm of Becoming existed in the universe of Being. Released

[at death] from the region of time and space, it returns to its former abode
. . . into communion with itself. After a season of quiet "alone with the
Alone," of assimilation of its earthly experiences and memories, refreshed
and invigorated, it is seized again by the desire for further trials of its
strength, further knowledge of the universe, the companionship of former
friends, by the desire to keep in step and on the march with the moving
world. There it seeks out and once more animates a body, the medium of
communication with its fellow travellers, and sails forth in that vessel upon
a new venture in the ocean of Becoming. . . .

Our lives are part of the universe and will last as long, but we must
wait for the secrets of the history to come. . . . And before we can attain
to that final harmony between the universe and ourselves, to which we look
forward as the consummation of existence, how much we have to learn
about both! In respect of our true natures, of what in truth we are and are
capable of becoming, to what heights in knowledge, wisdom, power, the
soul can climb, of all this science and philosophy have so far hardly yet
spoken. Nor can any boundary be set, any "Thus far and no farther" to the
expansion of the mind. In our present life we have acquired at the most the
alphabet of this knowledge; and as for the universe, of the modes of existence and happiness of what it permits, of its possibilities as an abode for
progressive beings like ourselves, we know less than nothing, and no single
life could teach us what they may be. Nor can any reason be advanced why
we should not in the end become its masters, mould it to our hearts' desires, and make of it a home, the natural and happy estate of the immortal
spirits to whom it indefeasibly belongs.

The Human Situation

GUSTAVE GELEY (1868–1924)
French Physician

[The book under consideration is Geley's *From the Unconscious to the
Conscious*, translated by Stanley de Brath.[1] In addition to his medical research activities, Dr. Geley was Director of the Institut Metapsychique International, having been selected for the post by Charles Richet, Camille
Flammarion, and other French scientists. Among the propositions which
the volume seeks to establish are: "(1) That which is 'essential' in the
universe is eternal and indestructible; permanent through all the transitory
appearances of things. (2) That which is essential in the universe passes, by
evolution, from the unconscious to the conscious. (3) Individual con-

[1] New York: Harper and Row, 1920.

sciousness is an integral part of that which is essential in the universe, and itself indestructible and eternal, it evolves from unconsciousness to consciousness."]

Starting without preconceived ideas, and proceeding to the study of subconscious psychology without heed to the formulae and dogmas of classical teaching, we experience a great surprise. The subconscious appears as the very essence of individual psychology. That which is most important in the individual psychism is subconscious. The foundation of the Self, its characteristic qualities, are subconscious. All the innate capacities are subconscious; likewise the higher faculties—intuition, talents, genius, artistic or creative inspiration. . . . The greater part of [these faculties] escape from the will . . . and show their existence only by bringing to light intermittent and apparently spontaneous results. This subconscious psychic activity, powerful in itself, is reinforced by a still more potent and infallible memory which leaves the feeble and limited conscious memory far behind. . . . No remembrance, no vital or psychological experience is lost. . . .

All conscious acquisitions are assimilated and transmuted into faculties. This is noticeable in the course of existence. . . . Psychological progress can be the result only of this transmutation of knowledge into faculties. And this transmutation is subconscious. It does not take place among the unstable and ephemeral cerebral molecules; it necessitates a deep-seated and continuous elaboration in the essential and permanent part of the being; that is, in his subconscious dynamo-psychism. Thus the perpetual disintegration of the conscious personality is of small importance. The permanent subconscious individuality retains the indelible remembrance of all the states of consciousness which have built it up. From these states of consciousness which it has assimilated it constructs new capacities. . . .

Since then in the course of our existence we find the origin of a part only of the contents of subconsciousness, it is at least permissible to seek the remainder in anterior experiences. . . . It is not hard to understand how the essential dynamo-psychism objectifying itself in new organic representations should retain the deep memory of experiences realized in previous representations. If in place of a single existence, we include a series of successive existences, the acquisition of consciousness by the primitive unconsciousness can readily be understood. . . . It is thus that the living being passes little by little from unconsciousness to consciousness. Against this inference of rebirth, no objections of a scientific kind can be raised. We may seek in vain for a single one in the whole stock of knowledge. Forgetfulness of previous existences has but slight importance for modern science. Remembrance plays but a secondary part in normal psychology; forgetfulness is habitual and is the rule. . . .

On the other hand, above this cerebral memory is the subconscious memory—the infallible memory of the true and complete individuality, [which] is indestructible as the being itself. In this essential memory there are engraved permanently all the events of the present life, and all the remembrances and conscious acquisitions of the vast series of antecedent lives.

In the light of the . . . propositions just stated, individual evolution can be understood and all naturalistic and philosophical problems relating to the individual can be resolved. No doubt from the metaphysical point of view the concept gives a large range to hypothesis, but from the psychological standpoint, there is no enigma on which it does not shed light.

From the Unconscious to the Conscious[2]

MOHANDAS K. GANDHI (1869–1948)
Indian Social Philosopher, Apostle of Nonviolence

[From *Gandhi's Letters to a Disciple*,[1] the disciple being Madeleine Slade, a British Admiral's daughter who renounced position and comfort to follow Gandhi:]

The more I observe and study things, the more convinced I become that sorrow over separation and death is perhaps the greatest delusion. To realize that it is a delusion is to become free. There is no death, no separation of the substance. And yet the tragedy of it is that though we love friends for the substance we recognize in them, we deplore the destruction of the insubstantial that covers the substance for the time being. Whereas real friendship should be used to reach the whole through the fragment. You seem to have got the truth for the moment. Let it abide forever. . . .

What you say about rebirth is sound. It is nature's kindness that we do not remember past births. Where is the good either of knowing in detail the numberless births we have gone through? Life would be a burden if we carried such a tremendous load of memories. A wise man deliberately forgets many things, even as a lawyer forgets the cases and their details as soon as they are disposed of. Yes, "death is but a sleep and a forgetting." . . .

[Your] Mother is slowly going. It will be well if the end comes soon. It is better to leave a body one has outgrown. To wish to see the dearest ones as long as possible in the flesh is a selfish desire and it comes out of

[2] Pp. 122–123, 225–226, 299.

[1] New York: Harper and Row, 1950, pp. 31, 87, 89.

weakness or want of faith in the survival of the soul after the dissolution of the body. The form ever changes, ever perishes, the informing spirit neither changes nor perishes. True love consists in transferring itself from the body to the dweller within and then necessarily realizing the oneness of all life inhabiting numberless bodies.

Gandhi's Letters to a Disciple

If for mastering the physical sciences you have to devote a whole lifetime, how many lifetimes may be needed for mastering the greatest spiritual force that mankind has known? [2] For if this is the only permanent thing in life, if this is the only thing that counts, then whatever effort you bestow on mastering it is well spent.

Harijan, March 1936

Having flung aside the sword, there is nothing except the cup of love which I can offer to those who oppose me. It is by offering that cup that I expect to draw them close to me. I cannot think of permanent enmity between man and man, and believing as I do in the theory of rebirth, I live in the hope that if not in this birth, in some other birth I shall be able to hug all humanity in friendly embrace.

Young India, April 2, 1931, p. 54

D. T. SUZUKI (1870–1966)
Japanese Zen Buddhist Philosopher

[Alan Watts writes of this renowned university teacher: "What he said was always openended. . . . He rambled, he digressed, he dropped hints, he left you suspended in mid-air, he astonished you with his learning (which was prodigious) and yet charmed you with scholarship handled so lightly and unpretentiously. . . . Every so often his eyes twinkled as if he had seen the Ultimate Joke, and as if, out of compassion for those who had not, he were refraining from laughing out loud." Watts goes on to tell of Suzuki's address to the final meeting of the 1963 World Congress of Faiths in London. "The theme was 'The Supreme Spiritual Ideal,' and after several speakers had delivered themselves of volumes of hot air, Suzuki's turn came. . . . 'How can a humble person like myself talk about such a grand thing as the Supreme Spiritual Ideal? . . . Really I do not know what Spiritual is, what Ideal is, and what Supreme Spiritual Ideal is.' Whereupon he devoted the rest of his speech to a description of his house and garden in

---

[2] *Ahimsa*: harmlessness, nonviolence, universal compassion. (Eds.)

Japan, contrasting it with the life of a great city. This from the translator of the *Lankavatara Sutra!* And the audience gave him a standing ovation." [1] (In Part Two, Erich Fromm's enthusiastic comments were quoted regarding a week's conference of some fifty psychiatrists and psychologists with Dr. Suzuki, held under the auspices of the Medical School of the National University of Mexico, in Cuernavaca.)]

When the Master Daito saw the Emperor Godaigo (reigned 1318–1338) who was another student of Zen, the Master said, "We were parted many thousands of Kalpas ago, yet we have not been separated even for a moment. We are facing each other all day long, yet we have never met."

Here we have the same idea as expressed by [Buddha] himself in the *Saddharma-Pundarika.* . . . In spite of the historical fact that he attained Enlightenment near Buddhagaya at a definite moment of time, he says that he was fully enlightened even before the world was created. The historical fact of his Enlightenment is a record which we time-minded make with the intellect, because the intellect likes to divide, and cuts time into years and days and hours, and constructs history, whereas time itself underlying history knows no such human artificial cuttings. We are living partly in this time-space-conscious history but essentially in history-transcending time-space. Most of us would recognise the first, but not the second phase of our life. Daito the Master here wishes to remind the Emperor of this most fundamental experience. . . .

We are now in a position to say something about Karma. Human suffering is due to our being bound in Karma, for all of us, as soon as we are born, carry a heavy burden of past Karma. . . . In this sense, human beings are the only beings which have their Karma. All others move in accordance with the laws of their being, but it is human beings alone that can design and calculate and are conscious of themselves and of their doings. . . . From thinking, from thinking consciously, we develop the faculty of seeing, designing, and planning beforehand, which demonstrates that we are free, and not always bound by the "inevitable laws" of Nature. . . .

Not only are we wrapped up in our Karma but we know the fact that we are so wrapped up. . . . This very fact of our being aware of the Karma-bondage is the spiritual privilege of humanity. For this privilege, implying freedom, means our being able to transcend Karma. . . . We must make full use of it, and, accepting the Karma-bondage as far as it extends, reso-

---

[1] "The 'Mind-less' Scholar: A Memoir," *Bulletin of the Society for Comparative Philosophy*, Autumn, 1966.

lutely face all forms of suffering and thereby qualify ourselves for transcending them.

The Essence of Buddhism[2]

BERTRAND RUSSELL (1872–　)
British Mathematician and Philosopher

I find my boy still hardly able to grasp that there was a time when he did not exist; if I talk to him about the building of the Pyramids or some such topic, he always wants to know what he was doing then, and is merely puzzled when he is told that he did not exist. Sooner or later he will want to know what "being born" means, and then we shall tell him.

Education and the Good Life (Chap. 12)

FRANCIS M. CORNFORD (1874–1943)
British Philosopher, Cambridge University

The most primitive of these [cardinal doctrines of mysticism] is reincarnation (palingenesis). . . . This life, which is perpetually renewed, is reborn out of that opposite state, called "death," into which, at the other end of its arc, it passes again. In this idea of reincarnation . . . we have the first conception of a cycle of existence, a Wheel of Life, divided into two hemicycles of light and darkness, through which the one life, or soul, continuously revolves. . . . Caught in the wheel of Time, the soul, preserving its individual identity, passes through all shapes of life. This implies that man's soul is not "human"; human life is only one of the shapes it passes through. Its substance is divine and immutable, and it is the same substance as all other souls in the world. In this sense, the unity of all life is maintained; but, on the other hand, each soul is an atomic individual, which persists throughout its . . . cycle of reincarnations.

From Religion to Philosophy[1]

[Dr. Cornford's wife, the poet Frances Cornford, has written a delightful reincarnation poem entitled "Pre-existence." See *Reincarnation, An East-West Anthology*, p. 143.]

[2] London: Buddhist Society, 1947, pp. 27–30.
_____
[1] London: Edward Arnold, 1912, pp. 161, 229.

CARL G. JUNG (1875–1961)
Swiss Psychiatrist and Psychologist

[Volume 9 of Jung's *Collected Works*,[1] Part I, *Archetypes and the Collective Unconscious*, reprints his lecture, delivered at the Eranos Meeting of 1939, entitled "Concerning Rebirth" (revised 1950). After carefully defining five main types of rebirth, namely, metempsychosis, reincarnation, resurrection, rebirth within one life, and transformation, he concerns himself not with reincarnation as a philosophical and metaphysical truth, but with the psychology behind all these concepts of rebirth. Quoting from the lecture:[2]]

1. *Metempsychosis.* The first of the five aspects of rebirth to which I should like to draw attention is that of metempsychosis, or transmigration of souls. According to this view, one's life is prolonged in time by passing through different bodily existences; or, from another point of view, it is a life-sequence interrupted by different reincarnations. . . . It is by no means certain whether continuity of personality is guaranteed or not: there may be only a continuity of *karma*. . . .

2. *Reincarnation.* This concept of rebirth necessarily implies the continuity of personality. Here the human personality is regarded as continuous and accessible to memory, so that, when one is incarnated or born, one is able, at least potentially, to remember that one has lived through previous existences and that these existences were one's own, i.e., that they had the same ego-form as the present life. As a rule, reincarnation means rebirth in a human body. . . .

[Speaking generally of all the named forms of rebirth, Dr. Jung states:] Rebirth is not a process that we can in any way observe. We can neither measure nor weigh nor photograph it. It is entirely beyond sense perception. We have to do here with a purely *psychic* reality, which is transmitted to us only indirectly through personal statements. One speaks of rebirth; one professes rebirth; one is filled with rebirth. This we accept as sufficiently real. . . . I am of the opinion that the psyche is the most tremendous fact of human life. . . . The mere fact that people talk about rebirth, and that there is such a concept at all, means that a store of psychic experiences designated by that term must actually exist.

Rebirth is an affirmation that must be counted among the primordial

1 New York: Pantheon, 1959.
2 Pp. 113, 116–117.

affirmations of mankind. These primordial affirmations are based on what I call archetypes. . . . There must be psychic events underlying these affirmations which it is the business of psychology to discuss—without entering into all the metaphysical and philosophical assumptions regarding their significance.

"Concerning Rebirth"

[In the chapter "On Life After Death" in Jung's remarkable posthumous autobiography, *Memories, Dreams, Reflections*,[3] he says that hitherto he had "never written expressly about a life after death" but now he would like to state his ideas. "Perhaps one has to be close to death to acquire the necessary freedom to talk about it." Jung indicates, however, that most of his life he has pondered the subject and that all his works "are fundamentally nothing but attempts, ever renewed, to give an answer to the question of the interplay between the 'here' and the 'hereafter.' " [4] It is interesting to note that years ago he wrote in a commentary on an old Chinese text:

Death is psychologically just as important as birth, and . . . an integral part of life. It is not the psychologist who must be questioned as to what happens finally to the detached consciousness. Whatever theoretical position he assumed, he would hopelessly overstep the boundaries of his scientific competence. He can only point out that the views of our text with respect to the timelessness of the detached consciousness, are in harmony with the religious thought of all times and with that of the overwhelming majority of mankind. He can say, further, that anyone who does not think this way would stand outside the human order, and would, therefore, be suffering from a disturbance in his psychic equilibrium. As physician then, I make the greatest effort to fortify, so far as I have the power, a belief in immortality, especially in my older patients to whom such questions come menacingly near.[5]

In *Memories, Dreams, Reflections*[6] Jung informs us that he has listened attentively to the Indian teaching of reincarnation and looked around in the world of his own experience to find authentic signs justifying such a belief, for the idea must be demonstrated empirically before he could accept it. Nothing convincing in this respect could be discovered until recently he had a series of dreams which seemed to describe the process of reincarnation in a deceased person of his acquaintance. Since then he viewed the problem of rebirth in another light, though without being able to give a definite opinion. However, he writes in the same volume:[7]]

[3] New York: Pantheon, 1963.
[4] P. 299.
[5] *The Secret of the Golden Flower* (A Chinese Book of Life), trans. Richard Wilhelm, with Commentary by C. G. Jung. London: Kegan Paul, 1938, p. 124.
[6] P. 319.
[7] Pp. 291, 318–319, 321–322, 332–333.

My life as I lived it had often seemed to me like a story that has no beginning and no end. I had the feeling that I was a historical fragment, an excerpt for which the preceding and succeeding text was missing. . . . I could well imagine that I might have lived in former centuries and there encountered questions I was not yet able to answer; that I had to be born again because I had not fulfilled the task that was given to me. When I die, my deeds will follow along with me—that is how I imagine it. I will bring with me what I have done. In the meantime it is important to insure that I do not stand at the end with empty hands. . . .

The meaning of my existence is that life has addressed a question to me. Or, conversely, I myself am a question which is addressed to the world, and I must communicate my answer, for otherwise I am dependent upon the world's answer. That is a suprapersonal life task, which I accomplish only by effort and with difficulty. . . . My way of posing the question as well as my answer may be unsatisfactory. That being so, someone who has my karma—or I myself—would have to be reborn in order to give a more complete answer. It might happen that I would not be reborn again so long as the world needed no such answer, and that I would be entitled to several hundred years of peace until someone was once more needed who took an interest in these matters and could profitably tackle the task anew. I imagine that for a while a period of rest could ensue, until the stint I had done in my lifetime needed to be taken up again. . . .

It seems probable to me that in the hereafter . . . there exist certain limitations, but that the souls of the dead only gradually find out where the limits of the liberated state lie. Somewhere "out there" there must be a determinant, a necessity conditioning the world, which seeks to put an end to the after-death state. This creative determinant—so I imagine it—must decide what souls will plunge again into birth. Certain souls, I imagine, feel the state of three-dimensional existence to be more blissful than that of Eternity. But perhaps that depends upon how much of completeness or incompleteness they have taken across with them from their human existence. . . .

In my case it must have been primarily a passionate urge toward understanding which brought about my birth. For that is the strongest element in my nature. This insatiable drive toward understanding has, as it were, created a consciousness in order to know what is and what happens, and in order to piece together mythic conceptions from the slender hints of the unknowable. . . .

The old question posed by the Gnostics, "Whence comes evil?" has been given no answer by the Christian world. . . . Today we are compelled to meet that question; but we stand empty-handed, bewildered, and perplexed. . . . As the result of the political situation and the frightful, not to say diabolic triumphs of science, we are shaken by secret shudders and dark forebodings; but we know no way out, and a very few persons indeed draw the conclusion that this time the issue is the long-since-forgotten *soul of man.*

Memories, Dreams, Reflections

GUSTAF STRÖMBERG (1882–1962)
Swedish-American Astronomer and Physicist

[Albert Einstein wrote concerning Dr. Strömberg's book *The Soul of the Universe:* "What impressed me particularly was the successful attempt to pick out of the bewildering variety of researches that which is of essential value, and to present it in such a way that the concept of the Oneness of all knowledge can for the first time be stated with definite intent." According to the author, "the study is based mainly on facts from physics, biology, and physiology. The facts are well known to students, the new things lie in the emphasis, the viewpoints, and the interpretations." For these facts the reader must of course consult the book itself. Here we merely present the conclusions on immortaity and reincarnation, taken from chapter eleven, entitled "The Soul," to be followed by excerpts from Strömberg's later work *The Searchers* where he speaks more affirmatively as to rebirth. *The Soul of the Universe* was published originally by David McKay.[1] A paperback was issued in 1965 by Educational Research Institute.[2]]

There is no doubt about the existence of the human *soul* if we define it properly. The human soul is in the first place the *ego* of the human being, a perceiving, feeling, willing, thinking and remembering entity. It is, for instance, not a set of memories, but the possessor of a particular group of memories, most of which never rise to the level of consciousness. . . . The soul is something which gives unity to the mental complex of a man. That such a unity should be recognized and given a name was felt very early in the history of mankind. Although the "observation" of this unity is not made with the aid of our sense organs, it must, nevertheless, be regarded as valid; in fact, this observation is more direct than ordinary sense observations which only give us shadow pictures of the external world. We have become so accustomed to this unity within ourselves that it takes a mental effort to describe it in proper terms and to realize its significance. . . .

[1] New York: 1940.
[2] North Hollywood, Calif.

Our memories are indelibly "engraved" in our brain field, that is, the electrical field which determines the structure and functions of our brain. By analogy we conclude that our brain field, and the "memory genie" associated with it, contract in unchanged form [at death] and disappear from the physical world, that is, the world of matter, radiation and force fields. Where does the brain field go to? Presumably it goes back to the same world from which it originally came. Since it no longer has any size, or at least any definable size, its properties can not be described in the language used in the science of physics. In other words, it disappears into a *nonphysical world*. . . .

The realization of this "principle of conservation of mental categories" led to the theory of the nature and origin of mental qualities described earlier in this book. This theory has an important relationship to Plato's idea of a *recollection* by our soul of conditions in the world from which it originally came. The conclusion at which we arrive is that in the non-physical world to which we return at death, there is the space and time of our perception, but not the metrical space and time of physics. . . . There are therefore good reasons for making the following important assertion: *A soul is indestructible and immortal. It carries an indelible record of all its activities*. . . .

Some souls have had a few years of development on earth, while others are completely blank; they are nothing but potentialities. The opportunities for development differ tremendously among different souls. If we assume that the earthly development has a *meaning*, an ulterior purpose, our inherent sense of justice tells us that it would be unfair for the different souls as individual entities to have such unequal opportunities, even if we do not consider the apparent waste involved in the unsuccessful emergence of so many undeveloped souls. Furthermore, the earthly development of most human souls is far from inspiring. The lack of opportunity from which the majority of people suffer while on earth leads to the hypothesis of a development after death. This development probably takes place in a "form" which can not be described in terms based on the present mental characteristics of the human race. Perhaps it may take the form of a new earthly or planetary incarnation, or in the permanent or temporary submergence of our souls in the realm beyond space and time.

Opinions differ whether human souls can be reincarnated on the earth or not. In 1936 a very interesting case was thoroughly investigated and reported by the governmental authorities in India. A girl (Shanti Devi from Delhi) could accurately describe her previous life (at Muttra, five hundred miles from Delhi) which ended about a year before her "second birth." She gave the name of her husband and child and described her home and life history. The investigating commission brought her to her former relatives, who verified all her statements. Among the people of India reincarnations are regarded as commonplace; the astonishing thing for them in this case was the great number of facts the girl remembered. This and similar cases can be regarded as additional evidence for the theory of the indestructibility of memory. . . .

Many questions could be asked, but our observations tell us very little. We must have recourse to intuitions, although naturally great caution must be exercised. It is difficult to estimate [their] value . . . because in general they can not be subjected to unequivocal tests. But having realized the existence of a world beyond space and time where ideas have their origin we see them in a new light.

The Soul of the Universe

The question whether or not the world is what it looks like has been asked by thinking men since time immemorial. . . . Most men of the present time are *realists* who claim that the world is what it appears to be to their sense organs, and they are interested in action and not in speculation about ultimate things. . . . There are also men of another type who regard the material objects of the realist as fleeting *phenomena* in their own minds. Plato was perhaps the first to give these ideas a systematic form. His philosophy was characterized by a certain contempt for a knowledge directly derived from our senses. The real world is not a world of matter, but a world of *ideas*. Our mind is able to discover and to study this world behind that of our sense perceptions, because our soul, that is, the personality behind our mind, is born with a true knowledge of fundamental realities. This knowledge is in a subconscious form, but by intellectual efforts, stimulated and aided by observations, we can bring it up to the level of consciousness. Then, and only then, do we know something about the real nature of the world and about the meaning of our own lives. . . .

Our real selves, our souls, belong before our birth, during our organic life and after our death to the non-physical world. . . . All the memories of our last and our previous lives can be reviewed [there] in full details in an instant, since there are no atoms which in the physical world block and slow down all our mental activities. . . . (The atoms form a screen or veil that makes it possible for us to concentrate on the immediate requirements of our earthly life. When this veil disappears at death, our memories from this and perhaps from earlier lives crowd in upon us without hindrance, tormenting us or blessing us). . . . The memories of the cruel acts we have committed against men and animals follow us through eternity. The victims of a tyrant are all there, and the memories of their suffering haunt their oppressor. The torment he suffers will probably produce a strong urge in his mind to make a new "emersion" into the physical world, partly in order to escape temporarily from the pangs of his conscience and partly to make an attempt to improve his record. . . .

(I am convinced that we live in eternity now, but like an unborn child we are in deep sleep. Occasionally we have lucid moments when we realize that the world is not what it looks like. When we really wake up we may find eternity dimly spread out in front of us and our past clearly distinguishable behind us.)

The Searchers[3]

HERMANN WEYL (1885–1955)
German Mathematician

[Dr. Weyl is well known for his work in relativity theory, quantum mechanics, differential equations, and the philosophy of mathematics. He taught for many years at Princeton University. The following is from *The Open World*,[1] lectures on the metaphysical implications of science.]

Physics has never given support to that truly consistent determinism which maintains the unconditioned necessity of everything which happens. . . . Kant's solution of the dilemma [regarding free will and determinism] can only be carried through honestly if one believes in the existence of the individual from eternity to eternity, in the form of a Leibniz monad, say, or by metempsychosis as the Indians and Schopenhauer believe. Nevertheless, it is of sufficient importance that physics has always admitted a loophole in the necessity of Nature.

The Open World

SIR JULIAN HUXLEY (1887–   )
British Biologist

Egg and sperms carry the destiny of the generations. The egg realizes one chance combination out of an infinity of possibilities: and it is confronted with millions of pairs of sperms, each one actually different in the combination of cards which it holds. Then comes the final moment in the drama—

---

[3] New York: David McKay, 1948, pp. ix, 198–199, 237–238. The two extracts placed in parentheses are the remarks of one of Strömberg's characters in this dialogue story. All the rest is Dr. Strömberg himself speaking, either in the introduction or epilogue.

[1] Yale University Press, 1932, pp. 45–46.

the marriage of egg and sperm to produce the beginning of a large individual. . . . Here too, it seems to be entirely a matter of chance which
particular union of all the millions of possible unions shall be consummated. One might have produced a genius, another a moron . . . and so
on. . . . With a realization of all that this implies, we can banish from
human thought a host of fears and superstitions. No basis now remains for
any doctrine of metempsychosis.

What Dare I Think [1]

[A reported conversation between Sir Julian and the Irish writer George
Russell (Æ), concerning Russell's supposed remembrances of former
lives:]

One evening it was about the intuitions he had had of his own incarnations that [Æ] talked. "They tell me that my recollections and visions are
ancestral memories—a mere phrase. I talked to Julian Huxley about it
once. You tell me, I said, that a man cannot transmit musical knowledge, or
a language he has mastered, or a craft, to his children? No, he said, you may
transmit a tendency, but everything has to be learnt afresh. And yet you tell
me, I said, that when I get a glimpse of strange cities and buildings I have
never seen, vivid and alive in every detail, the figures in the streets, the
sharp shadows, it has nothing to do with me, but is a memory of some
hypothetical ancestor of mine who may have gone on the Crusades? Huxley
didn't know what to say. He told me he had sat up all night once trying to
find a flaw in one of my arguments, and had to give up!" [2]

C. D. BROAD (1887–   )
British Philosopher, Cambridge University

In the Thirteenth F. W. H. Myers Memorial Lecture (1958) entitled
"Personal Identity and Survival," Dr. Broad stated (pp. 22–23): "Speaking
for myself, I would say that [reincarnation] seems to me on general
grounds to be much the most plausible form of the doctrine of survival,
though I would not go so far as Hume, who said, in his essay *Of the Immortality of the Soul*, '. . . Metempsychosis is the only system of this kind
that philosophy can hearken to.' " [1] In this lecture as it appears in revised
form in Broad's volume, *Lectures on Psychical Research*,[2] part of the above

[1] New York: Harper and Row, 1931, pp. 82–83.
[2] John Eglinton, *A Memoir of Æ*. London: Macmillan, 1937, pp. 272–273.

[1] London: Society for Psychical Research, 1958.
[2] New York: Humanities Press, 1962, p. 413.

remarks was amended to read: "I do think that the doctrine of reincarnation, as at any rate one conceivable form of human survival, is of sufficient theoretical interest and *prima facie* plausibility to deserve considerably more attention from psychical researchers, and from philosophers who concern themselves with the nature and destiny of human beings, than it has hitherto received."

In his book *Examination of McTaggart's Philosophy*,[3] Broad stated that the theory of pre-existence and plurality of lives seems to be one "Which ought to be taken very seriously, both on philosophical grounds and as furnishing a reasonable motive for right action. . . . We shall behave all the better if we act on the assumption that we may survive; that actions which tend to strengthen and enrich our characters in this life will probably have a favorable influence on the dispositions with which we begin our next lives; and that actions which tend to disintegrate our characters in this life will probably cause us to enter on our next life 'halt and maimed.' If we suppose that our future lives will be of the same general nature as our present lives, this postulate, which is in itself intelligible and not unreasonable, gains enormously in concreteness and therefore in practical effect on our conduct."

ALBAN G. WIDGERY (1 8 8 7 –   )
American-Born Philosopher

[Professor Widgery was Stanton Lecturer on the Philosophy of Religion at Cambridge University, and later Professor of Philosophy at Duke University in the United States. He has also resided for a number of years in India in various capacities.]

A contemporary Christian missionary in India is only repeating what has too often been said when he writes that the doctrines of transmigration and of karma have a paralysing influence throughout India, which must be freed from them if it is to progress at all. There can be no doubt that bad consequences may follow, and have indeed followed, misunderstanding of these doctrines. But there have been pernicious results also from the misinterpretation of doctrines regarded by others as important. . . .

The doctrine of Reincarnation involves a particular conception of the continuation of human existence: one that may be favourably compared with other views. Many Jews, Christians, and Muslims have the very vaguest notions as to what they believe (if indeed they believe anything) as

[3] Cambridge University Press, 1938, p. 639.

to the nature of the existence of the soul after death. . . . Reincarnation affirms a series of lives sufficiently alike and with such continuity that a progress in self-realization may reasonably be conceived in accordance with it. Though the incidents of births and deaths may appear abrupt breaks, continuity is involved, analogous to some extent to going to sleep and waking up in the same room. . . .

The doctrine of karma [is] of fundamental importance for the life of the individual, especially on the ethical side. . . . It does not allow shifting responsibility on to others or accusing others for suffering that comes to the individual himself . . . [it] tends to cultivate self-respect, a central attitude in morality. . . .

The doctrine of reincarnation, bound up as it is with the law of karma, also has implications for the State. And these are contrary to those associated with the [misunderstood] statement previously mentioned from the American Declaration of Independence, that "all men are created equal." For it affirms that men are not born equal . . . and this affirmation appears to be more in accordance with the facts. . . . Men are regarded as different at birth: the differences being due to the manner in which in past lives they have built up their nature through the action of the law of karma. Owing to these differences they are fit for particular positions in the State. . . . Thus there is a basis for a hierarchical form of social organization. . . . This does not necessitate any artificial restrictions and is no justification for the pernicious attitudes and practices too often found in the Indian caste system.

"Reincarnation and Karma, Their Value to the Individual and the State" [1]

SARVEPALLI RADHAKRISHNAN (1888–   )
Oriental Philosopher, President of India (1962–   )

[Charles Moore, Professor of Philosophy at the University of Hawaii and editor of *Philosophy East and West*, writes: "Radhakrishnan is a versatile genius, universally recognized and acclaimed for his remarkable ability as teacher, lecturer, scholar, and administrator, as philosopher, statesman, and India's cultural ambassador throughout the East and the West. His deep learning, his brilliant style, and his absolute tolerance have brought him recognition not only as the greatest living interpreter of Indian philosophy, religion, and culture, but also as an original and creative thinker of the first order. . . . According to Radhakrishnan, *máyá* has not meant to Indian philosophers . . . that the world is illusion. The world of everyday events and things is not ultimate reality, to be sure, but neither is it unreality. He

[1] *Aryan Path*, Bombay, October, 1936.

has defended the reality of the empirical world; it finds its basis in the Absolute. The Absolute is the source of its many transformations. . . . In this way he . . . paves the way for much greater understanding of India's greatest heights of thought and for a possible meeting of the minds of East and West." [1] For many years Radhakrishnan was Spalding Professor of Eastern Religions and Ethics at Oxford University.]

The way to realisation is a slow one. Hindu and Buddhist thought, the Orphic mysteries, Plato and some forms of early Christianity maintain that it takes a long time for realising the holy longing after the lost heaven. . . . The Hindu holds that the goal of spiritual perfection is the crown of a long patient effort. Man grows by countless lives into his divine self-existence. Every life, every act, is a step which we may take either backward or forward. By one's thought, will and action one determines what one is yet to be. According to Plato, the wise man turns away from the world of the senses, and keeps his inward and spiritual eye ever directed to the world of the eternal idea, and if only the pursuit is maintained, the individual becomes freed from the bonds of sensualism. . . .

Our feet are set on the path of the higher life, though they wander uncertainly and the path is not seen clearly. There may be the attraction of the ideal but no assent of the whole nature to it. The utter self-giving which alone can achieve the end is not easy. But no effort is wasted. We are still far from realising the implications of the spiritual dignity of man in matters of conduct, individual and social. It requires an agelong effort carried on from life to life and from plane to plane. . . . If only we can support this higher life, the long labour of the cosmic process will receive its crowning justification and the evolution of centuries unfold its profound significance. . . .

The world process reaches its consummation when every man knows himself to be the immortal spirit. . . . Till this goal is reached, each saved individual is the centre of the universal consciousness. . . . To be saved is not to be moved from the world. Salvation is not escape from life. The individual works in the cosmic process no longer as an obscure and limited ego, but as a centre of the divine or universal consciousness embracing and transforming into harmony all individual manifestations. It is to live in the world with one's inward being profoundly modified. The soul takes possession of itself and cannot be shaken from its tranquillity by the attractions and attacks of the world.

The spiritual illumination does not make the individual life impos-

[1] *A Source Book in Indian Philosophy*, ed. S. Radhakrishnan and Charles Moore. Princeton University Press, 1957, pp. 610–611.

sible. If the saved individuals escape literally from the cosmic process, the world would be forever unredeemed. It would be condemned to remain for all time the scene of unending strife and darkness. . . . Mahâyâna Buddhism declares that Buddha standing on the threshold of nirvâna took the vow never to make the irrevocable crossing so long as there was a single undelivered being on earth. The *Bhâgavata Purâna* [a Hindu scripture] records the following prayer: "I desire not the supreme state with all its eight perfections nor the release from rebirth; may I assume the sorrow of all creatures who suffer and enter into them so that they may be made free from grief." The self-fulfilment which they aspire to is inconsistent with [their] failure to achieve similar results in others. This respect for the individual as individual is not the discovery of modern democracy.

An Idealist View of Life[2]

JOSEPH WOOD KRUTCH (1893–   )
American Naturalist, Educator, Essayist, Critic

[It comes as no surprise to encounter passing but suggestive references to the possibility of rebirth in Krutch's writing. He is one who has truly absorbed the philosophic tone set by the "transcendentalists" Thoreau and Emerson, and also seems to have a special affinity for Wordsworth—and to all these men the idea of reincarnation had meaning. Speaking, in *The Desert Year*,[1] of his first associations with the "austere" yet inspiring desert, Krutch writes:]

For three successive years following my first experience I returned with the companion of my Connecticut winters to the same general region, pulled irresistibly across the twenty-five hundred miles between my own home and this world which would have been alien had it not almost seemed that I had known and loved it in some previous existence.

The Desert Year

[As a naturalist, Krutch often has provocative things to say about the evolutionary processes, and why more and more Darwinists are dissatisfied with current evolutionary theory as the complete answer to the development of form and intelligence. The possibility of a pre-existing intelligence in evolution seems implicit in this selection from Krutch's autobiography, *More Lives Than One:*[2]]

[2] London: Allen & Unwin, 1929, Chap. 3. Reprinted in *A Source Book in Indian Philosophy*, pp. 634–636.

[1] New York: Wm. Sloane, 1952, p. 7.
[2] New York: Wm. Sloane, 1962, pp. 322–323.

"The soul" is indeed a vague conception and the reality of the thing to which it refers cannot be demonstrated. But consciousness is the most self-evident of all facts. . . . The physiologists are very fond of comparing the network of our cerebral nerves with a telephone system but they overlook the significant fact that a telephone system does not function *until someone talks over it.* The brain does not create thought (Sir Julian Huxley has recently pointed out this fact); it is an instrument which thought finds useful. Biologists have sometimes referred to the origin of life as "an improbable chemical accident." But is not the assumption of an "improbable chemical accident" which results ultimately in something capable of discussing the nature of "improbable chemical accidents" a staggering one? Is it not indeed preposterous? Is it not far easier to believe that thought in some potential form must be as primary as matter itself?

More Lives Than One

J. B. RHINE (1 8 9 5 –)
American Parapsychologist

[Dr. Rhine hardly needs an introduction, as he is an internationally renowned psychic researcher, was director for many years of the Parapsychology Laboratory at Duke University and now heads the Institute for Parapsychology. The extracts that follow are from an article in *The American Weekly* for April 8, 1956 entitled "Did You Live Before?" in which Dr. Rhine, at the request of the editors of the *Weekly*, discussed the famous case of Bridey Murphy. When granting permission to use his article, Dr. Rhine made some minor changes therein.

Over a million copies were sold of Morey Bernstein's *The Search for Bridey Murphy*,[1] the book having been printed in more than thirty countries. For a follow-up survey of the facts in this much discussed case, see chapter "How the Case of The Search for Bridey Murphy Stands Today" in Professor C. J. Ducasse's book *A Critical Examination of the Belief in a Life after Death.*[2]]

In brief, *Bridey Murphy* is the story of Ruth Simmons, a young housewife living in Pueblo, Colorado. . . . One evening in 1952 she agreed to be the subject of a hypnotism experiment. The hypnotist was a young businessman, Morey Bernstein. At first he led her back through what we commonly call age-regression. . . . Eventually she remembered the toys she loved when she was only one year old. There was nothing unusual about this, but in a second session the hypnotist suggested, "Your mind will be

[1] New York: Doubleday, 1956.
[2] Springfield, Ill., Charles C. Thomas, 1961; Bernstein, *op. cit.*, 2d ed., 1965, pp. 241–277.

going back . . . back until you find yourself in some other scene, in some other place, in some other time. You will be able to talk to me about it and answer my questions."

The gist of her response was that she was a little Irish girl named Bridey Murphy, who lived in Cork with her mother Kathleen, her barrister father Duncan, and one brother. . . . The year was 1806. She told how, at fifteen, she attended Mrs. Strayne's school in Cork "studying to be a lady," and how she later married Brian Mac Carthy and went to live in Belfast. As the sessions continued, all recorded on tape, the life story carried on through the years, up to Bridey's death at the age of sixty-six. She claimed that, after bodily death, Bridey existed in the spirit world for forty years, then was reborn in Iowa, in 1923, to take up her life as Ruth—the present Ruth Simmons.

Checking later with the Irish Consulate, the British Information Service, the New York Public Library and other sources, Mr. Bernstein learned that a number of Bridey's statements were consistent with historical fact. If Ruth, who never had visited Ireland, had no normal way of knowing these things, didn't this raise the question: Does reincarnation really occur? . . .

In the first place nobody knows, and there is no way of finding out, that the hypnotized girl did not already have all the verified facts somewhere in her memory. . . . What had she read or otherwise absorbed that could have been woven into the tale of Bridey? . . . It also is possible that this young woman could have gained her knowledge through telepathy or clairvoyance, two forms of which we call extrasensory perception (ESP). Science has shown by careful experiment that ESP, or the acquisition of knowledge beyond the reach of the senses, is a normal capacity of human beings. . . . [Also] for a careful study of so important a matter as reincarnation, it would be necessary to know what went on in the conversations that took place with the girl awake, between sessions, as well as when hypnotized. . . .

If we are to consider the question seriously, and try to find some proof of reincarnation, leading a person back through hypnotic regression—as was done in this case—is the wrong road to take. Science should first attempt to discover whether there is a spirit personality which can exist apart from its body. . . .

Let us make our explorations as carefully as possible and go as cautiously into interpretations and applications as the gravity of the issues deserves. Let us get to the facts about men as we do about atoms. As we anxiously scan the skies for the new menace science has brought out of the hidden resources of nature, it is timely, is it not, for the scientist to peer over the edge of his physical foundations and ask: What, if anything, may follow the final obliterating blast?

"Did You Live Before?"

[Although research into mental telepathy and other forms of extrasensory perception receives a great deal of prominence today, many persons fail to appreciate the implications involved if such phenomena are proved to be a fact. Dr. Rhine suggests these implications in the *New York Herald Tribune*.[3]]

A type of lawfulness peculiar to mind and contrary to physics is increasingly evident in the extra-sensory perception and psychokinetic researches. Without these researches and with only the facts of the biological sciences to go on, it is hard to see how any kind of immortality would be possible. The brain-dominating, or cerebro-centric view of personality, would not allow it. In that view the brain is primarily and completely the center of man. But if the psyche is a force and a factor in its own right, with laws and ways peculiarly non-physical, the survival hypothesis has at least a logical chance.

If the mind is different from the physical brain system, it could have a different destiny, could perhaps be independent, separable, unique. This degree of simple possibility must not, of course, be mistaken for probability; but the mere logical possibility is itself very important. . . . Is it not then provocative, to say the least, to discover certain capacities of mind that appear to operate beyond the boundaries of space and time within which our sensorial, bodily system has to live and move? Here, surely, if ever, "hope sees a star" and the urge toward an inquiry into the question of survival receives valuable impetus and encouragement.

A. C. EWING (1899–)
British Philosopher

[Professor Ewing is well known for his work at Cambridge University having been Lecturer in Moral Science for many years and later taught philosophy there. In an article in *The Aryan Path*,[1] "The Philosophy of McTaggart, with Special Reference to the Doctrine of Reincarnation," Professor Ewing concludes with some of his own ideas on rebirth:]

[3] February 27, 1944.

[1] February, 1957.

A common objection made by Christians to the belief in reincarnation [is] on account of its alleged bad effects. It is said that the belief has commonly induced people . . . to be unsympathetic towards those suffering misfortune and to do little to help them because it was supposed that their misfortune was only a punishment for sins in a former life and that, if one did anything to alleviate it, the victim would only be punished in some other fashion.

Any such evil effects would be due not to the belief in reincarnation as such but to the further belief that one's good or bad fortune was proportioned to one's previous goodness or badness. . . . It may indeed be doubted whether there is any meaning in the conception of an exact proportion between such incommensurables as goodness and happiness, sin and suffering, and whether there is not an unworthy mercantile flavour about the conception. A universe in which there was a strict proportion between moral goodness and happiness, moral badness and unhappiness, would be one in which there could be ultimately no righteous self-sacrifice. . . .

Granting previous lives, it would seem . . . plausible to suppose that the cases where good people live in a specially unhappy environment were either cases of voluntary choice before birth. . . . for the same kind of motives as have made exceptionally altruistic people go to live in slums or work among lepers . . . or cases where it was necessary for his own sake to suffer . . . because his faults . . . were of such a kind as to necessitate a more painful route to salvation.

[Two ancient aphorisms on Karma seem appropriate to present: "Karmic causes already set in motion must be allowed to sweep on until exhausted, but this permits no man to refuse to help his fellows and every sentient being." "No man but a sage or true seer can judge another's Karma. Hence while each receives his deserts, appearances may deceive, and birth into poverty or heavy trial may not be punishment for bad Karma, for Egos continually incarnate into poor surroundings where they experience difficulties and trials which are for the discipline of the Ego and result in strength, fortitude, and sympathy." (The Path.[2])]

RAYNOR C. JOHNSON (1901–   )
British Physicist

In scientific work it is often the exceptional happening which offers us clues to wider understanding. . . . We are told that Sir William Hamilton at

[2] New York: March, 1893, pp. 367, 369.

the age of five, could answer a difficult mathematical question and would then "run off cheerfully to play with his little toy cart." If we are prepared to recognise the possibility of previous lives, then we might have a basis for explaining these things as a rare example of overflow of previously attained ability into a succeeding life. The permanent soul which stores the wisdom, goodness, artistic sensitivity, interest, and skills of the past, surely influences in some degree the new personality which it is sending forth into the world.

Normally, we should expect some of these interests or capacities to awaken as the child develops. Some may remain wholly latent, for a soul may desire to broaden its experience rather than to intensify certain aspects of it. Plato has a theory that the kind of knowledge which comes easily is "old" knowledge, in the sense that we have laid foundations for it in prior lives, while the learning in which at first we find little interest or which presents difficulty, is probably being met for the first time. On this view, the child prodigy would be the reincarnation of a soul of very specialised development. It is sometimes found that the genius fades out at an early age, as though the soul, as soon as it was able to do so, threw up other fields of interest and withdrew the exceptional one, for the sake of a wider and more balanced development. . . .

The only satisfactory solution of man's dilemma is to be found in his discovery of the enormous resources of his inner self. This is no easy quest or achievement, but it is a possible one, and the only satisfying one. In this way he may ride out the storms of this modern age with inner serenity, in the assurance that come what may, there is nothing really to fear.

A Religious Outlook for Modern Man[1]

ERNEST J. ÖPIK

Estonian-born Astronomer

[Dr. Öpik, an internationally known astronomer, is Research Associate of Armagh Observatory in Northern Ireland. Quoting from his book *The Oscillating Universe:*[1]]

Life is brief and ends in the unknown. The whole life of humanity is but a moment of the cosmic time scale, and we know that despite all efforts toward self-preservation, mankind will vanish eventually. . . . Yet we can firmly believe that there are elsewhere others of our semblance, some very much farther advanced on the track of evolution.

The whole cosmos is performing a giant oscillation. At present it expands, shot out of the chaos of the primeval focal point and, while in flight,

[1] London: Hodder and Stoughton, 1963, Introduction and pp. 178–180.

[1] New York: Mentor paperback, 1960, pp. 136–137.

sheltering the wondrous metamorphoses of life. After many thousands of millions of years, expansion will cease, and the world will collapse into its former focus, the primeval atom, where material individuality will melt and disappear; only to rebound and precipitate itself into new expansion, creating new worlds, with new metamorphoses and dreams.

Material things are born, vanish, and are born again. This is the rhythm of the physical world. All that can be measured, weighed, and timed obeys the rhythm. Yet there is something in us which has neither measure, weight, nor time: our consciousness, the "I," individually different from, yet similar to other "I's." Is it not a droplet or atom of the Great Cosmic Consciousness? The first reality of our knowledge, the only existence of which we have no doubt, our only gate and window through which we perceive the world . . . does it upon death rejoin the Great Consciousness? Or does it remain an atom by itself, to awaken elsewhere with the same feeling of identity and individuality? Being outside space and time, time intervals would not matter to it; when awakening somewhere after billions of billions of great cosmic oscillations, would it not be filled with the same fresh sense of individuality that it has now, or had billions of cosmic oscillations before our time? Maybe this consciousness is only the superficies of subconscious depths reaching to the root of all things. Maybe there is analogy with chemical affinity, an element of consciousness (or soul) combining with a suitable organism. . . . Only from such a standpoint would it not seem strange and unbelievable that we exist.

The Oscillating Universe

IAN STEVENSON (1918–   )
Canadian-born American Psychiatrist

[In 1960, Dr. Stevenson's 44-page essay "The Evidence for Survival from Claimed Memories of Former Incarnations" was the prize-winning essay in the American Society for Psychical Research contest in honor of William James, one of its early presidents. Parts I and II appeared respectively in the April and July issues of the Journal of the Society.[1] Dr. Stevenson, who is Chairman of the Department of Neurology and Psychiatry at the University of Virginia School of Medicine, studied hundreds of instances where children or adults seemed to remember a past life, and presents a select few "in the evaluation of which reincarnation becomes a very serious contender as the most plausible explanation of the empirical facts." With one excep-

[1] The essay has been published in pamphlet form and is available from M. C. Peto, 16 Kingswood Road, Tadworth, Surrey, England.

tion, the claimed memories upon which Dr. Stevenson bases the conclusions presented below, arose naturally and spontaneously in normal states of consciousness.

In reviewing the essay, the *Postgraduate Medical Journal* (Advances in Neurology) for July, 1961, states: "It is interesting and encouraging to read Dr. Stevenson's essay, which exhibits all the care and precision of the trained scientific observer, combined with the open and unprejudiced outlook of the philosopher. His thesis is worthy of that profound thinker, William James, in honour of whose memory this essay was composed. We congratulate the author on his approach to this difficult subject."]

The writer of a review of this kind has the privilege and perhaps the obligation of saying how he personally interprets the data. I will say, therefore, that I think reincarnation the most plausible hypothesis for understanding the cases of this series. This is not to say that I think they prove reincarnation either singly or together. Indeed, I am quite sure they do not. But for each of the alternative hypotheses I find objections or shortcomings which make them for me unsuitable explanations of all the cases, although they may apply to some. . . .

A large number of cases in which the recall of true memories is a plausible hypothesis should make that hypothesis worthy of attention. I think the number of cases in the present collection confers that respectability on the hypothesis, even though many of these cases may have particular aspects which make some other hypothesis more plausible in such cases. Expectations can harmfully influence perceptions. If we proceed in an investigation with the expectation of confirming a particular hypothesis, we may think we discover more evidence for it than we do. But the reverse type of misperception can also occur with equal harm. If we reject offhand, as most Westerners are inclined to do, the hypothesis of reincarnation, we may exclude from our investigations those conditions which could permit further relevant data to emerge.

The evidence I have assembled and reviewed here does not warrant any firm conclusion about reincarnation. But it does justify, I believe, a much more extensive and more sympathetic study of this hypothesis than it has hitherto received in the West. Further investigation of apparent memories of former incarnations may well establish reincarnation as the most probable explanation of these experiences. Along this line we may in the end obtain more convincing evidence of human survival of physical death than from other kinds of evidence. In mediumistic communications we have the problem of proving that someone clearly dead still lives. In evaluating apparent memories of former incarnations, the problem consists in judging whether someone clearly living once died. This may prove the easier task and, if pursued with sufficient zeal and success, may contribute decisively to the question of survival.

"The Evidence for Survival from Claimed Memories of Former Incarnations"

[Under the title *Twenty Cases Suggestive of Reincarnation,* a 354-page book by Dr. Stevenson was published in 1966 by the American Society for Psychical Research. Dr. Stevenson traveled to Europe, the Near East, Asia, South America, Alaska and other parts of the United States to conduct on-the-spot investigations of reported cases. "This is not a fantastic, but a thoroughly factual book," writes one reviewer, "and possibly an important milestone in the exploration of a staggering idea." (*The Ottawa Citizen.*[2]) Quoting from the volume:[3]]

So far, most of the best evidence bearing on reincarnation has come from spontaneous cases. Relevant material does not often arise in the laboratory under circumstances where we can exert even moderate control. Some of the earliest and most thorough investigators of the evidence for reincarnation used hypnosis to regress subjects back in time to supposed "previous lives." . . . The "personalities" usually evoked during hypnotically-induced regressions to a "previous life" seem to comprise a mixture of . . . the subject's current personality, his expectations of what he thinks the hypnotist wants, his fantasies of what he thinks his previous life ought to have been, and also perhaps elements derived paranormally. . . .

In the international census of cases suggestive of reincarnation which I have undertaken, I now have nearly six hundred cases listed. Of these my colleagues and I have personally investigated about a third. . . . The twenty cases presented in this volume provide a representative sample of the cases I have investigated at first hand. . . . I believe . . . that the evidence favoring reincarnation as a hypothesis for the cases of this type has increased since I published my review in 1960.

Twenty Cases Suggestive of Reincarnation

GINA CERMINARA
American Psychologist

[Dr. Cerminara was mentioned in the item on Edgar Cayce. Her books on Cayce, particularly *Many Mansions*—reprinted numerous times—have evoked considerable interest in reincarnation in the West.]

[2] Oct. 1, 1966.
[3] Pp. 1–3, 351.

If it could be demonstrated scientifically that man is not merely a body, but also a soul inhabiting a body; and that, further this soul existed before birth and will continue to exist after death, the discovery would transform psychological science. It would be as if a shaft had been dropped from surface levels of soil to deep-lying strata of the earth; modern "depth" psychology would appear as superficial as a two-inch hole for the planting of an onion by comparison with a two-mile shaft for the extraction of oil. First of all, such an added dimension of time would enlarge man's understanding of personality traits. Psychologists have for some time been making close statistical and clinical studies of the qualities that compose personality. These studies are monuments to the ingenuity of man's mind; they have had many practical applications in personnel work, vocational guidance, and clinical psychology—and yet they represent what would seem to be only the narrow foreground of man.

Acceptance of the reincarnation principle throws a floodlight of illumination on the unnoticed background. The landscape so illumined has a strange and beautiful fascination of its own, but its principal importance is that within it can be discerned the slow, winding paths by which traits and capacities and attitudes of the present were achieved. Or, to change the analogy, it is as if reincarnation revealed the submerged eight-ninths of an iceberg, of which psychologists had been painstakingly examining the visible ninth. . . . Psychiatrists concur in the view that the major life attitudes of the psyche arise from the unconscious. The reincarnation principle merely expands the scope of the unconscious to include the dynamics of past-life experience.

Many Mansions[1]

It becomes clear that anyone who accepts the idea of reincarnation cannot, with impunity, despise at wholesale any alien race or nation; for if he does so, he thereby runs the risk of despising his own past or future self. It must constantly be remembered, in the matter of race as in everything else, that man *is* a soul, and *has* a body, which he uses. . . . A proper understanding of this relationship of soul to body is . . . the first intellectual step towards a tolerance that shall be thorough and scientific rather than superficial and sentimental. When one recognizes that the body is merely the transitory expression and vehicle of the soul, one must of necessity see that to despise a man for his race, nationality, or color, is as absurd and unreasonable as to despise an actor for the costume he is wearing.

The longer one reflects upon the matter, in fact, the more does one's sense of separativeness and self-importance tend to dissolve. For if my soul has incarnated in black bodies and white, in red bodies and brown bodies

[1] New York: Wm. Sloane, 1950, pp. 102–103, 105.

and yellow; if each of these peoples has at one time or another been the creator of great civilizations equal to, comparable to, or even superior to our own, in the great moving kaleidoscope of history; if I participated in those colors and those civilizations, whether as an inferior or a superior member, whether as peasant or prince, whether as moron or as mastermind—how then can I remain smugly convinced of the unique importance and superiority of the race or nation to which I happen to belong in the present?

A passage in the Buddhist scriptures shows us an interesting fragment of conversation between Ananda, one of Buddha's disciples, and Buddha on the subject of karma. "How deep is this causal law!" Ananda exclaims. "How deep it seems! . . ." And Buddha answered, saying, "Say not so Ananda, say not so. Deep indeed is this causal law, and deep it appears to be. But it is by not knowing, by not understanding, by not penetrating this doctrine that the world of men has become entangled like a ball of twine, unable to pass beyond the Way of Woe and the ceaseless round of rebirth." Buddha, seems completely persuaded of the fact that *ignorance* of karma and reincarnation can be a hindrance to spiritual progress, and conversely that *knowledge* of them can be immeasurably helpful.

Not that a noble and beautiful and fruitful life cannot be lived without this knowledge. Countless men and women of many religious faiths have lived great and even saintly lives in complete ignorance of, or disbelief in, reincarnation. And yet it seems likely, to the present writer at least, that at a certain stage of evolution, a knowledge of reincarnation is indispensable for full comprehension of oneself and of life in general. The final redemption of self could hardly be made without a conscious dredging of the past and conscious transmutation of it. Perhaps we have reached a stage of our history where this knowledge is necessary to us—otherwise it would not be appearing in so many places.

The World Within[2]

IRA PROGOFF (1921–   )
American Psychologist

[Dr. Progoff is Director of the Institute for Research in Depth Psychology at Drew University, and author of the widely read book, *The Death and Rebirth of Psychology*. In a later work, *The Symbolic and the Real*,[1] he discusses Plato's dialogue *Meno*, and comments:]

[2] New York: Wm. Sloane, 1957, pp. 136–137, 199–200.

[1] New York: Julian Press, 1963, pp. 48–53.

Socrates undertook to prove that a slave boy who had never been taught mathematics could have a knowledge of certain mathematical facts drawn forth from him by a skillful teacher. To do this, Socrates questioned the boy carefully, evoking from him by the processes of thought which he stirred in him, new insights of which the boy had not before been aware. From this Socrates deduced that teaching is not a matter of something being placed in one person by another, but is a question of eliciting something that is already present, although only implicitly and latently, at hidden depths of the individual's mind.

On the face of it, this demonstration accords very well with the style of modern thinking. The modern mind is quite prepared to understand what Socrates was doing and to agree with him in principle that the process of education at its best is a drawing forth of capacities of knowledge that are present but undeveloped in the individual. . . . But Socrates had quite another view of what was to be inferred from his demonstration with the untutored slave boy. To him the facility with which he was able to draw new insights out of the boy was proof that the boy had known these things all along, but that he had not been aware of them. He had *forgotten* that he knew them. . . . To Socrates it was self-evident that the boy's capacity was the result of an experience he had had in a previous lifetime. What has been called Socrates' "favorite doctrine" was at the base of this. It was a doctrine with a very ancient lineage, the belief that the immortality of the individual soul is expressed in many incarnations at different points in history. . . .

The great task, then, as Socrates envisioned the problem of gaining knowledge, is to remember the things that one has known in earlier lifetimes. It seems clear in this connection that Socrates was interested primarily not in recalling the personal events of previous existences, but in recalling the underlying capacities of knowledge which had been accumulated in the course of its past lives by the person (or specifically by his "soul" as Socrates conceived of the soul). He would not see much point, for example, in attempting to identify the names and places of persons in whose form an individual had lived during previous incarnations; neither did he care to remember daily events, nor to recall emotional, personal encounters. These would have a subjectivity and pettiness that would place them beyond the pale of his primary concerns.

He would be interested, however, in establishing a connection and a new relationship with the qualities of cognition which had been developed in past experiences, such as one's relationship with mathematics, or with medicine, or with poetry. Such qualities of experience, representing underlying capacities of knowledge, would be of great relevance because they would provide access to larger awareness for the person in his present life. . . . Socrates' goal as a goad was to stir men up so that the traces of knowledge garnered through the timeless journey of the soul could come alive again . . . in order that it might serve as an inward source of truth.

We can see at this point a striking similarity between the calling of Socrates and the trend of work emerging in modern depth psychology. Both proceed on the hypothesis that the resources of wisdom are hidden in the depths of the human being, and that they are best able to unfold in meaning when they are stirred to full expression. . . . Both modern psychology and the Socratic way are instances of man's disciplined attempts to reach toward reality in modes of thought that fit the tone and temper of their times. Beyond their differences in style lies a quality of integrity that unites them; and from this unity we may eventually be able to draw the model of a psychological and spiritual perspective that will answer our modern need.

The Symbolic and the Real

HERBERT FINGARETTE (1921–   )
American Philosopher and Psychologist

[Dr. Fingarette is professor of philosophy at the University of California, Santa Barbara. The selections presented are from his book *The Self in Transformation*,[1] called a major contribution to psychoanalytic thought. Assuming the truth of a number of Freud's remarkable discoveries, the author suggests the direction in which they lead when more fully worked out. However, as Benjamin Nelson points out in the Harper paperback edition, "Fingarette escapes the logical and spiritual blunders which have regrettably dogged orthodox Freudianism from the time the earthshaking insights of psychoanalysis were prematurely encased in rigid molds."

The extracts are chiefly from the chapter "Karma and the Inner World." Unfortunately only samplings from these seventy pages can be offered. Fingarette has an unusual approach to the subject. He is not concerned with "proving" reincarnation and karma, but in investigating the Self-transforming potentials resident in these concepts, and in so doing reveals a number of significant parallels between the insights achieved by Freud and those of the ancient psychologists of the East. The author states: "I am not psychologizing reincarnation. I want to present it as a reality, not a metaphor. . . . I am trying to preserve it whole."

[1] New York: Basic Books, 1963; Harper Torchbook, 1965. Pp. 105, 171–172, 178–182, 218, 231, 234, 236.

Dr. Louis De Rosis, reviewing the book in *The Library Journal*, states: "The volume is a high-powered microscope used by a brilliant philosopher to bring profound illumination into psychoanalysis—not only to its basic theoretical underpinnings but to its relationships in the whole scheme of man's being. This is truly required reading for all psychiatrists, psychoanalysts, and clinical psychologists of any school or persuasion. It should also have more than passing meaning for the informed layman."]

The doctrine of karma, whether we accept it or not, poses profound questions about the structure, transformation, and transcendence of the Self. It raises in new ways general questions of ontology. We may be parochial and dismiss the doctrine, especially its theses on reincarnation, as obvious superstition. Or we may recall that it was not any self-evident spiritual superficiality but the historical accident of official Christian opposition which stamped it out as an important Greek and Roman doctrine, a doctrine profoundly meaningful to a Plato, as well as to the masses. Perhaps more significant, it has remained, from the first millennium B.C. until the present, an almost universal belief in the East, even among most of the highly trained and Western-educated contemporary thinkers. . . .

Certainly we can avoid some irrelevant psychological hurdles if it be stressed at once that, in our discussion of karma and reincarnation, we will not have jumped into an antiscientific position, nor will we be treating reincarnation as "pseudo" or as "super" science. The real issues are philosophical. They have nothing to do with amassing reports of *wunderkinder*, Indian yogis, or the periodic newspaper sensationalisms exploiting fakes or unfortunates claiming inexplicable knowledge of past events. These "marvels" are as philosophically uninteresting to us as it turns out that they are to the great prophets of karma. . . .

The assumption in this chapter is that joining a fresh examination of karmic doctrine to an examination of certain aspects of psychoanalytic therapy will throw a new light on therapy, on the meaning of the karmic doctrine, and on certain of our major philosophical and cultural commitments. The task of the reader in such a discussion is to see what the evidence and the argument say rather than to read into the words the Westerner's stock interpretation of "esoteric" doctrines.

The Judaeo-Christian apprehends life on earth as a unique cosmic event, a coming out of nothing, a staking of all on the one chance, and, finally, a reaping of eternal reward or punishment. The Far Eastern image is of a multitude of interconnected lives, a slow and arduous struggle toward spiritual enlightenment. The physicalistic image is of a cosmically meaningless life, beginning and ending in nothingness. . . .

In the West, we tend to think of heaven and hell as analogues to our penological practices: the punishment is physical discomfort and psychic isolation (prison) regardless of the specific nature of the criminal act. The karmic law is much closer to the old Greek notion of cosmic justice, or to the notion of "poetic justice." The punishment exactly fits the crime. But poetic justice must operate within a life, if not this one, then another one. It cannot be realized if life terminates in an essentially static heaven or hell. . . . Karmic law is not the edict of an All-Powerful Disciplinarian, not an expression of will accompanied by the threat of sanctions. It purports to be factual description: Somehow or other, things do eventually "balance out" in the moral realm; each moral action produces, eventually, its quite specific moral reaction. And our constant strivings are constantly producing new "karma" as well as bringing past karma to fruition; the weary round of births and deaths is perpetuated.

In the course of spiritual progress toward freedom from the round of births and rebirths one eventually achieves the power of remembering past lives. One then sees their connection with the present life. The ordinary person can neither remember nor understand: "And what happened to you in your mother's womb, all that you have quite forgotten." [2] The greater the spiritual progress, the greater the ability and the easier the task. Knowledge of one's former lives is one of the "five kinds of superknowledge." [3] In achieving this "superknowledge," one is concurrently achieving liberation from the karmic bonds. As in psychoanalysis, this knowledge is not the goal, but it is a distinctive ingredient in the achievement of freedom. Spiritual knowledge and spiritual freedom are born as one. . . .

[In terms of responsibility, comparison is made between the karma-reincarnation view of many lives or selves extending over long periods of time, and the psychoanalytic view of many lives or selves experienced within the span of one life. Of the latter view Dr. Fingarette states:]

We become responsible agents when we can face the moral continuity of the familiar, conscious self with other strange, "alien" psychic entities— our "other selves." We should perhaps speak of an "identity" with other selves rather than a "continuity." For we must accept responsibility for the "acts" of these other selves; we must see these acts as ours. As Freud said of our dream lives, they are not only in me but act "from out of me as well."

2 *Saddharmapundarika*, V, 70, in *Buddhist Texts*, E. Conze, Philosophical Library, New York, 1954, p. 125.
3 *Ibid.*, V, 71, p. 125.

Yet identity is, in another way, too strong a term. . . . The psycho-analytic quest for autonomy reveals the Self in greater depth; it reveals it as a *community* of selves. The genuinely startling thing in this quest is not simply the discovery that these other, archaic selves exist, nor even that they have an impact in the present. What startles is the detailed analysis of the peculiarly close, subtle, and complex texture of the threads which weave these other selves and the adult conscious self into a single great pattern.

It is a special, startling kind of intimacy with which we deal. It calls for me to recognize that I suffer, whether I will or no, for the deeds of those other selves. It is an intimacy which, when encountered, makes it self-evident that I must assume responsibility for the acts and thoughts of those other persons as if they were I. Finally and paradoxically, in the morally clear vision which thus occurs, there emerges, as in a montage, a new Self, a Self free of bondage to the old deeds of the old selves. For it is a Self which sees and therefore sees through the old illusions which passed for reality. . . . The self moving through the rich flux of experience is now not blinded and hobbled by the old superimposed and stereotyped fantasies which formed a tightly and dynamically interrelated community of selves generating its own repetitive destiny. . . .[4]

The karmic notion is that the old self acts, and the later selves, though they did not commit the acts, legitimately inherit their fruits as those fruits ripen in the course of time. This is an occurrence which need not involve generations or epochs; it may be from moment to moment or day to day: Coomaraswamy summarizes and emphasizes that "it is constantly over-looked that the majority of references [in Hindu scripture] to . . . re-peated birth and repeated death refer to this present life. . . ." And he refers to the concept of *punar bhava* ("becoming") as meaning that "man dies and is reborn daily and hourly in this present life." [5]

I am interested . . . in the karmic doctrine as . . . an expression of the genuine dialogue of spirit. . . . The doctrine's spiritual function . . . is that of providing a conceptual and action framework within which a person may explore and reorganize the psychomoral community of selves which constitute the person. . . .

Siwek has expressed the view that the doctrine of reincarnation is morally enervating: for not only are we assured of an indefinite number of lives in which to rectify our ways, but the widespread desire to keep on living

---

[4] In the various schools of Hindu philosophy it is held that at the root of these multiple selves is the Changeless Self—the witness and spectator, the Real I. "All things hang on me as precious gems upon a string." (The Bhagavad-Gita). (Eds.)

[5] A. K. Coomaraswamy, "Eastern Religions and Western Thought," *The Review of Religion* 6 (1942), p. 137.

on earth is a powerful motive to "sin" *in* order to assure rebirth. This view is understandable as "external," a result of seeing the words of the doctrine rather than its meaning as it functions in the appropriate context. . . . The doctrine of reincarnation does not receive its spiritual impulse and quality from theoretical discussion. I have tried to set the stage for detailed analysis by suggesting that karmic insight emerges in the situation of one who is driven by anxiety and suffering, who seeks self-awareness, and who is grappling in a highly personal and direct way with the fragmented, enslaving lives which he has lived, is living, and hopes to escape. For one who is not urgently concerned with suffering and illusion, who does not feel despair and the need for illumination, the doctrine of reincarnation is indeed a devilish snare. . . . We cannot toy with the idea of reincarnation as an intellectual or cultural curiosity having a certain piquant and quaint validity and still discover its power and its worth. . . . One earns a vision by living it, not merely thinking about it.

The Self in Transformation

What a handful of dust is man to think such thoughts! Or is he, perchance, a prince in misfortune, whose speech at times betrays his birth? I like to think that, if men are machines, they are machines of a celestial pattern, which can rise above themselves, and, to the amazement of the watching gods, acquit themselves as men. I like to think that this singular race of indomitable, philosophising, poetical beings, resolute to carry the banner of Becoming to unimaginable heights, may be as interesting to the gods as they to us, and that they will stoop to admit these creatures of promise into their divine society.

W. MACNEILE DIXON

Acknowledgments

Very grateful thanks are due to the following authors, publishers, or copyright holders, for granting permission to quote from the works indicated below:

Abingdon-Cokesbury Press, Nashville, Tenn. *The Christian Agnostic* by Leslie Weatherhead.

Allen & Unwin, Ltd., London. *The Art of Creation* by Edward Carpenter; *Pre-Existence and Reincarnation* by W. Lutoslawski; *Thus Spake Zarathustra* by Friedrich Nietzsche, trans. Thomas Common; *The Hibbert Journal*, "Varieties of Belief in Reincarnation" by E. G. Parrinder; *An Idealist View of Life* by S. Radhakrishnan; *Rumi, Poet and Mystic*, trans. R. A. Nicholson; *Education and the Good Life* by Bertrand Russell.

American Society for Psychical Research, Inc., New York, and Ian Stevenson. "The Evidence for Survival from Claimed Memories of Former Incarnations," and *Twenty Cases Suggestive of Reincarnation*, by Ian Stevenson.

Anthroposophical Pub. Co., London. *Reincarnation and Karma, Their Significance in Modern Culture* by Rudolph Steiner.

Anthroposophic Press, New York. *Reincarnation and Karma; How Karma Works* by Rudolph Steiner; *Reincarnation as a Phenomenon of Metamorphosis* by Guenther Wachsmuth.

Edward Arnold (Publishers) Ltd., London. *From Religion to Philosophy* by Francis M. Cornford; *The Human Situation* by W. Macneile Dixon; *Human Immortality and Pre-Existence* by J. E. McTaggart.

The Aryan Path, Bombay, India. Extracts from six articles.

Basic Books, New York, and Herbert Fingarette. *The Self in Transformation* by Herbert Fingarette, © 1963 by Basic Books, Inc.

Beacon Press, Boston. *Indian Thought and Its Development* by Albert Schweitzer; *Socrates, the Man and His Thought* by A. E. Taylor.

Blaisdell Publishing Company, a Division of Ginn and Company, Waltham, Mass. *Classic Myths in English Literature and Art* by Charles Mills Gayley, pp. 359–360.

The Bodley Head Ltd., London. *The Creed of Buddha* by Edmond Holmes.

Bollingen Foundation, Inc., New York. *The Hero with a Thousand Faces* by Joseph Campbell, Bollingen Series XVII, Pantheon Books, pp. 3–4; *The Myth of the Eternal Return* by Mircea Eliade, trans. from the French by Willard R. Trask, Bollingen Series XLVI, Pantheon Books, pp. 86–89, 98–99; *The Archetypes and the Collective Unconscious* by C. G. Jung, Bollingen Series XX, Pantheon Books, pp. 113, 116–117; *The Collected Works of C. G. Jung*, Vol. 11, "Psychology and Religion: West and East," trans. from the German by R. F. C. Hull, Bollingen Series XX.11, Pantheon Books, p. 529.

Albert & Charles Boni, Inc., New York. *Prophets of the New India* by Romain Rolland.

Ellen Bosanquet. *Value and Destiny of the Individual* by Bernard Bosanquet.

George Braziller, Inc., New York. *The Wisdom of the Serpent* by Joseph L. Henderson and Maud Oakes.

Buddhist Society, London. *The Essence of Buddhism* by D. T. Suzuki.

Cambridge University Press. *Examination of McTaggart's Philosophy* by C. D. Broad; *The Nature of Existence* by J. E. McTaggart; *Realm of Ends* by James Ward; *The Neoplatonists* by Thomas Whittaker.

The Clarendon Press, Oxford. *The Elements of Theology*, trans. E. R. Dodds; *Aristotle —Fundamentals of the History of His Development* by Werner Jaeger.

Cresset Press, London. *Exploring English Character* by Geoffrey Gorer.

Cunningham Press, Alhambra, Calif. The Dhammapada; *The Upanishads and Tao Te King*.

Diogenes, Chicago University Press. "The Gnostic Manuscripts of Upper Egypt" by Eva Meyerovitch, trans. by James H. Labadie. Permission granted by present publisher, Revue Internationale des Sciences Humains, Paris.

Dodd, Mead & Company, New York. *Our Eternity* and *Treasure of the Humble* by Maurice Maeterlinck.

Doubleday & Company, Inc., New York. *Collected Verse of Rudyard Kipling;* "The Sack of the Gods" from *Naulahka* by Rudyard Kipling. Permission for latter confirmed by Mrs. George Bambridge. *The Summing Up* by W. Somerset Maugham, © 1938 by W. Somerset Maugham. *The Sufis* by Idries Shah, © 1964 by Idries Shah.

E. P. Dutton & Co., Inc., New York. *Seven Years in Tibet* by Heinrich Harrer; *The Life of Mazzini* by Bolton King; *Leibniz' Philosophical Writings*, trans. Mary Morris; *Lucretius' The Nature of Things*, trans. W. E. Leonard; *The Story of San Michele* by Axel Munthe.

Faber & Faber, London, and Alfred A. Knopf, New York. *James Joyce's Ulysses* by Stuart Gilbert.

Funk & Wagnalls, New York. *Victor Hugo's Intellectual Autobiography*, trans. Lorenzo O'Rourke.

Victor Gollancz, Ltd., London. *Puzzled People; Lord Riddell's Intimate Diary of the Peace Conference and After*, confirmed by Harcourt, Brace & World, New York.

Harper & Brothers, New York. *Pleasant Valley* by Louis Bromfield; *Gandhi's Letters to a Disciple* by Mohandas K. Gandhi, © 1950 by Harper & Brothers; *From the Unconscious to the Conscious* by Gustave Geley; *The Perennial Philosophy* by Aldous Huxley; *The Imprisoned Splendor* by Raynor C. Johnson; *Sweet Rocket* by Mary Johnston; *The Naked Truth* by Clare Sheridan; *The Religions of Man* by Huston Smith; *Zen Buddhism and Psychoanalysis* by Suzuki, Fromm, and De Martino; *Letters from the Earth* by Mark Twain; "My Platonic Sweetheart" from *The Mysterious Stranger* and Other Stories by Mark Twain.

Harvard Divinity Bulletin, Cambridge, Mass. "Symbols of Eternal Life" by Paul Tillich.

Harvard University Press, Cambridge, Mass. *The Dawn of Philosophy* by Georg Misch; *Metempsychosis* by G. F. Moore; *The Odes of Pindar*, trans. Sir John Sandys.

William Heinemman Ltd., London. *I Have Been Here Before* by J. B. Priestley, reprinted by permission of A. D. Peters & Co.

Hodder & Stoughton Limited, London. *The Light and the Gate* and *A Religious Outlook for Modern Man* by Raynor C. Johnson.

Hogarth Press, London. *The Standard Edition of the Complete Psychological Works of Sigmund Freud,* Vol. XIV.

Holt, Rinehart and Winston, New York. *Anthony Adverse* and *Bedford Village* by Hervey Allen; *The Forgotten Language* by Erich Fromm; *Complete Poems of Robert Frost,* © 1916, 1947 by Holt, Rinehart and Winston, Inc., © 1944 by Robert Frost.

The Johns Hopkins Press, Baltimore. "The Phædrus and Reincarnation" by R. S. Bluck, from *American Journal of Philology.*

Houghton Mifflin Company, Boston. *The Soul of the Indian* by Charles Eastman; *Religion and Immortality* by G. Lowes Dickinson; *John of the Mountains* by John Muir.

Julian Press, New York. *The Symbolic and the Real* by Ira Progoff.

Alfred A. Knopf, Inc., New York. *Ireland's Literary Renaissance* by Ernest Boyd; *Merely Players* by Claude Bragdon.

J. B. Lippincott Company, Philadelphia. *Meditation, The Inward Art,* by Bradford Smith.

Liveright Publishing Corporation, New York. *The Dybbuk* by S. Ansky, © 1954 by Henry G. Alsberg and Winifred Katzin, translators.

Longmans, Green, London. *The Philosophy of Plotinus* and *The Platonic Tradition in English Religious Thought,* by W. R. Inge.

David McKay, New York. *The Searchers* and *The Soul of the Universe* by Gustaf Strömberg.

The Macmillan Company, New York. *The Story of the Faith* by W. A. Gifford, © 1946 by The Macmillan Company; "A Creed" from *Collected Poems* by John Masefield, © 1912 by The Macmillan Company, renewed 1940 by John Masefield; "A Prelude and a Song" from *The Hill of Vision* by James Stephens; "Under Ben Bulben" from *Collected Poems* of W. B. Yeats, © 1940 by Georgie Yeats.

Macmillan & Co., Ltd., London. *The Soul of a People* and *The Inward Light* by H. Fielding Hall; *Northern Tribes of Central Australia* by Spencer and Gillen.

Dr. W. H. Magee (John Eglinton). *A Memoir of AE* by John Eglinton.

MD Publications, New York. *Centaur, Essays on the History of Medical Ideas* by Félix Martí-Ibáñez.

William Morrow & Company, Inc., New York. *Many Mansions* and *The World Within* by Gina Cerminara, © 1950 and 1957, respectively, by Dr. Cerminara; *More Lives Than One* and *The Desert Year* by Joseph Wood Krutch, © 1962, and 1951 and 1952, respectively, by Prof. Krutch; *Male and Female* by Margaret Mead, permission confirmed by Dr. Mead; *In the Wet* by Nevil Shute, © 1953 by William Morrow & Company, Inc.

John Murray, London. *Musings of a Chinese Mystic,* ed. by Lionel Giles.

The New Age Magazine, Washington, D. C. "Freemasonary and Reincarnation" by C. I. McReynolds.

The New American Library, Inc., New York. *The Oscillating Universe* by Ernest J. Öpik.

New Directions, New York. *Siddhartha* by Hermann Hesse, trans. Hilda Rosner, © 1951 by New Directions.

New York Herald Tribune, article in *Today's Living,* "Dali Greets the World" by Ben Martin.

The New York Times Magazine, "Tragic Decline of the Humane Ideal" by André

Maurois; article on Jean Sibelius by Howard Taubman; "Kandinsky, No Great Master But a Great Influence," by Hilton Kramer.

W. W. Norton & Company, Inc., New York. *Toward a Philosophy of History* by José Ortega y Gasset.

Oxford University Press. *Some Sayings of the Buddha*, trans. F. L. Woodward.

Open Court Publishing Company, La Salle, Illinois. *Nature, Mind, and Death* by C. J. Ducasse, confirmed by Dr. Duacsse; "The Religion of the Spirit and the World's Need" by S. Radhakrishnan, from *The Philosophy of Sarvepalli Radhakrishnan*.

Pantheon Books, New York, a Division of Random House, Inc. *Memories, Dreams, Reflections* by C. G. Jung, recorded and edited by Aniela Jaffee, © 1962, 1963 by Random House, Inc.

Philosophical Library, New York. *The Diary and Sundry Observations of Thomas Alva Edison; The Splendour That Was Egypt* by Margaret A. Murray.

Princeton University Press. *A Source Book in Indian Philosophy*, ed. S. Radhakrishnan and Charles Moore, © 1957 by Princeton University Press.

G. P. Putnam's Sons, New York. *The Nazarene* by Sholem Asch, © 1939 by Mr. Asch; *The Century of the Renaissance in France* by Louis Batiffol; *Zones of the Spirit* by August Strindberg, © 1913 by G. P. Putnam's Sons; *Goethe* by Emil Ludwig, © 1928 by G. P. Putnam's Sons; *Life of Appollonius of Tyana* by Philostratus, trans. F. C. Conybeare.

Random House, Inc., New York. *Birdman of Alcatraz* by Thomas E. Gaddis, © 1955 by Thomas E. Gaddis; "The Great God Brown," by Eugene O'Neill, © 1926 and renewed 1954 by Carlotta Monterey O'Neill, reprinted from *Nine Plays By Eugene O'Neill*.

Dr. J. B. Rhine. "Did You Live Before?" from *The American Weekly*.

Ross, Nancy Wilson, *The Return of Lady Brace*.

Routledge & Kegan Paul Ltd., London. *Giordano Bruno, His Life, Thought and Martyrdom* by William Boulting; *The Life of Paracelsus* by Franz Hartmann; *The World As Will and Idea* by Arthur Schopenhauer, trans. by Haldane and Kemp; *The Secret of the Golden Flower* by Richard Wilhelm.

Russell & Russell, New York. *Complete Works of Friedrich Nietzsche*, vol. 16, essay "Eternal Recurrence."

Rutgers University Press, New Brunswick, N. J. *The Expulsion of the Triumphant Beast*, by Giordano Bruno, trans. Arthur D. Imerti.

Saturday Review, New York. "Walt Whitman's Buried Masterpiece" by Malcolm Cowley.

SCM Press, London. *Teenage Religion* by Harold Loukes.

Charles Scribner's Sons, New York. *From Here to Eternity*, pp. 647, 648, 723, by James Jones, © 1951 by James Jones; *Look Homeward Angel*, pp. 1, 36–7, 63 and 662, by Thomas Wolfe, © 1929 Charles Scribner's Sons, renewal © 1957 Edward C. Aswell, Administrator, C.T.A., and/or Fred Wolfe.

Julio M. Seton. *The Gospel of the Red Man* by Ernest Thompson Seton and Julia M. Seton.

G. Bernard Shaw, The Public Trustee of, and The Society of Authors, London. *Saint Joan* and *Back to Methuselah* by Bernard Shaw.

Irving Shepard, Jack London Ranch, Glen Ellen, Calif. *The Star Rover* by Jack London.

Stanford University Press, Stanford, Calif., *Who Is Man?* by Abraham J. Heschel.

Sunrise, Pasadena, Calif. "The Transcendentalists on Reincarnation."

The Theosophical Publishing House, Adyar, Madras, India. *Reincarnation*, and *The Ancient Wisdom* by Annie Besant; *Reincarnation in Islam* by N. K. Mirza; *Buddhist Stories*, trans. F. L. Woodward.

Theosophy Company, 245 W. 33rd St., Los Angeles, Calif. *The Key to Theosophy*,

Isis Unveiled, The Secret Doctrine, The Voice of the Silence, by H. P. Blavatsky; *The Ocean of Theosophy* by W. Q. Judge; *The Bhagavad-Gita* and *Patanjali's Yoga Aphorisms,* trans. W. Q. Judge.

Theosophy in Pakistan, "Reincarnation, Islamic Conceptions," by M. H. Abdi.

University Books, New York. *The Candle of Vision* by George W. Russell.

Vedanta Society of Southern California. As publisher and copyright holder of The *Bhagavad-Gita,* trans. by Swami Prabhavananda and Christopher Isherwood.

The Viking Press, Inc., New York. *The Masks of God: Oriental Mythology* by Joseph Campbell; *The River* by Rumer Godden; *A Prison, a Paradise* by Loren Hurnscot.

John M. Watkins, publishers. *Fragments of a Faith Forgotten* and *The Thrice Great Hermes,* by G. R. S. Mead; *The Masonic Initiation* by W. L. Wilmshurst.

Leslie D. Weatherhead, and M. C. Peto, England. "The Case for Reincarnation" by Leslie D. Weatherhead.

H. G. Wells, Executors of estate of. *The Dream* by H. G. Wells.

The Yale Review, New Haven, Conn. "Belief in a Future Life" by J. Paul Williams.

Yale University Press, New Haven, Conn. *After Life in Roman Paganism* by Franz Cumont.

Index

Note

To increase the usefulness of the Index, the usual method of indexing words rather than ideas is not consistently followed. Consequently, to locate references under such subject headings as those listed below, examine the printed page for the idea implicit in the subject, not simply the wording of the subject.

After-Death States
Animals, Error that Humans Incarnate as
Animals, Reincarnation of
Antiquity of Reincarnation Belief
Art, Modern
Birth, Human
Brotherhood and Unity
Children
Consciousness
Cycles
Education
Emancipation
Enlightenment and Self-Knowledge
Esotericism in Religion
Evolution
Free Will
Genius
Health and Reincarnation Belief
Heredity
Identity, Preservation of
Individuality and Personality, Distinction Between
Innate Ideas

Karma and Justice
Love and Friendship
Meaning of Existence
Memory of Past Lives
Mind
Music and Composers
Nirvana
Population
Procrastination, Does Rebirth Encourage
Psychology
Purpose of Rebirths
Races and Nations Reincarnating
Reincarnation, Not Selfishly Escaping
Reincarnation of Great Men
Self, The
Sleep and Dreams
Soul
Suicide
Time Between Incarnations
Time, Beyond
Worlds, Incarnating in Other
Worlds Reborn